Italian Yearbook
of Human Rights 2014

P.I.E. Peter Lang

Bruxelles · Bern · Berlin · Frankfurt am Main · New York · Oxford · Wien

Director
Antonio Papisca

Research and editorial committee
Andrea Cofelice, Pietro de Perini,
Paolo De Stefani, Marco Mascia,
Antonio Papisca, Claudia Pividori

Editors
University Human Rights Centre
University of Padua
via Martiri della Libertà, 2
35137 Padua

tel. 049.8271817; fax 049.8271816

centro.dirittiumani@unipd.it
www.italianhumanrightsyearbook.eu
http://unipd-centrodirittiumani.it/en/

Italian Yearbook
of Human Rights 2014

Italian Yearbook of Human Rights

UNESCO Chair
Human Rights, Democracy and Peace

Cover picture: © *The ideal city (interpolation)*, 2011, Venezia, Marsilio Editori.

First Italian edition: *Annuario italiano dei diritti umani 2014*, Venezia, Marsilio Editori, 2014.

© P.I.E. PETER LANG S.A.
  Éditions scientifiques internationales
  Brussels, 2014
  1 avenue Maurice, B-1050 Bruxelles, Belgique
  info@peterlang.com ; www.peterlang.com

ISSN 2294-8848
ISBN 978-2-87574-217-9
D/2014/5678/83

Printed in Germany

CIP available from the British Library, GB and the Library of Congress, USA.

Bibliographic information published by "Die Deutsche Nationalbibliothek"

"Die Deutsche Nationalbibliothek" lists this publication in the "Deutsche Nationalbibliografie"; detailed bibliographic data is available in the Internet at http://dnb.d-nb.de.

Table of Contents

List of Acronyms 11

**Italy and Human Rights in 2013: the Challenges
of Social Justice and the Right to Peace** 15

   I. Regulatory and Infrastructural Human Rights Situation 22

   II. Implementation of International Obligations
      and Commitments: Implementation of ECtHR Case-law 26

   III. Adoption and Implementation of Policies 27

   IV. Structure of the 2014 Yearbook 31

**UPR: Towards the Second Cycle
of the Universal Periodic Review** 35

Italian Agenda of Human Rights 2014 41

PART I. IMPLEMENTATION OF INTERNATIONAL
HUMAN RIGHTS LAW IN ITALY

International Human Rights Law 49

   I. Legal Instruments of the United Nations.............................. 49

   II. Legal Instruments on Disarmament and Non-proliferation....... 49

   III. Legal Instruments of the Council of Europe 50

   IV. European Union Law.. 50

Italian Law 55

   I. The Constitution of the Italian Republic 55

   II. National Legislation 55

   III. Municipal, Provincial and Regional Statutes 58

   IV. Regional Laws 59

PART II. THE HUMAN RIGHTS INFRASTRUCTURE IN ITALY

National Bodies with Jurisdiction over Human Rights 69

   I. Parliamentary Bodies.. 70

   II. Prime Minister's Office (Presidency)................................... 95

   III. Ministry of Foreign Affairs... 101

   IV. Ministry of Labour and Social Policies 105

   V. Ministry of Justice 109

VI. Judicial Authorities 110

VII. National Economy and Labour Council (CNEL) 110

VIII. Independent Authorities.. 111

IX. Non-governmental Organisations 119

X. Human Rights Teaching and Research
in Italian Universities... 120

Sub-national Human Rights Structures.. 131

I. Peace Human Rights Offices in Municipalities,
Provinces and Regions... 131

II. Ombudspersons in the Italian Regions and Provinces.......... 132

III. National Coordinating Body of Ombudspersons.................. 136

IV. Network of Ombudspersons for Children and Adolescents....... 137

V. National Coordinating Network of Ombudspersons
for the Rights of Detainees 138

VI. National Coordinating Body of Local Authorities
for Peace and Human Rights 139

VII. Archives and Other Regional Projects for the Promotion
of a Culture of Peace and Human Rights............................. 140

Region of Veneto.. 143

I. Regional Department for International Relations................. 144

II. Committee for Human Rights and the Culture of Peace 144

III. Committee for Development Cooperation............................ 146

IV. Regional Archive "Pace Diritti Umani – Peace
Human Rights" 146

V. Venice for Peace Research Foundation................................ 148

VI. Ombudsperson for Children and Adolescents 148

VII. Ombudsperson 150

VIII. Regional Commission for Equal Opportunities
between Men and Women.. 152

IX. Regional Observatory on Social Policies 152

X. Regional Observatory on Immigration 154

PART III. ITALY IN DIALOGUE WITH INTERNATIONAL
HUMAN RIGHTS INSTITUTIONS

The United Nations System 159

I. General Assembly... 159

II. Human Rights Council 168

III. High Commissioner for Human Rights (OHCHR) 192

    IV. High Commissioner for Refugees (UNHCR)...................... 194
    V. Human Rights Treaty Bodies.. 198
    VI. Specialised United Nations Agencies, Programmes
    and Funds... 205
    VII. International Organisations with Permanent
    Observer Status at the General Assembly............................ 215

Council of Europe 217
    I. Parliamentary Assembly 218
    II. Committee of Ministers 221
    III. European Court of Human Rights 225
    IV. Committee for the Prevention of Torture............................ 226
    V. European Committee of Social Rights 235
    VI. Commissioner for Human Rights 242
    VII. European Commission against Racism and Intolerance....... 246
    VIII. Advisory Committee on the Framework Convention
    for the Protection of National Minorities............................. 246
    IX. European Commission for Democracy through Law 247
    X. Group of Experts on Action against Trafficking
    in Human Beings 250
    XI. Group of States against Corruption 252

European Union 255
    I. European Parliament.. 255
    II. European Commission.. 256
    III. Council of the European Union 257
    IV. Court of Justice of the European Union 258
    V. European External Action Service....................................... 258
    VI. Special Representative for Human Rights 258
    VII. Fundamental Rights Agency.. 259
    VIII. European Ombudsman 261
    IX. European Data Protection Supervisor.................................. 262

Organisation for Security and Cooperation in Europe 263
    I. Office for Democratic Institutions and Human
    Rights (ODIHR)... 263
    II. High Commissioner on National Minorities......................... 264
    III. OSCE Representative on Freedom of the Media.................. 264
    IV. Special Representative and Co-ordinator for Combating
    Trafficking in Human Beings 266

International Humanitarian and Criminal Law 269

    I. Adapting to International Humanitarian
    and Criminal Law 269

    II. The Italian Contribution to Peace-keeping and Other
    International Missions 269

PART IV. NATIONAL AND INTERNATIONAL CASE-LAW

Human Rights in Italian Case-law 275

    I. Dignity of the Person and Principles of Biolaw 275

    II. Asylum and International Protection 279

    III. Discrimination 283

    IV. Rights of Persons with Disabilities 283

    V. Social Rights 287

    VI. Laws Affecting Individual Rights with
    Retroactive Effect 290

    VII. Immigration 292

    VIII. Right to Privacy, Right to Property 298

    IX. Children's Rights 300

    X. Fair Trial and Pinto Law 303

    XI. Torture, Prison Conditions, Rights of Detainees 307

    XII. Criminal Matters 309

**Italy in the Case-law of the European Court
of Human Rights** 319

    I. Pilot Judgments and Related Cases 319

    II. Other Cases Decided by the Chambers
    and Committees of the Court 325

**Italy in the Case-law of the Court of Justice
of the European Union** 335

**Legal Approach to the Chairperson-Rapporteur's
Draft Declaration in Light of the Current Debate
on the Right of Peoples to Peace** 341

Index 413

Table of Cases 419

Research and Editorial Committee 431

List of Acronyms

AGCM	Regulatory Authority for Electricity and Gas (Autorità garante della concorrenza e del mercato)
AGCOM	The Communications Regulatory Authority (Autorità per le garanzie nelle comunicazioni)
ANCI	National Association of Italian Municipalities (Associazione Nazionale dei Comuni Italiani)
C.l.	Constitutional law (Legge costituzionale)
CARA	Reception Centre for Asylum Seekers (Centro di accoglienza per richiedenti asilo)
CAT	Convention against Torture and other Cruel, Inhuman or Degrading Treatment or Punishment
CFSP	Common Foreign and Security Policy of the European Union
CEDAW	Convention on the Elimination of all Forms of Discrimination against Women
CFREU	Charter of Fundamental Rights of the European Union
CFSP	Common Foreign and Security Policy of the European Union
CIDU	Inter-Ministerial Committee for Human Rights (Comitato interministeriale per i diritti umani)
CIE	Identification and Expulsion Centre (Centro di identificazione ed espulsione)
CM	Committee of Ministers of the Council of Europe
CNEL	National Economy and Labour Council (Consiglio nazionale dell'economia e del lavoro)
CoE	Council of Europe
CPED	International Convention for the Protection of All Persons from Enforced Disappearance
CPT	European Committee for the Prevention of Torture and Inhuman or Degrading Treatment or Punishment
CRC	Convention on the Rights of the Child

CRPD	Convention on the Rights of Persons with Disabilities
CSM	National Council of the Judiciary (Consiglio Superiore della Magistrarura)
CSDP	Common Security and Defence Policy of the European Union
D.p.c.m.	Decree of the President of the Council of Ministers (Decreto del Presidente del Consiglio dei Ministri)
D.p.r.	Decree of the President of the Republic (Decreto del Presidente della Repubblica)
ECHR	European Convention for the Protection of Human Rights and Fundamental Freedoms
ECJ	Court of Justice of the European Union
ECOSOC	United Nations Economic and Social Council
ECRI	European Commission against Racism and Intolerance
ECtHR	European Court of Human Rights
EP	European Parliament
ESC-R	European Social Charter (revised)
EU	European Union
FAO	Food and Agriculture Organisation of the United Nations
FRA	Fundamental Rights Agency of the European Union
GA	General Assembly of the United Nations
ICC	International Criminal Court
ICCPR	International Covenant on Civil and Political Rights
ICERD	International Convention on the Elimination of All Forms of Racial Discrimination
ICESCR	International Covenant on Economic, Social and Cultural Rights
ICRMW	International Convention on the Protection of the Rights of all Migrant Workers and their Families
ILO	International Labour Organisation
IOM	International Organisation for Migration
L.	Law

LGBT/LGBTI	Lesbian, Gay, Bisexual, Transexual (and Intersex)
L.d.	Law-decree (decreto legge)
Lgs.d.	Legislative decree (decreto legislativo)
MIUR	Ministry of Education, University and Research
NATO	North Atlantic Treaty Organisation
NGO	Non-governmental Organisation
ODIHR	Office for Democratic Institutions and Human Rights (OSCE)
OHCHR	Office of the High Commissioner of the United Nations for Human Rights
OPCAT	Optional Protocol to the Convention against Torture
OSCE	Organisation for Security and Cooperation in Europe
P.l.	Provincial law
PACE	Parliamentary Assembly of the Council of Europe
R.l.	Regional law
SPRAR	Protection System for Asylum Seekers and Refugees (Sistema di protezione per richiedenti asilo e rifugiati)
TEU	Treaty on European Union
TFEU	Treaty on the Functioning of the European Union
UN-HABITAT	United Nations Human Settlements Programme
UNACLA	United Nations Advisory Committee of Local Authorities
UNAR	Office for the Promotion of Equal Treatment and the Fight against Racial Discrimination (Ufficio per la promozione della parità di trattamento e la rimozione delle discriminazioni fondate sulla razza e sull'origine etnica)
UNDEF	United Nations Democracy Fund
UNDP	United Nations Development Programme
UNEP	United Nations Environmental Programme
UNESCO	United Nations Educational, Scientific and Cultural Organisation
UNFPA	United Nations Population Fund
UNHCR	United Nations High Commissioner for Refugees

UNICEF	United Nations Children's Fund
UNRWA	United Nations Relief and Works Agency for Palestine Refugees in the Near East
UPR	Universal Periodic Review
WHO	World Health Organisation

Italy and Human Rights in 2013: the Challenges of Social Justice and the Right to Peace

In autumn 2014, the United Nations Human Rights Council will conduct its second Universal Periodic Review of Italy, primarily in order to ascertain the degree of compliance reached in Italy following the recommendations made during the first round of reviews. The *2014 Yearbook* aims to provide empirical evidence which should prove useful, in addition to supporting the preparation for this operation, in enacting a comprehensive human rights system in Italy which is compliant with the principles and guidelines repeatedly recommended by the United Nations and the Council of Europe. The most important step is to establish the National Human Rights Commission as an independent body for the protection and promotion of fundamental rights. Italy made a commitment to this when putting its own candidature forward for a second mandate as a member of the Human Rights Council. It should be noted that, in the last years, there have been a series of bills *in re*, yet none of them have come to fruition in any way. Meanwhile, the Inter-ministerial Committee for Human Rights at the Ministry of Foreign Affairs has been reconstituted, and this body is charged with operating in the area of governmental functions.

The *2014 Yearbook*, like the previous edition, cannot but report the protracted state of great suffering for rights in Italy, particularly economic and social rights, starting from the right to work and to social security: the general unemployment rate is 13%, and youth unemployment stands at 42.3% (ISTAT data, March 2014).

The woes of social and economic rights are also spreading to the field of civil and political rights, creating difficulties for the very practice of democracy and fanning the fires of corporate egoism, inter-generational conflict, racist sentiment and anachronistic nationalism, as well as heightening the lack of confidence in public institutions at the national, European and international level. Social cohesion and even territorial cohesion are at risk. It is well to recall here just how peremptory are the provisions of the second paragraph of article 20 of the 1966 International Covenant on Civil and Political rights, ratified by Italy in 1977: "Any advocacy of national, racial or religious hatred that constitutes incitement to discrimination, hostility or violence shall be prohibited by law".

Again, in the previous editions of the Yearbook, emphasis was put on the fact that, in virtue of the principle of the interdependence and indivisibility of all human rights – economic, social, civil, political and cultural – policies which comply with the requirements of social justice are for all States an obligation, not an *optional* extra; it is reiterated that the social state and the rule of law are two indissociable infrastructural attributes of sustainable statehood. For the Member States of the European Union, this obligation is specifically mentioned in the Treaty of Lisbon, where it establishes that the Union shall work for sustainable development, based, specifically, on "a highly competitive social market economy, aiming at full employment and social progress" (article 3(3)). It should also be remembered that the EU Charter of Fundamental Rights includes civil and political rights as well as economic, social and cultural rights, and that the Lisbon Treaty itself makes specific reference, in its Preamble, to the 1961 European Social Charter and the 1989 Community Charter of the Fundamental Social Rights of Workers.

The *2013 Yearbook* quoted the warning from the United Nations High Commissioner for Human Rights, Navanethem Pillay, "the right to work is a fundamental human right which is inseparable from human dignity", to make the strongest possible statement that unemployment prevents the full realisation of the person, takes away the sense of ethics of one's "vocation", restricts horizons of freedom and the promotion of human dignity, and undermines education and training processes at their roots. It is useful to repeat, *opportune et inopportune*, that a Civilisation of Law comes to fulfilment when, in recognising all the rights relating to human dignity, it meets and espouses the Civilisation of Labour, obliging Governments and the other actors in economic processes to face market challenges with a compass of fundamental rights. These are a series of practical truths – as Jacques Maritain defined them – which predicate their true incarnation on individual and social behaviours, on public policies, on positive measures and on comprehensive investments in education. In other words, they constitute a "political agenda" which feeds into good governance processes in the multilevel *glocal* space which stretches from the town hall to the United Nations.

And so it is necessary, once and for all, to go beyond the limits and determinisms of the pervasive and malignant sub-culture which distinguishes, but in actual fact separates, the subject of fundamental rights from that of political action and decision-making, that is, cutting off the right from the corresponding obligation to implement it.

It should be strongly emphasised here that human rights, in addition to being "the parents of Law", as Amartya Sen typically argued, are political agenda, the alpha and omega of good governance.

The imperative of good governance is, of course, incumbent on intergovernmental and supranational organisations as well as on States, as they promote international human rights law and monitor its application by all States. However, the issue of monitoring and possibly applying penalties for the violation of rules is not the sole function of these international institutions. Indeed, they determine and implement veritable Government programmes, which affect a broad range of vitally important sectors. And so, like States, they too are bound to the respect of human rights, the rule of law and democratic principles, setting a good example in pursuing the objectives set by the overarching *human development* and *human security* strategies. For this to happen, it is necessary that the States making up the inter-governmental organisations respect the statutes of the same, and hence fulfil their obligation to make them function effectively, to provide them with the necessary human and financial resources and allow their structure and functioning to be made more democratic. As concerns Italy's responsibilities in this area, article 11 of the Constitution clearly states that: "Italy rejects war as an instrument of aggression against the freedom of other peoples and as a means for the settlement of international disputes. Italy agrees, on conditions of equality with other States, to the limitations of sovereignty that may be necessary to a world order ensuring peace and justice among the Nations. Italy promotes and encourages international organisations furthering such ends".

The dynamics of human rights must be considered not only in a vision of the plurality of its contents in substance, but also in the light of a territorial and functional context which, as previously mentioned, has a glocal dimension, and wherein the "responsibility to protect" human rights, that is, the commitment to guarantee them, must necessarily be shared between all institutions operating at the various levels from towns up to the highest supranational bodies.

In this respect, it is well to refer back to article 1 of the 1999 United Nations Declaration on the Right and Responsibility of Individuals, Groups and Organs of Society to Promote and Protect Universally Recognized Human Rights and Fundamental Freedoms: "Everyone has the right, individually and in association with others, to promote and to strive for the protection and realization of human rights and fundamental freedoms at the *national and international levels* (*italics added*). So there are no borders limiting the actions of human rights defenders, be they individuals, associations or local government bodies, the latter in their capacity as "organs of society". One should note that, pursuant to the Italian Constitution, Municipalities and Regions are part of the Republic, not of the State.

The reference to borderless space for the realisation of human rights calls to mind the model of world order the DNA of which is found in the United Nations Charter and in the Universal Declaration of Human Rights. It is the order of positive peace as defined in article 28 of the Declaration: "Everyone is entitled to a social and international order in which the rights and freedoms set forth in this Declaration can be fully realized".

It is essential to keep this model in the spotlight, to avoid being paralysed in the situation of liquidity – synonym of precariousness and insecurity – evocatively diagnosed by Zygmunt Baumann with reference to the human condition in the globalised world.

One will realise that not everything is "liquid". If one knows how to look for it, there is ample empirical evidence of the existence of "solids", identifiable in the genuine presence of elements of good governance of an infrastructural nature. First of all comes the "normative solid", constituted specifically by the universal code of human rights and the relative machinery to implement them. Then there is the "organisational solid", made up of the legitimate international institutions operating at the dual regional and universal level: from the United Nations Organisation to the European Union, from UNESCO and the ILO to the African Union, ASEAN, and the OAS, etc.

These organisations are "common houses" which exist in order to be enjoyed by all members of the human family, and for the proper running of which the member States are responsible. Significantly, the genuine commitment of Governments is measured according to their active participation in the functioning of these organs, but also according to the funds they allocate as their voluntary contributions to the organisations they belong to. In 2013, Italy's contribution to the Office of the United Nations High Commissioner for Human Rights was approximately $ 68,000 (ranking it 42nd as a donor), representing a decrease of about $ 25,000 compared to the previous year (when it was in 40th place). As concerns the budget of the High Commissioner for Refugees, in 2013, Italy contributed $ 9.3 million, a decrease of about $ 3.4 million dollars compared to the previous year.

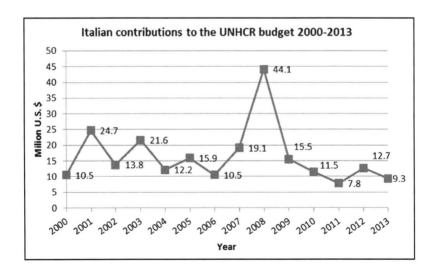

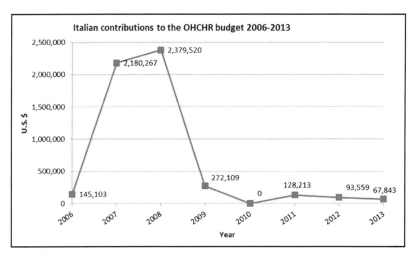

Source: OHCHR, *United Nations Human Rights Appeal 2014.*

In 2013, Italy's participation in the work of the United Nations Human Rights Council was particularly distinguished by the fact that over half of the 95 resolutions adopted by the Council saw Italy's direct participation (as a sponsor) or diplomatic support (as a co-sponsor), and that Italy's position was "winning" in 15 of the 28 votes cast. It is pointed out that two of the four "thematic" resolutions promoted by Italy refer to the contributions of national Parliaments to the completion of the Universal Periodic Review and to the World Programme for human rights education respectively.

In the education field, it should be noted that Italy was an active member of the platform of States which worked for the drafting and approval in 2011 of the United Nations Declaration on Human Rights Education and Training. There is now an expectation that the Italian Government, on the strength of its active role at the world level, should promptly adopt comprehensive plans to develop education in human rights, peace and democratic citizenship for schools at all levels. It is within this area that efforts must finally be made to recapitulate the various rivulets of sectorial education (on sustainable development, citizenship, legality, environment, etc.) around the human rights paradigm. The guidelines for this operation can be found in three fundamental international documents: the Resolution and Programme of Action on a Culture of Peace and Human Rights; the Declaration on Human Rights Education and Training, both from the United Nations, and the Council of Europe Charter on Education for Democratic Citizenship and Human Rights Education. In Italy, the Government is expected to feel spurred on in this direction by the example set by the good number of universities which continue to offer teaching and develop research in the specific field of human rights. Indeed, in 2013 there were 109 units specifically devoted to human rights, taught in 38 different universities. Over half of these units are included in degree courses in the area of politics and social sciences (numbering 61, or 56%), whereas a third are in the Law area (36 units, or 33%); 9 are in the areas of history, philosophy, pedagogy and psychology (8%) and 3 in the area of economics and statistics (3%). Top of the list of universities is the University of Padua with 20 units, followed by the University of Turin with 8. The strong presence of courses in the political and social sciences area is proof that the prevalent approach is decidedly policy and action-oriented, in line with the natural theoretical approach to the subject: or the axio-practical approach.

Since 2012, an inter-governmental working group tasked with drafting a Declaration on the Right to Peace has been operating within the United Nations Human Rights Council. From the outset, carrying out this mandate has proven fraught with difficulties because certain States declared their *a priori* rejection of the draft document being debated. One of their objections is that since current international law does not include a specific right to peace, such a right cannot be introduced by a Declaration. Another objection is that if peace were to be recognised as a fundamental right of the person and of peoples, all formally recognised human rights would be weakened as a consequence. These are clearly spurious arguments. A number of non-governmental organisations with consultative status at ECOSOC are taking an active part in the work of the aforementioned inter-governmental working group and are, as is to be expected, aligned in favour of the initiative. In Italy, the ongoing debate in Geneva has attracted the attention of a number of Municipal Councils, which have included the so-called "peace human rights norm" in their respective Statutes; this norm makes reference to the Italian Constitution and international human rights law to recognise peace as a fundamental right of the person and of peoples. Following a proposal from, and with the support of, the Human Rights Centre of the University of Padua, the Italian Coordination of Local Authorities for Peace and Human Rights asked municipal (and provincial) councils to approve a detailed petitionary motion supporting the initiative of the Human Rights Council. As the current edition of the Yearbook is going to print, there are news that about a hundred Municipal Councils large and small, from the Alps in the north to the southernmost tip of Italy, from east to west, in Sicily and in Sardinia, have approved the motion and are sending a delegation to deliver a copy of each to the Chairperson-Rapporteur of the Working Group, Ambassador Christian Guillermet Fernandez (Costa Rica), to the High Commissioner for Human Rights, Navi Pillay, and to the Head of the

Italian Mission, Ambassador Maurizio Enrico Serra. The Human Rights Centre of the University of Padua accompanied this virtuous mobilisation of local administrations with a special edition of its review "Pace diritti umani/Peace human rights" entirely devoted to *"The right to peace"* (Marsilio Editori, 2013, 240 pages), published with the collaboration of the Permanent Mission of Costa Rica to the United Nations (Geneva), specifically from the aforementioned Ambassador Guillermet and his legal advisor, David Fernàndez Puyana. Their Mission also distributed the magazine to the representatives of Human Rights Council member States and in other areas of the United Nations.

The debate over the recognition of peace as a fundamental right of the person and of peoples is strong proof of the need to bring back into peacebuilding the lofty aspirations expressed in the Preamble of the United Nations Charter ("We, the peoples of the United Nations, determined to save succeeding generations from the scourge of war...") and the Preamble of the Universal Declaration ("recognition of the inherent dignity and of the equal and inalienable rights of all members of the human family is the foundation of freedom, justice and peace in the world").

Paradoxically, despite the contents of article 28 of the Universal Declaration and those of the statutes of the international organisations, starting with the United Nations Charter and the UNESCO Constitution, peace continues to be a fundamental human right for the *vox populi* but not yet so, formally, under current international *ius positum*. The ongoing efforts within the Human Rights Council are directed at rendering visible that which is already immanent in new international law.

The advocacy of Italian towns in favour of the recognition of peace as a right of the person and of peoples is an expression of a "city diplomacy" exercised based on the principle of subsidiarity and with reference to the provisions of the aforementioned article 1 of the 1999 United Nations Declaration on the Right and Responsibility of Individuals, Groups and Organs of Society to Promote and Protect Universally Recognized Human Rights and Fundamental Freedoms. In their petitionary motion, the Municipal Councils wish to particularly emphasise that peace, as such, is grounded in the right to life and is hence, like the right to life, a precondition for the enjoyment of all human rights, and that the formal inclusion of peace as a right of the person and of peoples in the universal code of human rights requires States to meet specific obligations, starting from disarmament and the commitment to fully implementing the provisions of the United Nations Charter for the effective deployment of a collective security system. Specifically, it is a question of consigning to the past, once and for all, the right to make war – *ius ad bellum* – as an essential attribute of the constituent shape of national statehood, and to replace it with the duty to peace – *officium pacis* –. This would cut to the roots the right of States over the life and death (*ius necis ac vitae*) of their own and other citizens and would give a firmly operative meaning to the concept of security contained in the United Nations Charter.

In this context, the establishing of Civilian Peace Corps pursuant to the provisions of the so-called "2014 Stability Law" (l. 27 December 2013, No. 147, art. 253), with a budget of 9 million euros to be spent over a three-year period, becomes truly meaningful.

I. Regulatory and Infrastructural Human Rights Situation

Ratification Process Completed, Underway and Neglected

In 2013, Italy was involved in the ratification process for several important international legal instruments concerning human rights. Specifically, on 3 April 2013, the ratification process for the Optional Protocol to the Convention against Torture (OPCAT) was completed, the respective law for implementation and ratification having been adopted by the Italian Parliament on 9 November 2012). Consequently, Italy must proceed without further delay to set up a relevant nationwide preventive mechanism, in line with the provisions of the Protocol itself. On disarmament, the Arms Trading Treaty was signed (2 April 2013) and in October of the same year, Parliament adopted law 118/2013 authorising its ratification and execution (the ratification instrument was deposited on 2 April 2014).

As concerns the legal instruments adopted by the Council of Europe, Italy ratified the Convention on the Protection of Children Against Sexual Exploitation and Sexual Abuse ("Lanzarote Convention", 3 January 2013); the Framework Convention on the Value of Cultural Heritage for Society (27 February 2013) and the Convention on Preventing and Combating Violence against Women ("Istanbul Convention", 10 September 2013). In addition, during the year the ratification instruments were finally deposited concerning the Civil Law Convention and the Criminal Law Convention on Corruption (13 June 2013); the respective ratification and implementation laws were adopted by Parliament in June of the previous year (l. 110/2012 and l. 112/2012). On the other hand, no recent legislative action has been taken concerning the acceptance of the Optional Protocol to the Criminal Law Convention on this subject, which completes the provisions designed to protect the judiciary from corruption (the Protocol was signed on 15 June 2003).

Italy has also signed, on the date on which they opened for signature, the two new additional Protocols to the European Convention on Human Rights adopted in 2013. Protocol XV adds, in the Preamble of the ECHR, references to the principle of subsidiarity and to the States' margin of appreciation as they hold primary responsibility for the functioning of the ECtHR; Protocol XVI allows the highest national courts to suspend their proceedings and request the Grand Chamber to provide an advisory opinion on the interpretation or the application of the rights and freedoms in the ECHR or the additional Protocols thereto.

On the contrary, there has been no progress in the completion of some essential legal human rights instruments on which Italy had already started the respective ratification processes, in some cases, several years ago. These include, at the global level: the International Convention for the Protection of All Persons from Enforced Disappearances (signed in 2007), the Optional Protocol to the International Covenant on Economic, Social and Cultural Rights (signed in 2009) and the Third Optional Protocol to the Convention on the Rights of the Child on a Communications Procedure (signed in 2012); at the European regional level: Protocol No. 12 to the Convention for the Protection of Human Rights and Fundamental Freedoms, prohibiting discrimination (signed in 2000) and the Convention on Human Rights and Biomedicine (Oviedo Convention), for which the Italian Parliament adopted and implemented a law in 2001 (l. 145/2001). Since the ratification instrument of this Convention has not yet been deposited, Italy does not figure as a Party to it. Of the core international human rights treaties, the 1990 International Convention on the Protection of the Rights of all Migrant Workers and their Families is the only international legal instrument which has not been the object of any initiative for its ratification.

Implementation of Social Rights Standards

In January 2014, the Council of Europe European Committee of Social Rights adopted its *Conclusions 2013* on Italy, relative to the thematic group of provisions of the European Social Charter (revised) on "Health, Social Security and Social protection". Of the 19 provisions in this thematic group, the Committee adopted 8 conclusions of conformity (in some cases requesting further information be presented), 7 of non-conformity and 4 requests for more in-depth information. Still regarding the degree of Italy's compliancy with the European system of protection of social rights, Italy has not yet presented its first report on the provisions of the revised Charter which it did not accept, that is, only art. 25, which recognises workers' right to protection of their credit in case of insolvency of their employer. According to the Committee of Ministers' communication, this report should have been presented back in 2004, that is, five years after Italy's ratification of the European Social Charter (revised) (on 5 July 1999). Finally, on the subject of social security, the Committee of

Ministers expressed a substantially positive assessment of Italy's implementation of the European Code of Social Security (see Part III, Council of Europe, II).

Requested legislative Actions

Several international bodies have requested Italy to take action to change legislation relative to the offence of defamation and, specifically, the provisions of the Italian criminal code by which prison sentences of up to three years can be imposed on journalists and editors found guilty of the "aggravated" form of such misdemeanour. Despite the sentences of the European Court of Human Rights and the prompts from organisations such as the United Nations, the Council of Europe and the OSCE, unanimous in judging a prison sentence disproportionate punishment for defamation through printed media (libel), Italy still has not completed the process of amending the legislation concerning the aforementioned issues. An additional concern is that the bill on the matter currently being examined in Parliament (Act C 925), despite being a step in the right direction as it would replace prison sentences with fines, does not appear to be going for complete decriminalisation of the offence of defamation, which was what the European and international organisations had suggested.

Finally, the failure to introduce the crime of torture into the Italian criminal code continues to be criticised by a number of international monitoring bodies. Specifically, in 2013 the Council of Europe Committee for the Prevention of Torture once again highlighted how the absence of the specific offence of torture in the Italian criminal code has made it difficult to prosecute behaviour constituting this serious violation of human rights. In this case, too, not one of the bills aiming to remedy this shortcoming (of which twelve were presented in 2013 alone) has to date been finalised.

Regional Legislation

As in previous years, in 2013 too, the Italian Regions and Autonomous Provinces adopted a number of laws on issues relevant to human rights. It should be pointed out that some of these legislative acts require amendments to previously adopted laws, whereas others are cross-cutting and regard more than one of the thematic categories used in this Yearbook. Bearing this in mind, the total number of laws examined in 2013 was 71, distributed as follows over the various thematic categories: Peace, human rights, development cooperation and fair trade: 3; Equal opportunities, gender issues: 9; Minorities: 1; Migrations: 1; Ombudspersons and Ombudspersons for Children: 2; Persons with disabilities: 5; Workers' rights: 24; Solidarity, social promotion and support to families: 23; Education in citizenship and legality: 3. What stands out in this list is the large (and growing) number of regional laws for the protection of workers' rights (+ 13 compared to 2012) and the promotion of solidarity and support to families (+ 1), data which confirm the efforts certain local and regional bodies have put into tackling the social impact that the protracted Italian economic and employment crises are having at the territorial level.

Infrastructural Shortcomings: National Human Rights Institutions

Despite the numerous and repeated recommendations received from Europe and international institutions, Italy has still not created an independent national Institution for human rights in line with the Paris principles.

Concerning the establishing of the National Commission for Human Rights, in 2013 two bills were presented: one to the Chamber of Deputies and one to the Senate. Each of them has been assigned to its respective parliamentary commission, however neither branch of Parliament has yet started examining them. Moreover it should be remembered that, now the Optional Protocol to the Convention against Torture has been ratified, the National Commission can also take on the functions of the national mechanism for the prevention of torture which said Protocol envisages, in line with the provisions in art. 3(3) of the law authorising its ratification and implementation (l. 195/2012).

Regarding Ombudspersons, no legislative measures to establish an Ombudsperson at the national level have been taken. On the other hand, the activity of the regional, territorial and provincial Ombudspersons has continued, protecting the rights and interests of individuals in dealings with the public administration, with the support of the National Coordinating Body of Ombudspersons and the Italian Ombudsman Institute. In 2013, an Ombudsman was appointed for the Campania Region (the post was vacant in 2012), bringing the total number of incumbent Regional Ombudspersons to 15, out of a total of 19 Regions and Autonomous Provinces (17 + 2) whose statutes contemplate this institution. The figure of the Ombudsperson also exists in 24 ordinary Provinces. In 16 of these, the Ombudsperson performs the duties of territorial Ombudsperson, with responsibility also for the territories of the Municipalities with whom an agreement has been made.

In December 2013, the Government adopted l.d. 146/2013, which in art. 7 provides for the establishment of a National Ombudsperson for the rights of persons detained or deprived of their personal freedom. The National Ombudsperson is collegial and will have the function of acting as a watchdog to ensure that the execution of custodial sentences and of other forms of restriction of personal freedom is implemented in compliance with the regulations and principles established by the Constitution, by international human rights conventions and by the laws of the State. It is hoped that immediate action will be taken to appoint the members of this new independent authority and to provide it with the resources necessary for it to be able to fulfil its institutional duties.

II. Implementation of International Obligations and Commitments: Implementation of ECtHR Case-law

2013 practice confirmed the positive trend of Italian judges, from the Constitutional Court and the Supreme Court downwards, to consciously and extensively resort to international sources on human rights issues, including, especially, the European Convention of Human Rights. However, despite the increasing efforts of the judiciary to harmonise the national and the international, on certain specific issues the Italian legal system as a whole continues to prove itself somewhat impermeable, or incapable of adapting to some consolidated orientation from case-law developed by the Court of Strasbourg.

Issues relating to the excessive duration of judicial proceedings, including proceedings to establish redress for the excessive duration of previous proceedings, continue to cause concern in this regard, not least because of their structural nature. Specifically, in redress proceedings, the amendments to the Pinto law, the objective of which was to speed up the procedure for ascertaining the damages payable for the unreasonable duration of proceedings, appears not only to have failed to produce the results expected, but doubts have also been raised as to its compliancy with the Constitution.

Another issue which has brought Italy a series of censures from Europe over the years, culminating in the pilot judgment in the January 2013 *Torreggiani and others* case, is the structural inadequacy of the Italian prison system. It should be noted that, in addition to the problems of overcrowding, in itself a situation which the Strasbourg Court considers potentially damaging to human dignity, the shortcomings of the Italian prison system have also led to a number of judgments against Italy for violation of art. 3 ECHR as applied to the conditions for prisoners with particular pathologies. Finally, the ECtHR continues to receive cases questioning the compatibility with art. 6 ECHR ("fair trial") of certain legal instruments presented as "interpretative", but which in effect make retroactive changes to legal positions that citizens believed established by reason of consolidated case-law orientation. The most significant example of these problems in 2013 is the pilot judgment in the *M.C. and others* case during which, among other things, further examples of violation of the principle of pre-eminence of the law emerged, because the Italian authorities had failed to implement a ruling of the Constitutional Court.

On the other hand, two 2013 rulings by the Italian Constitutional Court deserve mention as examples of a positive convergence, or exemplary use of ECtHR case-law. In the first, concerning the implications of *Scoppola* (2) case-law, the Court recognised the general applicability of the ruling by the Strasbourg Court and declared that the law object of censure in Europe was unconstitutional in all those cases where it had brought about identical prejudice. In the second, the Constitutional Court, in effect making a legal about-turn, accepted the opinion expressed by the ECtHR in the *Godelli* case as to the right of an adopted child to know his family origins versus the request for anonymity expressed at the time of his birth by his biological mother.

III. Adoption and Implementation of Policies

Prison Conditions: Overcrowding and Ill-treatment

As highlighted in the special-focus paragraphs above, concerning the desirable legislative actions and acceptance of ECtHR case-law, the question of prison conditions is a particularly pressing issue in the overall framework of the human rights situation in Italy. One of the main problems connected to this subject is, as is well known, that of overcrowding in prisons. According to data provided by the Prisons Administration Department (DAP), updated to April 2014, there are 59,683 people in prison in Italy (2,524, or 4.2% of the overall number, are women; 20,521, or 34%, are foreigners). The regular total capacity of Italy's 205 prisons is 49,091. Compared to the previous year (DAP data from December 2012), the total number of detainees has decreased by 6.018, while the overall capacity has increased by 2,051. The ratio between number of detainees and places officially available is now 1.2 (approximately 120 detainees for every 100 available places), whereas in 2012 it was about 1.4 (140 detainees for every 100 places).

However, despite the aforementioned decrease in the prison population, the measures aimed at reducing prison overcrowding implemented in recent months by the Italian Government still appear insufficient to provide a systematic and definitive solution to this serious structural issue, as imposed by the European Court of Human Rights with the *Torreggiani* "pilot judgment" (which became final in May 2013). Moreover, as highlighted in the reports published in 2013 by the Council of Europe Committee for the Prevention of Torture (CPT), there are still situations in some Italian prisons where the minimum requisite of 4 m² per detainee (in multiple occupation cells) is not respected. It is therefore incumbent upon the Italian authorities, over a year since the *Torreggiani* sentence became final, to adopt remedies of a structural nature, to act in parallel at the administrative and normative level, and consider more frequent recourse to alternative, non-custodial sentences and reducing the use of pre-trial detention, as recommended by the international monitoring bodies.

Another particularly pressing issue which emerges from the recommendations of the international monitoring bodies, especially in the CPT reports, is on the question of ill-treatment in prison (see Part III, Council of Europe, IV). The measures recommended in this area are mainly directed towards: strengthening the effectiveness of investigations into those responsible, where there are reports or signs that ill-treatment has occurred while a person was in police custody or in prison; ensuring that all persons deprived of personal freedom have full access to all procedures designed to protect them from any ill-treatment; boosting efforts aimed at preventing any instances of ill-treatment through initiatives such as establishing an independent inspection system.

Progress of the National Strategy for the Inclusion of Roma, Sinti and Traveller Communities

The condition of Roma and Sinti and the process for the social inclusion of members of these communities in Italy is another issue on which the attention and concern of international monitoring bodies and civil society organisations are focused. A paradigm shift compared to the "emergency" approach long taken by the Italian authorities towards these social groups (calling it the "Nomad Emergency") began in February 2012, with the Government's adoption of the National Strategy for the Inclusion of Roma, Sinti and Traveller Communities. The Strategy develops an inter-ministerial participatory approach, aiming to open up a new stage in relations with the members of these communities. One of the pillars of this new approach is its emphasis on territorial cooperation, to be effected through the planning of activities involving local institutions and non-institutional actors (including representatives of the Roma, Sinti and traveller communities), with special attention focused on protection of the human rights of the people involved in the social inclusion process.

Since late 2012, a number of roundtables have been established, involving civil society organisations and representatives of local and regional bodies, in order to implement the principles and the provisions relative to the four areas identified in the Strategy for priority action: education, work, housing and healthcare. Of the roundtables, two are particularly important: the Legal one (first meeting in January 2013), which is charged, *inter alia*, with the complex task of finding solutions for the situation of over 15,000 *de facto* stateless Roma born in Italy to stateless parents from the former Yugoslavia (see *2012 Yearbook*, p. 35) and the Housing Policy roundtable. The latter, which convened for the first time on 18 November 2013, is tasked with contributing to the abandonment of the practice of "clearing" Roma camps and with finding suitable housing solutions as an alternative to living in settlements. Indeed, these two issues are those most frequently mentioned in the recommendations made to Italy by regional and international human rights organisations.

Moreover, following stimuli from UNAR and the Italian State-Regions Conference, eight Regions have set up regional working groups to strengthen territorial cooperation and foster the participation of the various local actors concerned in drawing up the details of plans for inclusion. There is also an active statistics task force involving ISTAT, ANCI and the EU Fundamental Rights Agency (FRA), set up to gather specific, non-aggregate data on the presence of Roma in Italy, essential to the adoption of effective measures which are functional in relation to the objectives and the inclusive approach the Strategy has developed.

In September 2013, the inter-ministerial steering committee charged with guiding the integration process over the medium and long term met in order to boost the general advancement of the Strategy and enhance the channels for dialogue and cooperation between the national and sub-national levels. However, at present it is difficult to find any detailed information on the current state of progress of the various activities of the aforementioned roundtables, and hence, on the real state of implementation of this stage of the Strategy. The initiatives undertaken to date show a gradually developing commitment based on securing the participation of all the different types of actors involved in the process of social inclusion of Roma and Sinti, and also close attention to the many problematic issues raised by civil society and the main international organisations monitoring human rights. In order to comply with the medium and long-term commitments made (the reference period for the implementation of the Strategy is 2012–2020), local and national authorities will therefore have to continue and redouble the efforts made thus far, together with civil society organisations and the representatives of the Roma community, including plans to adopt some normative provisions. On this issue, it should be remembered that in the first half of 2013 two bills were presented in the Senate which could support their efforts: Act S 560 (Ratification and execution of the European Charter for Regional or Minority Languages, done in Strasbourg on 5 November 1992) which in art. 3, provides for linguistic and cultural protection afforded by the Charter to be applied to these minorities too (in addition to those already protected under l. 482/1999) and Act 770 (Provisions for the Protection and Equal Opportunities for Roma and Sinti minorities). To date, however, examination of these bills by their respective parliamentary committees has not yet started.

The Rights of Migrants, Refugees and Asylum-Seekers

In Italy the migratory phenomenon has for quite some time now become a structural phenomenon. According to estimates in the *2013 File on Immigration Statistics* (Dossier Statistico Immigrazione 2013), published by the "Centro studi e ricerche IDOS/Immigrazione", together with the UNAR, the number of foreign citizens regularly present in Italy in 2012 was 5,186,000, of whom about 4,388,000 with residency status, equivalent to 7.4% of Italy's total population.

2013 was marked by a large number of migrant landings in the Mediterranean, some of which ending in tragic shipwrecks, such as that on 3 October 2013 off the island of Lampedusa, which caused the death of hundreds of refugees and migrants, prevalently from Eritrea. Partly due to these arrivals, the number of asylum requests registered in Italy in 2013 were 27,800 (+60% compared to 2012, but well below the spike at 34,100 requests in 2011, the year of the so-called "Arab Spring" in north African Countries). These figures place Italy seventh out of the 44 industrialised Countries by number of asylum requests received (about 5% of the total number of requests).

In this area, the most critical aspects concern not only access to and living conditions on Italian soil (violations of the principle of *non-refoulement*, difficulties in accessing the procedures to request asylum, protracted detention in the Centres for Identification and Expulsion, problems in the identification and reception of unaccompanied minors), but also the many cases of discrimination targeting migrants who are regular residents of Italy. In 2012, UNAR recorded 659 cases of racial discrimination, an increase of 22% compared to 2010. The mass-media (particularly the Internet) are the arena in which the greatest number of cases of discrimination occurred. In the workplace, the condition of migrants is often marked by occupying jobs for which they are over-qualified and widespread instances where work is temporary, underground, exploited and on the verge of slavery, as well as subject to a high level of workplace accidents (15.9% of all work accidents, according to the *2013 File on Immigration Statistics*, without taking into account the so-called "invisible accidents", because they were not reported: 164,000 according to INAIL – the Italian national work accident insurance institute). In the area of education, the drop-out rate of foreign children and adolescents is higher than that of Italians, both at middle school (0.49% for foreigners compared to 0.17% for Italians) and at high school (2.42%

compared to 1.16%). Migrants are particularly subject to discrimination also as concerns their right to housing (the *Immigration Statistics File* estimates that about 20% of migrants live in unsuitable and precarious housing) and their right to healthcare (only 6 of the Regions and Autonomous Provinces have formally ratified the agreement approved by the permanent State-Regions Conference on the elimination of unequal access of immigrants to health services). Cases of racism are on the rise in the world of sport, too: there were 699 instances of racism involving fans during the 2012–2013 football championship season (including Serie A and lower divisions, the Coppa Italia, the under-20 league championship and friendly matches), involving 29 clubs and ensuing in fines for almost 500,000 euros.

The Yearbook makes reference to the frequent recommendations made to Italy by international bodies and experts, specifically the UNHCR and the United Nations Special Rapporteur on the human rights of migrants, that Italy eliminate discrimination and promote the full enjoyment of rights and equal opportunities for migrants (see Part III, United Nations, II, C and IV). In any event, all agree on one essential element: Italy needs to get away from a purely emergency and security-oriented view and manage the migratory phenomenon as a structural one, the systematic planning for which must be regulated through ordinary instruments and multi-level governance involving the Ministries concerned, the Regions, local administrations and civil society.

IV. Structure of the 2014 Yearbook

The objective of the *Italian Yearbook of Human Rights 2014* is to provide a snapshot of the human rights situation in Italy both from the legislative and the "infrastructural" point of view, and from that of the practical implementation of policies and initiatives to promote and protect them. The reference timeframe of the book is calendar year 2013. The level of detail and further background supplied in the various sections allow for cross-cutting and targeted reading, which can also be developed by consulting the analytical indexes.

The information presented in the first three Parts of the Yearbook come from documents in the public domain, normally consultable via the official web pages of each body examined. For Part IV the databases of the courts mentioned were used (for Italian case-law, the Giuffrè "De Iure" database was that used the most). From this edition of the Yearbook, the complete and updated lists of the international legal instruments adopted and Italy's behaviour in relation to them (ratifications, signatures, no action) have been made available online in the specific section hosted on the "Pace Diritti Umani" website (www.italianhumanrightsyearbook.eu, Attachments") managed by the University of Padua Human Rights Centre pursuant to art. 2 of Veneto regional law 55/1999.

Part I of the Yearbook illustrates the main developments in Italy's incorporation of international and regional laws into its own domestic legal order. This overview starts from the universal level (United Nations), moves on to the regional level, comprising legislation drawn up by the Council of Europe and the European Union, before presenting domestic legislation which has implemented international obligations through national and regional laws.

Part II illustrates the human rights infrastructure in Italy and is divided into three chapters. The first presents the structure, functions and activities of State bodies: Parliament, Government, the Judiciary and independent authorities; it also covers the activities of civil society organisations and academic institutions which operate at the national level. The second chapter refers to the sub-national level of the Italian order and illustrates the variegated local and regional human rights infrastructure and the relative co-ordinating bodies at the national level. The third chapter is devoted to the peace and human rights infrastructure and the local and international initiatives in this area developed by the Region of Veneto. The specific focus on this Region is explained by the pioneering commitment shown by Veneto, dating back to its regional law 18/1988, in promoting a culture of human rights, peace and international solidarity.

Part III examines Italy's position with reference to the regional and international bodies and mechanisms for monitoring the implementation of human rights. Ample space is given to the evaluations and recommendations that these bodies have made on Italy following specific visits to the Country and periodic monitoring activities. Italy's role within these organisations and the contribution of its representatives for the promotion of human rights at regional and global level are highlighted. This Part is divided into five chapters. The first focuses on the United Nations system, concentrating mainly on the activities of the General Assembly, the Human Rights Council and the specialised Agencies. The second chapter turns to the Council of Europe, whereas the third is on the European Union. These two chapters complement the information presented in part I (concerning legislation) and Part IV (concerning case-law), relative to EU and Council of Europe activities in 2013. The fourth chapter is on the Organisation for Security and Cooperation in Europe (OSCE) and its bodies for the promotion of the human dimension of security. The fifth and final chapter is on international humanitarian and criminal law and in this area, it provides updates on the level of implementation of their provisions in Italy and also a list of the international peace missions which saw the participation of Italian troops in 2013.

Finally, Part IV presents a selection of domestic and international case-law concerning Italy over the reference period. In the three chapters into which it is divided, the cases are subdivided according to the issues to which the various judgments refer. The chapters address domestic case-law (mainly the Constitutional Court, the Supreme Court and the Council of State), case-law of the European Court of Human Rights and case-law of the Court of Justice of the European Union respectively, the latter with reference to cases directly involving Italy. A targeted reading of the case-law can also be made by using the index of referenced case-law at the end of the book.

In consideration of the great significance of the Italian Municipalities' initiative regarding the international recognition of peace as a fundamental right of the person and of peoples, this Yearbook includes an exceptional addition: an essay by Ambassador Christian Guillermet Fernandez, Deputy Permanent Representative of Costa Rica to the United Nations in Geneva and Chairperson/Rapporteur of the Intergovernmental Working Group on the right to peace established by the Human Rights Council in 2012, and by Dr. David Puyana Fernandez, Legal Advisor to the Chairperson of the Working Group. The Draft Declaration attached to the essay, published on 24 June 2014, is the subject of serious criticism, in particular by the several NGOs that are calling for the recovery of the substantial part of the Draft that was previously adopted by the Advisory Committee of the Human Rights Council. Article 1 of the previous Draft reads:

1. Individuals and peoples have a right to peace. This right shall be implemented without any distinction or discrimination for reasons of race, descent, national, ethnic or social origin, colour, gender, sexual orientation, age, language, religion or belief, political or other opinion, economic situation or heritage, diverse physical or mental functionality, civil status, birth or any other condition.

2. States, severally and jointly, or as part of multilateral organizations, are the principal duty-holders of the right to peace.

3. The right to peace is universal, indivisible, interdependent and inter-related.

4. States shall abide by the legal obligation to renounce the use or threat of use of force in international relations.

5. All States, in accordance with the principles of the Charter of the United Nations, shall use peaceful means to settle any dispute to which they are parties.

6. All States shall promote the establishment, maintenance and strengthening of international peace in an international system based on respect for the principles enshrined in the Charter and the promotion of all human rights and fundamental freedoms, including the right to development and the right of peoples to self-determination.

UPR: Towards the Second Cycle of the Universal Periodic Review

How is Italy preparing for its second Universal Periodic Review before the United Nations Human Rights Council (October 2014)? To what degree have the recommendations received during the first Universal Periodic Review (2010) been implemented? These questions persuaded the members of the Yearbook's research and editorial committee to prepare an analysis, presented in the coming pages and based on the contents of the *2014 Yearbook* and the three previous editions (2011, 2012 e 2013), of the status of implementation of the recommendations made to Italy in 2010. This analysis is further backed by the information contained in the reports adopted, over the same period, by international bodies (the United Nations, the Council of Europe, the European Union and the OSCE) and civil society organisations (particularly Upr.info, Amnesty International, Human Rights Watch and the Comitato per la promozione e protezione dei diritti umani – Italian Committee for the Promotion and Protection of Human Rights).

In the course of the first Universal Periodic Review, Italy received 92 recommendations, relative to 19 thematic areas, from 51 different Countries (doc. A/HRC/14/4). The overwhelming majority of these recommendations (83%) belong to 8 thematic areas:

1. *the rights of migrants, refugees and asylum-seekers* (recommendations Nos. 9–10 and 67–82): within this area, the most recurrent recommendations request Italy to rethink its policy of criminalising irregular migrants and the push-back policies implemented in the Mediterranean;

2. *racial discrimination* (recommendations Nos. 18–33): particular concern is expressed over the increase in the number of cases of discrimination reported by the UNAR, with particular reference to the increased number of public speeches inciting racial hatred;

3. *the rights of national minorities* (recommendations Nos. 56–66), with particular reference to the need to improve the conditions of the Roma, Sinti and travellers communities;

4. *ratification of international instruments* (recommendations Nos. 1–7): Italy is specifically requested to ratify the United Nations Convention on the Rights of Migrant Workers, the International Convention for the Protection of All Persons from Enforced Disappearances and the Optional Protocol to the Convention against Torture;

5. *the rights of children* (recommendations Nos. 37–44): the recommendations are above all on the need to combat the phenomenon of violence against and ill-treatment of children, and the need to establish mechanisms to enshrine their right to be heard in court and/or administrative proceedings which concern them directly;

6. *trafficking in human beings* (recommendations Nos. 83–88): Italy has been invited to redouble previous efforts to stamp out human trafficking, offer adequate protection to victims, particularly women and children, and to prosecute traffickers;

7. *lack of human rights structures at the national level* (recommendations Nos. 11–15): Italy should correct this structural shortcoming in the shortest possible time by creating an independent national human rights institution in line with the Paris Principles;

8. *Independence of the media and freedom of the press* (recommendations Nos. 50–54): the Human Rights Council invites Italy to implement suitable measures to enhance the independence of the information system and protect freedom of the press, with particular reference to the protection of journalists from attack by organised criminal groups.

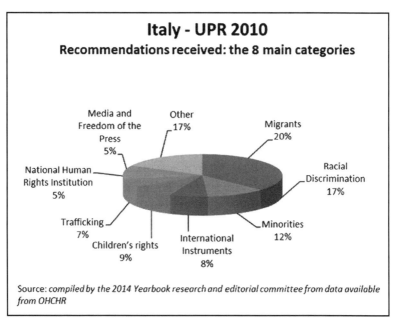

Italy - UPR 2010
Recommendations received: the 8 main categories

Media and Freedom of the Press 5%

Other 17%

Migrants 20%

National Human Rights Institution 5%

Racial Discrimination 17%

Trafficking 7%

Children's rights 9%

International Instruments 8%

Minorities 12%

Source: compiled by the 2014 Yearbook research and editorial committee from data available from OHCHR

Other equally serious, albeit less frequent, recommendations highlight shortcomings and critical issues in the national system for protecting human rights, such as, for example, the fact that the crime of torture is not envisaged in the Italian legal order, overcrowding in prisons, the spreading of the scourge of violence against women.

Of the 92 recommendations received, Italy accepted 80, therefore committing to their implementation within four years, and rejected 12 of them. Included in the latter group are the recommendations on the need to: introduce torture as a specific crime in the Italian criminal code; abrogate the laws which criminalise irregular immigration; ratify the United Nations Convention on the Rights of Migrant Workers (for a more detailed illustration of these recommendations, see *2011 Yearbook*, pp. 169–173). Italy's commitment to implementing the recommendations it accepted was moreover reconfirmed in 2011, when the Italian Government presented its candidature for election to the United Nations Human Rights Council: thanks in part to this commitment, Italy was indeed elected for the three-year period June 2011-June 2014.

On the basis of data collected in the 2011–2014 Yearbooks, it is apparent that as of May 2014, Italy had only fully implemented 14% of the recommendations accepted[1]. Specifically, Italy has: ratified the Optional Protocol to the Convention against Torture, committing to introducing the required domestic preventive measure and ratified the Council of Europe Convention on Combating Trafficking in Human Beings; drawn up the Third two-year National Action Plan for the Protection of the Rights and Development of Children and Adolescents 2010–2011, the National Strategy for the Inclusion of Roma, Sinti and travellers 2012–2020 and the National Plan against Racism, Xenophobia and Intolerance for the three-year period 2013–2015; strengthened the measures adopted to combat trafficking in human beings and to especially protect women and child victims of trafficking. Recommendation No. 73 is also one of those fully implemented (striking out the aggravating factor connected to the status of irregular immigrants: criminal code art. 61, No. 11-bis) although initially rejected by Italy during the Periodic Review: the Constitutional Court declared this circumstance unconstitutional in judgment No. 249 of 8 July 2010, (see *2011 Yearbook*, pp. 277–278).

28% of the recommendations have been partially implemented, or certain positive actions have been undertaken towards implementing them, but these are still not sufficient to ensure fully achieving the objective established[2]. In effect, some of the recommendations include long-term objectives which require the activation of a complex legislative process

---

[1] Recommendation Nos. 3, 4, 7, 18, 19, 42, 43, 73, 74, 82-84, 87.

[2] Recommendation Nos. 6, 11, 15, 20-22, 26, 28-30, 32, 34-36, 40, 45, 46, 57, 62, 67, 72, 75, 80, 85, 86, 88, 89, 92.

or several cycles of public policies, which makes it very difficult to complete them all in a timeframe of only 4 years. Some examples are:

– *recommendations Nos. 21, 22, 26, 28–30, 32*: despite efforts deployed at the national level to combat all forms of racism and racial discrimination, through campaigns and education and awareness-raising initiatives promoted above all by the Department for Equal Opportunities, the Ministry of Labour and Social Policies and the Ministry for Integration, between 2010 and 2012 UNAR recorded an increase of 22% in the number of instances of racial discrimination (see, in this Yearbook, Part II, National Bodies with Jurisdiction over Human Rights, II, A);

– *recommendations Nos. 45–46*: As already mentioned in the focus section above on prison conditions, the Prison Administration Department estimates that between December 2012 and April 2014, the ratio between detainees and number of places available in prison has moved from 1.4 (140 detainees per 100 places) to 1.2 (approximately 120 detainees per 100 places). However, these improvements still appear insufficient to systematically and permanently resolve the serious problem of prison overcrowding.

– *recommendation No. 72*: on 17 May 2014, law 67/2014 came into effect, under which the Government is to abrogate the criminal offence of a first irregular entry and stay in Italy, making it an administrative offence. This will be effected through a legislative decree, to be presented by the Minister of Justice with the agreement of the Minister of Economy and Finance, and which must be adopted within eighteen months from the date the law came into effect. This recommendation, too, had been initially rejected by Italy.

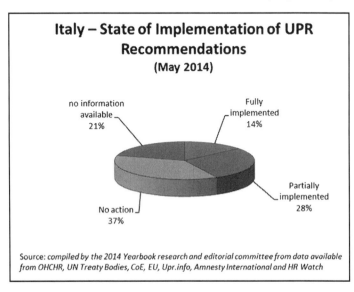

Italy – State of Implementation of UPR Recommendations (May 2014)

no information available 21%; Fully implemented 14%; Partially implemented 28%; No action 37%

Source: compiled by the 2014 Yearbook research and editorial committee from data available from OHCHR, UN Treaty Bodies, CoE, EU, Upr.info, Amnesty International and HR Watch

Overall, then, Italy has made progress in the implementation of 42% of the 92 recommendations received, including two which it initially rejected (striking out the "aggravating circumstance" of being an irregular immigrant and decriminalising the offence of irregular entry and stay in Italy).

On the other hand, no action has been taken concerning 37% of the recommendations received[3]. Specifically, Italy has not withdrawn the reservations it expressed on the International Covenant on Civil and Political Rights (recommendation No. 1); it has not ratified the International Convention on the Protection of the Rights of All Migrant Workers and Members of Their Families nor that against enforced disappearances (recommendations Nos. 2 and 5); it has not yet introduced the crime of torture into the national legal order, nor has it established the independent National Commission for Human Rights (recommendations Nos. 8 and 11–15), despite several bills having been presented on the issues (see, in this Yearbook, Part II, National Bodies with Jurisdiction over Human Rights, I, D); it has not adopted legislative measures to strengthen the mandate and operational capacities of the UNAR (recommendation No. 16); it has not made human rights training compulsory for police and justice sector workers (recommendation No. 31); it has not amended national legislation in order to recognise the Roma and Sinti communities as national minorities (recommendations Nos. 56 and 58); it has not made a significant increase to its official development assistance (stuck at only 0.16% of GDP in 2013) in order to reach the objective of 0.7% GDP established by the United Nations (recommendations Nos. 90 and 91).

Finally, it is impossible to assess the situation of about 20% of the recommendations because the terms in which they are formulated are so generic as to make it impossible to establish clearly whether or not the objectives set have been achieved[4].

The Italian Government has only a few months left to further improve the level of implementation of the recommendations received in 2010 and to realise at least the most inescapable of the commitments made on international human rights standards before the now imminent second Universal Periodic Review. The research and editorial committee of the Yearbook hereby expresses once again its hope that the preparatory stage for the Review before the United Nations Human Rights Council be seized as an opportunity to promote the diffusion of a human rights culture in Italy, bringing together the efforts and the commitment of public institutions, private bodies and civil society organisations.

---

[3]   Recommendation Nos. 1, 2, 5, 8, 12-14, 16, 17, 24, 25, 27, 31, 38, 41, 44, 50-54, 56, 58, 60, 69-71, 77, 79, 81, 90, 91.

[4]   Recommendation Nos. 9, 10, 23, 33, 37, 39, 47-49, 55, 59, 61, 63-66, 68, 76, 78.

Italian Agenda of Human Rights 2014

For the third year running, the research and editorial committee of the *Italian Yearbook of Human Rights*, based at the Human Rights Centre of the University of Padua, has compiled an "Italian Agenda of Human Rights", drawing on analysis of the recommendations made to Italy at the international level and the most critical issues identified in the successive editions of the Yearbook itself. The Agenda can be used as a practical guide to choosing the main actions to be undertaken on the legislative, infrastructural and policy-making fronts in order to strengthen the Italian system of promoting and protecting human rights (the 2012 and 2013 Agendas are available online at www.italianhumanrightsyearbook.eu).

Only 5 of the items (and sub-items) on the 2013 Agenda were actually met during the year. Italy did deposit the instruments of ratification of the Civil Law Convention and Criminal Law Convention on Corruption and also ratified the Council of Europe Convention on Preventing and Combating Violence against Women and Domestic Violence. Moreover, Italy presented the outline of its National action plan against racism, xenophobia and intolerance 2013–2015, in line with the spontaneous commitment made in 2011, when Italy submitted its candidature for election to the Human Rights Council; the National Action Plan for the promotion of the rights of persons with disabilities was also adopted. Finally, the Government has requested the publication of the two reports drawn up by the Council of Europe Committee for the Prevention of Torture following its visits to Italy in 2010 and 2012 to assess the conditions of people deprived of their personal liberty. Consequently, these five points are not mentioned in the 2014 Agenda.

On the remaining points, on the other hand, some distinctions should be made. In certain areas, significant progress has been made, but a longer time-frame is considered necessary to assess whether Italy has actually met its commitments. Consequently, these points are reformulated, based on the developments observed and appear again in the 2014 Agenda, to allow for a longitudinal assessment of their implementation. Other issues have not been the object of any specific initiatives by the Italian authorities and so the research and editorial committee considers special attention should be directed to them. These points are therefore confirmed again, in the same words as last year, in the 2014 Agenda. Finally, some new points have been added to the Agenda in consideration of the most recent developments at the national and international level concerning the promotion and protection of human rights, including the human right to peace.

Generally speaking, the points listed in the *Italian Agenda of Human Rights 2014* coincide with most of the recommendations which were rejected, implemented only in part or not at all out of those made to Italy during the 2010 Universal Periodic Review (see the previous section). And so the 2014 Agenda is also offered as a practical contribution to the preparatory process for Italy's second cycle of UPR, scheduled for October 2014.

Italian Agenda of Human Rights 2014

Normative Level	1) Ratify the following legal instruments at the United Nations and the Council of Europe: a. International Convention on the Protection of the Rights of All Migrant Workers and Members of their Families b. International Convention for the Protection of All Persons from Enforced Disappearances c. Optional Protocol to the International Covenant on Economic, Social and Cultural Rights d. Optional Protocol to the Convention on the Rights of the Child on a Communications Procedure; e. United Nations Convention on the Reduction of Statelessness; f. Protocol 12 to the Convention for the Protection of Human Rights and Fundamental Freedoms; g. Protocol 15 to the Convention for the Protection of Human Rights and Fundamental Freedoms; h. Protocol 16 to the Convention for the Protection of Human Rights and Fundamental Freedoms; i. European Convention on Nationality; j. Additional Protocol to the Criminal Law Convention on Corruption.
	2) Deposit the instruments of ratification for the following legal instruments for which Parliament has already adopted the relative ratification and implementation laws: a. Convention on Human Rights and Biomedicine (Oviedo Convention); b. Additional Protocol to the Convention on Human Rights and Biomedicine concerning Transplantation of Organs and Tissues of Human Origin.
	3) Support the adoption of the draft Declaration on the right to peace (A/HRC/20/31), presented to the Human Rights Council by its own Advisory Committee in February 2012.
	4) Accept article 25 of the European Social Charter (revised), which recognises the right of workers to the protection of their claims in the event of insolvency of their employer.

	5) Withdraw the declaration which excludes the application for Italy of Chapter C of the European Convention on the Participation of Foreigners in Public Life at Local Level and, accordingly, provide for the introduction of active and passive voting rights in local elections for foreigners who have been residing in Italy for a certain number of years.
	6) Include hate motivation as an aggravating circumstance in article 61 of the Italian criminal code.
	7) Include the crime of torture in domestic legislation.
	8) Expressly recognise representative non-governmental organisations within Italian jurisdiction having particular competence in issues regulated by the European Social Charter (revised) the right to present collective complaints pursuant to the 1995 Protocol.
	9) Complete the adoption process of parliamentary bill No. 925 on defamation laws in light of the of United Nations, Council of Europe and OSCE standards.
	10) Continue efforts to reform the system for the prevention and repression of corruption in both the public and private sector.
Infrastructural Level	11) Complete the system of independent national human rights institutions in line with the Paris principles adopted by the United Nations: a. establish the National Human Rights Commission; b. establish the National Ombudsperson; c. appoint the members and allocate the necessary resources to the National Ombudsperson for the rights of detainees and persons deprived of their personal freedom, established by law-decree 146/2013; d. establish an independent and adequately funded national preventive mechanism against torture (OPCAT), pursuant to law 195/2012.
	12) Ensure the existence of a permanent parliamentary Human Rights Commission, in one or both Chambers.
	13) Assign all Ministries an ad hoc human rights office.
Implementation of International Obligations and Commitments	14) Complete the legislative process for the implementation of the Statute of the International Criminal Court as concerns substantive law.
	15) Submit the reports due to the international monitoring bodies, particularly: a. VI report to the United Nations Committee on Civil and Political Rights (overdue since October 2009); b. VI report to the United Nations Committee against Torture (overdue since July 2011); c. I report to the Council of Europe European Committee of Social Rights on the provisions of the European Social Charter (revised) which have not been accepted (overdue since 31 July 2004).

	16) Execute the judgments of the European Court of Human Rights and improve Italy's capacity to adjust to the standards defined by the same.
	17) Address as a matter of urgency the issue of the excessive duration of legal proceedings, including those initiated to seek remedy for their excessive duration.
Adoption of policies	18) Hold an annual debate on Human Rights in Parliament.
	19) Adopt the following national action plans, providing them with suitable tools for monitoring and assessment: a. National action plan against trafficking of human beings; b. National action plan on the human rights situation within detention structures; c. National programme on education for democratic citizenship and education and training on human rights d. Fourth National action plan for the protection of rights and of the development of children and adolescents e. National plan against racism, xenophobia and intolerance for the three-year period 2013–2015, based on the outline prepared by UNAR in 2013; f. Extraordinary Action Plan against Sexual and Gender-Based Violence, as per art. 5 of law-decree 14 August 2013, No. 93, as amended and converted into law by law 15 October 2013, No. 119.
	20) Provide information on the impact of the following national action plans: a. National Strategy for the Inclusion of Roma, Sinti and travellers – 2012–2020; b. National Strategy for Preventing and Combating Discrimination on grounds of gender identity or sexual orientation; c. Two-year action plan for the promotion of rights and the integration of persons with disabilities.
	21) Allocate UNAR sufficient human and financial resources to fulfil its functions.
	22) Allocate sufficient public social spending in the various categories (illness, disability, family support, unemployment, social housing and combating social exclusion).
	23) Resolve the problem of overcrowding in prisons through structural measures and deflation mechanisms, with the objective of bringing down the numbers of detainees to the official number of places available.

Initiatives in specific fields	
Rights of Women	24) Promote actual equality between men and women in all aspects of public and private life, specifically through adoption of policies and actions directed at: a. reducing the deficit in the number of women represented in the highest decision-making roles in political bodies, including Parliament and Regional Councils, the public administration including the Diplomatic Service and in the private sector b. reducing the salary gap between men and women c. fostering a more balanced sharing of family duties between men and women, both in running the home and in care-giving duties d. eliminating stereotypical attitudes on the roles and responsibilities of women and men in the family, in society and in the workplace e. encouraging plans for the integration of foreign women; f. tackling and resolving the phenomenon of resignations without a justified reason ("blank resignation letters") for pregnant women and working mothers.
	25) Adopt further institutional, political and administrative initiatives to continue to combat the phenomenon of violence against women and reinforce the support services for victims of violence, including: a. correcting the current fragmentation of legislation on violence against women and fostering the use of current legislation which is best able to ensure effective protection of victims b. completing the framework of regional laws on violence against women c. carrying out an audit on the performance of the activities to prevent and contrast gender-based violence and stalking planned in the relative National Plan. d. encouraging growth in the numbers of anti-violence centres and multi-agency work on the issue, including in the prevention of violence stage e. encouraging correct information on the real circumstances and dimensions of the phenomenon of violence against women, with a particular regard to femicides.
Rights of Children	26) Adopt a general legislative measure which enshrines the right of children to be listened to in court, in administrative bodies, in the institutions, at school and in the family in every issue which concerns them directly and establish suitable mechanisms and procedures to this end, to ensure that the participation of children really takes place.

	27) Amend the criminal code so as to explicitly forbid and criminalise the recruitment and the deployment, by either the armed forces or armed groups, of young people under the age of 18 in the course of armed conflicts.
	28) Adopt legislation prohibiting and criminalising the sale of light and small calibre arms to Countries which deploy child soldiers.
	29) Amend legislation so as to prohibit the expulsion of children, even on public order or State security grounds, when there are substantiated reasons to believe there is a real risk of irreparable damage to the child.
Rights of Migrants, Refugees and Asylum Seekers	30) Address migratory flows as a structural phenomenon, the systematic planning for which must be assigned to instruments of an ordinary nature (rather than to emergency measures linked to a purely security-oriented viewpoint) and to multi-level governance with the involvement of the relevant Ministries, Regions, local administrations and civil society.
	31) Respect the principle of non-refoulement, the right of asylum seekers to an individual examination of their case, as well as immediate access to asylum procedures and other forms of national and international protection, including where there are bilateral agreements for return or for cooperation in management of migratory flows.
	32) Support the activities of the "Roundtable on the Legal Status of Roma", established on 30 January 2013 as part of the National Strategy for Inclusion of the members of these communities, with the objective of finding solutions to the situation of statelessness of large numbers of Roma originally from the former Yugoslavia, and of their children born in Italy (the so-called "de facto stateless people").
	33) Develop a more expeditious identification system, in order to reduce as far as possible the period that migrants are detained while waiting for the identification procedures to be completed.
	34) Re-examine laws on citizenship in the light of the principle of ius humanae dignitatis, continuing in the direction taken by the simplification of the process for acquiring citizenship status pursuant to art. 33 of legal decree 21 June 2013, No. 69.

PART I

IMPLEMENTATION OF INTERNATIONAL HUMAN RIGHTS LAW IN ITALY

International Human Rights Law

The first Part of the Yearbook is divided into two chapters. The first is devoted to the review of the major international human rights instruments that Italy has ratified, as well as to the identification of both those international instruments signed but not ratified by the Country and those adopted in 2013 that have not been subjected to any initiative of acceptance yet.

The framework of Italy's international obligations takes into consideration the universal conventions adopted within the system of the United Nations, the conventions of the Council of Europe as well as the European Union treaties and secondary law. Accordingly, the information provided are preliminary to the presentation of the national normative apparatus – the Constitution, national and regional laws – which is the subject of the following chapter.

The complete list, updated to December 2013, of the 111 international legal instruments on human rights considered into this publication (43 of the United Nations, 16 on disarmament and non-proliferation and 52 of the Council of Europe) and of Italy's acceptance status (ratification, signature, no initiative) is available online at: www.italianhumanrightsyearbook.eu, in the section "attachments".

I. Legal Instruments of the United Nations

On 3 April 2013, Italy ratified the Optional Protocol to the Convention against Torture and Other Cruel, Inhuman or Degrading Punishment.

The complete list, updated to December 2013, of the legal instruments of the United Nations and of Italy's acceptance status (ratification, signature, no initiative) is available online at: www.italianhumanrightsyearbook.eu, in the section "attachments".

II. Legal Instruments on Disarmament and Non-proliferation

In 2013, the United Nations adopted and opened to signature the Arms Trade Treaty. Italy signed this instrument on 2 April 2013; in October, moreover, law 118/2013 through which Parliament authorises the President of the Republic to ratify the Arms Trade Treaty, entered into force. However, as of 31 December 2013, the related instrument of ratification has not been yet deposited with the United Nations General Secretariat (see Part III, International Humanitarian and Criminal Law).

The complete list, updated to December 2013, of the legal instruments on disarmament and non-proliferation and of Italy's acceptance status (ratification, signature, no initiative) is available online at: www.italianhumanrightsyearbook.eu, in the section "attachments".

III. Legal Instruments of the Council of Europe

In 2013, the Council of Europe adopted and opened to signatures two new Protocols to the Convention for the Protection of Human Rights and Fundamental Freedoms: No. 15 (24 June 2013) and No. 16 (2 October 2013). Italy signed both Protocols in the dates in which they were opened to signatures.

Moreover, in the same year, Italy ratified the following legal instruments of the Council of Europe:

– the Convention on the Protection of Children against Sexual Exploitation and Sexual Abuse (deposit of instrument of ratification on 3 January 2013);

– the Framework Convention on the Value of Cultural Heritage for Society (27 February 2013);

– the Criminal Law Convention on Corruption (13 June 2013);

– the Civil Law Convention on Corruption (13 June 2013);

– the Convention on Preventing and Combating Violence against Women and Domestic Violence (10 September 2013).

The complete list, updated to December 2013, of the legal instruments of the Council of Europe and of Italy's acceptance status (ratification, signature, no initiative) is available online at: www.italianhumanrightsyearbook.eu, in the section "attachments".

IV. European Union Law

A. Treaties

As envisaged by the Treaty of Lisbon, since 1 December 2009 the EU legal framework has consisted of two fundamental instruments: the Treaty on the European Union (TEU) and the Treaty on the Functioning of the European Union (TFEU). Article 6 of the TEU attributes the status of primary law to the Charter of Fundamental Rights of the EU, and also refers specifically to the rights guaranteed by the European Convention for the Protection of Human Rights and Fundamental Freedoms (ECHR) and those deriving from the constitutional traditions common to the Member States, which are part of EU law insofar as they are general principles.

Furthermore, in the Preamble of the TEU, explicit reference is made to the 1989 Community Charter of Fundamental Social Rights of Workers and the 1961 European Social Charter of the Council of Europe (revised in 1996). Both these instruments are also mentioned in the TFEU in the context of Title X on Social Policy (art. 151).

On 5 April 2013 representatives of the European Union and of the 47 Member States of the CoE reached agreement on the text for EU accession to the European Convention for the Protection of Human Rights and Fundamental Freedoms (ECHR). The final adoption of this instrument now awaits the completion of a number of legal procedures and internal policies. As regards the Member States of the EU, it is necessary to wait, first of all, for the opinion of the EU Court of Justice on the compatibility of the accession text with the institutive Treaties, and secondly, the unanimous adoption by the EU Council of a decision authorising the signing of the agreement. As far as the Council of Europe is concerned, all the States that are parties to the ECHR are requested to ratify the accession document.

The agreement reached is in line with the provisions of article 6(2) of the Treaty of Lisbon, and represents an important step forwards towards the reinforcement of human rights protection in Europe. The EU's accession to the ECHR will in fact make it possible, subject to the exhaustion of appeals to the Court of Justice of the European Union, to submit individual pleas to the European Court of Human Rights in the event of presumed violations of fundamental rights on the part of EU institutions.

B. EU Law in 2013

During 2013 the European Parliament and the Council of the EU adopted a number of directives, regulations and decisions with particular relevance for human rights. For its part, the European Commission presented significant communications and legislative proposals.

During 2013 directives were adopted on the following matters: the right of access to a lawyer in criminal proceedings and in European arrest warrant proceedings, and on the right to have a third party informed upon deprivation of liberty and to communicate with third persons and with consular authorities while deprived of liberty (2013/48/EU of 22 October 2013); standards regarding the reception of applicants for international protection (2013/33/EU of 26 June 2013); on common procedures for granting and withdrawing international protection (2013/32/EU of 26 June 2013).

Regulations adopted in 2013 with particular significance for human rights include: regulation No. 1381/2013 of the European Parliament and of the

Council of 17 December 2013, establishing a Rights, Equality and Citizenship Programme for the period 2014 to 2020; regulation No. 604/2013 of the European Parliament and of the Council of 26 June 2013 establishing the criteria and mechanisms for determining the Member State responsible for examining an application for international protection lodged in one of the Member States by a third-country national or a stateless person; regulation No. 603/2013 of the European Parliament and of the Council of 26 June 2013 on the establishment of 'Eurodac' for the comparison of fingerprints; regulation No. 585/2013 of the Commission, of 20 June 2013, amending Council Regulation (EC) No. 1236/2005 concerning trade in certain goods which could be used for capital punishment, torture or other cruel, inhuman or degrading treatment or punishment.

A number of decisions of particular relevance to the theme considered here were also adopted: Council decision No. 2013/488/EU of 23 September 2013, on the security rules for protecting EU classified information; Council decision No. 252/2013/EU of 11 March 2013, establishing a Multiannual Framework for 2013–2017 for the European Union Agency for Fundamental Rights.

Finally, as regards the communications adopted by the Commission in 2013, it is worth drawing attention to the ones concerning: female genital mutilation (COM/2013/0833 final); steps forward in implementing national Roma integration strategies (COM/2013/0454 final); preparing for the 2014 European elections (COM/2013/0126 final); the report under article 25 TFEU on progress towards actual EU citizenship 2011–2013 (COM/2013/0270 final); European Citizenship report 2013: EU citizens: your rights, your future (COM/2013/0269 final).

Since the adoption of law 24 December 2012, No. 234, two instruments are employed to bring Italian legislation into line with European law: the European Law and the Law of European Delegation. While the former contains norms for the direct implementation of EU law, designed to remedy situations where European norms have been implemented incorrectly, the latter contains the authorisation provisions necessary for implementing the directives and other acts of the Union.

On 6 August 2013, respectively with law No. 96 and No. 97, Parliament adopted the 2013 Law of Delegation and the 2013 European Law. With particular reference to the protection of fundamental rights, the first of these instruments delegated the Italian Government to implement: the directive regarding the right to interpretation and translation in criminal proceedings (2010/64/EU of 20 October 2010, deadline for transposition: 27 October 2013); the directive on preventing and combating trafficking in human beings and on protecting victims (2011/36/EU of 5 April 2011, deadline for transposition: 6 April 2013); the directive amending directive 2003/109/EC, to extend its scope to beneficiaries of international protection (2011/51/EU of 11 May 2011, deadline for transposition: 20 May 2013); the directive on the term of protection of copyright and certain related rights (2011/77/EU); the directive on combating sexual abuse and sexual exploitation of minors and child pornography (2011/93/EU); the directive on the standards of qualification for third-country parties or stateless persons as beneficiaries of international protection, for a uniform status for refugees or for persons eligible for subsidiary protection, and for the content of the protection granted (2011/95/EU of 13 December 2011, deadline for transposition: 21 December 2013); directive on the right to information in criminal proceedings (2012/13/EU of 22 May 2012, deadline for transposition: 2 June 2014); directive establishing minimum standards on the rights, support and protection of victims of crime, and replacing Council framework decision 2001/220/GAI (2012/29/EU of 25 October 2012, deadline for transposition: 16 November 2015).

On the other hand, as regards European Law in 2013, interventions concerning the protection of fundamental rights concerned: amendments to the regulatory code regarding access to jobs with public administrations (EU Pilot cases 1769/11/JUST and 2368/11/HOME); provisions regarding fixed-term employment (infringement proceeding 2010/2045, closed on 20 November 2013); provisions to remedy the incorrect implementation of directive 2004/38/EC on the rights of citizens of the Union and their family members to move and reside freely (infringement proceeding 2011/2053, closed on 10 December 2013); provisions for the correct implementation of directive 2003/109/EC concerning the status of third-country nationals who are long-term residents (infringement proceeding 2013/4009); amendment to legislative decree 28 January 2008, No. 25, concerning territorial Commissions for the granting of international protection (infringement proceeding 2012/2189).

Finally, it should be mentioned that, in exercising the faculty as per article 29 of law 234/2012, on 22 November 2013 the Government presented in Parliament two further bills (European Law bis) for implementing another group of European regulations and to close various proceedings for infringements of EU law.

With regard to the latter, the data provided by the Department of European Affairs of the Prime Minister's Office show that, as of 10 December 2013, 104 infringement proceedings were pending against Italy, of which 55 started in 2013. Of particular note in relation to human rights issues is proceeding No. 2013/4199, whereby Italy received a letter of formal notice (ex article 258 TFEU) for the non-compliance of law 22 December 2011, No. 214 (Reform of the pension system) with EU legislation on the parity of treatment between men and women (directive 2006/54/EC); proceeding No. 2013/0398, whereby Italy received a letter of formal notice (ex article 258 TFEU) for failure to implement directive 2010/64/EU of 20 October 2010 on the right to interpretation and translation in criminal proceedings; procedure No. 2013/0276, whereby Italy received a letter of formal notice (ex art. 258 TFEU) for failure to implement directive 2011/51/EU of 11 May 2011, which amended Council directive 2003/109/EC to extend its scope of application to the beneficiaries of international protection; proceeding No. 2013/0228, whereby Italy received a letter of formal notice (ex article 258 TFEU) for failure to implement directive 2011/36/EU of 5 April 2011 on preventing and combating the trafficking of human beings and on protecting the victims.

Finally, as regards the continuing evolution of infringement proceedings initiated in previous years, it should be noted that on 26 September 2013 the European Commission referred Italy to the EU Court of Justice as per article 260 TFEU for the non-compliance of law 13 April 1988, No. 117, with EU legislation regarding payment of damages caused in the exercising of judicial functions and the civil responsibility of magistrates (infringement proceeding No. 2009/2230 (see *2012 Yearbook*, pp. 364–365). On 17 October 2013 the Commission also decided to present a reasoned opinion as per article 258 TFEU for Italy's poor application of directive 2004/80/EC regarding compensation for victims of crime (infringement proceeding No. 2011/4147).

Italian Law

I. The Constitution of the Italian Republic

"The Republic recognises and guarantees the inviolable rights of the persons, both as an individual and in the social group where the human personality is expressed. The Republic expects that the fundamental duties of political, economic and social solidarity be fulfilled" (article 2).

"All citizens have equal social dignity and are equal before the law, without distinction of sex, race, language, religion, political opinion, personal and social conditions.

It is the duty of the Republic to remove those obstacles of an economic or social nature which constrain the freedom and equality of citizens, thereby impeding the full development of the human person and the effective participation of all workers in the political, economic and social organisation of the Country" (article 3).

"The Italian legal system conforms to the generally recognised principles of international law. The legal status of foreigners is regulated by law in conformity with international provisions and treaties. A foreigner who, in his home Country, is denied the actual exercise of the democratic freedoms guaranteed by the Italian constitution shall be entitled to the right of asylum under the conditions established by law. A foreigner may not be extradited for a political offence" (article 10).

"Italy rejects war as an instrument of aggression against the freedom of other peoples and as a means for the settlement of international disputes. Italy agrees, on conditions of equality with other States, to the limitations of sovereignty that may be necessary to a world order ensuring peace and justice among the Nations. Italy promotes and encourages international organisations furthering such ends" (article 11).

The whole of Part I of the Constitution (articles 1–54) is devoted to the fundamental rights and duties of citizens, which are grouped into four areas: civil relations, ethical and social relations, economic relations and political relations.

II. National Legislation

During the year 2013, the Parliament and the Government passed a number of legislative acts (laws, law-decrees, legislative decrees) relating, directly or indirectly, to the safeguarding and protection of internationally recognised human rights. The following list of legislative acts is structured on the same lines as the classification of international instruments:

a) general legislative acts (the judiciary in general);

b) legislative acts dealing with specific issues (public order and security; peacekeeping missions and international cooperation; crimes, criminal procedure and issues relating to the prison system; culture and mass media; education; environmental protection, health);

c) legislative acts concerning the protection of particular groups (children and adolescents; victims of disasters; equal opportunities, gender; workers).

a) *General legislative Acts*

The Judiciary in General

L. 14 January 2013, No. 5 (Adhesion of the Italian Republic to the United Nations Convention on Jurisdictional Immunities of States and Their Property, signed in New York on 2 December 2004, and regulations for compliance by Italy's legal system).

b) *Legislative Acts Dealing with Specific Issues*

Public Order and Security

L. 4 October 2013, No. 118 (Ratification and execution of the Arms Trade Treaty adopted by the UN General Assembly in New York on 2 April 2013).

Peacekeeping Missions and International Cooperation

L. 1 February 2013, No. 12 (Conversion into law, with amendments, of law-decree 28 December 2012, No. 227, containing provisions for the extension of the international missions of the armed forces and police, cooperation initiatives to develop and support processes of reconstruction and participation in the initiatives of international organisations for the consolidation of peace and stabilisation processes).

L. 9 December 2013, No. 135 (Conversion into law, with amendments, of law-decree 10 October 2013, No. 114, containing provisions for the extension of the international missions of the armed forces and police, cooperation initiatives to develop and support processes of reconstruction and participation in the initiatives of international organisations for the consolidation of peace and stabilisation processes).

Crimes, Criminal Procedure and Issues Relating to the Prison System

L. 7 February 2013, No. 14 (Ratification and execution of the Agreement between the Government of the Italian Republic and the Government of the Arab Republic of Egypt regarding the transfer of convicted persons, reached in Cairo on 15 February 2001).

L. 9 August 2013, No. 94 (Conversion into law, with amendments, of law-decree 1 July 2013, No. 78, containing urgent provisions regarding execution of the sentence).

L.d. 23 December 2013, No. 146 (Urgent measures concerning the protection of the fundamental rights of prisoners and the controlled reduction of the prison population).

Culture and Mass Media

Lgs.d. 14 March 2013, No. 33 (Reorganisation of the rules concerning the obligations of publicity, transparency and dissemination of information by public authorities).

L. 9 August 2013, No. 100 (Ratification and execution of the Memorandum of Understanding between the Government of the Italian Republic and the UN Organisation for Education, Science and Culture regarding the operating, in Perugia, Italy, of the UNESCO Programme Office on Global Water Assessment, which houses the Secretariat of the World Water Assessment Programme, signed in Paris on 12 September 2012).

L. 7 October 2013, No. 112 (Conversion into law, with amendments, of decree-law 8 August 2013, No. 91, containing urgent provisions for the protection, valorisation and promotion of Italy's cultural heritage, cultural activities and tourism).

Education

L. 8 November 2013, No. 128 (Conversion into law, with amendments, of law-decree 12 September 2013, No. 104, containing urgent measures regarding education, the university system and research).

Environmental Protection, Health

L. 1 February 2013, No. 11 (Conversion into law, with amendments, of law-decree 14 January 2013, No. 1, containing urgent provisions for overcoming critical situations regarding waste management and some cases of environmental pollution).

L. 23 May 2013, No. 57 (Conversion into law, with amendments, of law-decree 25 March 2013, No. 24, containing urgent health care provisions).

L.d. 10 December 2013, No. 136 (Urgent provisions for tackling environmental and industrial emergencies and for assisting the development of the areas concerned).

c) *Legislative Acts Devoted to the Protection of Social Groups*

Children and Adolescents

L. 9 August 2013, No. 98 (Conversion into law, with amendments, of law-decree 21 June 2013, No. 69, containing urgent measures to revive the economy), art. 33 (Simplification of the procedure for the acquisition of citizenship to foreigners born in Italy).

Migrants, Refugees and Asylum Seekers

L. 13 December 2013, No. 137 (Conversion into law, with amendments, of law-decree 15 October 2013, No. 120, containing urgent measures for balancing the public finances and regarding immigration).

Equal Opportunities, Gender

Constitutional law 7 February 2013, No. 3 (Amendment of articles 15 and 16 of the Special Status of Sardinia, as per Constitutional law 26 February 1948, No. 3, concerning the composition and election of the Regional Council).

L. 27 June 2013, No. 77 (Ratification and execution of the Council of Europe Convention on Preventing and Combating Violence against Women and Domestic Violence, opened for signature in Istanbul on 11 May 2011).

L. 15 October 2013, No. 119 (Conversion into law, with amendments, of law-decree 14 August 2013, No. 93, containing urgent provisions regarding security, the fight against gender violence, civil protection and the placing the Provinces under external administration).

Workers

L. 9 August 2013, No. 99 (Conversion into law, with amendments, of law-decree 28 June 2013, No. 76, containing initial urgent measures to promote employment, especially among the young, social cohesion and with regard to Value Added Tax (VAT) and other urgent financial measures).

L. 23 September 2013, No. 113 (Ratification and execution of the Maritime Labour Convention No. 186, with Appendixes, adopted by the International Labour Organisation (ILO) in Geneva on 23 February 2006 during the 94th session of the ILO's General Conference, together with domestic compliance regulations).

L. 27 December 2013, No. 147 (Provisions for the preparation of the State's annual and multiyear).

III. Municipal, Provincial and Regional Statutes

Since 1991, after the adoption of law 8 June 1990, No. 142 (Local authorities system), the so called "peace human rights norm", originally contained in article 1 of Veneto regional law 30 March 1988, No. 18 (then updated by regional law 55/1999) on "Regional measures for the promotion of a culture of peace", has been included in the statutes of several Italian Municipalities, Provinces and Regions. The original wording of this norm reads:

"The Municipality [...] (the Province [...], the Region [...]), consistent with the Constitutional principles sanctioning the repudiation of war as a means of resolving international controversies, and the promotion of human rights, the democratic freedoms and international cooperation, recognises peace as a fundamental human and peoples' right.

To this end the Municipality [...] (the Province [...], the Region [...]) promotes the culture of peace and human rights through cultural, research, education, cooperation and information initiatives aimed at making the Municipality a land of peace.

In order to achieve these goals, the Municipality [...] (the Province [...], the Region [...]) will take direct initiatives and foster the initiatives by local authorities, associations, cultural institutions, volunteers and international cooperation groups".

Among the local and regional authorities that have included this norm in their Statutes, it is worth mentioning, for example, the Municipalities of Catania, Cuneo and Riccione, the Provinces of Alessandria, Foggia and Perugia, the Region of Marche and the Region of Veneto. Quantitative data concerning the spread of the "peace human rights norm" in Italy are available (in Italian) at the website of the Human Rights Centre of the University of Padua: http://unipd-centrodirittiumani.it/it/database/Enti-locali-pace-e-diritti-umani/4.

Moreover, there are also many statutes, at the municipal, provincial and regional levels, that make explicit references to international provisions and principles on human rights and territorial self-government, in particular the Charter of the United Nations, the Universal Declaration of Human Rights, the International Covenant on Civil and Political Rights, the International Covenant on Economic, Social and Cultural Rights, the International Convention on the Rights of the Child, the EU Charter of Fundamental Rights and the European Charter on Local Self-Government.

No significant changes are observed in 2013, compared with what reported the previous years (see *2013 Yearbook*, p. 70).

IV. Regional Laws

This section lists the laws on human rights, equal opportunities, development cooperation, fair trade, minorities, migration, Ombudspersons and the protection of children's rights, workers' rights, the rights of persons with disabilities, solidarity, social advancement, family assistance, and citizenship and legality education adopted by the Councils of the Italian Regions and Autonomous Provinces in 2013. The laws are divided according to topics and listed, for each authority, in chronological order.

Peace, Human Rights, Development Cooperation, Fair Trade

R.l. Abruzzo 15 October 2013, No. 35 (Amendments to r.l. 10 September 1993, No. 56 (New regulations concerning cultural promotion), to r.l. 11 February 1999, No. 5, to r.l. 22 February 2000, No. 15 and to r.l. 10 January 2013, No. 2 and contributions in favour of the "Associazione Onlus Kabawil" of Pescara).

R.l. Marche 30 September 2013, No. 30 ("Limes" – Border Territories – Proposals and joint and cofunded projects for the development and integration of border areas).

R.l. Molise 15 July 2013, No. 8 (Implementation in Molise of the European Progress Microfinance instrument).

Equal Opportunities, Gender

R.l. Abruzzo 28 August 2013, No. 29 (Amendments to r.l. 14 June 2012, No. 26 (Establishment of the Regional Commission for the achievement of equal opportunities and legal and substantive parity between men and women), amendments to r.l. 14 September 1999, No. 77 and amendment to r.l. 28 January 2004, No. 10).

R.l. Emilia-Romagna 24 October 2013, No. 16 (Integration of r.l. 15 July 2011, No. 8 (Institution of the Regional Commission for the Promotion of Complete Parity between Women and Men).

R.l. Marche 30 April 2013, No. 8 (Promotion of institutional actions to combat violence against women and to combat discrimination based on sexual orientation).

R.l. Molise 10 October 2013, No. 15 (Measures to prevent and combat gender violence).

R.l. Sardinia 12 September 2013, No. 26 (Measures to prevent and combat gender violence and stalking. Amendments and integrations to r.l. 7 August 2007, No. 8 (Regulations for the establishment of antiviolence centres and shelters for women victims of violence)).

R.l. Sicily 10 April 2013, No. 8 (Norms regarding gender representation and dual gender preference).

P.l. Trent 14 March 2013, No. 2 (Measures to prevent and combat mobbing and to promote organisational wellbeing in the workplace, and amendments to p.l. 18 June 2012, No. 13, regarding equal opportunities).

R.l. Valle d'Aosta 25 February 2013, No. 4 (Measures to prevent and combat gender violence and measures to support women who are victims of gender violence).

R.l. Veneto 23 April 2013, No. 5 (Regional measures to prevent and combat violence against women).

Minorities

R.l. Friuli-Venezia Giulia 7 February 2013, No. 3 (Establishment in the city of Trieste of an information office for the Serb community living in the Region of Friuli Venezia Giulia).

Migration

R.l. Friuli-Venezia Giulia 27 December 2013, No. 22 (Intersectorial norms governing access to social services on the part of Italian citizens and migrants).

Ombudspersons and Children's Ombudspersons

R.l. Marche 14 October 2013, No. 34 (Amendments to r.l. 28 July 2008, No. 23 (Ombudspersons for children and adolescents and for adults – regional Ombudsperson) and to r.l. 13 October 2008, No. 28 (Integrated regional system for measures to assist adults and minors subject to rulings issued by the judicial authorities and to assist former convicts)).

R.l. Veneto 24 December 2013, No. 37 (Regional Ombudsperson for the rights of the person).

Persons with Disabilities

R.l. Abruzzo 25 November 2013, No. 44 (Regional Observatory on the condition of persons with disabilities).

R.l. Abruzzo 7 June 2013, No. 15 (Amendments and integrations to l. 11 December 2007, No. 41 (Establishment and regulatory code of the Council of Local Autonomies) and amendment to r.l. 19 June 2012, No. 27 (Regulatory code for granting the use of sports facilities owned by public entities of the Region of Abruzzo, measures on behalf of Paralympic athletes and a regulatory code for the granting of funding to support sports facilities as per Title XI of r.l. 20/2000)).

R.l. Marche 16 September 2013, No. 29 (Recognition of the specificity of the multidisplinary activities carried out by the Lega del Filo d'Oro).

R.l. Valle d'Aosta 15 April 2013, No. 10 (Amendments to r.l. 22 July 2005, No. 16 (Regulatory code for the voluntary sector and for social promotion associationism. Amendments to r.l. 21 April 1994, No. 12 (Funding for associations and bodies operating in Valle d'Aosta whose mission is to protect invalid, maimed and handicapped citizens), and the repeal of r.l. 6 December 1993, No. 83, and r.l. 9 February 1996, No. 5) and to r.l. 23 December 2009, No. 52 (Regional measures for access to social credit)).

R.l. Valle d'Aosta 18 November 2013, No. 17 (Provisions regarding funding for the insertion of persons with disabilities into the workplace. Amendments to r.l. 11 August 1981, No. 54, and 28 December 1983, No. 89).

Workers' Rights

R.l. Abruzzo 18 June 2013, No. 16 (Measures to support the minimum guaranteed wage).

R.l. Abruzzo 27 September 2013, No. 30 (Establishment of the Remembrance Day for agricultural workers who have died in the fields).

R.l. Apulia 5 August 2013, No. 23 (Guidelines for training pathways designed to provide job orientation and to assist entry into the labour market).

R.l. Calabria 15 July 2013, No. 35 (Integration to r.l. 14 August 2008, No. 28 (Norms for the reassigning to other employment of workers who receive ordinary and extraordinary social safety net allowances, including wage guarantee funds)).

R.l. Calabria 2 August 2013, No. 39 (Amendment to r.l. 19 April 2012, No. 13 (Provisions to ensure work safety and quality, and to combat and to formalise irregular work)).

R.l. Calabria 2 August 2013, No. 40 (Guidelines for the use of currently un-used workers in the Region for community work).

R.l. Campania 9 August 2013, No. 11 (Provisions concerning safety in the workplace and the quality of work).

R.l. Emilia-Romagna 19 July 2013, No. 7 (Provisions concerning internships. Amendments to r.l. 1 August 2005, No. 17 (Norms for promoting employment and the quality, safety and regularity of work)).

R.l. Friuli-Venezia Giulia 9 August 2013, No. 9 (Urgent measures to support and boost production sectors and employment. Amendments to r.l. 2/2012, r.l. 11/2009 and r.l. 7/2000).

R.l. Liguria 21 November 2013, No. 36 (Provisions concerning social agriculture).

R.l. Lombardy 24 December 2013, No. 21 (Measures in support of contracts and union agreements of solidarity).

R.l. Sardinia 10 January 2013, No. 1 (Setting up of the fund for paying social safety net benefits, including wage guarantee allowances, also in view of sums due to the assisted from the National employment fund, and urgent measures regarding local government bodies).

R.l. Sardinia 8 February 2013, No. 3 (Abolition of Sardinia's optimum territorial authority – Provisional regulations, urgent provisions regarding local government bodies, social safety net benefits, labour policies and amendments to r.l. No. 1 of 2013).

R.l. Sardinia 29 April 2013, No. 10 (Urgent provisions concerning labour and the social sector).

R.l. Sardinia 26 July 2013, No. 17 (Further urgent provisions concerning labour and the social sector).

R.l. Sardinia 2 August 2013, No. 22 (Urgent guidelines for the implementation of article 4 of r.l. 29 April 2013, No. 10 (Urgent provisions concerning labour and the social sector)).

R.l. Sardinia 26 September 2013, No. 27 (Amendments and integrations to r.l. 26 July 2013, No. 17, in relation to social safety net benefits).

R.l. Sardinia 20 December 2013, No. 38 (Guidelines concerning work services, provisions for implementing r.l. 29 April 2013, No. 10 (Urgent provisions concerning labour and the social sector) and measures on behalf of environmental protection workers).

R.l. Trentino-Alto Adige 18 March 2013, No. 2 (Amendments to r.l. 27 November 1993, No. 19 (Regional indemnity for unemployed workers enrolled in the provincial workers' mobility lists and provisions regarding supplementary pensions) and subsequent amendments, and to r.l. 27 February

1997, No. 3 (Supplementary pension measures to support regional pension funds) and subsequent amendments)).

P.l. Trento 14 March 2013, No. 2 – cited above: Equal Opportunities, Gender.

R.l. Tuscany 2 August 2013, No. 45 (Funding support measures on behalf of families and workers in financial difficulty, to promote social cohesion and combat social alienation).

R.l. Tuscany 10 December 2013, No. 74 (Amendments to r.l. 2 August 2013, No. 45 (Funding support measures on behalf of financially vulnerable families and workers, to promote social cohesion and combat social alienation)).

R.l. Umbria 17 September 2013, No. 16 (Measures for preventing falls from a height).

R.l. Umbria 17 September 2013, No. 17 (Further amendments and integrations to r.l. 21 October 1981, No. 69 (Regulations for the regional training system) and 23 March 1995, No. 12 (Help to promote youth employment by supporting new business initiatives)).

R.l. Veneto 28 June 2013, No. 14 (Measures regarding social agriculture).

Solidarity, Social Promotion and Assistance to Families

R.l. Abruzzo 18 June 2013, No. 16 – cited above: Workers' Rights.

R.l. Abruzzo 29 October 2013, No. 40 (Provisions for preventing the spread of forms of pathological gambling).

R.l. Abruzzo 25 November 2013, No. 43 (Amendments to r.l. 24 June 2011, No. 17 (Reorganisation of public assistance and charitable institutions (IPAB), and regulation of public companies providing services to the person (ASP)).

R.l. Apulia 13 December 2013, No. 43 (Combating the spread of Pathological Gambling (PG)).

P.l. Bolzano 17 May 2013, No. 81 (Family development and support in Alto Adige).

R.l. Calabria 29 March 2013, No. 15 (Guidelines for pre-school education services).

R.l. Calabria 2 May 2013, No. 19 (Measures to promote social inclusion and health and social service integration, and to combat poverty in high-density population urban agglomerates).

R.l. Calabria 21 March 2013, No. 10 (Temporary regulatory code for the granting of funds to bodies using subjects engaged in community work).

R.l. Emilia-Romagna 4 July 2013, No. 5 (Guidelines for combating, preventing and reducing the risk of pathological gambling, in addition to the correlated problems and pathologies).

R.l. Friuli-Venezia Giulia 11 November 2013, No. 18 (Urgent provisions concerning culture, sport and solidarity).

R.l. Lazio 5 August 2013, No. 5 (Provisions for the prevention and treatment of pathological gambling).

R.l. Lombardy 21 October 2013, No. 8 (Guidelines for the prevention and treatment of pathological gambling).

R.l. Lombardy 24 December 2013, No. 21 – cited above: Workers' Rights.

R.l. Marche 5 February 2013, No. 3 (Regional measures for recovering, returning and donating unexpired medicines with a view to their reuse).

R.l. Molise 30 September 2013, No. 14 (Establishment of the solidarity fund for measures to deal with special and unforeseen situations).

R.l. Sardinia 2 August 2013, No. 21 (Poverty alleviation and various measures).

R.l. Sardinia 4 December 2013, No. 33 (Urgent measures to assist the areas hit by the floods of November 2013, pursuant to r.l. No. 32 of 2013).

P.l. Trento 15 May 2013, No. 9 (Further measures to support the economic system and families).

R.l. Tuscany 2 August 2013, No. 45 – cited above: Workers' Rights

R.l. Tuscany 19 September 2013, No. 50 (Guidelines for alleviating the hardship of separated parents).

R.l. Tuscany 18 October 2013, No. 57 (Provisions for responsible gambling and for the prevention of problem gambling).

R.l. Tuscany 9 December 2013, No. 72 (Emergency financial aid for the populations of the Municipalities affected by the floods in September and October 2013).

R.l. Tuscany 10 December 2013, No. 74 – cited above: Workers' Rights

R.l. Umbria 8 February 2013, No. 3 (Regulations for the reconstruction of areas hit by the earthquake of 15 December 2009).

R.l. Umbria 23 January 2013, No. 1 (Further integrations to r.l. 22 December 2005, No. 30 (Integrated system of social and educational services for infants)).

R.l. Valle d'Aosta 15 April 2013, No. 12 (Promotion and coordination of policies to support young people. Repeal of r.l. 21 March 1997, No. 8 (Promotion of social, educational and cultural initiatives on behalf of the young)).

R.l. Valle d'Aosta 18 December 2013, No. 20 (Refunding, for 2013, of regional laws concerning family support and the establishment of a rotation fund for microcredit. Amendment to r.l. 15 February 2010, No. 4 (Regional measures to offset electricity costs for domestic users. Amendment to r.l. 18 January 2010, No. 2)).

Education for Citizenship and Legality

R.l. Marche 25 June 2013, No. 15 (Activities of the Region of Marche to uphold the values of the Resistance, of anti-Fascism and of the principles of the Republican Constitution).

R.l. Piedmont 12 August 2013, No. 18 (Amendments to r.l. 18 June 2007, No. 14 (Measures for crime prevention and the setting up of the Regional Day of Remembrance and Action in memory of mafia victims)).

R.l. Tuscany 9 May 2013, No. 23 (Amendments to r.l. 10 March 1999, No. 11 (Measures for Tuscan schools and universities and for civil society, to contribute, through education promoting legality and the development of a democratic civic conscience, to the fight against organised and widespread crime and against the various hidden powers). This section lists the laws on human rights, equal opportunities, development cooperation, fair trade, migration, ombudspersons, children's rights, workers' rights and the rights of persons with disabilities, adopted by the Councils of Italian Regions and Autonomous Provinces in 2012. The laws are divided according to topics and listed, for each authority, in chronological order.

PART II

THE HUMAN RIGHTS INFRASTRUCTURE IN ITALY

National Bodies with Jurisdiction over Human Rights

International human rights law requires States to set up structures adequately specialised in promoting and protecting fundamental rights. In this regard, a distinction shall be made between, on the one hand, strictly governmental bodies and, on the other, independent structures directly emanating from civil society. The latter in particular, through channels different from those classically used by governmental powers, aim at participating in policy-making, promoting and developing a human rights culture as well as preventing violations.

In this Part the composition, mandate and activities of the following institutions will be illustrated:

Parliamentary bodies: the Special Commission for the Promotion and Protection of Human Rights of the Italian Senate; the Permanent Committee on Human Rights instituted within the Foreign Affairs Commission (III) of the Italian Chamber of Deputies; the Parliamentary Commission for Children and Adolescents; the Parliament-Government Observatory Monitoring the Promotion and Protection of Fundamental Rights (data are lacking on the actual functioning of this Observatory in 2013).

Governmental bodies: bodies established within the Prime Minister's Office: Committee of Ministers for Orientation and Strategic Guidance for the Protection of Human Rights (data are lacking on the actual functioning of this Observatory in 2013); Department for Equal Opportunities; Commission for International Adoptions; National Committee on Bioethics; bodies established within the Ministry of Foreign Affairs: Inter-Ministerial Committee for Human Rights; National Commission for UNESCO; bodies established within the Ministry of Labour and Social Policies: National Observatory for Children and Adolescents; National Observatory Monitoring the Condition of Persons with Disabilities; as well as the departments and bureaus of the Ministry of Justice specifically involved in human rights matters.

Judicial authorities: the Constitutional Court and the Court of Cassation, acting as the supreme judge of legitimacy.

The *National Economy and Labour Council* (CNEL) as a constitutional body;

Independent authorities: the Communications Regulatory Authority; the Data Protection Authority; the Committee Guaranteeing the Implementation of the law on Strikes Affecting Essential Public Services; the National Ombudsperson for Children and Adolescents.

Finally, Italy's national human rights infrastructure is completed by academic institutions promoting not only research, but also education and training in human rights issues, and by several non-governmental organisations, some of which function through networking.

I. Parliamentary Bodies

A. *Senate of the Republic: Special Commission for the Protection and Promotion of Human Rights*

The Senate's Special Commission for the Protection and Promotion of Human Rights was first set up during the 14th legislature (motion 20, 1 August 2001) and is the fruit of long experience by the Committee against Capital Punishment (1996–2001). Since the Commission is not of a permanent nature, it must be instituted formally at the beginning of each legislature, and the Senate did so both during the 15th legislature (motion 20, 12 July 2006), the 16th legislature (motion 13, 26 June 2008) and the 17th legislature (motion 7, 26 March 2013). In the latter motion, the Senate decided to commence the proceedings for the establishment of a permanent human rights commission.

> The Commission has the task of studying, observing and taking initiatives on issues concerning the protection and promotion of internationally recognised human rights. To this end, it can establish relations with institutions of other Countries and with international bodies; carry out missions in or outside Italy, in particular with foreign Parliaments, even – if necessary – in order to establish agreements fostering human rights or to facilitate other forms of collaboration; it can carry out informational procedures and formulate proposals and Assembly reports; and provide its advisory opinions on proposed legislation as well as on matters deferred to other Commissions.

> The Commission is made up of 25 members, present in proportion to the size of the parliamentary groups to which they belong. Among these members, the Commission elects the bureau, made up of the Chair, two Vice Chairs and two Secretaries.

> In 2013 the Commission was composed as follows: Chair: Luigi Manconi; Vice Chairs: Ciro Falanga, Daniela Donno; Secretaries: Giovanni Bilardi, Paola De Pin; Members: Bruno Alicata, Silvana Amati, Federica Chiavaroli, Franco Conte, Peppe De Cristofaro, Aldo Di Biagio, Enzo Fasano, Emma Fattorini, Elena Ferrara, Miguel Gotor, Sergio Lo Giudice, Riccardo Mazzoni, Emanuela Munerato, Venera Padua (from 4 November 2013), Francesco Palermo, Lucio Romano, Francesco Russo, Manuela Serra, Ivana Simeoni, Mario Tronti (until 4 November 2013), Guido Viceconte.

In 2013 the Commission focused chiefly on the following issues: human rights in relation to sexual orientation; the rights of persons with disabilities; the rights of migrants, refugees and asylum seekers; the expulsion of Alma Shalabayeva; prisoners' rights and jail conditions; cyberbullying; the right to health; children's rights; the rights of the Roma and Sinti; the Universal Periodic Review of the United Nations. In the ambit of the survey of the various levels and systems of human rights protection currently in place in Italy and abroad, the Commission held 27 hearings of representatives from associations, organisations and institutional bodies, and of individual experts, as reported below.

- 12 June: Pietro Marcenaro, former Chair of the Special Commission for the Protection and Promotion of Human Rights in the 16th legislature.

- 19 June: delegation of activists for the rights of lesbian, gay, bisexual, transgender and intersex persons (LGBTI) from France, Russia and Uganda, accompanied by Carlotta Sami, Director general of Amnesty International Italy.

- 26 June: Luisa Panattoni and Alessandra Incoronato, affected by seriously invalidating pathologies, and Maria Teresa Agati, president of Confindustria's Study and Research Centre for Technical Aids for Disabled Persons.

- 3 July: Grazia Naletto, President of the association Lunaria, and Alberto Barbieri, General Coordinator of Medici per i diritti umani ("Doctors for human rights"), regarding Italy's identification and expulsion centres.

- 4 July: Diego Loveri, justice of peace, on possible breaches of the Constitution connected with the treatment of migrants in identification and expulsion centres.

- 9 July: delegation of the Open Dialog Foundation, on the human rights situation in Kazakhstan and in particular on the case of Alma Shalabayeva.

- 16 July: the lawyers Riccardo and Federico Olivo, and Ernesto Gregorio Valenti, defence counsel for Alma Shalabayeva.

- 17 July: prefect Alessandro Pansa, Chief of Police, on the Alma Shalabayeva case.

- 23 July: Gioia Passarelli and Matteo Massimi, from the association "A Roma, insieme – Leda Colombini", and Lia Sacerdote, President of the association "Bambini senza sbarre", on the conditions of women in prison and their children.

- 24 July: Raffaela Milano and Cristiana De Paoli, from Save the Children, on cyberbullying.

- 31 July: Beatrice Lorenzin, Minister of Health, on the updating of the tariff tables.

- 24 September: Giusi Nicolini, Mayor of Lampedusa.

- 1 October: Ali Abdul Atumane, on conditions in the Ponte Galeria Identification and Expulsion Centre.

– 2 October: Marilina Intrieri, Ombudsperson for children and adolescents of Calabria.

– 8 October: representatives from UNHCR, Save the Children, IOM and the Italian Red Cross, engaged in the *Praesidium* project, following the tragedy off Lampedusa on 3 October.

– 9 October: Hélèna Behr and Andrea De Bonis from UNHCR.

– 22 October: Maria Cecilia Guerra, Deputy Minister of Labour and Social Policies, with responsibility for equal opportunities, on Italy's strategy for dealing with discrimination against the LGBTI community.

– 29 October: Vincenzo Spadafora, Ombudsperson for children and adolescents, on cyberbullying.

– 30 October: Luigi Pagano, substitute deputy head of the Department of the Prison Administration.

– 6 November: representatives from Amnesty International, for the presentation of the report entitled "Double standards. Italy's housing policies discriminate the Roma".

– 28 November: Enrico Rossi, President of the Region of Tuscany, on initiatives taken by the Region to tackle prison conditions.

– 11 December: Marco Rossi Doria, Undersecretary for Education, University and Research, and Beatrice Morano, teacher, on cyberbullying.

– 17 December: Ambassador Gian Ludovico De Martino, Chair of the Inter-Ministerial Committee for Human Rights, on the UN's Universal Periodic Review (UPR).

– 18 December: Maryam Rajavi, President of the National Council of Iranian Resistance.

– 18 December: Cécile Kyenge, Minister of Integration, on the national strategy for the inclusion of Roma, Sinti and traveller communities

– 19 December: David Matas, nominated for the Nobel Peace Prize in 2010, and representatives from the Italian association Falun Dafa.

Moreover, the Commission adopted two resolutions concerning immigration: the resolution "Access to structures that receive and assist immigrants" (22 October 2013) and the resolution "Second reception" (28 November 2013).

In 2013, the Commission also conducted many visits and missions. In particular, from 11 to 15 September, a delegation of the Commission went on a mission to Kazakhstan, during which it was able to meet Alma Shalabayeva, her daughter Alua and the Kazakh authorities.

With regard to the execution of sentence, the Commission made visits, respectively to the high-security prison of Nuoro (17 June), the Venice open prison for mothers with young children (9 September) and Opera prison (16 September).

In relation to immigration issues, between July and December the Commission visited the CIEs of Bari, Ponte Galeria, Gradisca d'Isonzo and Trapani, and the CARAs in Castelnuovo di Porto and Gradisca d'Isonzo.

On 19 September 2013, the Commission organised the presentation of the Italian Human Rights Yearbook 2013, in conjunction with the Ministry of Foreign Affairs' Interministerial Committee for Human Rights and the Human Rights Centre of the University of Padua. The speakers were Luigi Manconi, Chair of the Senate of the Republic's Special Commission for Human Rights; Emma Bonino, Minister of Foreign Affairs; Marco Mascia, Director of the Human Rights Centre of the University of Padua; Antonio Papisca, Chief Editor of the Human Rights Yearbook; and members of the Yearbook's research and editorial board.

Finally, in 2013 the Commission organised the following conferences and seminars:

- 27 June: "The criminalisation of irregular immigration: legislation and practices in Italy";
- 17 July: "Some yes and some no. The role of the commissions for the right to asylum";
- 17 September: "Roma, Sinti and travellers in Italy: a bill for the recognition, protection and social advancement of the minority";
- 4 December: "Necessary clemency. Amnesty, pardon and reform of the justice system".

B. Chamber of Deputies: Permanent Committee on Human Rights

The international protection of human rights is one of the focal points of the activities performed by the Commission for Foreign and European Union Affairs (3rd Commission) of the Chamber of Deputies. As from the 10th legislature (1987–1992), the Commission set up within it the Permanent Committee on Human Rights, which, especially through hearings, ensures that Parliament is kept continually informed and up-to-date with regard to the status of international human rights. The Committee also has the task of following the course of individual human rights measures, performing preliminary tasks pertinent to the activities of the Commission. The Committee for the current legislature (17th) was set up on 16 July 2013.

In 2013 the Committee consisted of the following: Chair: Mario Marazzitti; Vice Chair: Emanuele Scagliusi; Secretary: Michele Nicoletti; Members: Renata Bueno, Maria Rosaria Carfagna, Khalid Chaouki, Eleonora Cimbro, Edmondo Cirielli, Rocco Crimi (until 28 November 2013), Daniele Del Grosso, Claudio Fava, Enzo Lattuca (until 12 November 2013), Gianluca Pini, Marietta Tidei.

In 2013, the Committee convened 15 times. Sessions of particular significance were the following:

- 7 August: start of the preliminary examination of the European Union Guidelines on the promotion and protection of freedom of religion or belief (preliminary examination 11491/2013, rapporteur Michele Nicoletti);
- 19 September: meeting with the United Nation's Special Rapporteur on Trafficking of Persons, Joy Ngozi Ezeilo;
- 15 October: communications of the Chair, Mario Marazzitti, on the mission to New York for the 68th session of the UN General Assembly (23–27 September 2013), and of the Vice Chair, Michele Nicoletti, on the mission to Brussels for the Interparliamentary Meeting organised by the Committee on Foreign Affairs and the Subcommittee on Human Rights (25 September 2013);
- 22 October: meeting with a delegation from the Committee for Ethnic and Religious Affairs of the Chinese People's Political Consultative Conference;
- 23 October: hearing of Father Javier Giraldo Moreno, human rights activist in Colombia, and representatives from the Peace Community of San José de Apartado and the association "Colombia vive!";
- 11 November: hearing of representatives from the Palestine-Israel Group of the Euro-Mediterranean Human Rights Network;
- 14 November: hearing of Zainab Hawa Bangura, the UN Secretary-General's Special Representative on Sexual Violence in Conflict;
- 14 November (in joint session with the Permanent Committee on Africa and Global Issues): meeting with Mohamed Abdelaziz, Secretary-General of the Polisario Front;
- 26 November (in joint session with the Permanent Committee on the Post-2015 Agenda, Development Cooperation and Public-Private Partnership): hearing of a delegation of Afghan women parliamentarians;
- 26 November (in joint session with the Permanent Committee on Foreign Affairs and the External Relations of the European Union): hearing of the OSCE Chief of Mission for the monitoring of the presidential elections in Georgia, Matteo Mecacci;
- 28 November: hearing of NGO representatives concerning the military exploitation of children;
- 28 November: hearing of participants in the 8th International Conference "No Justice without Life" (Rome, 29–30 November 2013);
- 10 December: communications of the President on the occasion of the Human Rights Day and the meeting with the Ambassador of the Republic of South Africa, Nomatemba Tambo, on the occasion of the commemoration of the death of former President Nelson Mandela.

C. Bicameral Bodies: Parliamentary Commission for Children and Adolescents

The Parliamentary Commission for Children and Adolescents was set up by law 23 December 1997, No. 451, although its name and responsibilities were modified by law 3 August 2009, No. 112.

Essentially, the Commission is entrusted with a supervisory and policymaking role related to the enforcement of international obligations and domestic law on children's rights. It may also present to the two Houses of Parliament observations and proposals concerning the effects and limitations of current legislation, and the possible need to amend it to ensure compliance with international law concerning the rights of the child.

The Commission is composed of 20 Senators and 20 Representatives appointed, respectively, by the Chair of the Italian Senate and the Chair of the Italian Chamber of Deputies, proportionately to the total number of members in the various parliamentary groups. The Commission then elects its Chair, two Vice Chairs and two Secretaries. In 2013 the Commission was composed as follows: *Chair*: Michela Vittoria Brambilla; *Vice Chairs*: Rosetta Enza Blundo, Sandra Zampa; *Secretaries*: Antimo Cesaro, Maria Antezza; *Members from the Chamber of Deputies*: Luigi Bobba, Renata Bueno, Annagrazia Calabria, Vittoria D'Incecco, Gabriella Giammanco, Silvia Giordano, Maria Tindara Gullo, Vanna Iori, Loredana Lupo, Alessandra Moretti (until 12 November 2013), Gaetano Nastri, Marisa Nicchi, Giovanna Petrenga, Chiara Scuvera (since 12 November 2013), Giorgio Girgis Sorial, Irene Tinagli, Giorgio Zanin; *Members from the Senate*: Ornella Bertorotta, Laura Bianconi (until 5 November 2013), Valeria Cardinali, Nunzia Catalfo, Mario Ferrara (since 5 November 2013), Rosanna Filippin, Antonio Gentile, Stefania Giannini, Manuela Granaiola, Donella Mattesini, Alessandra Mussolini, Venera Padua, Franco Panizza, Francesca Puglisi, Antonio Razzi, Maria Rizzotti, Mariarosaria Rossi, Annalisa Silvestro, Maria Spilabotte, Erika Stefani.

On 4 December 2013 the Commission decided to carry out two surveys:

– *Child poverty survey*. The aim of the survey is to investigate the impact and consequences of the protracted economic crisis in Italy on minors, and to identify legislative and administrative instruments that could be adopted by Government institutions to combat the phenomenon and to deliver concrete responses to the difficulties faced by children and adolescents. In the ambit of the survey, the following were heard: Maria Cecilia Guerra, Deputy Minister of Labour and Social Policies (10 December); Giorgio Pighi, Mayor of Modena with responsibility for immigration for ANCI; and Luca Pacini, responsible for the welfare sector for ANCI (18 December).

– *Child prostitution survey.* The aim of the survey is above all to up-date the overall picture of the phenomenon built up during the survey conducted in the previous legislature (16th), in order to gauge if and to what extent forms of systematic monitoring have been introduced by the institutionally competent bodies; such monitoring is the prerequisite for developing effective instruments for combating and stamping out this form of exploitation of minors. Moreover, the survey also intends to learn more about the social context of the phenomenon by analysing the under-lying causes (economic, educational, social), with a view to identifying possible preventative initiatives.

D. Parliamentary Initiatives Concerning Human Rights

Presented below is a synthetic overview of the main human rights ini-tiatives taken by the Italian Parliament in 2013, subdivided into bills and guideline and watchdog initiatives (motions, interpellations, questions for an oral or a written answer, resolutions, agenda proposals). The proposer or first signer, the code (the letter 'C' indicates that the initiative was pre-sented in the Chamber of Deputies, the letter 'S' that it was presented in the Senate), the title, the date of presentation and the most recent update are listed for each initiative.

In the first year of the 17th legislature, Parliament adopted 143 human rights initiatives, including 92 bills, 14 motions, 5 interpellations, 4 ques-tions for an oral answer, 12 questions for a written answer, 2 questions submitted to Commissions, 4 Commission resolutions, 1 final resolution and 9 Assembly agenda proposals.

Bills

The 92 bills presented concerned the following issues: prison conditions and the rights of prisoners (15); the right to vote (13); the rights of migrants (including citizenship rights), refugees and asylum seekers (13); the intro-duction of the crime of torture into the Italian legal system (12); freedom of opinion and expression (6); economic, social and cultural rights (6); the rights of women (5); the right to a private and family life (4); the protec-tion of personal data (4); the ratification of international instruments (4); the right to health (4); national human rights institutions (3); homophobia and transphobia (1); the rights of persons with disabilities (1); the rights of Roma, Sinti and travellers (1).

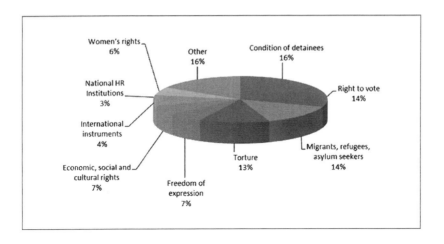

Prison Conditions and the Rights of Prisoners

Date	Initiative	Latest update
15/03/2013	Salvo TORRISI (NCD) and others – S.210 Establishment of the regional, provincial and municipal Ombudsperson for the fundamental rights of prisoners and their reintegration into society	03/07/2013 currently under examination by the Commission
26/03/2013	Luigi COMPAGNA (NCD) and others – S.299 Amendments to l. 26 July 1975, No. 354, regarding the ban on granting prison and differentiated prison regime benefits	09/05/2013 assigned (examination not yet begun)
03/04/2013	Donatella FERRANTI (PD) – C.631 Amendments to the code of criminal procedure regarding pre-trial detainment measures	09/01/2014 approved
04/04/2013	Lucio BARANI (GAL) and others – S.380 Amendments to articles 274, 275, 284 and 308 of the code of criminal procedure, regarding pre-trial detainment measures	09/05/2013 assigned (examination not yet begun)
04/04/2013	Lucio BARANI (GAL) and others – S.383 Establishment of the national Ombudsperson for the protection of the fundamental rights of prisoners and persons deprived of liberty, and amendments to articles 35 and 69 of l. 26 July 1975, No. 354, regarding the jurisdictional protection of prisoners' rights	03/07/2013 currently under examination by the Commission

Date	Initiative	Latest update
16/04/2013	Luisa BOSSA (PD) – C.782 Establishment of the Ombudsperson for the rights of persons in prison or deprived of their liberty	01/07/2013 assigned (examination not yet begun)
17/05/2013	Sandro GOZI (PD) – C.973 Establishment of the national Ombudsperson for the protection of the fundamental rights of prisoners and persons deprived of liberty, and amendments to articles 35 and 69 of l. 26 July 1975, No. 354, regarding the jurisdictional protection of prisoners' rights	07/08/2013 assigned (examination not yet begun)
17/05/2013	Sandro GOZI (PD) – C.976 Amendment to article 28 of the criminal code and repeal of article 32 of said code, and of paragraphs 1 and 2 of article 85 of the consolidated text as per decree of the President of the Republic, 9 October 1990, No. 309, with regard to alternative punishments to facilitate the reintegration of convicted prisoners into society and employment	02/08/2013 assigned (examination not yet begun)
21/05/2013	Luigi MANCONI (PD) – S. 668 Establishment of the Ombudsperson for the rights of persons deprived of liberty	03/07/2013 currently under examination by the Commission
19/06/2013	Sandro GOZI (PD) – C.1235 Amendments to article 303 of the code of criminal procedure, for the reduction of the maximum term of protective custody, and to article 54 of l. 26 July 1975, No. 354, regarding the simplification of procedures for early release	14/11/2013 assigned (examination not yet begun)
28/06/2013	Nicola FRATOIANNI (SEL) – C.1285 Amendments to l. 26 July 1975, No. 354, concerning the introduction of special early release from prison	10/10/2013 assigned (examination not yet begun)
06/08/2013	LETTA Government – S. 896-B Conversion into law, with amendments, of l.d. 1 July 2013, No. 78, containing urgent provisions regarding execution of sentence	08/08/2013 passed as law
06/08/2013	Mauro Maria MARINO (PD) – S. 1002 Establishment of the national Ombudsperson for the rights of prisoners or persons deprived of liberty	19/11/2013 assigned (examination not yet begun)
12/09/2013	Enrico BUEMI (Aut-PSI) – S. 1039 Provisions for the protection of the right to be forgotten of subjects subjected to criminal procedure	12/09/2013 still to be assigned

| 26/09/2013 | Sandro GOZI (PD) – C.1635
Amendments to the code of criminal procedure and to
the regulations for the implementation and coordination
of the said code, and temporary provisions therein,
as per lgs.d. 28 July 1989, No. 271, regarding the
reexamination of trial sentences following the ruling of
the European Court of Human Rights | 04/10/2013
assigned
(examination not
yet begun) |

Sources: TESEO classification system (search criteria: "human rights", "civil and political rights", "rights of foreigners" and "mistreatment and torture") and openparlamento (search criteria: "human rights", "rights of the person").

Right to Vote

Date	Initiative	Latest update
15/03/2013	Popolare – C. 10 Regulations for taking part in general and local elections and for the franchise without discrimination on the basis of citizenship and nationality	07/05/2013 assigned (examination not yet begun)
15/03/2013	Albrecht PLANGGER (Mixed) – C.79 Provisions for voting by post in political, European and local elections, and in referendums envisaged by the Constitution	15/03/2013 still to be assigned
15/03/2013	Karl ZELLER (Aut-PSI) – S. 39 Amendments to l. 27 December 2001, No. 459, regarding the exercising of the right to vote on the part of Italian citizens resident abroad	18/06/2013 assigned (examination not yet begun)
15/03/2013	Federica MOGHERINI REBESANI (PD) – C.117 Amendments to the consolidated text as per decree of the President of the Republic 30 March 1957, No. 361, to the consolidated text as per lgs.d. 20 December 1993, No. 533, and to l. 24 January 1979, No. 18, concerning the exercising of the right to vote of university students in elections for the Chamber of Deputies, the Senate of the Republic and the European Parliament	15/03/2013 still to be assigned
15/03/2013	Luigi BOBBA (PD) – C.162 Amendments to the consolidated text as per decree of the President of the Republic 20 March 1967, No. 223, for the attribution of franchise, for local elections alone, to citizens who have reached the age of sixteen	03/06/2013 assigned (examination not yet begun)
16/04/2013	Luisa BOSSA (PD) – C.779 Rule and regulations for the exercising of the right to vote in elections for the Senate of the Republic, the Chamber of Deputies and for the members of the European Parliament reserved for Italy, on the part of maritime workers at sea	05/07/2013 assigned (examination not yet begun)

Date	Initiative	Latest update
07/05/2013	Antonio DECARO (PD) – C.889 Amendment to article 48 of the Constitution, with regard to the extension of suffrage for elections for regional, provincial, local and ward councils, to sixteen-year-olds and to non-EU foreigners resident in Italy for at least five years	07/05/2013 still to be assigned
27/05/2013	Marco MELONI (PD) – C.1056 Rules and regulations for the exercising of the right to vote on the part of Italian citizens who are temporarily abroad	24/09/2013 assigned (examination not yet begun)
18/09/2013	Enrico BUEMI (Aut-PSI) – S. 1054 Rules and regulations for the depriving of electoral rights pursuant to article 48, paragraph four of the Constitution	18/09/2013 still to be assigned
25/09/2013	Aldo DI BIAGIO (PI) and others – S. 1059 Provisions for the exercising of the right to vote on the part of Italian citizens temporarily living abroad	25/09/2013 still to be assigned
15/10/2013	Francesco RUSSO (PD) – S. 1111 Provisions for the exercising of the right to vote on the part of Italian citizens who are temporarily abroad	16/12/2013 assigned (examination not yet begun)
17/10/2013	Fabio PORTA (PD) – C.1704 Amendments to l. 27 December 2001, No. 459, regarding the exercising of the right to vote on the part of Italian citizens temporarily living abroad	17/10/2013 still to be assigned
13/11/2013	Antonio DE POLI (PI) and others – S. 1170 Amendments to article 1 of l. 7 May 2009, No. 46, containing urgent provisions for some electors to vote from home	13/11/2013 still to be assigned

Sources: TESEO classification system (search criteria: "human rights", "civil and political rights", "rights of foreigners" and "mistreatment and torture") and openparlamento (search criteria: "human rights", "rights of the person").

Rights of Migrants (Including Citizenship Rights), Refugees and Asylum Seekers

Date	Initiative	Latest update
18/03/2013	Antonello GIACOMELLI (PD) – C.327 Organic code of guidelines for the right to asylum, refugee status and subsidiary protection, together with provisions for implementing directives 2003/9/EC, 2005/85/EC and 2011/95/EC	18/12/2013 currently under examination by the Commission
09/05/2013	Gennaro MIGLIORE (SEL) – C.908 Amendments to articles 48 and 51 of the Constitution with regard to the granting of the franchise and of eligibility to foreigners	23/07/2013 assigned (examination not yet begun)

09/05/2013	Gennaro MIGLIORE (SEL) – C.909 Amendment to article 2 of the consolidated text of provisions concerning immigration and norms on the condition of foreigners, as per lgs.d. 25 July 1998, No. 286, regarding the granting of the franchise and eligibility to foreigners in elections and in local-level referendums	16/07/2013 assigned (examination not yet begun)
13/05/2013	Loredana DE PETRIS (Mixed) – S. 640 Amendments to articles 48 and 51 of the Constitution concerning the granting of the franchise and eligibility to foreigners	19/11/2013 assigned (examination not yet begun)
13/05/2013	Loredana DE PETRIS (Mixed) – S. 639 Amendment to article 2 of the consolidated text as per lgs.d. 25 July 1998, No. 286, regarding the granting of the franchise and eligibility to foreigners in elections and in local referendums	17/07/2013 assigned (examination not yet begun)
14/05/2013	Gennaro MIGLIORE (SEL) – C.944 Regulations regarding humanitarian protection and the right to asylum	18/12/2013 currently under examination by the Commission
25/06/2013	Loredana DE PETRIS (Mixed) – S. 875 Regulations regarding humanitarian protection and the right to asylum	18/10/2013 assigned (examination not yet begun)
25/07/2013	Andrea COLLETTI (M5S) and others – C.1422 Establishment of a parliamentary Commission of inquiry into the expulsion of Alma Shalabayeva and her daughter from Italy to Kazakhstan	02/08/2013 assigned (examination not yet begun)
30/07/2013	Titti DI SALVO (SEL) – C.1444 Introduction of article 01 of l.d. 30 December 1989, No. 416, converted, with amendments, from l. 28 February 1990, No. 39, concerning the identification of subjects possessing the right to asylum and the granting of the same right to women victims of violence	18/12/2013 currently under examination by the Commission
01/08/2013	Michele BORDO (PD) – C.1462 Establishment of the Fund for the security of the communities that host reception centres for asylum seekers and the integration of foreigner asylum seekers	27/11/2013 assigned (examination not yet begun)
02/08/2013	Delia MURER (PD) – C.1476 Amendments to articles 48, 50, 51 and 75 of the Constitution, with regard to the political rights of foreigners resident in Italy	17/12/2013 assigned (examination not yet begun)
22/11/2013	LETTA Government – S. 1174 Conversion into law, with amendments, of l.d. 15 October 2013, No. 120, containing urgent measures for balancing the public finances and regarding immigration	11/12/2013 passed as law

Date	Initiative	Latest update
17/12/2013	Marco CAUSI (PD) – C.1898 Amendments to articles 48 and 51 of the Constitution, regarding the extension of the right to franchise and to eligibility for general, regional and local elections, and of the right to accede to public offices to citizens belonging to Member States of the European Union	17/12/2013 still to be assigned

Sources: TESEO classification system (search criteria: "human rights", "civil and political rights", "rights of foreigners" and "mistreatment and torture") and *openparlamento* (search criteria: "human rights", "rights of the person").

Introduction of the Crime of Torture into the Italian Legal System

Date	Initiative	Latest update
15/03/2013	Gianclaudio BRESSA (PD) – C.276 Introduction of articles 613-bis and 613-ter of the criminal code and other provisions concerning torture	11/06/2013 assigned (examination not yet begun)
15/03/2013	Pino PISICCHIO (Misto) – C.189 Introduction of articles 613-bis and 613-ter of the criminal code concerning torture	07/05/2013 assigned (examination not yet begun)
15/03/2013	Luigi MANCONI (PD) – S. 10 Introduction of the crime of torture into the criminal code	22/10/2013 examination by the Commission completed
28/03/2013	Gennaro MIGLIORE (SEL) and others – C.588 Introduction of article 608-bis of the criminal code and other provisions concerning the crime of torture	27/05/2013 assigned (examination not yet begun)
04/04/2013	Lucio BARANI (GAL) and others – S. 388 Introduction of article 593-bis of the criminal code, concerning the crime of torture, and other norms regarding torture	22/10/2013 examination by the Commission completed
08/04/2013	Loredana DE PETRIS (Mixed) – S. 395 Introduction of the crime of torture into the criminal code	22/10/2013 examination by the Commission completed
03/05/2013	Maria Teresa BERTUZZI (PD) – S. 601 Introduction of articles 613-bis and 613-ter of the criminal code regarding torture	04/09/2013 assigned (examination not yet begun)
17/05/2013	Sandro GOZI (PD) – C.979 Introduction of article 593-bis of the criminal code, concerning the crime of torture, and other norms regarding torture	07/08/2013 assigned (examination not yet begun)

19/06/2013	Maurizio BUCCARELLA (M5S) – S. 849 Introduction of the crime of torture into the criminal code	22/10/2013 examination by the Commission completed
25/06/2013	Salvo TORRISI (NCD) and others – S. 874 Introduction of article 613-bis of the criminal code and other provisions concerning torture	22/10/2013 examination by the Commission completed
07/08/2013	Mario MARAZZITI (PI) and others – C.1499 Introduction of articles 613-bis and 613-ter of the criminal code and other provisions concerning torture	05/09/2013 assigned (examination not yet begun)
12/11/2013	Fausto RACITI (PD) – C.1801 Introduction of article 608-bis of the criminal code and other provisions concerning the crime of torture	12/11/2013 still to be assigned

Sources: TESEO classification system (search criteria: "human rights", "civil and political rights", "rights of foreigners" and "mistreatment and torture") and *openparlamento* (search criteria: "human rights", "rights of the person").

Freedom of Opinion and Expression

Date	Initiative	Latest update
15/03/2013	Pino PISICCHIO (Mixed) – C.175 Amendment to article 21 of the Constitution, concerning the right to information	07/05/2013 assigned (examination not yet begun)
13/05/2013	Enrico COSTA (NCD) and others – C.925 Amendments to l. 8 February 1948, No. 47, to the criminal code and to the code of criminal procedure with regard to defamation, libel by the press and other media, offence to personal dignity and the conviction of the plaintiff	17/10/2013 approved
06/06/2013	Stefano DAMBRUOSO (SCpI) – C.1165 Amendments to l. 8 February 1948, No. 47, to the consolidated text as per l.d. 31 July 2005, No. 177, and to the criminal code with regard to crimes committed by the press, television broadcasts or other media, and to defamation and offence to personal dignity	17/10/2013 absorbed
12/06/2013	Mirella LIUZZI (M5S) – C.1190 Amendments to the criminal code, the code of civil procedure and l. 8 February 1948, No. 47, concerning the crimes of offence to personal dignity, defamation and press libel, and the relative damages	17/10/2013 absorbed
20/06/2013	Nicola MOLTENI (Lega) – C.1242 Amendments to the criminal code and to l. 8 February 1948, No. 47, with regard to offence to personal dignity, defamation and press libel, and the publication of responses and rectifications	17/10/2013 absorbed

Date	Initiative	Latest update
18/10/2013	Enrico COSTA (NCD) e altri – S. 1119 Amendments to l. 8 February 1948, No. 47, to the criminal code and to the code of criminal procedure with regard to defamation, libel by the press and other media, offence to personal dignity and the conviction of the plaintiff	20/12/2013 currently being examined by the Commission

Sources: TESEO classification system (search criteria: "human rights", "civil and political rights", "rights of foreigners" and "mistreatment and torture") and *openparlamento* (search criteria: "human rights", "rights of the person").

Economic, Social and Cultural Rights

Date	Initiative	Latest update
15/03/2013	Pino PISICCHIO (Misto) – C. 174 Amendment to article 2 of the Constitution, concerning recognition of the right to water	07/05/2013 assigned (examination not yet begun)
27/03/2013	Maurizio BIANCONI (FI-PdL) – C.560 Amendments to articles 3, 9, 17, 18 and 19 of the Constitution, regarding the principle of substantive equality, the protection and promotion of the landscape and of the historic, artistic and cultural heritage, freedom of assembly, freedom of association and freedom of religion	07/05/2013 assigned (examination not yet begun)
10/04/2013	Antonio DE POLI (PI) and others – S. 516 Provisions concerning the self-government of schools, families' freedom of educational choice and the reform of the juridical status of teachers	10/04/2013 still to be assigned
19/04/2013	Massimo CASSANO (NCD) and others – S. 556 Introduction of temporary regulations for the suspension of the seizure, due to debts, of non-luxury homes and property required for work activities	19/04/2013 still to be assigned
07/08/2013	Pietro ICHINO (SCpI) – S. 1006 Code of labour relations. Amendments to Book V of the civil code	19/11/2013 assigned (examination not yet begun)
08/08/2013	LETTA Government – C.1248-B Conversion into law, with amendments, of l.d. 21 June 2013, No. 69, containing urgent measures for boosting the economy	09/08/2013 passed as law

Sources: TESEO classification system (search criteria: "human rights", "civil and political rights", "rights of foreigners" and "mistreatment and torture") and *openparlamento* (search criteria: "human rights", "rights of the person").

Women's Rights

Date	Initiative	Latest update
30/04/2013	Simona VICARI (NCD) and others – S. 592. Delegation to Government with regard to measures in favour of women and other subjects who are victims of violence or abuse	30/04/2013 still to be assigned
09/05/2013	Franca Maria Grazia BIONDELLI (PD) – C.912. Regulations regarding measures in favour of pregnant women and mothers and designed to guarantee confidentiality of delivery and the rights of the new-born	05/07/2013 assigned (examination not yet begun)
20/05/2013	Anna ROSSOMANDO (PD) – C.1010. Regulations regarding measures in favour of pregnant women and mothers and designed to guarantee the confidentiality of delivery for women who do not intend to recognise their new-born	10/09/2013 assigned (examination not yet begun)
29/05/2013	Francesca PUGLISI (PD) – S. 724. Provisions to promote female subjectivity and to combat feminicide	17/10/2013 currently being examined by the Commission
20/06/2013	Daniela SBROLLINI (PD) – C.1241. Provision for combating violence and discrimination for reasons relating to sex or to sexual orientation, and for promoting female subjectivity	30/07/2013 assigned (examination not yet begun)

Sources: TESEO classification system (search criteria: "human rights", "civil and political rights", "rights of foreigners" and "mistreatment and torture") and *openparlamento* (search criteria: "human rights", "rights of the person").

Right to a Private and Family Life

Date	Initiative	Latest update
15/03/2013	Luigi MANCONI (PD) – S. 14. Rules and regulations for civil unions	10/12/2013 currently being examined by the Commission
03/07/2013	Alessia PETRAGLIA (Misto) – S. 909. Regulations regarding civil unions and mutual aid unions	10/12/2013 currently being examined by the Commission
08/08/2013	Basilio CATANOSO (FI-PdL) – C.1523. Provisions for protecting the dignity and confidentiality of family members of the victims of serious crimes	08/08/2013 still to be assigned

Date	Initiative	Latest update
19/12/2013	Andrea MARCUCCI (PD) – S. 1211 Amendments to the civil code with regard to the rules and regulations for civil unions and cohabitation agreements	19/12/2013 still to be assigned

Sources: TESEO classification system (search criteria: "human rights", "civil and political rights", "rights of foreigners" and "mistreatment and torture") and *openparlamento* (search criteria: "human rights", "rights of the person").

Protection of Personal Data

Date	Initiative	Latest update
25/03/2013	Guglielmo VACCARO (PD) – C.499 Amendments to 615-ter of the criminal code and to the code as per lgs.d. 30 June 2003, No. 196, concerning the protection of personal data on the Internet	03/06/2013 assigned (examination not yet begun)
08/08/2013	Basilio CATANOSO (FI-PdL) – C.1522 Amendments to l. 31 October 1955, No. 1064, regarding the use of personal particulars	21/01/2014 assigned (examination not yet begun)
05/09/2013	Jonny CROSIO (Lega) and others – S. 1027 Amendments to articles 7, 129 and 130 of the code regarding the protection of personal data, as per lgs.d. 30 June 2003, No. 196, concerning the processing of data for advertising or telephone sales purposes	05/09/2013 still to be assigned
25/11/2013	Renato BRUNETTA (FI-PdL) – C.1846 Amendments to the criminal code, the code of criminal procedure, lgs.d. 8 June 2001, No. 231 and to the code regarding the protection of personal data, as per lgs.d. 30 June 2003, No. 196, concerning the rules and regulations for telephone and telematic tapping and for bugging	03/12/2013 assigned (examination not yet begun)

Sources: TESEO classification system (search criteria: "human rights", "civil and political rights", "rights of foreigners" and "mistreatment and torture") and *openparlamento* (search criteria: "human rights", "rights of the person").

Ratification of International Instruments

Date	Initiative	Latest update
21/03/2013	Daniela SBROLLINI (PD) – C.459 Ratification and execution of the Council of Europe Convention on Preventing and Combating Violence against Women and Domestic Violence, opened for signature in Istanbul on 11 May 2011, and other provisions for combating violence and discrimination for reasons relating to sex or sexual orientation, and for the promotion of female subjectivity	14/05/2013 assigned (examination not yet begun)
18/07/2013	Marietta TIDEI (PD) – C.1374 Ratification and execution of the UN Convention on the Protection of All Persons from Enforced Disappearance, adopted in New York on 20 December 2006	18/07/2013 still to be assigned

06/11/2013	Enrico BUEMI (Aut-PSI) – S. 1158 Ratification and execution of Protocol No. 16 to the Convention on the Protection of Human Rights and Fundamental Freedoms, and provisions regarding the executive efficacy of the equitable indemnity recognised by the European Court of Human Rights to the Italian State	16/12/2013 assigned (examination not yet begun)
06/11/2013	Enrico BUEMI (Aut-PSI) – S. 1159 Ratification and execution of Protocol No. 15 to the Convention on the Protection of Human Rights and Fundamental Freedoms	06/11/2013 still to be assigned

Sources: TESEO classification system (search criteria: "human rights", "civil and political rights", "rights of foreigners" and "mistreatment and torture") and *openparlamento* (search criteria: "human rights", "rights of the person").

Right to Health

Date	Initiative	Latest update
15/03/2013	Benedetto FUCCI (FI-PdL) – C.256 Amendment to article 2 of the Constitution, regarding the principle of the inviolability of the right to life	15/03/2013 still to be assigned
04/06/2013	Matteo MANTERO (M5S) – C.1142 Rules and regulations regarding informed consent and advance health care directives designed to avoid futile medical care	09/07/2013 assigned (examination not yet begun)
01/07/2013	Lucio BARANI (GAL) and others – S. 9 01 Urgent measures for the protection of the right to health and of freedom of treatment. Amendments to the consolidated text as per decree of the President of the Republic 9 October 1990, No. 309	23/10/2013 assigned (examination not yet begun)
09/09/2013	Stefano VACCARI (PD) – S. 1026 Amendments to l. 4 July 2005, No. 123, containing norms for the protection of subjects with coeliac disease	09/09/2013 still to be assigned

Sources: TESEO classification system (search criteria: "human rights", "civil and political rights", "rights of foreigners" and "mistreatment and torture") and *openparlamento* (search criteria: "human rights", "rights of the person").

National Human Rights Institutions

Date	Initiative	Latest update
20/05/2013	Khalid CHAOUKI (PD) – C.1004 Establishment of the National Commission for the Promotion and Protection of Human Rights	29/07/2013 assigned (examination not yet begun)
21/06/2013	Emma FATTORINI (PD) – S. 865 Establishment of the Italian Commission for the Promotion and Protection of Human Rights	23/10/2013 assigned (examination not yet begun)

Date	Initiative	Latest update
24/06/2013	Barbara POLLASTRINI (PD) – C.1256 Establishment of the Parliamentary Commission for the Promotion and Protection of Human Rights	24/06/2013 still to be assigned

Sources: TESEO classification system (search criteria: "human rights", "civil and political rights", "rights of foreigners" and "mistreatment and torture") and *openparlamento* (search criteria: "human rights", "rights of the person").

Homophobia and Transphobia; Rights of Persons with Disabilities; Rights of Roma, Sinti and Travellers

Date	Initiative	Latest update
28/05/2013	Renato BRUNETTA (FI-PdL) – C.1071 Amendment to article 61 of the criminal code with regard to the common aggravating circumstances for crimes committed for reasons of discrimination, approved with the new title "Provisions concerning the fight against homophobia and transphobia"	19/09/2013 approved in unified text
04/06/2013	Francesco PALERMO (Aut (SVP, UV, PATT, UPT) – PSI) and others – S. 770 Norms for the protection and equal opportunities of the Roma and Sinti minorities	30/10/2013 assigned (examination not yet begun)
05/06/2013	Antonio GENTILE (NCD) and others – S. 804 Establishment of the Ombudsperson for the protection of the rights of persons with disabilities	12/09/2013 assigned (examination not yet begun)

Sources: TESEO classification system (search criteria: "human rights", "civil and political rights", "rights of foreigners" and "mistreatment and torture") and *openparlamento* (search criteria: "human rights", "rights of the person").

Motions

Of the 14 motions presented, 4 concerned violence against women, 3 were about the protection of human rights at an international level (with particular reference to Syria and Afghanistan), 3 regarded the ratification of international instruments, while the other 4 related respectively to prison conditions, the rights of refugees and asylum seekers, national civil service and national human rights institutions.

Violence against Women

Date	Initiative	Latest update
14/05/2013	Paola BINETTI (PI) and others – C.1/00036 Violence against women	04/06/2013 concluded
15/05/2013	Renato BRUNETTA (FI-PdL) – C.1/00041 "Whereas: the concept of feminicide…"	04/06/2013 concluded
16/05/2013	Mara MUCCI (M5S) – C.1/00042 "Whereas: the statistics for violence in Italy are sadly known. One woman in three aged between 16 and 70 has been a victim of some form of violence; …"	04/06/2013 concluded

03/06/2013	Giorgia MELONI (FdI) and others – C.1/00065 "Whereas: violence against women is the most widespread human rights violation in the world…"	04/06/2013 concluded

Source: *openparlamento* (search criteria: "human rights", "rights of the person").

Protection of Human Rights at an International Level

Date	Initiative	Latest update
16/04/2013	Manlio DI STEFANO (M5S) – C.1/00022 "Whereas: with the 12 years of direct involvement on the part of our Country, the war in Afghanistan is the most long-lasting…"	16/04/2013 presented
29/05/2013	Gennaro MIGLIORE (SEL) – C.1/00060 "Whereas: almost 12 years have gone by since the beginning of the NATO mission in Afghanistan…"	29/05/2013 presented
03/06/2013	Maria MUSSINI (M5S) – S. 1/00054 "Whereas: a civil war has been under way in Syria since March 2011…"	appending of new signatures

Source: *openparlamento* (search criteria: "human rights", "rights of the person").

Ratification of International Instruments

Date	Initiative	Latest update
29/05/2013	Silvana AMATI (PD) – S. 1/00049 "Whereas: the text of the Arms Trade Treaty was adopted on 2 April 2013…"	29/05/2013 presented
04/06/2013	Roberto SPERANZA (PD) – C.1/00067 Ratification and execution of the Council of Europe Convention on preventing and combating violence against women	04/06/2013 accepted
12/06/2013	Emma FATTORINI (PD) – S. 1/00064 "Whereas: on 28 May 2013 the Chamber of Deputies approved, on the first reading, the bill regarding the Ratification and execution of the Council of Europe Convention on Preventing and Combating Violence against Women…"	19/06/2013 accepted

Source: *openparlamento* (search criteria: "human rights", "rights of the person").

Prison Conditions; Rights of Refugees and Asylum Seekers; National Civil Service; National Human Rights Institutions

Date	Initiative	Latest update
26/03/2013	Luigi ZANDA (PD) – S. 1/00007 The establishment, in the Senate, of the Special Commission for the Protection and Promotion of Human Rights	16/04/2013 accepted
13/06/2013	Manuela SERRA (M5S) – S. 1/00068 "Whereas: the origin of the word 'asylum' lies in the Greek term *asylon*;…"	13/06/2013 presented

Date	Initiative	Latest update
13/06/2013	Francesca BONOMO (PD) – C.1/00097 "Whereas: the current National Civil Service is rooted in the fight for the right to conscientious objection, ..."	11/07/2013 appending of new signatures
21/06/2013	Gregorio GITTI (PI) and others – C.1/00115 "Whereas: the problem of prison overcrowding does not just concern the moral and social sphere of our democracy..."	29/07/2013 appending of new signatures

Source: *openparlamento* (search criteria: "human rights", "rights of the person").

Interpellations

Date	Initiative	Latest update
16/04/2013	Arturo SCOTTO (SEL) – C.2/00024 Regarding the diplomatic initiative undertaken in recent months by Christopher Ross, the UN Secretary-General's Personal Envoy for the Western Sahara	16/04/2013 presented
30/04/2013	Gennaro MIGLIORE (SEL) – C.2/00030 On the arrest of Lander Fernandez Arrinda on 13 June 2012	16/05/2013 concluded
08/05/2013	Teresa BELLANOVA (PD) – C.2/00037 On the collapse, in Dhaka, Bangladesh on 23 April 2013, of a nine-storey building housing five clothing factories	08/05/2013 presented
20/06/2013	Alessandro ZAN (SEL) – C.2/00108 On the law, approved by the Russian Parliament on 11 June 2013, banning homosexual propaganda between minors	16/07/2013 concluded
26/06/2013	Gianni MELILLA (SEL) – C.2/00114 On migrants detained in Italy in inhumane centres such as the identification and expulsion centres	26/06/2013 presented

Source: *openparlamento* (search criteria: "human rights", "rights of the person").

Questions for an oral answer

Date	Initiative	Latest update
02/04/2013	Giuseppina MATURANI (PD) – S. 3/00014 To the Minister of the Interior – Whereas: with l. 3 March 2009, No. 18, Parliament authorised the ratification of the UN Convention on the Rights of Persons with Disabilities...	24/07/2013 concluded
30/04/2013	Luigi MANCONI (PD) – S. 3/00044 To the Ministers of Justice and Foreign Affairs – Whereas: Lander Fernandez Arrinda was arrested during a police operation on 13 June 2012...	30/04/2013 presented
03/06/2013	Peppe DE CRISTOFARO (Mixed) – S. 3/00100 To the Ministers of Foreign Affairs and of the Interior – Whereas: Libya is a nation in which the rule of law is currently absent, the central Government...	03/06/2013 presented

| 18/06/2013 | Maurizio GASPARRI (FI-PdL) – S. 3/00147
GASPARRI
To the Minister of Justice – Whereas: prison conditions
overall in our nation have now become unsustainable,
with reference to the poor ratio between… | 18/06/2013
presented |

Source: *openparlamento* (search criteria: "human rights", "rights of the person").

Questions for a written answer

Of the 12 questions for a written answer, 5 concerned prison conditions and the rights of prisoners, 4 related to the rights of migrants, refugees and asylum seekers, 1 regarded children's rights, 1 the protection of human rights at an international level (with particular reference to the Western Sahara) and 1 the freedom of religion.

Prison Conditions and the Rights of Prisoners

Date	Initiative	Latest update
15/03/2013	Ermete REALACCI (PD) – C.4/00016 The Constitution of the Italian Republic clearly establishes that prison punishment cannot consist of treatments contrary to human dignity and must aim at rehabilitating the convicted…	02/09/2013 reminder
26/03/2013	Benedetto FUCCI (FI-PdL) – C.4/00107 In its meeting of 20 March 2013, the Provincial Council of the Province of Barletta-Andria-Trani unanimously approved an agenda proposal requesting immediate intervention, on the part of the Ministry of Justice, to reopen the prison of Spinazzola (BT)…	16/07/2013 concluded
16/04/2013	Renata BUENO (Mixed) – C.4/00211 On 27 March 2008 the Government of the Italian Republic and the Government of the Federative Republic of Brazil signed the treaty concerning the transfer of convicted persons in order…	15/07/2013 concluded
06/05/2013	Paola DE PIN (Mixed) and others – S. 4/00138 To the Ministers of Justice and of Food, Agriculture and Forestry – Whereas the Report on the status of human rights in prison institutions and in centres…	06/05/2013 presented
04/06/2013	Ettore ROSATO (PD) – C.4/00703 On 8 January 2013 the European Court of Human Rights in Strasbourg ruled that Italy was guilty of "inhumane and degrading treatment" following a plea lodged by seven detainees that…	04/06/2013 presented

Source: *openparlamento* (search criteria: "human rights", "rights of the person").

Rights of Migrants, Refugees and Asylum Seekers

Date	Initiative	Latest update
09/04/2013	Marisa NICCHI (SEL) – C.4/00163 As from the early months of 2011, the mothers and families of around 500 Tunisian migrants heading for Italy and Europe, and with regard to whom, except for 14 persons whose arrival has been ascertained...	09/04/2013 presented
04/06/2013	Sandro GOZI (PD) – C.4/00690 The UN High Commission for Refugees (UNHCR), the International Organisation for Migration (IOM) and Save the Children – which, since 2006, have been working as partners in the ambit...	04/06/2013 presented
05/06/2013	Benedetto DELLA VEDOVA (SCpI) – S. 4/00316 To the Ministers of the Interior and of Foreign Affairs – Whereas: the United Nations High Commission for Refugees (UNHCR), the International Organisation for...	05/06/2013 presented
12/06/2013	Walter RIZZETTO (M5S) – C.4/00825 The law establishing the Identification and Expulsion Centres, passed during the last Berlusconi Government, extends to 18 months the period of stay...	12/06/2013 presented

Source: *openparlamento* (search criteria: "human rights", "rights of the person").

Protection of Human Rights at an International Level; Freedom of Religion

Date	Initiative	Latest update
22/05/2013	Renzo CARELLA (PD) – C.4/00551 The UN Security Council convened on 25 April 2013 to discuss the conclusions and recommendations of the UN Secretary General's report on the situation in the Western Sahara...	16/07/2013 concluded
27/05/2013	Andrea CECCONI (M5S) – C.4/00593 The citizens' human rights and family aid committee of Brescia has been contacted by a mother in great distress due to the "enforced" admission of her seven-year-old son to the psychiatric ward of Brescia hospital...	27/05/2013 presented
19/06/2013	Maria Elisabetta ALBERTI CASELLATI (FI-PdL) – S. 4/00374 To the Ministers of the Interior, of Justice, of Education, University and Research, and of Health – Whereas: in the light of the disturbing spread of religious sects in Europe, the Council of Europe...	19/06/2013 presented

Source: *openparlamento* (search criteria: "human rights", "rights of the person").

Questions submitted to Commissions

Date	Initiative	Latest update
12/06/2013	Marietta TIDEI (PD) – C.5/00326 Gerardo Hernàndez, Ramòn Laba-ñino, Antonio Guerrero, Fernando Gonzàles and René Gonzàles were arrested on Saturday 12 September 1998 on the charge of espionage, and were held for 17 months in...	30/07/2013 Concluded
12/06/2013	Emanuela CORDA (M5S) – C.5/00328 Various press sources indicate that five hundred marines have been transferred to Sicily in the last few days from the Rota base in Spain. The men form part of the Marine Air Ground...	13/06/2013 concluded

Source: *openparlamento* (search criteria: "human rights", "rights of the person").

Commission resolutions

Date	Initiative	Latest update
16/05/2013	Gianluca PINI (Lega) – C.7/00006 Whereas: one can observe with great dismay the intensity of the violence taking place in Syria, on the part both of forces still loyal to President Bashar al-Assad and on the part of...	16/05/2013 presented
22/05/2013	Mario MARAZZITI (PI) and others – C.7/00016 On the global moratorium on the death penalty	05/06/2013 accepted
17/06/2013	Emanuela CORDA (M5S) – C.7/00042 Whereas: as can be read on its official website, http://www.eurogendfor.org, the European Gendarmeria Force (EGF) is a multinational initiative of 5 Member States...	17/06/2013 presented
17/06/2013	Manlio DI STEFANO (M5S) – C.7/00043 On the ratification of the Arms Trade Treaty	26/06/2013 accepted

Source: *openparlamento* (search criteria: "human rights", "rights of the person").

Final resolutions

Date	Initiative	Latest update
26/06/2013	Manlio DI STEFANO (M5S) – C.8/00005 On the ratification of the Arms Trade Treaty	26/06/2013 approved

Source: *openparlamento* (search criteria: "human rights", "rights of the person").

Assembly Agenda Proposals

Of the 9 agenda proposals adopted in the Assembly, 5 concerned women's rights and 4 related to prison conditions and the rights of prisoners.

Women's Rights

Date	Initiative	Latest update
28/05/2013	Delia MURER (PD) – C.9/00118-A/001 Whereas: the Istanbul Convention, now open for ratification, in referring to the preventing and combating of violence against women and violence…	28/05/2013 accepted
28/05/2013	Paola BINETTI (PI) and others – C.9/00118-A/003 Whereas: in August 2011, the Committee on the Elimination of Discrimination against Women (CEDAW), promoted by the UN and…	28/05/2013 accepted
28/05/2013	Rosa Maria VILLECCO CALIPARI (PD) – C.9/00118-A/005 Whereas: the Council of Europe Convention on Preventing and Combating Violence against Women and Domestic Violence…	28/05/2013 accepted
28/05/2013	Maria Rosaria CARFAGNA (FI-PdL) – C.9/00118-A/006 Pursuant to the issuing of guidelines and the inspective supervision which, in the last legislature, demanded, in both branches of Parliament, Italy's accession to, and ratification of, the Istanbul Convention against Violence towards Women	28/05/2013 accepted
28/05/2013	Giulia DI VITA (M5S) – C.9/00118-A/008 Having examined the unified text concerning the ratification and execution of the Council of Europe Convention Preventing and Combating Violence against Women …	28/05/2013 accepted

Source: *openparlamento* (search criteria: "human rights", "rights of the person").

Prison Conditions and the Rights of Prisoners

Date	Initiative	Latest update
3/07/2013	Lucio BARANI (GAL) and others – S. 9/00896/001 Considering that the overcrowding in Italian jails, and more generally, the precarious prison conditions have a negative impact on the rights guaranteed by the Constitution…	23/07/2013 accepted
04/07/2013	Mario MARAZZITI (PI) and others – C.9/00331-A/004 Whereas: the European Court of Human Rights in Strasbourg has confirmed its ruling against Italy, rejecting the request for a reexamination of the Torreggiani petition to the Great	04/07/2013 accepted as recommendation

| 04/07/2013 | Paola BINETTI (PI) and others – C.9/00331-A/008 Whereas: the statistics supplied by the Ministry of Justice (updated to last 10 June) indicate that there are 65,891 (1,176 interned, 40,118 convicted, 24,697 awaiting judgement)… | 04/07/2013 accepted |
| 23/07/2013 | Maurizio Giuseppe ROSSI (PI) and others – S. 9/00896/002 Whereas: article 27 of the Italian Constitution establishes that prison punishment cannot consist of treatments contrary to human dignity and must aim at rehabilitating the convicted. | 23/07/2013 accepted as recommendation |

Source: *openparlamento* (search criteria: "human rights", "rights of the person").

II. Prime Minister's Office (Presidency)

The organisation of the Prime Minister's Office is regulated by the decree of the Prime Minister of 1 October 2012. The Prime Minister's Office has a number of departments and offices (the so-called general structures), which the Prime Minister draws on for guideline and coordination functions regarding specific political and institutional fields. Of particular importance for human rights is the Department for Equal Opportunities.

A number of committees and commissions with specific tasks of economic and social relevance operate within the ambit of the Prime Minister's Office. These include the Commission for International Adoptions and the National Committee on Bioethics.

In addition, in 2007 the Committee of Ministers for Orientation and Strategic Guidance for the Protection of Human Rights was established, in order to ensure effective policy and coordination between ministries with regard to the protection of human rights; however, no data are available about the actual functioning of this Committee in 2013.

Finally, in April 2013, Enrico Letta's Government established the Ministry of Integration under the auspices of the Prime Minister's Office. The Ministry is responsible for the following areas: integration, youth policies, national civil service, international adoptions, the fight against racial discrimination, the National Strategy for the Inclusion of Roma, Sinti and Travellers Communities. Cécile Kyenge was appointed as the Minister.

A. Department for Equal Opportunities: UNAR and Observatory for the Fight against Paedophilia and Child Pornography

The Department for Equal Opportunities, established under the auspices of the Prime Minister's Office, plans and coordinates legislative, administrative and research initiatives in all areas pertaining to equal opportunities policies. In June 2013, the Deputy Minister of Labour and Social Policies, Maria Cecilia Guerra, with responsibility for equal opportunities, was entrusted with the direction of the Department.

> The Department was instituted by the d.p.c.m. of 28 October 1997, No. 405, subsequently amended by various decrees (the most recent being M.D. 4 December 2012). It comprises three offices: the Office of General Affairs, International Affairs and Social Measures; the Office for Measures to Promote Equality and Equal Opportunities; and the National Anti-Racial Discrimination Office (UNAR).

> UNAR was established by lgs.d. 9 July 2003, No. 215, in compliance with the European Community directive 2000/43/CE. Its mission is to guarantee observance of the principle of equal treatment of individuals, to monitor the efficacy of current instruments against discrimination, and to help to stamp out forms of discrimination based on race or ethnic origin, while analysing their diversified impact on gender, and their connection with other forms of racism of a cultural and religious nature.

In July 2013, UNAR published the figures relating to ethnic and racial discrimination in Italy in 2012. UNAR received a total of 1,283 pertinent reports in 2012, that is, cases which, when examined, proved to be actual instances of discrimination. Of these, 659 (51.4%) regarded the ethnic-racial sphere, 326 (25.4%) were age-related, 144 (11.2%) concerned sexual orientation, 93 (7.2%) regarded disability, 31 (2.4%) gender and 30 (2.3%) religious orientation. Therefore, although, as from 2011, the Office began to systematically deal with all the factors of discrimination, racism and ethnic intolerance continue to be its principal field of activity.

Analysis of the 659 cases of racial discrimination (there were 799 in 2011 and 540 in 2010) reveals that the largest number of reports came from Lombardy (19.6%) and Lazio (14.4%), followed by Emilia Romagna (11.2%), Veneto (9.7%), Tuscany (9.1%) and Piedmont (8.2%). These are Regions where immigrants form a significant component of society (see below, Statistical Dossier on Immigration). Overall, 53.6% of all cases brought to the attention of UNAR in 2012 were from northern Italy, while 27.6% were from the centre and 14% from the south.

Just as in 2010 and 2011, so too in 2012 the largest number of cases of discrimination (19.6%) concerned the mass media (especially Internet), followed by the workplace (18.2%, with particular reference to access to employment) and public life (17%). These three areas represented 54.8% of all cases. A little over one case in ten (11.5%) related to the provision of services by public bodies, and another one tenth (11.4%) took place in the field of leisure. Discrimination in access to housing and schools accounted for respectively 7.3% and 5% of all cases. Other areas obtained lower percentages: provision of services by public utilities (3.2%), the forces of law and order (2.6%), public transport (2.3%), the provision of financial services (1.1%) and health (0.9%).

In November 2013 the new edition of the Statistical Dossier on Immigration ("From discrimination to rights") was presented, edited for the first time by the IDOS/Immigration Study and Research Centre in collaboration with UNAR. The Dossier estimates that the number of foreigners legally present in Italy in 2012 was 5,186,000, of whom about 4,388,000 were resident, equivalent to 7.4% of the overall population. The prevalent continent of origin was Europe, accounting for 50.3% (of whom 27.4% are EU citizens), followed by Africa (22.2%), Asia (19.4%), America (8.0%) and Oceania (0.1%). Non-EU Countries accounting for large groups of foreigners included: Morocco (513,000), Albania (498,000), China (305,000), Ukraine (225,000), the Philippines (158,000), India (150,000) and Moldova (149,000). The largest group of EU citizens was from Romania (about 1 million). The principal areas of residence continue to be the Regions of the north (61.8%) and centre (24.2%), while a sixth of all foreign residents (16.9%) were in the Provinces of Milan and Rome alone.

A section of the report is devoted to an analysis of the forms of discrimination of which migrants are victim, with particular reference to the following areas.

– *Housing*. The Dossier estimates that about 20% of immigrants live in difficult and uncertain housing conditions.

– *Work*. Problem areas concerning the access and integration of migrants in the workplace include: jobs for which they are over-qualified (concerning 41.2% of foreigners in work); the spread of irregular work; the increase in exploited and semi-slave labour; the prevalence of temporary job opportunities; reduced access to good-quality jobs; high incidence of workplace accidents (15.9% of the total, without mentioning "invisible accidents", namely those that are not reported: 164,000 according to INAIL).

– *Education*. The Italian education system is characterised by: bureaucratic requirements that are sometimes excluding (for example, the need to have a fiscal code to enrol is an obstacle for irregulars); inadequacy of measures to support the learning of Italian; "selective" orientations (80.7% of secondary school immigrant children are in technical and job-oriented schools); dropping out, both in middle schools (0.49%, compared to 0.17% for Italians) and in high schools (2.42%, compared to 1.16%).

– *Health*. Only 6 of the Regions and autonomous Provinces have formally ratified the agreement approved by the Permanent Conference for

Relations between the State and the Regions, regarding the elimination of inequality of access for immigrants to health services.

– *Legal and institutional*. This area encompasses discriminatory effects that can be related to the action of public institutions, with particular reference to welfare provision (e.g.: benefits for those living in rented accommodation; health services and assistance for the disabled; benefits for large families; registry office enrolment; access to state-sector jobs and self-employment; admission to civil service).

– *Freedom of religion*. An organic law on religious freedom, which moves beyond the 1929 law on "permitted religions" and the agreements with non-Catholic confessions, has still to be passed.

– *Racism in sport*. In the 2012–2013 football league championship there were 699 racist episodes involving fans (in Serie A, Serie B, 1st and 2nd divisions, the Coppa Italia, the under-20 league championship and friendly games); fines amounting to a total of almost half a million euro were issued to 29 clubs.

To overcome discrimination and promote the full affirmation of the rights and equal opportunities of migrants, the Dossier highlights three possible areas of intervention: the use of language, the issue of citizenship and resources for integration.

Finally, in 2013 UNAR carried out a series of activities in relation to the following national strategies:

– *National strategy for preventing and combating discrimination based on sexual orientation and gender identity*. UNAR published the national strategy in April 2013, in response to the programme promoted by the Council of Europe, "Combating discrimination on grounds of sexual orientation or gender identity", for the implementation of recommendation CM/REC (2010)5 of the Committee of Ministers. The goal of the national strategy, drawn up and coordinated by UNAR in conjunction with various institutional bodies, LGBT associations and social actors, is to create a three-year plan of integrated and multidisciplinary pilot actions (2013–2015) designed to prevent and combat discrimination in this field.

– *National plan against racism, xenophobia and intolerance for the three-year period 2013–2015*. In July 2013, the Minister of Integration and the Deputy Minister of Labour and Social Policies (who has responsibility for equal opportunities) presented the outline of the National Plan of action against racism. Prepared by UNAR, the outline represents a point of departure for drawing up a national plan agreed on by all the public and private bodies concerned (ministries, local and regional government bodies, unions, civil society). The National Plan will be organised around five key topic areas: work, housing, education, mass media and sport, safety.

– National Strategy for the Inclusion of Roma, Sinti and Travellers Communities, 2012–2020. Approved by the Council of Ministers in February 2012 (see *2013 Yearbook*, p. 99). In September 2013 the political steering committee began its work, the aim being to draw on the competence of all the government bodies involved to give impetus to the implementation of the Strategy.

Besides the three above-mentioned offices, the following collegial bodies are also part of the Department for Equal Opportunities: the Inter-Ministerial Committee to Support Victims of Human Trafficking, Violence and Severe Exploitation (as per the decree of the President of the Republic of 14 May 2007, No. 102); the Committee for the Prevention of Female Genital Mutilation; the Committee to Evaluate the Legitimacy to Act on Behalf of People with Disabilities; the Committee for Equal Opportunities between Men and Women; the Observatory for the Fight against Paedophilia and Child Pornography.

The Observatory for the Fight against Paedophilia and Child Pornography was established in accordance with l. 3 August 1998, No. 269, as modified by l. 6 February 2006, No. 38, with the task of acquiring and monitoring data and information relating to activities carried out by all Government bodies to prevent and stamp out the sexual abuse and sexual exploitation of minors. Amongst the other tasks of the Observatory, there is, in particular, the drawing up of the National Plan to prevent and fight the sexual abuse and sexual exploitation of minors.

In 2013, the Observatory took part in a wide range of initiatives, including:

– the European programme *Safer Internet 2009–2013*, an intervention plan regarding new media and the protection of minors;

– the European Commission programme *Prevention and Fight against Crime 2007–2013*, with a project entitled "Development of a methodology to identify and support children who have been sexually exploited for the production of pornographic images", in conjunction with Save the Children, the Italian Association of Services to Combat the Mistreatment and Abuse of Children, and the Postal and Communications Police;

– the European Commission's Daphne III programme, running from 2007 to 2013, the aim of which is to fund projects submitted by institutional and other subjects and designed to help protect children, young people and women against any form of violence.

B. Commission for International Adoptions

Article 6 of the Hague Convention on the Protection of Minors and Cooperation in Respect of Intercountry Adoption, which was adopted on

29 May 1993 and entered into force on 1 May 1995, requires States Parties to establish a central authority guaranteeing that adoptions of foreign children occur in respect of the principles established by the Convention itself. In order to comply with this requirement, Italy, via law 31 December 1998, No. 476, instituted the Commission for International Adoptions, operative through the Prime Minister's Office. The Commission is Italy's central authority for implementing the Hague Convention.

> The Commission is composed of a Chair, appointed by the President of the Council of Ministers (in 2013: Cécile Kyenge, Minister of Integration), and by the following members: three representatives of the Prime Minister's Office; a representative of the Ministry of Foreign Affairs; a representative from the Ministry of Education; a representative from the Ministry of Labour and Social Policies; a representative from the Ministry of the Interior; two representatives from the Ministry of Justice; a representative from the Ministry of Health; a representative from the Ministry of Economy; four representatives from the Conference between State and Regions; three representatives from family associations; experts in the field.

In 2013, the Commission authorised the entry into Italy of 2,825 children (down on the 3,106 authorisations of 2012 and the 4,022 of 2011), from 56 Countries. A total of 2,291 couples successfully completed the adoption procedure, compared to 2,469 in 2012 and 3,154 in 2011. Compared to 2012, then, there was a 9.1% decrease in the number of adopted minors, and a 7.2% fall in adoptive couples: this drop was mainly due to the slowing down of activities in Colombia, Brazil and Ukraine. The Russian Federation remained the first Country of origin, with 730 minors entering Italy in 2013 (25.8% of the total). Ethiopia, with 293 minors (10.4%), was the second-ranked Country of origin, followed by Poland with 202 minors (7.2%), Brazil with 187 (6.6%) and Colombia with 179 (6.3%). The 1,591 children from these five Countries represented about 56.4% of the minors adopted by Italian couples in 2013.

In 2013 the Commission published two studies: *Education Paths in International Adoptions. The Evolution of the Path and International Contributions. Activities 2010–2011* and *Paths of International Adoption: the Point of View of Families.*

C. National Committee on Bioethics

The National Committee on Bioethics performs an advisory role vis-à-vis the Government, Parliament and other institutions, with a view to providing guidelines on legislative and administrative instruments designed to define the criteria to use in medical and biological practice in order to protect human rights. It also has a role in informing the public and in raising awareness with regard to ethical problems arising in connection with progress in scientific research and in technological applications in the life sciences and in healthcare.

The Committee was established by the d.p.c.m. of 28 March 1990. It is made up of the following bodies: Chair (Francesco Paolo Casavola, President Emeritus of the Constitutional Court); Vice Chairs (Riccardo Di Segni, Chief Rabbi of Rome; Lorenzo d'Avack, Professor in the Philosophy of Law; Laura Palazzani, Professor in the Philosophy of Law); Office of the President (made up of the Chair and the Vice Chairs); Assembly.

One of the tasks of the Committee is to produce studies and make recommendations that can also be used for legislative purposes. The Committee's documents offer in-depth focus and reflection on ethical and legal issues that arise as knowledge in the field of the life sciences advances. According to their nature and purpose, the documents are classified as: opinions (approved in the Committee's assembly on the basis of inquiries conducted by working groups); motions (urgent documents approved with a two-thirds majority of those present in the assembly); responses (documents in which the Committee makes recommendations on issues about which its opinion has been sought by other bodies or by physical persons).

No motions were approved in 2013. However, the following opinions were approved: "Human rights, medical ethics and enhancement technologies in the military sphere" (22 February); "Neurosciences and pharmacological cognitive enhancement: bioethical profiles" (22 February); "Donation of the human body post mortem for study and research purposes" (19 April); "Illegal trafficking in human organs between living persons" (23 May); "Intensive care 'open' to family visiting" (24 July); "Mental disability in the developmental age: the case of autism" (19 April); "Conjoined twins and separation procedures: bioethical considerations" (19 July); "Health within the walls" (27 September).

III. Ministry of Foreign Affairs

The Ministry of Foreign Affairs has a number of directorate-generals and offices that deal specifically with human rights, disarmament and cooperation. In 2013, the delegated responsibility for issues arising in the United Nations was held by the Deputy Minister Lapo Pistelli.

Particularly worthy of note is Office II – Human rights advocacy and international humanitarian law, Council of Europe, which falls within the directorate-general for Political Affairs and Security. Other offices in the same directorate are: Office I – The United Nations system and the institutional reform process, peacekeeping operations and preventive diplomacy; Office V – Disarmament, arms control and nuclear, biological and chemical non proliferation, Office of the national authority for the banning of chemical weapons; Office VI – Organisation for Security and Cooperation in Europe.

The theme of human rights also relates across the board to the directorate-general for Global Affairs (Office IV – Energy, environmental protection and sustainable global development policies), the directorate-general for the European Union (Office III – European space of freedom, security and justice, the free movement of people and migratory flows towards the European Union) and the directorate-general for Development Cooperation (Office I – Development of cooperation policies within the European Union; Office II – Multilateral development cooperation; Office VI – Emergency and humanitarian aid; Office VIII – Planning and monitoring of the cooperation budget; gender issues, the rights of children and people with disabilities).

A. Inter-Ministerial Committee for Human Rights (CIDU)

The Inter-Ministerial Committee for Human Rights (CIDU) was established by decree of the Minister of Foreign Affairs on 15 February 1978, No. 519; its composition was updated by d.c.p.m. on 11 May 2007. In 2012–2013 CIDU underwent a reorganisation: initially phased out as a result of the spending review, it was reestablished on 5 September 2013, maintaining its functional competences because it was considered indispensable for providing advice and strategic guidance with regard to the promotion and protection of human rights and correct compliance with obligations assumed by Italy following the signature and ratification of conventions and international agreements in this field. The first plenary session of the reestablished Committee took place on 9 February 2013.

CIDU is chaired by a functionary of the diplomatic service appointed by the Minister of Foreign Affairs: in 2013, Gian Ludovico De Martino. Committee members include representatives of the Prime Minister's Office, of various Ministries and of many different institutions (such as the National Council on Economy and Labour (CNEL); the Association of Italian Municipalities (ANCI); the Conference of Presidents of the Regions and Autonomous Provinces; the Union of Italian Provinces (UPI); the National Commission for UNESCO; the Italian Committee for UNICEF; the Italian Society for International Organisation (SIOI); as well as three eminent personalities in the field of human rights.

CIDU has the following tasks: to promote measures necessary for ensuring full compliance with international obligations assumed by Italy; to facilitate the implementation of international conventions in Italy; to draft the reports Italy is required to submit to the pertinent international organisations; to maintain and develop appropriate relations with civil society organisations engaged in promoting and protecting human rights.

On 10 December 2013 the Minister of Foreign Affairs, Emma Bonino, delivered to the Office of the President of the Chamber of Deputies a report on the activities carried out by CIDU, and on the protection and respect of human rights in Italy in the course of 2012 (doc. CXXI, No. 1).

The report provided Parliament with the results of the collaborative activities conducted with UN and Council of Europe bodies with regard to the presentation of the periodic reports envisaged by the international human rights instruments to which Italy is a party, and the visits arranged by these organisations in order to obtain specific information or to directly appraise the situation in areas considered to be particularly sensitive for human rights. The activities carried out by CIDU in 2013 were as follows:

United Nations

– Drafting of Italy's 5th periodic report regarding the implementation of the international Covenant on Economic, Social and Cultural Rights;

– discussion of the 16th, 17th and 18th periodic reports regarding the Convention on the Elimination of All Forms of Racial Discrimination (Geneva, 5 March 2012);

– contribution to the drafting of Italy's 1st periodic report on the implementation of the Convention on the Rights of Persons with Disabilities;

– overseeing of procedures for the implementation, in Italy, of Security Council resolution 1325 (2000) on "Women, Peace and Security";

– activities to implement the recommendations made to Italy by the Human Rights Council following the Universal Periodic Review;

– the visit to Italy of the UN Special Rapporteur on violence against women, Rashida Manjoo (15–26 January 2012);

– the visit to Italy of the Executive Director of UN Women, Michelle Bachelet (10–11 July 2012);

– the visit to Italy of the UN Special Rapporteur on the human rights of migrants, Francois Crépeau (1–8 October 2012);

– the visit to Italy of the UN Special Rapporteur on the promotion and protection of the right to freedom of opinion and expression, Frank La Rue (29–30 November 2012).

Council of Europe

– the visit to Italy of the Committee for the Prevention of Torture (12–27 May 2012);

– the visit to Italy of the Commissioner for Human Rights, Nils Muiznieks (3–6 July 2012).

In relation to its study and analysis activities, in 2012 CIDU organised the following meetings and conferences:

– Series of seminar sessions on "Promoting human rights: from theory to practice", for students on master's degree courses at the main public and private universities of Rome;

– Conference on "Human rights and foreign policy" (13–14 December 2012), jointly organised by the Chamber of Deputies, the Senate of the Republic and the Council of Europe;

– International conference: "The centrality of the person and the protection of human rights in the contemporary world" (12 December 2012);

– Presentation of the *Italian Yearbook of Human Rights* (20 September 2012), organised in conjunction with the Human Rights Centre of the University of Padua and the Italian Society for International Organisation (SIOI);

– Meetings organised in the ambit of the Observatory on religious freedom, including "Religious liberty: God's gift to all nations is our responsibility to defend" (28 June 2012); "Stop the massacre of Christians in Nigeria. Initiatives by Italy" (19 July 2012).

B. Italian National Commission for UNESCO

The Commission was established by inter-ministerial decree on 11 February 1959, at the Ministry of Foreign Affairs, two years after Italy entered the Organisation, and pursuant to article 7 of the UNESCO Charter.

Its composition has been regulated and updated by a series of successive decrees, the most recent one dating back to 24 May 2007. Members of the Commission include representatives from Parliament, the Prime Minister's Office, various Ministries, public and private agencies, local authorities and civil society.

The Commission's mission is to promote the implementation of UNESCO programmes in Italy; to spread the ideals of the Organisation, especially among the younger generations; to disseminate information on its principles, goals and activities, thus stimulating action by institutions, civil society and the world of culture, education and science. The Commission also advises the Government regarding its dealings with UNESCO.

In 2013 the President, nominated by the Ministry of Foreign Affairs, was Giovanni Puglisi, while the post of Secretary General was held by Lucio Alberto Savoia.

The Italian National Commission for UNESCO receives funding for institutional activities and its functioning through chapter 2471/10 of the budget forecast of the Ministry of Foreign Affairs. Funding has continued to drop over the years, with allocated funds falling in 2013 to approximately 17,000 euros (in 2012 it was 25,000 euros), which covers nothing more than the mere functioning of the Commission, and makes it extremely difficult to perform its public activities.

Despite these shortages, in 2013 the Commission carried out many activities (seminars, conferences, meetings in schools, competitions, exhibitions, workshops, shows) in various Italian cities, above all on the occasion of the various UN International Days, including the International Mother Language Day (21 February), the World Poetry Day (21 March), the World Book and Copyright Day (23 April) and the International Jazz Day (30 April). Moreover, the Commission ran specific projects in schools, and further reinforced the network of UNESCO associated schools. Finally, from 18 to 24 November the National Commission co-ordinated and promoted the eighth edition of the Week of Education for Sustainable Development, devoted to the theme "Landscapes of Beauty: from Valorisation to Creativity". The Week falls within the framework of the Decade of Education for Sustainable Development, 2005–2014 (DESD), a world campaign set up by the United Nations and coordinated by UNESCO.

IV. Ministry of Labour and Social Policies

A number of the departments and offices belonging to the Ministry of Labour and Social Policies deal specifically with human rights.

The following are particularly worthy of note:

- *Directorate-general for employment service policies.* Functions: guidance, promotion and coordination of employment services in order to sustain employment policies; initiatives to combat ir-regular labour; guidance, coordination and initiatives to facilitate entry and reentry to the labour market of persons with disabilities; promotion of female employment; promotion of equal opportuni-ties for entry into the labour market; support for the activities of parity advisors.

- *Directorate-general for inclusion and social policies.* Functions: promoting policies to combat poverty, social exclusion and severe marginalisation; promoting and monitoring policies for children and adolescents, and the protection of minors; coordination policies for the social inclusion, protection and promotion of the rights and opportunities of persons with disabilities; managing the National Fund for Social Policies, the National Fund for the Non-self-sufficient, the National Fund for Childhood and Adolescence and other funds for financing social policies and monitoring transferred resources; study, research and investigations concerning social policies; participation in all the pertinent internationally signifi-cant activities, and managing relations with the European Union, the Council of Europe, the International Labour Organisation, the United Nations and the Organisation for Economic Cooperation and Development.

- *Directorate-general for the third sector and social groups.* Functions: promoting and supporting the activities carried out by third sector subjects, especially initiatives relating to social promotion and voluntary associations, in order to facilitate the growth of an active society welfare to support policies of social inclusion and integration.
- *Directorate-general for immigration and integration policies.* Functions: programming migratory flows, and managing and monitoring entry quotas of foreign workers as well as bilateral cooperation agreements with Countries of origin; coordinating policies for social and job integration of foreign immigrants and initiatives designed to prevent and combat discrimination, xenophobia and racism; developing international cooperation for activities to prevent and study social and employment emergencies, and for initiatives regarding work-related migratory flows.

In 2012 the Directorate-general for immigration and integration policies took over the functions of the Committee for Foreign Minors, suppressed in accordance with the decree on the so-called spending review (article 12, para. 20 of l.d. 95/2012, converted into law, with amendments, in l. 135/2012). The Directorate-general is therefore responsible for monitoring the presence, and modes thereof, of foreign minors temporarily present on Italian territory, whether they be unaccompanied minors present on Italian soil or admitted minors.

As regards unaccompanied minors, the Directorate-general may adopt two kinds of measures: the first is "no repatriation", which amounts to activating the procedures for integrating the person into Italy; the second is "assisted repatriation", designed to reunite the child with his or her family in their Country of origin. As regards the first option, responsibility for managing and monitoring the measures is put in the hands of local authorities. The most frequent choice made for unaccompanied minors in Italy is to place them in protected communities.

As regards admitted minors, the Directorate-general makes decisions, following due appraisal and according to predetermined criteria, at the request of organisations, associations or Italian families, regarding the temporary admission of children in the framework of humanitarian programmes; the Committee then makes decisions on temporary fostering and the minors' repatriation. It keeps a register of minors already admitted in the framework of humanitarian programmes and predefines criteria for assessing requests for the admission of temporary admitted minors.

During 2013, 8,461 unaccompanied foreign minors were referred to the Directorate-general (compared to 7,066 in 2012), of which 7,908 were male (93.5%) and 553 female (6.5%). The chief Countries of origin were Egypt (21.6%), Bangladesh (13.1%) and Afghanistan (12.8%). Of these minors, 31.4% were admitted in Sicily, 12.5% in Lazio and 10% in Lombardy.

A. *National Observatory for Children and Adolescents*

The Observatory performs a role of coordination among central administrations, local and regional bodies, associations, professional groups and non-governmental organisations dedicated to children's issues.

It was instituted by law 23 December 1997, No. 451, and is currently regulated by decree of the President of the Republic (d.p.r.), No. 103, 14 May 2007, which assigns it joint chairmanship by the Ministry of Labour and Social Policies and the Undersecretary of State to the Prime Minister's Office mandated with family policies. It is made up of representatives from national and local public administrations, associations and professional orders, voluntary and third sector organisations as well as experts in the field of children's rights.

Presidential decree 103/2007 assigns to the Observatory the task of preparing three documents about the condition of childhood and adolescence in Italy:

– The *National Plan of action and of measures to safeguard the rights and development of children and adolescents*. Drawn up every two years, the plan contains the fundamental strategic guidelines and concrete commitments that the Government intends to pursue in order to develop a satisfactory policy for children and adolescents in Italy. The third action plan (2010–2011) was adopted by presidential decree on 21 January 2011 (see *2012 Yearbook*, p. 113).

– The *Report on the condition of children and adolescents in Italy*, which aims to provide an updated picture of the aspects and phenomena characterising the condition of children and adolescents in Italy, and of the system of social services and measures for promoting and protecting the rights of children and adolescents. The latest report published by the Observatory refers to the two-year period 2008–2009.

– The *Periodic report of the Government to the UN Committee on the Rights of the Child regarding the application of the 1989* International Convention on the Rights of the Child, pursuant to article 44 of the Convention. The latest report (combining the 3rd and 4th reports) was sent by Italy in January 2009, and discussed in October 2011 (*see 2012 Yearbook*, p. 114).

In carrying out its functions, the National Observatory makes use of the National Centre of Documentation and Analysis for Children and Adolescents, which performs documentation, analysis, research, monitoring and training tasks. In 2013, the chair of the Centre was Simonetta Matone, while the Coordinator of scientific activities was Maria Burani Procaccini.

More specifically, the National Centre of Documentation deals with:

- collecting and disseminating regional, national, European and international norms and regulations, as well as statistical data and scientific studies;
- creating an annually updated map, based on information provided by regional authorities, of public, private and non-governmental services, including social and health care services, and of financial resources dedicated to children at the national, regional and local level;
- analysing the situation of childhood and adolescence in Italy, including the conditions of foreign minors;
- preparing an outline, based on National Observatory directives, of the biennial report on the condition of children in Italy, and of the Government report to the United Nations Committee on the Rights of the Child on the domestic implementation of the Convention on the Rights of the Child;
- formulating proposals, also at the request of local authorities, for the creation of pilot projects designed to improve children's living conditions as well as to assist mothers during the prenatal period.

B. *National Observatory Monitoring the Condition of Persons with Disabilities*

The Observatory is an advisory body offering technical and scientific support in defining national policies regarding disabilities.

It was instituted by law 3 March 2009, No. 18, at the Ministry of Labour, Health and Social Policies. It is chaired by the Ministry of Labour and includes a maximum number of 40 members, who are appointed by ministerial decree and represent central administrations involved in defining and implementing disability-related policies; regional and local authorities; social security institutions; the National Statistics Institute; trade unions; and most representative associations and organisations of persons with disabilities, joined by a maximum number of five experts of proven experience in the field of disabilities.

The strategic and scientific guidance of the Observatory's activities is provided by a Technical and Scientific Committee. In 2013 the composition of the Committee was the following: Matilde Leonardi (Committee coordinator), Raffaele Tangorra (Ministry of Labour and Social Policies), Enrico Agosti (Ministry of Health), Beatrice Bartolini (Conference of Regions and

Autonomous Provinces), Paolo Anibaldi (ANCI), Giovanni Pagano (FAND), Pietro Vittorio Barbieri (FISH), Carlo Francescutti (expert), Mario Melazzini (expert).

The Observatory's tasks include the following: to promote the implementation of the United Nations Convention on the Rights of Persons with Disabilities and to prepare, together with CIDU, the national report for the monitoring procedure established by that Convention; to prepare a biennial Plan of action on disability implementing national and international laws; to promote and develop statistic-based studies and research that may contribute to defining priorities and needs.

In 2013 the Observatory drew up the first *Two-year action plan for promoting the rights and for the integration of persons with disabilities*, adopted by presidential decree on 4 October 2013. The action plan consists of seven areas for priority intervention: 1) revision of the access system, recognition of the certification of disability and the model for social and healthcare intervention; 2) work and employment; 3) policies, services and organisational models for independent life and inclusion in society; 4) promotion and implementation of the principles of accessibility and mobility; 5) educational processes and inclusion in the school system; 6) health, the right to life, habilitation and rehabilitation; 7) international cooperation.

V. Ministry of Justice

Within the Ministry of Justice there are various departments and bureaus specifically involved with human rights. The most relevant are:

– *Office for studies, research, legislation and international relations* (Office of the Head of Department – Department of penitentiary administration): it deals in particular with coordinating activities with international organisations devoted to the protection and promotion of human rights of adult prisoners; it also handles pleas lodged by inmates with the European Court of Human Rights;

– *Office II*: (Directorate-general for litigation and human rights – Department of legal affairs): it is actively involved in examining cases pending before the European Court of Human Rights and in procedures relating to compliance with international obligations, and to the amendment of domestic law in accordance with the provisions of international instruments;

– *Office III: Protection and support for the rights of minors. Promotion of measures in favour of subjects who risk the greatest degree of social exclusion* (Directorate-general for the enforcement of judgments – Department of juvenile justice): the office deals with promoting and protecting the rights of unaccompanied foreign minors and of persons at risk of social exclusion.

VI. Judicial Authorities

The judiciary, that is to say the various organs of justice – ordinary, administrative and auditing – constituting judicial power, is the fundamental guarantee of rights and legality in a State that respects the principles of democracy, the division of powers and the rule of law. The Italian courts – the Constitutional Court, which delivers judgments regarding the constitutionality of laws, the Supreme Court, which is the court of last resort, the penal and civil tribunals and trial courts, and those concerned with administrative, audit and military matters – deal in a contentious manner with cases which often affect human rights in the most various ways and according to the most disparate perspectives. Access to a judge to obtain a ruling on a right that a plaintiff claims has been breached is a fundamental human right, linked to which are the many other procedural rights that distinguish the fair trial.

Besides ruling on individual cases, the justice system contributes to building and to the evolution of applicable law, through its own case-law. In recent years, and in relation to the theme of fundamental rights in particular, Italian rulings have been strongly influenced by that of international courts, especially the European Court of Human Rights and the Court of Justice of the European Union. The interaction between national judicial organs and international courts with jurisdiction over human rights stresses the universal nature of the latter. The dialogue with international courts and with those of other Countries called upon to apply the same standards regarding individual human rights does not just concern the supreme courts of a State, but all judges, who can draw on rulings made in foreign or international courts to improve existing guarantees regarding fundamental rights, fully respecting the Constitution and the law.

Part IV of this Yearbook is specifically devoted to a summary presentation of cases in the Italian courts on which rulings were delivered in 2013 (with particular reference to those made by the Constitutional and the Supreme Court), and of case-law elaborated by the European Court of Human Rights or the Court of Justice of the European Union which directly concerns Italy, either because the Italian State was the "defendant" or because the intervention of the European judge regarded pleas presented by Italian citizens or related to Italian legal norms.

VII. National Economy and Labour Council (CNEL)

CNEL is a body provided for in article 99 of the Constitution. The Chair for the 9th council period (2010–2015) is Antonio Marzano.

The CNEL's function is essentially advisory. It expresses opinions at the request of Parliament, the Government and the Regions; on its own initiative it prepares observations and recommendations on proposed legislation, reports, studies and in-depth analyses.

The CNEL structure includes an Assembly, a Chair's office and committee, several specialised Commissions, as well as numerous committees and bodies (including the Observatory on the social economy; the Socio-economic Observatory on crime; the National body of coordination for policies of foreign citizens' social integration at the local level).

In 2013, CNEL produced 15 documents, subdivided as follows:

- 7 texts containing observations and recommendations, including those on: the national energy strategy (28 February); ICT, employment and productivity (28 February); annual analysis of growth 2013 (20 March); promotion of advanced-level technical education and training (22 May);
- 3 bills, including Measures concerning gender statistics (29 October);
- 2 reports, including The labour market 2012–2013 (1 October);
- the 2013 Annual Report to Parliament and the Government on the level and quality of service provision by central and local public administrations to businesses and citizens (10 December);
- 2 volumes containing conference and debate proceedings; of particular note was Public policies in welfare: sectorial analysis preparatory to the 2013 Annual Report to Parliament and the Government on the level and quality of service provision by central and local public administrations to businesses and citizens (25 July).

VIII. Independent Authorities

There are nine independent authorities in Italy: the Communications Regulatory Authority (AGCOM); the Data Protection Authority; the Committee Guaranteeing the Implementation of the Law on Strikes Affecting Essential Public Services; the Authority Protecting Free Competition and the Market (Antitrust Authority); the Italian Companies and Stock Exchange Commission (CONSOB); the Institute for Vigilance on Private Insurance and Insurances of Collective Interest (ISVAP); the Regulatory Authority for Electricity and Gas; the Authority for Vigilance on Contracts for Public Works, Services and Supplies; the National Ombudsperson for Children and Adolescents.

Furthermore, in December 2013 the Council of Ministers adopted l.d. 146/2013 "Urgent measures regarding the protection of the fundamental rights of prisoners and the controlled reduction of the prison population". Article 7 of the l.d. made provision for the establishment, in the Ministry of Justice, of the National Ombudsperson for the Rights of Persons in Prison or Deprived of Liberty. The National Ombudsperson is collegial, and consists of the Chair and two members, and will have the function of acting as a watchdog to ensure that the execution of custodial sentences and of other forms of restriction on liberty is implemented in compliance with the regulations and principles established by the Constitution, by international human rights conventions and by the laws of the State. It will also have the faculty to visit, without prior authorisation, prison institutions and any other structure used to house persons subject to measures depriving them of their liberty.

The four authorities that relate more pertinently to human rights are described below.

A. Communications Regulatory Authority (AGCOM)

AGCOM was set up by law 31 July 1997, No. 249. It has a dual mandate: to ensure correct competition among market actors and to guarantee the fundamental freedoms of citizens in the area of communications, particularly as regards the protection of minors.

> The composition of the Authority is disciplined by decree 6 December 2011, No. 201 (the so-called Save Italy decree), and its conversion into law (22 December 2011, No. 214). In 2013 the Authority was made up as follows: Chair: Angelo Marcello Cardani; members of the Services and Products Commission: Antonio Martusciello and Francesco Posteraro; members of the Commission for Infrastructure and Networks: Maurizio Dècina (until November 2013, replaced by Antonio Nicita) and Antonio Preto. The Council consists of the Chair and all the Commissioners.

As detailed in the 2013 annual report of its activities and work programmes (referring to the period May 2012-April 2013), the Authority devoted particular attention to acting as a watchdog on behalf of minors and users, especially in relation to local and national broadcasters, in order to ascertain whether violations had been committed and to punish them accordingly. To this end, in the period considered, the Authority issued 29 injunction orders for violation of the self-regulatory code regarding media and minors, and of various provisions laid down in lgs.d. 31 July 2005, No. 177 (Consolidated text on radio and audiovisual media services) and of l. 23 December 1996, No. 650 (Conversion into law, with amendments, of law-decree 23 October 1996, No. 545, containing urgent provisions for radio and television broadcasting. Measures for the reorganisation of RAI S.p.a., in the publishing and entertainment sector, for the television and radio broadcaster in the local sphere and for encoded television broadcasts).

From the regulatory point of view, following the entry into force of lgs.d. 28 June 2012, No. 120, which introduced a series of amendments to the Consolidated text on radio and audiovisual media services regarding the prohibition of television programmes that may seriously damage the physical, psychic and moral development of minors, the Authority was called upon to draw up new detailed regulations containing technical measures to take in order to prevent minors from viewing or listening normally to programmes for adults. The legislator listed among the technical measures to be adopted systems of authentication based on personal identification codes and filter or identification systems. Pursuant to the new norms, on 3 May 2013 the Authority adopted the Regulations regarding technical measures to take in order to prevent minors from viewing or listening to broadcasts made available by audiovisual media service providers on request that may seriously damage the physical, psychic and moral development of minors, in compliance with article 34 of lgs.d. 31 July 2005, No. 177, as amended and integrated in particular by lgs.d. 15 March 2010, No. 44, and as amended by lgs.d. 28 June 2012, No. 120 (deliberation No. 51/13/CSP).

B. Data Protection Authority

The Data Protection Authority was instituted by l. 31 December 1996, No. 675, later substituted by lgs.d. 30 June 2003, No. 196 (Personal data protection code), with the aim to ensure protection of the fundamental rights and freedoms and respect for the dignity of persons, in the processing of personal data.

The Data Protection Authority is a collegial body made up of four members elected by Parliament, who remain in office for a seven-year non-renewable mandate. The current body is made up of Antonello Soro (Chair), Augusta Iannini (Vice Chair), Giovanna Bianchi Clerici and Licia Califano.

During 2013 the Authority adopted 420 measures to protect the fundamental rights of individuals with regard to the processing and diffusion of personal data, with particular reference, among other things, to the following issues:

– *Right to be forgotten.* On-line archives of newspapers and availability of data regarding the person concerned through external search engines (24 January);

– *Journalism.* Adoption of amendments and integrations to the code of professional conduct regarding the processing of personal data in the exercising of journalistic activities (1 August);

– *Education.* Opinion on a draft ministerial decree concerning the modality and content of admission tests for limited-access degree and master's degree courses for the academic year 2013–2014 (11 April);

– *Work.* Communication of data regarding personal evaluations and disciplinary measures (3 October); closed-circuit surveillance systems installed on commercial premises and the rights of workers (12 September);

– *Health*. General authorisation for the processing of personal data for scientific research purposes (27 December).

C. Commission Guaranteeing the Implementation of the Law on Strikes Affecting Essential Public Services

The Commission was instituted by law 12 June 1990, No. 146, modified by law 11 April 2000, No. 83. It comprises nine members designated by the Chairs of the Chamber of Deputies and the Senate among experts in matters of constitutional law, labour law and industrial relations, and appointed by decree of the President of the Republic. In 2013, the members of the Commission were: Roberto Alesse (Chair), Pietro Boria, Alessandro Forlani, Elena Montecchi, Iolanda Piccinini, Nunzio Pinelli, Salvatore Vecchione.

Some of the Commission's main tasks are:

– assessing the capacity of essential services to guarantee protection of both the right to strike and the enjoyment of constitutionally guaranteed human rights;

– requesting that those calling the strike delay the date of abstention from work if the Commission intends to attempt conciliation, or if it finds that the abstention violates legal and/or contractual obligations for strikes in essential public services;

– pointing out to those calling the strike any violations of norms concerning advance notice or any other requirements relative to the phase preceding collective abstention;

– notifying the appropriate authority which can order strikers back to work of situations where the strike or collective abstention could give rise to an imminent, probable risk of infringing constitutionally protected human rights;

– taking note of behaviour by administrations or enterprises which provide essential public services in clear violation of the law;

– assessing behaviour of both parties and if any non-compliance or violation of legal or contractual obligations relative to essential services emerges, inflicting penalties pursuant to art. 4 of law 146/1990 as amended by art. 3 of law 83/2000, ordering the employer to apply the disciplinary actions.

On 2 July 2013 the Commission presented its 2013 annual report on activities in 2012. The data in the report show how conflict in essential services reflected the protracted duration of the economic crisis, bringing recession to both the public and private sector. This crisis hit small and medium-size enterprises particularly hard, causing a large number to close (according to Unioncamere data, over 380,000 companies closed in 2012); a situation which contributed to keeping social tension relatively high. Indeed, although the number of general strikes decreased in

2012 compared to the previous year (7 national general strikes against the 20 called in 2011), at the same time there was a significant increase in territorial strike actions, at the regional level (10 compared to 5 in 2011) and, particularly, at the provincial level (59 as compared to 9 the previous year), the latter being called mainly in the northern Italian Regions, where the economic crisis has hit the companies running public services particularly hard, as well as small and medium enterprises in general. As regards the causes behind the conflict, about 90% of strikes were called to back political claims (amendments to laws, or bills being debated in Parliament); only 10% were related to renewal or respect of their specific collective labour contracts.

The Commission reacted immediately to all the calls for national general strikes with advice, not so much attempting to have the strikes called off completely, but to highlight the partial illegitimacy of their nature and request the unions to alter the duration of the strike, its time-frame, to exclude some services from it or to postpone the strike, for several different reasons (to distance them from previously called strikes, multiple simultaneous strikes, violation of the election truce period). All of the Commission's interventions were accepted by those to whom they were addressed, consequently giving it a 100% compliance rate.

As regards the levels of conflict in the various sectors of essential public services, there were 2,330 strike calls in 2012 against 2,229 in 2011, showing an increase of about 5%. Strikes actually held, on the other hand, were 1,375, a very small increase over the 1,339 of 2011.

In more detail, conflict levels remained stable, but high, in the environmental services (refuse collection, decontamination and reclamation) sector (351 and 243 calls for strike respectively, compared to 355 and 187 in 2011). The number of strikes in the transport sector also remains high: there were increases in air transport (171 calls against 132 the previous year) in the railways (albeit minimal: 154 compared to 149 in 2011) and in maritime services (66 against 33 in 2011); On the contrary, local transport had fewer calls for strike (357 against 465 in 2011, a decrease of 23%).

The instrument most used by the Commission remained that of advance warning of illegitimacy, as per art. 13, para. 1, point d), of law 146/1990 and subsequent amendments. There were 514 such advance warnings in 2012, compared to 654 in 2011. The high level of compliancy by those who call strikes shows how effective the interventions of the Commissions are: following the Commission's 514 advance warnings of irregularities in the call for a strike, 338 strikes were called off or postponed and in 109 cases strikers complied with the decisions of the Commission (resulting in an approximately 87% success rate).

The significant success of the so-called ex ante phase relegated to a marginal role the committee's ex post activities, which involve the para-jurisdictional ascertaining of responsibilities following violations of the law, with the consequent activation of the powers to inflict penalties envisaged by article 4 of law 146. Indeed, there were only 27 closure of proceedings deliberations assessing the behaviour of the parties, of which 17 were negative: 8 concerning company behaviour, 7 concerning that of the trade unions and 2 the behaviour of individual workers, relative to wildcat strikes, or at any rate, actions called by people other than trade unions. The remaining 10 deliberations were formally closed with dismissal or with the finding that there were no grounds for a negative evaluation.

D. National Ombudsperson for Children and Adolescents

The National Ombudsperson for Children and Adolescents was established with law No. 112 of 12 July 2011. A monocratic organ, the holder of the post is appointed by the Presidents of the Chamber of Deputies and of the Senate, who choose a figure of unquestioned morality, independence and professional competence in the field of children's rights. The term of office is four years. In 2013 the post of Ombudsperson was held by Vincenzo Spadafora.

The Ombudsperson has, amongst others, the following responsibilities:

– to promote the implementation of the UN Convention on the Rights of the Child, and of other pertinent international and European instruments, and to ensure appropriate forms of collaboration with all the national and international bodies and organisations engaged in promoting and protecting children and adolescents;

– to express opinions on legislative initiatives concerning the protection of the rights of children and adolescents, and the report that the Government presents periodically to the UN Committee on the Rights of the Child;

– to inform the Government, Regions and other local or territorial bodies involved, in relation to their respective responsibilities, of all appropriate measures to ensure full promotion and protection of the rights of children and adolescents;

– to inform judicial authorities and bodies concerned of problem cases or risks of minors' rights being infringed, as well as serious cases of neglect of minors, so that they can be taken into care by the appropriate authorities;

– to enhance knowledge of the rights of children and adolescents, organising, to this end, awareness-raising activities, studies and research.

Article 6 of law 112 also allows anyone to address the Ombudsperson to report violation of rights or the risk thereof. Finally, article 3 states that the Ombudsperson is to establish appropriate forms of cooperation with the regional Ombudspersons or similar figures. The National Conference for the Rights of Children and Adolescents was set up for this purpose; coordinated by the National Ombudsperson, it brings together all the other Ombudspersons, where these have been established (see in this Part, II, D).

In April 2013, the Ombudsperson presented his second report to Parliament on the actions undertaken over the course of 2012 to benefit the approximately 11 million children and adolescents living in Italy (comprising about 17% of the population). The following are of particular note:

– *Work in the parliamentary area*. During 2012, the Ombudsperson was summoned to the Parliamentary Commission for Children and Adolescents in relation to its survey on the implementation of measures governing adoption and foster parenting and, informally, to the Chamber of Deputies Justice Commission, in connection with the bill on the recognition of children born out of wedlock. Parliamentary approval of the latter, on November 28th, is welcomed as it puts an end to discrimination between children born in, and out of, wedlock.

– *Creating institutional networks*. In order to strengthen national strategies relating to children and adolescents, regular contacts were established with the National Observatory for Children and Adolescents and with the Observatory for the Fight against Paedophilia and Child Pornography.

On 10 December 2012, the Ombudsperson signed a protocol with the Police Chief aiming to strengthen actions to prevent and stamp out crimes where the victims of abuse are minors and specifically to identify best practices to ensure uniformity of approach and method throughout Italy in tackling the problems connected with minors who are the victims, perpetrators or witnesses of crime. The signature was followed up by establishing a group of experts who identified two priority areas from which to start their work: reception of unaccompanied minors and the relationship of minors with the Internet.

In addition, promising discussions took place with RAI (the Italian state broadcaster) on producing awareness-raising campaigns on the rights of children, and with ISTAT (Statistics Office) to promote an in-depth study on adolescents and on indicators of well-being for children and adolescents.

– *International activity*. In 2012, the Ombudsperson took part in the 7th *European Forum on the Rights of the Child*, organised by the European Commission. The main focus of the Forum was "Supporting child protection systems through the implementation of the EU Agenda on the Rights of the Child.

In September 2012 the Ombudsperson was accepted as a full member of the European Network of Ombudspersons for Children – ENOC). As such, he attended the 16th Annual Conference and General Assembly in Cyprus in October, focusing on minors who are in trouble with the law.

– *Cooperation with civil society*. In 2012, the Ombudsperson's Office supported the *Working Group on the CRC* for the launch and distribution of its 2012 Supplementary Report; it began work on essential levels of service, together with the platform *Batti il cinque!* (Gimme five!); it met with the *Tavolo Nazionale Affido* (National round table on Foster Care) in order to identify a common project on the complex situation of minors living away from their family; it cooperated with individual associations in organising conventions and seminars on certain specific themes, such as that organised by *Terre des hommes* Italia to celebrate the first International Day of the Girl, established by the United Nations on 11th October, or the convention *"Sguardi Oltre – I ragazzi si riprendono le periferie"* (Looking further – The young are taking back their suburbs), organised by the association *L'Albero della Vita* (The Tree of Life) in Rome on November 6th. The Ombudsperson decided to invite reflections on the protection of children when their parents are in conflict, and thanks to cooperation with the association Associazione GeA-Genitori Ancora (Still Parents), which works in the field of family mediation, organised a round table in Rome on 28 November 2012, where judges, lawyers, social workers, psychologists, mediators and representatives from various associations could share their points of view.

In addition, the Ombudsperson supported the launch of the "Atlas of children (at risk)" published by Save the Children Italy. With this same organisation and *Telefono Azzurro* (Children's Helpline), the Ombudsperson also promoted the project "Safer Internet Centre", designed to combat cyber bullying and provide children and young people with the tools for a better online experience.

Finally, together with a number of associations, a detailed study on unaccompanied foreign minors was started. It covers issues related to their right to be taken in Italy, how to determine their age, the conditions of the reception communities and actions to dissuade the children from leaving them and the risk that children in transit fall prey to exploitation by organised criminals.

– *Reports*. In 2012, the Ombudsperson's Office received reports from individuals, associations and structures working with children and adolescents, but none coming directly from minors. The reports received were mainly relative to the following areas: contested custody of minors, family poverty, social exclusion (Roma and Sinti children), unaccompanied foreign minors, difficulties at school (children with disabilities or special needs), school buildings, health (particularly as regards administering medication to minors), TV advertisements and programmes unsuitable for a juvenile audience, gambling, children in prison with their mothers, insufficient funds for reception communities.

IX. Non-governmental Organisations

In Italy there are numerous non-governmental organisations active in promoting and protecting human rights. Some of them, organised in networks at the national and international level, have gained consultative status with international organisations and actively participate in the organisations' activities.

As of 31 December 2013, 95 Italian non-governmental organisations held consultative status with the United Nations Economic and Social Council (-4 compared to 2012), 9 of which have general status (-1); 69 have special status (-2) and 17 have roster status (-1). There are 159 non-governmental organisations with headquarters or representative offices in Italy that enjoy participatory status with the Council of Europe.

In addition, some of the most important international nongovernmental organisations have a local branch in Italy. These include Amnesty International, the International Federation on Human Rights, Save the Children, Médecins sans Frontières and Action Aid. The Italian associations Nessuno tocchi Caino (Hands off Cain – for worldwide abolition of the death penalty) and Non c'è pace senza giustizia (No Peace without Justice) also have a high profile internationally.

Particularly worthy of note, as well, is the Comitato per la promozione e protezione dei diritti umani, a network of 86 non-governmental organisations working to promote human rights, created in January 2002 on initiative of the Fondazione Basso (Basso Foundation), with the support of a group of human rights experts. In 2012, Barbara Terenzi acted as coordinator, while Carola Carazzone was the main spokesperson.

The Committee's main goal is to stimulate and support the Italian legislative process in order to create an independent national institution for human rights in Italy, in full compliance with the standards promoted by the United Nations General Assembly (resolution 48/134 of 20 December 1993) and the "Paris Principles". Alongside activities linked to the creation of the national institution for human rights, since 2005 the Committee has designed and implemented a systematic process for monitoring the respect of human, civil, political, economic, social and cultural rights in Italy, using the legal framework of the two relevant international Covenants in an integrated fashion.

In addition to its core activities, i.e. advocating the creation of a national human rights institution in Italy, and monitoring the respect for human rights at the national level, in 2013 the Committee organised an informal meeting between representatives of the Italian civil society and the new Commissioner for Human Rights of the Council of Europe, Nils Muižnieks, as well as a series of seminars on the topic "Promoting Human Rights: From Theory to Practice", in collaboration with the CIDU, SIOI and the universities Roma Tre, La Sapienza, LUISS, LUMSA, LUSPIO and Tor Vergata. Moreover, since 2013, the Committee is a member of the EU Civil Society Platform Against Trafficking in Human Beings.

X. Human Rights Teaching and Research in Italian Universities

The Italian world of academia has been showing growing interest in research and education on the subject of human rights. This issue is now included in the teaching programmes of a number of disciplines and in the curricula of various degree courses at the undergraduate and post-graduate level, as well as in cross-cutting interdisciplinary research programmes. The next pages offer an overview of the universities and research centres which are specifically involved with human rights issues, including the teaching on three-year degrees, Masters and PhD courses which were available in 2013 or opened for registration within the year. To be precise, the list comprises only the courses and structures which include the phrase "human rights" or equivalent expressions (rights of the person, fundamental rights) in their full title. The picture thus obtained is reasonably reliable proof as to how widespread and penetrating issues regarding the multifaceted aspects of the rights of the person have become in Italian academia.

University institutions and research centres
No change with respect to 2012

University	Name	Founding Year
University of Padua	University Human Rights Centre	1982
University of Salento	Inter-University Centre on Bioethics and Human Rights	1992
41 European universities in partnership	European Inter-University Centre for Human Rights and Democratisation (EIUC)	2002
University of Naples	Centre for Studies on Human Rights in the era of globalisation and conflicts	2003

University of Ca' Foscari, Venice	Interdepartmental Human Rights Research Centre (CIRDU)	2003
University of Salerno	Department of Individual Rights and Comparison	2011

Source: elaboration by the research and editorial committee.

Bachelor's degree courses

No change with respect to 2012

University	Name	Scientific Area
University of Padua	Political Science, International Relations, Human Rights	L-36: Political science and International Relations

Source: elaboration by the research and editorial committee.

Master's degree courses

In 2013, the University of Padua established an English-taught course on "Human rights and multi-level governance".

University	Name	Scientific Area
University of Bergamo	Human Rights and the Ethics of International Cooperation	LM-81: Cooperation development sciences
University of Bologna	International Cooperation, Protection of Human Rights and Ethno-cultural Heritage in the Mediterranean and Eurasia	LM-81: Cooperation development sciences
	International cooperation, development and human rights	LM-81: Cooperation development sciences
University of Padua	Human rights and multi-level governance	LM-52: International relations
	Institutions and Policies of Human Rights and Peace	LM-52: International relations

Source: elaboration by the research and editorial committee.

Teaching programmes

In 2013, a total of 109 human rights teaching programmes were run in 38 universities: 61 programmes were delivered in degree courses pertaining to the area of political and social science (56%); 36 to the area of law (33%); 9 to the area of history, philosophy, pedagogy and psychology (8%); and 3 to the area of economics and statistics.

As in 2010, 2011 and 2012, the university with the greatest number of human rights courses was Padua (20 programmes), followed by Turin (8), Bologna (6), Milan (6), Bari (5), and Palermo (5). 11 out of 109 human rights programmes are taught in English: 6 at the University of Padua, 3 at the University of Milan, 1 at the "La Sapienza" University of Rome, 1 at the University of Cagliari.

University	Scientific Area	Degree Course	Teaching
Aldo Moro University of Bari	Law	BA in Science of Law Service	International protection of human rights – human rights protection in the European Convention on Human Rights
		5-Year Degree in Law	Human rights
			International protection of human rights
	Political and social science	MA in International Relations	International protection of human rights
			Theory of human rights
University of Bergamo	History, philosophy, pedagogy and psychology	BA in Philosophy	Teaching on marginalisation and human rights
			Teaching on human rights and international cooperation
University of Bologna	Law	5-Year Degree in Law	Fundamental rights
	Political and social science	MA in International Cooperation, Protection of Human Rights and Cultural Heritage	Human rights and history of international law
			International human rights law and European law on cooperation
			Public law and protection of fundamental rights
		MA in Local and Global Development	Human rights, constitutions and institutions
		MA in International Relations and Diplomatic Affairs	International protection of human rights (seminar)
University of Cagliari	Law	5-Year Degree in Law	European Governance and Human Rights
University of Camerino	Economics and statistics	BA in Social Sciences for Non-Profit Organisations and International Cooperation	International protection of human rights
University of Ferrara	Law	5-Year Degree in Law	Human rights and humanitarian law in armed conflicts
University of Florence	Law	BA in Science of Law Service	Legal systems and protection of rights
			Welfare state and rights
		5-Year Degree in Law	International law, human rights and armed conflict
	History, philosophy, pedagogy and psychology	BA in Social Education	Human Rights

University	Scientific Area	Degree Course	Teaching
University of Genova	Law	5-Year Degree in Law	Civil and social rights
University of L'Aquila	Economics and statistics	BA in Economics	Theory of interpretation and human rights
University of Macerata	Political and social science	MA in Theories, Cultures and Techniques for Social Work	Social and citizenship-related rights
	History, philosophy, pedagogy and psychology	MA in Philosophy	Philosophy of rights and cultures
			Philosophy of rights and cultures II
University of Messina	Political and social science	MA in International Relations and European Studies	International organisations and human rights
University of Milan	Law	5-Year Degree in Law	Rights of religions and human rights
			International refugee and human rights law
			Advanced international refugee and human rights law
			International investment law and human rights
	Political and social science	BA in International Studies and European Institutions	International protection of human rights
		MA in Political Science and Government	Theories of fundamental rights
Bicocca University of Milan	Law	5-Year Degree in Law	European Constitutional law (fundamental rights)
			International protection of human rights
	Political and social science	MA in Programming and Management of the Political and Social Services	Cooperation and human rights protection
		MA in Sociology	Rights and European citizenship
Sacro Cuore Catholic University	Political and social science	BA in Political Science and International Relations	International protection of human rights
	Law	5-Year Degree in Law	Human rights
University of Modena and Reggio Emilia	Law	5-Year Degree in Law	Theory and practice of human rights
University of Molise	Political and social science	BA in Communication	Human rights and globalisation

University	Scientific Area	Degree Course	Teaching
Federico II University of Naples	Economics and statistics	MA in Economics and Business Law	International protection of human rights
	Political and social science	MA in Social Services and Political Science	International protection of human rights
Second University of Naples	Political and social science	BA in Political Science	Protection of rights in multi-cultural States
		MA in International Institutions and Markets	Constitutions and fundamental rights in Arab-Islamic systems
	Law	5-Year Degree in Law	International protection of human rights
Suor Orsola Benincasa University (Naples)	History, philosophy, pedagogy and psychology	BA in Education	Human rights
University of Padua	History, philosophy, pedagogy and psychology	BA in Primary Education	Pedagogy of childhood, adolescence and rights of the child
	Law	5-Year Degree in Law	Human rights and public ethics
	Political and social science	BA in Political Sciences, International Relations, Human Rights	Human rights
			Sociologia generale e dei diritti umani
			Sviluppo economico e diritti umani
			International protection of human rights
			Philosophy of human rights
			Public policy and human rights
		MA in Human Rights and Multi-level Governance	International and European Law of Human Rights
			European Union Law of Human Rights
			International Law of Human Rights and International Humanitarian and Criminal Law
			Human Rights and International Justice
			International Organisation for Human Rights and Peace
			Women's Human Rights

University	Scientific Area	Degree Course	Teaching
		MA in Institutions and Policies of Human Rights and Peace	Human rights and international justice
			Sport and human rights in the European Union law
			Human rights, monitoring, electoral observation, peace-keeping
			International organisation for human rights and peace
			Sociology of criminal law, prevention of deviance, prison conditions and rights of detainees
		MA in European Studies	Fundamental rights and European citizenship
University of Palermo	Political and social science	BA in Cooperation and Development	Theory and policy of human rights
		BA in Political Sciences and International Relations	Human rights and international criminal law
	Law	5-Year Degree in Law	Human rights
		5-Year Degree in Law (Trapani)	International protection of human rights
		5-Year Degree in Law (Agrigento)	International protection II – International protection of human rights
University of Pavia	Law	5-Year Degree in Law	Constitutional law and fundamental rights
University of Perugia	Political and social science	BA in Political Sciences and International Relations	Human rights and international crime
Amedeo Avogadro University of Eastern Piemonte	Political and social science	MA in Cultural Heritage and European Studies	Democracy, rights, religions
	Law	5-Year Degree in Law	Protection of fundamental rights
University of Pisa	Political and social science	BA in Sciences for Peace: international cooperation and conflict transformation	Legal and political theories of human rights
		MA in Sciences for Peace: international cooperation and conflict transformation	Monitoring, assessment and protection of human rights
	Law	5-Year Degree in Law	Multilevel protection of human rights

University	Scientific Area	Degree Course	Teaching
La Sapienza University of Rome	Political and social science	MA in Integrated Communication for Public and Non-for-profit Organisation	Communications of rights and active citizenship
		MA in International Relations	International human rights law
		MA in Development and International Cooperation Sciences	Human rights and bioethics Human rights
Roma Tre University	Political and social science	BA in Integrated Communication for non-profit organisations	International organisation and protection of human rights
		MA in International Relations	Protection of fundamental rights in the comparative law
		MA in European Studies	Theories of human rights
Libera Università Internazionale Studi Sociali "Guido Carli" LUISS-Roma	Law	5-Year Degree in Law	International protection of human rights
University of Salento	Political and social science	BA in International Relations	Human rights
University of Salerno	Law	5-Year Degree in Law	Human rights Human rights and biolaw International protection of human rights
University of Siena	Political and social science	BA in International Studies	International protection of human rights
		BA in Communication, Languages, Cultures	History of human rights
University of Teramo	Law	5-Year Degree in Law	Human rights
University of Torino	Law	5-Year Degree in Law	International humanitarian law and human rights protection Fundamental rights guarantees Social order, juridical hermeneutics and protection of fundamental rights
	Political and social science	MA in Political and Social Sciences	Citizenship, social rights, justice Vulnerable groups and human rights protection

University	Scientific Area	Degree Course	Teaching
		MA in International Studies	Human rights and globalisation
			History of human rights
		MA in Sociology and Social Research	Theories of human rights
University of Trieste	Political and social science	MA in Governmental Sciences and Public Policies	Human rights
		MA in Intercultural Cooperation for Development	Comparative human rights
University of Udine	Law	5-Year Degree in Law	Theories of human rights
Carlo Bo University of Urbino	Law	5-Year Degree in Law	Human rights
Ca' Foscari University of Venice	History, philosophy, pedagogy and psychology	MA in Cultural Anthropology, Ethnology, Anthropological Linguistics	Human rights
			Citizenship-related rights
University of Verona	Political and social science	MA in Social Services and Social Policies	Social and citizenship-related rights
			Protection of fundamental rights

Source: elaboration by the research and editorial committee on data available on universities websites.

Doctoral programmes (academic years 2012–2013 and 2013–2014)

University	Name	Area of Scientific Discipline
University of Camerino	Fundamental rights in the global society	M-STO/02; M-STO/04; M-DEA/01; M-FIL/03; M-FIL/06; IUS/04; IUS/08; IUS/09; IUS/13 – IUS/21 SECS-P/01; SECS P/02; SECS-P/04; SPS/01; SPS/02; SPS/04; SPS/06; SPS/07; SPS/11; SPS/12
University of Cassino and Southern Lazio	Human rights protection in national constitutional courts and other European courts case-law	IUS/08, IUS/09, IUS/10, IUS/13, IUS/14, IUS/21, IUS/12, IUS/20, IUS/16

University of Florence	Theory and history of law – Theory and history of human rights	IUS/18, IUS/19, IUS/20
University of Palermo	Human rights: evolution, protection and limits	IUS/01, IUS/09, IUS/12, IUS/20, SPS/02, IUS/13, IUS/19, IUS/10, SPS/09, SECS-P/01, IUS/O8
Amedeo Avogadro University of Eastern Piedmont	Local autonomies, public services and citizenship's rights	IUS/05, IUS/08, IUS/09 IUS/10, IUS/21
Scuola Superiore Sant'Anna in Pisa	Politics, human rights and sustainability	SPS/01, SPS/06, IUS/13, IUS/03, IUS/14, SPS/04, SECS-P/02, SECS-P/06, SECS-P/08
La Sapienza University of Rome	International Order and Human Rights	IUS/13, IUS/14, IUS/08, IUS/07, IUS/01
Libera Maria Santissima Assunta University – LUMSA	Fundamental rights and freedoms in contemporary legal systems	IUS/01, IUS/11, IUS/13, IUS/17, IUS/20, IUS/18, IUS/07
	International adoptions: issues on the protection of fundamental human rights	IUS/01, IUS/11, IUS/13
University of Salerno	Comparative human rights	IUS/01, IUS/02, IUS/07, IUS/13, IUS/14, IUS/16, IUS/17
University of Teramo	Protection of fundamental rights – Italian and European public law	IUS/08, IUS/09, IUS/10, IUS/21
Carlo Bo University of Urbino	Human rights and fundamental social rights	IUS/01, IJUS/02, IUS/07, IUS/10, IUS/11, IUS/13, IUS/15, IUS/16, IUS/17, IUS/18, IUS/19, IUS/12, SECS-P/03

Source: elaboration by the research and editorial committee.

Master degree programmes – postgraduate

University	Name	Level
University of Bologna	Human rights and humanitarian intervention	I
European Inter-University Centre for Human Rights and Democratisation (EIUC, 41 European partner universities)	European Master's Degree in Human Rights and Democratisation E.MA	I
Sant'Anna School of Advanced Studies of Pisa	Human rights and conflict management	I
University of Siena	European joint master of human rights and genocide studies	I

Libera Maria Santissima Assunta University – LUMSA	Bioethics and human rights	II
La Sapienza University, Rome	International protection of human rights "Maria Rita Saulle"	II
Roma Tre University	Peace studies: international cooperation, human rights and policies of the European Union	II
Italian Society for International Organisation (SIOI)	International relations and international protection of human rights	-

Source: elaboration by the research and editorial committee.

Sub-national Human Rights Structures

I. Peace Human Rights Offices in Municipalities, Provinces and Regions

At the sub-national level, especially by virtue of the inclusion of the "peace human rights norm" in thousands of municipal, provincial and regional statutes, and of the adoption of dedicated regional laws on this topic (see Part I, Italian Law, III), Italy has a number of consultancies, offices, departments, bureaux and centres for human rights, peace, equal opportunity, development cooperation and international solidarity. As was done in previous editions of the Yearbook, three of these structures will be briefly described, as examples.

Vicenza Municipality House for Peace: the House for Peace is the headquarters of the Vicenza Board for the promotion of a culture of peace but is also open to all local associations, groups and individual citizens working on issues relative to peace, nonviolence, human rights and international solidarity. It supports interventions and initiatives which opt for the use of the nonviolent method and promotes the pacific coexistence of the various foreign communities living in the area. One of the many hands-on activities the House for Peace hosts is a documentation centre and several info points on issues concerning peace, nonviolence and human rights.

"Annalena Tonelli" Peace Centre: thanks to an agreement with the Municipality and the Province of Forlì, to which it turns for policies concerning the promotion of peace and cultural integration, the Centre was created with the aim of increasing awareness and cultural growth on the following issues: peace, management and unarmed and nonviolent transformation of conflict, human rights, international cooperation, north-south relations, intercultural and multi-ethnic education. Its activities follow three main threads: peace, integration among peoples and cultural activities, as well as running a thematic library.

Milan Municipality House for Human Rights: opened in December 2013 and run by the Municipal Council on Social Policy and Health, it offers services and info points dedicated to defending rights and protecting them from all discrimination. It also has offices to support and listen to as well as help victims of violence, and promotes initiatives to defend human rights. Furthermore, it has an info point for "second generation people" (born in Italy to foreign national parents) and one for LGBT people, and it has a meeting room which it makes available for cultural activities organised by various local associations.

II. Ombudspersons in the Italian Regions and Provinces

In 2013 there were 15 incumbent Ombudspersons out of a total of 19 Regions and Autonomous Provinces (17 + 2) whose respective statutes or specific regional laws include provisions for such an institution: Abruzzo, Basilicata, Campania, Emilia-Romagna, Lazio, Liguria, Lombardy, Marche, Molise, Piedmont, Tuscany, Valle d'Aosta and Veneto, plus the Autonomous Provinces of Bolzano and Trento. The post is currently vacant in Sardinia and Umbria, while no Ombudsperson has ever been appointed in Calabria and Apulia. No legislative provision is made for the role by the Regions of Sicily and Trentino-Alto Adige (where, however, the Region has delegated full responsibility in their respective territories to the Ombudspersons of the Autonomous Provinces), while in Friuli-Venezia Giulia the law establishing this institution (dating back to 1981) was abrogated by a budget-balancing act in 2008 (r.l. 14 August 2008, No. 9).

The figure of the Ombudsperson is also present in 24 Provinces (in addition to the 2 Autonomous Provinces and in Aosta, where the provincial responsibilities are performed by the Region): Arezzo, Asti, Belluno, Caltanissetta, Como, Cremona, Lecce, Lecco, Lodi, Lucca, Milan, Modena, Naples, Novara, Padua, Perugia, Pisa, Pistoia, Prato, Rome, Rovigo, Savona, Turin and Venice. These include 16 territorial Ombudspersons (who, following the abolition of the municipal Ombudspersons pursuant to l. 23 December 2009, have taken on responsibilities relative to the Municipalities with which a convention has been stipulated). There are 8 provincial Ombudspersons (who have not yet stipulated any conventions with the Municipalities and therefore have responsibility only at the provincial level).

At the European and International level, Burgi Volgger, Ombudsperson for the Autonomous Province of Bolzano, is President of the European Ombudsman Institute (EOI) Executive Committee. Other Italian Committee members are Lucia Franchini, Ombudsperson for the Region of Tuscany, Vittorio Gasparrini, from the Region of Tuscany Ombudsperson's office and Vittorio Galatro, formerly Ombudsperson for the Municipality of Nocera Inferiore (in the Province of Salerno).

The Ombudspersons for the Region of Valle d'Aosta, Enrico Formento Dojot, the Autonomous Province of Bolzano, Burgi Volgger, the Region of Lombardy, Donato Giordano, the Region of Tuscany, Lucia Franchini, and the Region of Basilicata, Catello Aprea, are members of the International Ombudsman Institute (IOI).

The following paragraphs present, in summary form, data regarding the activities of some of the Ombudspersons for Italian Regions and

Autonomous Provinces in the course of 2013. The data were provided by the relative Offices themselves in response to a request made by the Yearbook research and editorial committee.

Lazio (Ombudsperson: Felice Maria Filocamo). In 2013 the Ombudsperson's Office dealt with 392 cases. The five main thematic areas were: management of the territory (74), transparency and efficiency of local authorities (47), public services and utilities (46), access to official documents (42), taxes and fines (33). Over the course of the year, 2338 letters were recorded between incoming and outgoing concerning the cases worked on

One of the more significant cases listed by the Office concerned a state school teacher employed by the Ministry of Education, Universities and Research, who was resident in Rome but detached in a managerial position to the Ministry of Foreign Affairs, to work in the Italian school in Addis Ababa. The Italian consular authorities in Addis Ababa requested the respective local authorities where their permanent teaching staff came from, to automatically record them in the Registry of Italians Resident Abroad (A.I.R.E.), since, pursuant to l. 470/88, working abroad for more than 12 months makes it compulsory to enrol in this registry. Under articles 1 para. 2 and 2 para. 1, sub a) of l. 470/88, the Civil Registry of each Municipality is made up of the individual and family records removed from the resident population registry due to the permanent transfer abroad of the people to whom they refer. Considering that the work performed by the teacher in Ethiopia is temporary and not continuous (indeed she returns to Italy frequently), so the requisite of uninterrupted residency abroad for over 12 months is not met, it appears clear that the teacher may not be automatically moved to the Registry of Italians Resident Abroad.

Liguria (Ombudsperson: Francesco Lalla; he also acts as Ombudsperson for Children and Adolescents). In 2013 the Ombudsperson's Office received a total of 433 requests. The claims made were mainly in the following thematic areas: environment and territory (79), social security and welfare (53), various taxes (48) and healthcare (44). To these areas one should add 116 claims from the accounting departments of the dioceses in Liguria reporting delays in the payment by Municipalities of their share relating to planning fees to be paid to religious groups under Regional law r.l. Liguria 4/1985. The five main bodies involved with the ombudsperson's actions in 2013 were: local authorities (239), local health services (ASL) (49), service supplying bodies (38), Liguria Regional administration (30) and the Housing Association ARTE (23). The Ombudsperson was a speaker at a number of seminars and round tables, thus contributing to the promotion and knowledge of the Ombudsperson's Office as an institution.

As concerns cases which have legal implications, the following were mentioned: a) action undertaken following the request of many inhabitants of Genoa to reduce the serious levels of noise pollution coming from the Docks and disturbing the neighbourhoods of Prà, Pegli and Voltri. The noise comes from the ships in dock and resolving the issue will prove problematic because the decree implementing the 1995 basic law has never been approved; b) issues reported by local citizens' groups, again in the Prà neighbourhood, concerning a large-scale coastal area renovation project, funded by the European Union, involving extremely controversial road planning and lifestyle choices by the Municipality; c) the time required to grant Italian citizenship, which often goes well beyond the legal maximum of two years. This time-frame is already very long, but despite this, it is not usually met.

Lombardy (Ombudsperson: Donato Giordano, who also acts as the Ombudsperson for Taxpayers and the Ombudsperson for Detainees). In 2013 the Office dealt with a large number of cases, which were primarily related to the following areas: environment (470 cases in all, of which 30 new, 254 ongoing and 186 closed during the year), territory (459, 131 new, 126 ongoing and 202 closed), institutional structures (448, 169 new, 79 ongoing and 200 closed), Ombudsman for Detainees (257, 118 new, 32 ongoing and 107 closed), social security (256, 104 new, 45 ongoing and 105 closed). Compared to 2012, the number of contacts with users increased by 49% and cases closed increased by 11%, also after a campaign publicising the Ombudsperson's Office throughout the Region using both traditional means (print and brochures) and through the website, presence on social media and the opening of Centres for receiving claims. Another activity of the Ombudsman's Office which is highlighted is the development of software called Di.As.Pro for the handling of claims, wholly designed by the Lombardy Ombudsperson's Office, assisted by a software company and using open source programmes.

Piedmont (Ombudsperson: Antonio Caputo). In every case activated, the objective "problem" of poor governance was always the major issue, impacting on so many other citizens, bodies, companies and organisations, all victims of this same "dysfunctionality". The Ombudsperson for Piedmont handled 2,315 claims in 2013, concerning the following issues: healthcare (implementation of the right to uninterrupted care for the chronically ill who are not self-sufficient and for people with disabilities and the issue of illegal "waiting lists", as well as cases of poor healthcare services); social care; education; disability; services to the person; territory and environment; taxes and charges; public transport including the local level, traffic and mobility; employment of civil servants; participation in local governance and the right of access; citizens' access pursuant to lgs.d. 33/2013 (Implementation for local healthcare bodies); obligations regarding "anti-corruption" and transparency measures governed by l. 190/2012; obligation to provide transparent accounting to ensure systemic consistency between "real hospitalisation and "financial hospitalisation"; protection of fundamental rights (personal, labour, educational, health, environmental and mobility-related); violence against women and gender discrimination; overcrowding of prisons and other issues relating to imprisonment; targeted placement of persons with disabilities; rights of access and participation in the appointment of Commissioners Ad Hoc; damages caused by omissions or delays in the issue of local government acts and measures; late payments by the Public Administration; dealings with the following authorities: power and gas, transport, the Italian Antitrust Commission, Ombudsperson for personal data protection).

Trento (Ombudsperson: Raffaello Sampaolesi, who also acts as Ombudsperson for Children and Adolescents; the data refer to 2012). In 2012, the Office investigated 937 claims. Of these, 71 received a verbal answer, 465 a written and therefore formal intervention and 401 were resolved thanks to explanations and further information supplied to the citizens in the Ombudsperson's Office. The main areas concerned in 2012 were: regulations (37%), territory and the environment (35%), social and cultural services (15%), labour and the economy (10%), and the public protection of minors (4%). The outcomes of the interventions by the Ombudsperson's Office were as follows: information supplied in 38% of cases; finding in favour 37%, finding against 12%; and finally, non-cooperation by the body in question in 3% of cases.

The promotional activities concerning the figure of the Ombudsperson took place mostly in connection with the numerous guided tours for school groups, an activity coordinated by the Provincial Council President's Office and during periodic meeting with citizens, organised at the request of and in cooperation with the University for Senior Citizens.

Valle d'Aosta (Ombudsperson: Enrico Formento Dojot, who also acts as the Ombudsperson for the Rights of Detainees). 507 cases were handled by the Ombudsperson in 2013. The issues mainly related to welfare support (99 cases: subsidies, housing crisis, council housing, social security and welfare services, citizenship and immigration) and connected to labour relations (141 cases). Building on initiatives undertaken in previous years, meetings were scheduled with high school pupils in order to foster greater civic awareness.

One case is highlighted as particularly interesting from the legal point of view and as an illustration of the effectiveness of the actions by the Office. Two citizens presented themselves to the Office in connection with the following: the call to apply for a professional training course for emergency workers specified that candidates should not be over 35 years of age. The citizens wanted to know whether those who have already celebrated their 35th birthday but not yet reached the age of 36 are eligible. The Ombudsperson explained to them that this question has seen two different positions in case-law. In order to settle the dispute, the Council of State met, in plenary session, producing ruling No. 21 on 2 December 2011, which equated the requisite of being not more than a certain number of years old with one's actual birthday. Hence, the Ombudsman considers that, should they go to court, the chances of victory for those citizens would be quite slim, inasmuch as the ruling by the Council of State, although not binding, represents a very authoritative indication of orientation, as it emerged from a Plenary Assembly. The citizens duly took note.

Veneto (Ombudsperson: Roberto Pellegrini). See, in this Part, Region of Veneto, VII.

III. National Coordinating Body of Ombudspersons

The National Coordinating Body of Regional and Autonomous Provinces' Ombudspersons is an associative body working to harmonise and enhance the institutional role of the Ombudsperson in Italy, and to guarantee every citizen, regardless of where he or she resides, protection in dealing with the public administration at all levels, whether State, regional or local.

> The Coordinating Body is made up of the incumbent Ombudspersons in the Regions and the Autonomous Provinces. It operates through the office of the Ombudsperson collectively elected from time to time and its Headquarters are in Rome, at the Network of the Presidents of the Legislative Assemblies of the Regions and the Autonomous Provinces, where it usually meets.

Since March 2013, the National Coordinator has been Lucia Franchini, Ombudsperson for the Region of Tuscany. The previous incumbent (2011–2013) was Antonio Caputo, Ombudsperson for the Region of Piedmont. The Coordinator also takes action if requested by the European Ombudsman towards the central State offices or those of the Italian Regions and local authorities which do not have their own regional or local Ombudsperson. Moreover, the incumbent interfaces as the Italian National Ombudsperson with the European Ombudsman and interacts with the other European Ombudsmen also through a liaison officer, who in 2013 was Vittorio Gasparrini.

Over the course of 2013, the Coordinating Body held six meetings. During the session on 4th March 2013, the new National Coordinator, Lucia Franchini, was unanimously elected; she presented her road map, underscoring the need for more coordination between the various regional situations. As a good example to follow, she mentioned the adoption of the new software for the computerised handling of claims. She also suggested that a national report should be produced and a database created which houses all the cases handled by the various offices pertaining to issues of common interest at the national level. Finally, the Coordinator reconfirmed her commitment, shared by all members of the Coordinating Body, to the introduction of the figure of a National Ombudsperson. In the course of the next two meetings on 6 May and 27 June, among other things, there were discussions about creating and managing a specific Internet website, which would serve to give enhanced visibility and raise citizens' awareness of the National Coordinating Body of Ombudspersons. At the 23 September meeting, the main focus was on the results of the general Assembly of the European Ombudsman Institute held on 20 September, the meeting with the European Ombudsman, and the possible development prospects for the institution in Italy, as well as the desirability of replicating at the national level the well-established local-level cooperation between the Ombudsperson's function and various associations. During the 18 November meeting, the new members of the board of governors of the Italian Ombudsman Institute were appointed. At this same meeting, the Coordinating Body hosted the National Ombudsperson for Albania, Igli Totozani, expressing its hope of signing a memorandum of understanding offering reciprocal protection to citizens of the two nations. The Coordinating Body also approved the "Ancona Charter" at this meeting, a document which reiterates the need to enshrine in law the autonomy and independence of the Ombudsperson, including functional independence, and hoping that, in Italy too, the Ombudsperson can take on the characteristics of an Institution for the non-jurisdictional protection of fundamental rights, bringing together in the same figure the functions of guarantor, in line with the criteria spelled out at the United Nations and the Council of Europe.

Finally, in 2013, the Coordinating body, together with the Human Rights Centre of the University of Padua and the Office of the Ombudsperson for the Region of Veneto, promoted three public seminars as part of the series of meetings on the subject of "The Function of the Ombudsperson and citizens' rights" inaugurated in December 2012: "The rapport between citizens and the Ombudsperson: access by the weak and the emarginated" (15 February); "Citizens and the right to health: how enforceable is it? The role of the Ombudsperson" (17 June); "Rights, environment, commons: what role should the Ombudsperson play?" (18 November).

IV. Network of Ombudspersons for Children and Adolescents

As of today, 18 Italian Regions and the Autonomous Provinces of Trento and Bolzano have approved legislation introducing a local Ombudsperson for Children and Adolescents or similar figure (Abruzzo, Basilicata, Calabria, Campania, Emilia-Romagna, Friuli-Venezia Giulia, Lazio, Liguria, Lombardy, Marche, Molise, Piedmont, Apulia, Sardinia, Tuscany, Trentino-Alto Adige, Umbria, Veneto); 12 Ombudspersons have actually been appointed (in Apulia, Calabria, Campania, Emilia-Romagna, Lazio, Liguria, Marche, Molise, Tuscany, the Autonomous Provinces of Trento and Bolzano and in Veneto).

The approval of l. 12 July 2011, No. 112 established the figure of Ombudsperson for Children and Adolescents at the national level and formally defined and established the National Network for the protection of the rights of children and adolescents, made up of the Regional Ombudspersons for children (or equivalent), charged with: identifying and adopting common lines of action of the Ombudspersons at national and regional level regarding the protection of the rights of children and adolescents, to be promoted and supported at the international level; identifying means for a constant exchange of data and information on the condition of minors at the national and regional level. The Network has drawn up a set of internal rules governing its functioning.

The Network met twice in 2013 to facilitate the exchange of information between its members concerning actions undertaken at the territorial level, on emerging issues and on transversal initiatives to be carried out jointly to further examine and promote the rights of children and adolescents.

V. National Coordinating Network of Ombudspersons for the Rights of Detainees

While awaiting the appointment of a national body for the rights of detainees (National Ombudsperson), established pursuant to l.d. 23 December 2013, No. 146 (Urgent measures concerning the protection of the fundamental rights of detainees and controlled reduction of numbers of prison occupants), many Ombudspersons for the rights of detainees at the local, provincial and regional level have continued to be active within a National Coordinating Network.

The aims of this body are to undertake joint actions regarding the rights of detainees, to find consensual answers to the main problems encountered by the individual Ombudspersons in Italy, and to all put their personal experience at the disposal of all the others. The National Coordinator since 2011 has been Franco Corleone, Ombudsperson for detainees of the Municipality of Florence (since October 2013, Ombudsperson for detainees for the Region of Tuscany). The Network is open to all local, provincial and regional Ombudspersons who wish to be part of it.

The Network met several times in 2013 and the following problems were discussed at length; the right to vote for detainees, the conditions in juvenile prisons and in the Centres for Identification and Expulsion of illegal immigrants, overcrowding, the level of drug addiction among detainees, the future of criminal psychiatric hospitals, issues connected to the prison commissary, as well as the establishment of an independent authority for the protection of rights in prisons, in the light of Italy's ratification, in April 2013, of the Optional Protocol to the United Nations Convention against Torture.

Moreover, in February 2013, the Network gave its backing to the campaign "3 Leggi per la Giustizia e i Diritti" (3 laws for Justice and Rights) set up to support three citizens' bills concerning torture, prisons and drugs, presented to the Supreme Court in January 2013 by 20 associations. In that same month, the Network sent a letter to the Italian President, Giorgio Napolitano, presenting a platform for the reform of the Italian prison system which the Network itself had approved. In addition to supporting the content of the three bills mentioned above, the platform considers it a priority to tackle the issues relating to pre-trial imprisonment and alternatives to custody, in line with proposals by the CSM's (the National Council of the Judiciary) "Giostra Commission", to approve a new criminal code, to finally close all criminal psychiatric hospitals, to draft new prison system regulations and to approve a law introducing the figure of the National Ombudsperson for the rights of detainees (adopted in December 2013).

VI. National Coordinating Body of Local Authorities for Peace and Human Rights

The National Coordinating Body is an association founded in 1986 which brings together over 700 Italian Municipalities, Provinces and Regions committed to promoting peace, human rights, solidarity and international cooperation. The Chair of this association is Marco Vinicio Guasticchi, President of the Province of Perugia; the Director is Flavio Lotti.

In 2013, the National Coordinating Body drafted and promoted two large projects aimed at investing in young people and developing their commitment to peace. The first is a two-year programme for schools on education for democratic citizenship. The second is the call for another peace march from Perugia to Assisi on 19 October 2014.

The Programme "Pace, fraternità e dialogo. Sui passi di Francesco" (Peace, fraternity and dialogue. In the footsteps of St. Francis) was drawn up by the National Coordinating Body, in agreement with the Directorate General for students, the involvement, participation and communication of the Ministry of Education, Universities and Research, the magazine "San Francesco Patrono d'Italia" (St. Francis, Patron Saint of Italy) and the Perugia-Assisi Network. The Programme takes its starting point from the decision of the Italian Parliament to celebrate the National Day of Peace, fraternity and dialogue between members of different cultures and religions on 4 October of each year, in honour of the Patron Saints of Italy, St. Francis of Assisi and Saint Catherine of Siena. The declared aim of the Programme is to turn the project of one day into a programme for a whole year, helping young people to rediscover the real meaning of the universal values of peace, fraternity and dialogue, and encouraging students to be centre stage. 151 schools and 64 local administrations have signed up to the Programme.

2013 also saw the launch of the preparatory activities for another edition of the Perugia-Assisi peace march, scheduled for the autumn of 2014. In this area, the Coordinating Body decided to promote a series of peace-related activities aimed at refreshing and increasing the tangible commitment of people in Italy against impoverishment, wars and indifference. The Coordinating Body kicked off the new year of work by promoting a "Week of Peace" from 29 September to 6 October 2013, in the centre of which fell the historic visit of Pope Francis to Assisi on 4 October and the celebration, that same day, of the IX National Day of Peace, Fraternity and Dialogue. The Week began and ended with two marches for peace; the first in Forlì on Sunday 29 September and the second in Lodi on 6 October.

On 5 December 2013, over 120 representatives of local administrations, schools and associations took part in the seminar "Perugia-Assisi. Dalla Marcia di un giorno alla marcia di tutti i giorni" (Perugia-Assisi: from the one-day March to the everyday march), held at the Holy Convent of St. Francis in Assisi with the objective of defining new ways to peace starting from towns. On that occasion, the text of a petitionary motion was distributed, for use by Italian Municipalities, Provinces and Regions, in support of the recognition of peace as a human right.

Finally, the Coordinating Body continued its commitment to the Middle Eastern peace process in 2013 and organised the European Forum of local authorities for Palestine, held in Dunkirk, France, on 28–29 November 2013. The Forum gave new impulse to the process of strengthening the European Network of Local Authorities for Peace in the Middle East and new firm proposals were defined to bolster the European Union's actions in favour of the construction of a just and lasting peace in the Middle East, through a broader involvement of European citizens and the development of European programmes of decentralised cooperation.

VII. Archives and Other Regional Projects for the Promotion of a Culture of Peace and Human Rights

Besides the "Pace Diritti Umani – Peace Human Rights" Archive of the Region of Veneto, established by r.l. 18/1988 and managed by the Human Rights Centre of the University of Padua (see in this Part, Region of Veneto, IV), there are other more recent archives and similar projects set up by Italian Regions and Autonomous Provinces to foster the promotion and dissemination of a culture of human rights and peace.

The "Peace and Human Rights" project of the Region Emilia-Romagna was established by the Regional Council in conjunction with the Office for Social Policies, Immigration, Youth Projects and International and the Management and Statistical Systems Control Service of the Regional Government. The project, which is run by the Europe Direct Centre for Emilia Romagna, draws inspiration from the content of r.l. 24 June 2002, No. 12 (Regional measures for cooperation with developing Countries and Countries in transition, for international solidarity and the promotion of a culture of peace) and its purpose is to support the activities described in said law. Its website is: http://www.paceediritti.it/.

Since 2013, the Regional Office for European Politics and International Relations – International cooperation – has joined the Project and has expanded the content of the website with news and information on the Region's programmes in the Provinces, as well as on peace and cooperation round tables at the international level. Moreover, further study and information activities have continued, with particular reference to the issues of "peace and cooperation" and "Europe and human rights". Two publications edited by the Studies, Research and Documentation office of the Europe Direct Centre came out in 2013, one on this latter subject and the other on data protection in the European Union.

The Forum "Trentino per la pace e i diritti umani" (Trentino for peace and human rights), is a permanent body created in 1991 by Trento Provincial Council by p.l. 10 June 1991, No. 11 (Promotion and dissemination of the culture of peace). Its website is: http://www.forumpace.it/.

For the year 2013–2014, the Forum chose the following cultural theme to which to devote its peace-building activities: *1914 – 2014. Indagine sulla pace nel secolo degli assassini* (Enquiry into peace in the century of assassins). The purpose of the project is to try, through in-depth analysis of the history, the cultures and the key places of the XXth Century, to understand how "war and peace chased after one another without managing to observe one another closely and understand the banality of good and evil". In the context of this thematic project, the Forum was an active party in organising and holding a series of events, lectures, exhibitions and public meetings in the Autonomous Province of Trento.

Region of Veneto

The Region of Veneto has been operating organically for the promotion of human rights, the culture of peace and international cooperation, ever since 1988, the year when the first specific law on such issues was adopted (regional law 30 March 1988, No. 18). During the same year, the Regional Council established the Ombudsperson (r.l. 28/1988) and the Ombudsperson for Children and Adolescents (r.l. 42/1988). In 1999, regional law 18/1988 was replaced by the current r.l. 16 December 1999, No. 55, on "Regional measures for the promotion of human rights, a culture of peace, development cooperation and solidarity". With r.l. 24 December 2013, No. 37, the Region has established the post of *Regional Ombudsperson for the Rights of the Person* who will integrate the functions of the Ombudsperson, of the Ombudsperson for Children and Adolescents as well as those of promotion and protection of the rights of persons deprived of their liberty. In the context of the Regional Government, issues concerning human rights pertain to the Councillor on Economy, Development, Research and Innovation, Marialuisa Coppola. Measures and activities concerning international relations and development cooperation respond directly to the Regional Governor, Luca Zaia, assisted by the Minister Plenipotentiary Stefano Beltrame.

In virtue of r.l. 55/1999, the Committee on Human Rights and the Culture of Peace (articles 12–13) and the Committee on Development Cooperation (articles 14–15) operate to fulfil their mandate of formulating three-year programmes and annual plans of implementation according to their respective areas of competence and intervention. In addition, the law promotes and supports the Regional Archive "Pace Diritti Umani – Peace Human Rights" (article 2), the Venice for Peace Research Foundation (article 17) (both established with r.l. 18/1988), the activities of the European Commission for Democracy through Law (Venice Commission) of the Council of Europe (article 19) and initiatives of decentralised cooperation promoted by the Ministry of Foreign Affairs and by the European Union (article 7). The regional infrastructure for peace and human rights is completed by the Commission for the Realisation of Equal Opportunities between Men and Women, the Regional Observatory on Social Policies and the Regional Observatory for Immigration. Moreover, by way of r.l. 28 December 1998, No. 33, the Region promotes and supports financially the European Master's degree Programme in Human Rights and Democratisation (E.MA), located in Venice. With the adoption of r.l. 22 January 2010, No. 6, the Region has recognised the social and cultural value of fair trade, proclaiming its support for the organisations which operate in this sector. Finally, the new regional law 23 April 2013, No. 5, envisages the creation, within the Regional Government, of a Regional Coordination Table for Preventing and Combating the Violence against Women. The Table will be joined by organisations, institutions and other stakeholders to ensure the widest possible participation.

I. Regional Department for International Relations

The Regional Department is the central administrative structure for the implementation of r.l. 55/1999. The Director managing this structure in 2013 was Diego Vecchiato.

> The Regional Department oversees a series of international activities undertaken by the Region, including: the management of international relations, the signature of memoranda of understanding with National and foreign institutions, the participation in international bodies and initiatives, international solidarity and all activities in the sectors of human rights, culture of peace, promotion of equal opportunities and protection of linguistic minorities. The Veneto Regional Committee for UNICEF is also hosted by the Department.

> In the specific area of promotion of human rights, the Department provides technical support to the Committee for human rights and the culture of peace; it oversees the organisation of events, takes part in the activities of the Council of Europe Venice Commission and fulfils the obligations deriving from the Region's participation in the European Master's Programme in Human Rights and Democratisation (E.MA).

The role of the Department is transversal to the activities of the various bodies described in the paragraphs below. It should also be noted that in 2013, the Department designed an online questionnaire for private and not-for-profit bodies operating in the field of the promotion of human rights in Veneto, in order to collect information and observations on regional activities promoting human rights. The initial objective of the questionnaire was specifically to sound out the appreciation or otherwise of so-called "education vouchers", a new way of financing that the Region might experiment with in order to create opportunities for meetings and exchanges of views between schools and associations on human rights issues.

II. Committee for Human Rights and the Culture of Peace

Established pursuant to art. 12 of r.l. 55/1999, the Committee contributes to drawing up three-year programmes and annual plans regarding initiatives promoted by the Region of Veneto on human rights and a culture of peace (art. 13). The Committee comprises representatives from local authorities, civil society, academia, the business world and social partners.

While awaiting approval of the new three-year programme, the Regional Government adopted the 2013 Annual Plan, with regional deliberation No. 1366 of 30 July 2013, concerning the implementation of regional measures to promote human rights and a culture of peace. A total of € 300,000 of the Regional budget for 2013 was designated for this purpose. In addition to supporting the "Peace Human Rights" Archive and the Venice for Peace Research Foundation, pursuant to r.l. 55/1999, the Regional Council contributed to financing 18 initiatives for a total of € 165,000. On the other hand, it proved impossible to undertake direct actions on these issues during the past year.

The initiatives financed through regional grant in the framework of the 2013 Annual Plan have been the following: *Percorsi di pace, polis e partecipazione*, by Alternativa Nord/Sud per il XXI secolo (Vicenza); *Peer Education – Diritti umani a più mani*, by Adelante soc. coop. soc. onlus (Bassano del Grappa, Vicenza); *Beni Comuni: Pensare globalmente – agire localmente*, by Gruppo Missioni Africa (Montagnana, Padua); *Mi Attivo! Diritti, cittadinanza, cooperazione*, by Associazione di cooperazione allo sviluppo-ACS (Padua); *Giovani, attori di cittadinanza, cooperazione e partecipazione*, by NATs per... onlus (Treviso); *I(')mpossible – Nothing is Impossible, the world itself says I'm possible*, by Sumo società cooperativa sociale (Venice); *Diritto chiama dovere: dall'impegno personale ad un'economia di condivisione*, by Incontro fra i Popoli (Padua); *Settimo, non sprecare – Giovani veneti attivi per un mondo sostenibile*, by ProgettoMondo Mlal onlus (Verona); *La mia città solidale*, by Pace e sviluppo società cooperativa sociale (Treviso); *Diritti +Umani. Immagini, documenti e storie sui diritti umani in Italia e nel mondo (ninth edition)*, by Associazione Diritti Umani – Sviluppo Umano – ADUSU (Padua); *Salute: diritto di tutti?*, by Medici per la Pace onlus (Verona); *A scuola di dialogo*, by Associazione di Volontari per Iniziative di Pace – AVIP onlus (Sant'Angelo di Piove di Sacco, Padua); *Nord, Sud, Ovest, Est. Dove i diritti trovano cittadinanza*, by Coordinamento delle Associazioni di Volontariato della Provincia di Treviso; *Essere rete per la pace e i diritti umani*, by Associazione di promozione sociale bNET (Treviso); *Percorsi di educazione alla cittadinanza europea ed interculturale "fare l'Europa è fare la Pace" (J. Monnet)*, by Amici dei Popoli Padova; *Assicurare l'istruzione primaria a tutti i bambini e le bambine – World Social Agenda Padova 2013–2014: Obiettivi di sviluppo del millennio meno due*, by Fondazione Fontana onlus (Trento); *ATTIVA(mente)*, by Centro internazionale per l'infanzia e la famiglia onlus (Turin); *A scuola con i diritti: conoscere, incontrarsi, agire*, by Associazione SOS diritti (Venice).

III. Committee for Development Cooperation

The Committee for Development Cooperation was established pursuant to art. 14 of r.l. 55/1999. The Committee is charged with contributing to the drafting of the three-year programmes and annual plans for decentralised development cooperation and international solidarity activities. The Committee comprises representatives from local administrations, civil society, academia, the business world and social partners.

In 2013, the Regional Council adopted deliberation 30 July 2013, No. 1337, concerning the 2013 Annual Plan for initiatives of decentralised development cooperation and international solidarity, providing funds for direct initiatives by the Region in partnership with public bodies from Veneto, for initiatives in which the Region is a partner, together with national and supra-national bodies and organisations, as well as for contributions to others' initiatives. The strategic priorities of the new Plan are those detailed in the *2013–2015 Three-year Programme* (adopted in 2012): the promotion of human and sustainable development; the protection, defence and appreciation of territories, their natural resources and the environmental heritage; the enhancement of the role of women; protection of children; the strengthening of democratic institutions and local administrations; supporting the active role of migrants in co-development initiatives.

IV. Regional Archive "Pace Diritti Umani – Peace Human Rights"

The Regional Archive was created pursuant to r.l. 18/1988 and reconfirmed by the subsequent r.l. 55/1999. The Archive is managed by the Human Rights Centre of the University of Padua, as laid down in art. 2 of the aforementioned law, which reads: "*1. The Region promotes and supports: [...] c) the Archive established by regional law 30 March 1988, No. 18, in cooperation with the Centre of Studies and Training on the Rights of Man and of Peoples of the University of Padua, according to a special agreement [...]*". It is one of the main instruments through which the Region of Veneto promotes the culture of human rights, peace, development cooperation and solidarity in Italy and abroad.

The Archive works to collect, elaborate and publish documents, thematic databases and informational resources on topics regarding regional law, particularly through the regular updating of the portal "Archivio Pace Diritti Umani" (http://unipd-centrodirittiumani.it), available in Italian and in English, and the distribution of knowledge on human rights through multi-media tools and social networks. In addition, it oversees publication of books, teaching aids, indepth studies and multi-media CD-ROMs and offers technical and scientific support to the actors most closely involved in the promotion and practice of the culture of peace, especially as concerns initiatives promoted by teachers, education staff and schools. In this area, in 2013 the Archive published and distributed 12 editions of the newsletter "Schools for human rights and democratic citizenship" to a long but qualified mailing list. The newsletter aims to support development activities relating to education on human rights and the culture of peace in schools.

During 2013, the Archive updated most of the databases available from the website, notably: the database of all the documents referenced in the various editions of the *Italian Yearbook of Human Rights (2011–2013)*; the Italian translations of the legal instruments concerning international human rights, humanitarian and criminal law and the rights of refugees; the publications of the Human Rights Centre of the University of Padua from 1982 to date; and the associations and NGOs operating in the human rights and development cooperation areas which are active in the Region of Veneto.

In addition to its usual activities of updating and providing in-depth studies and information through its website, the main social networks and regular newsletters, the Archive published three numbers of the four-monthly magazine "Pace diritti umani/Peace human rights" as well as several editions of Human Rights Academic Voice, in-depth reflections by university professors on current topics connected to human rights. The Archive also contributed to the publication of two "Quaderni" (Volumes) by the Human Rights Centre:

– *La protezione delle donne vittime di violenza nella prospettiva dei diritti umani* (the protection of women victims of violence from the human rights perspective), edited by Paola Degani and Roberto della Rocca;

– *Caschi bianchi oltre le vendette* (White helmets going beyond revenge), edited by Primo Di Blasio, Samuele Filippini, Francesco Tommasi and Ilaria Zom er. This book presents the findings of the research project by the same name carried out in the context of the National Civil Service Project run by the Associazione Comunità Papa Giovanni XXIII, Caritas Italy and Focsiv, with the scientific support of the Human Rights Centre of the University of Padua.

Finally, the Archive gave support to the organising of a series of initiatives together with national and international experts and organisations, particularly as concerns the documentation and multi-media aspects. These included:

– the first edition of the "Padua Human Rights Laboratory", a series of seminars organised in the context of the Master's degree course in Human Rights and Multi-level Governance at Padua University in order to encourage interaction between students and professors with experts, officials from international organisations, diplomats, professionals and academics involved in human rights-related issues (Padua, 11–14 November 2013).

– the three events promoted by the Human Rights Centre of the University of Padua in connection with the celebration of the 2013 International Day for Human Rights: "La città che sogna" (the city with dreams) (Padua, 9 December 2013), "The Italian Human Rights Agenda: approaching the 2014 UPR" (Padua, 10 December 2013) and "Violence against Women and Human Rights" (Castelfranco Veneto, TV, 11 December 2013).

V. Venice for Peace Research Foundation

As was the Regional Archive, the Foundation was established by r.l. 18/1988 and reconfirmed by r.l. 55/1999. The Foundation's main goal is to carry out research, partly in collaboration with national and international institutions, on matters of security, development and peace.

In recent years, the Foundation has focused its research activities on the following issues: "The role of memory in building peace and in the process of European integration" and "Access to natural resources, especially to water and to a sustainable climate, and the importance of this for the keeping of peace".

VI. Ombudsperson for Children and Adolescents

The Office of the Ombudsperson for Children and Adolescents was established by r.l. 9 August 1988, No. 42. The Ombudsperson is elected by the Regional Council, to which he or she presents a detailed report on an annual basis on the activities performed during the year. Since December 2010, the Ombudsperson for Children and Adolescents in Veneto has been Aurea Dissegna.

The Ombudsperson works towards the non-conflictual, non-jurisdictional protection of the rights of children and adolescents, freely and independently with respect to other public institutions. It is a monocratic authority which avails itself of a staff of experts and collaborators from various professions and disciplines; no charges are made for his or her services.

Over the years, the Office of the Ombudsperson for Children and Adolescents has trained and provided support to over a thousand voluntary legal guardians throughout the Region of Veneto, 75% of whom have declared their willingness to continue to act as legal guardians. In 2013 the Office continued its support, consultancy and training activities for both voluntary legal guardians and for the local spokespersons who represent the link between the Office and the local area, as well as a reference-point for the groups of guardians operating in each local healthcare catchment area. Some extra days of training were organised for the latter on the issue of the suitability/evaluation of guardians and on managing groups.

In 2013 the Office received 273 requests for voluntary legal guardians from the judicial authorities (ordinary and juvenile courts), affecting approximately 300 children and adolescents in the Region of Veneto.

The Office of the Ombudsman has over the years coordinated the publication of *Guidelines for the social and healthcare services in Veneto on the treating and reporting of problems concerning minors*, a precious tool which needs constant updating and reviewing in view of a forthcoming new edition, based on regional government decree (r.g.d.) 8 August 2008, No. 2416 (Regional guidelines for developing the services for protecting and safeguarding children and adolescents).

In connection with this, in view of the success of the workshop designed and held in the previous year ("Workshop for communications between the services and the judicial authorities", the outcome of which was recorded in the r.g.d. 779/2013 and serves as a guideline for social workers and healthcare workers), in 2013 the Office proposed and coordinated the second stage of the Workshop, which also brought in representatives of the police, the magistrates' courts, the Appeal Court (juvenile section) as well as social and healthcare workers from the whole Region. The objective was to strengthen and improve the means of communicating and cooperating between the Services and the police force in making reports to the juvenile and ordinary courts, the implementation of measures ordered by the judiciary (particularly the removal of minors from their families) and the communications between Services and Judiciary at ordinary and appeal level, as well as to clarify the role, duties and responsibilities of court-appointed experts and the Services in procedures regarding minors.

Alongside the workshop activities, mention should also be made of some inter-institutional thematic round tables set up and coordinated by the Ombudsperson's Office on specific issues concerning minors: the right to education of children with health problems, minors who have drug addictions, young children who are in prison with their mothers and minors subject to criminal proceedings.

Over the years, the institutional listening and counselling activity (counselling, mediating and offering guidance) has taken on an increasingly important role in supporting the various public and private bodies involved in actions for the promotion and defence of the rights of children and adolescents (public and private service providers, local administrators, private citizens, etc.). In 2013, 375 files were opened concerning institutional listening, mediating and counselling, following requests from various different institutions (Municipalities, Local Health Authorities, schools, the judiciary...) and from private individuals (citizens, parents and relatives). The requests from social and healthcare services remain constantly high, comprising about 66% of the total.

Moreover, in 2013 the Office organised a regional convention aiming to foster the development of a "culture of listening to minors", through joint reflection and discussions with those who, in their workplace or their daily lives, are required to activate relational processes. The objective was to show the extent to which the practice of listening, or not listening, influences interpersonal relations, which are fundamental experiences in the evolutionary processes of children and adolescents.

Concerning the activity relative to the *Guidelines for communications between schools and welfare and healthcare services*, the Office of the Ombudsperson for Children and Adolescents, in conjunction with the Regional School Office, the Regional Department of Social Services and the Training Directorate of the Region of Veneto ran one regional seminar in 2013 which was the final one in a teaching-training series for professionals from schools, vocational training, social and healthcare services envisaged as a chance to get to know one another, exchange experience of and reflect on best practices for interactions between school, vocational training, social services and healthcare services, for the best possible well-being of children and adolescents.

Finally, the research-action on the subject of the legal institution of placing children in care has been concluded. The research project was promoted by the Ombudsperson for Children and Adolescents of the Region of Veneto and coordinated by the Human Rights Centre of the University of Padua and also involved the Ombudspersons from the Regions of Lazio and Emilia Romagna. The results of this research will be discussed and examined at the national level with the objective of supporting the production of guidelines for social workers, but also for people working in the Courts, to foster greater mutual understanding and agreement over the use and interpretation of the meanings and the responsibilities created by the adoption of legal provisions to put a child into care.

VII. Ombudsperson

The Ombudsperson of the Region of Veneto was established by r.l. 6 June 1988, No. 28. The post is currently occupied by Roberto Pellegrini, who was appointed by the President of the Regional Council on 7 December 2010 and took office on 20 January 2011.

The Ombudsperson is a monocratic authority with freedom to act completely independently and freely to defend the rights and the interests of citizens in cases of maladministration or abuse of power by public authorities. The Ombudsperson has the support of an Office comprising a staff of legal experts who are qualified in the specific areas covered by the Ombudsperson's activities. His services are given free of charge. The Ombudsperson is elected by the Regional Council from among the citizens possessing the necessary qualifications and experience in legal and administrative matters and remains in office for five years; every year the Ombudsperson presents the Regional Assembly with a detailed report on the activity of the previous year. In April 2013, the Ombudsperson prepared his report relative to the year 2012 and the first quarter of 2013.

In 2013, the Veneto Regional Ombudsperson's Office received a total of 713 claims, 577 of which were resolved within the year, whereas 136 are still open and awaiting decisions. Moreover, 30 cases which had been carried over from previous years were resolved. The five main areas to which the claims referred were: territorial issues (189 new cases in 2013, of which 133 closed, 56 cases from previous years resolved in 2013); taxes, levies, subscriptions and fines (120 new cases in 2013 of which 102 closed, 18 cases from previous years closed in 2013); participatory instances and administrative procedures (129 new cases in 2013 of which 119 closed, 10 back cases closed in 2013); general and institutional affairs and organisation (80 new cases in 2013, of which 45 closed, 35 back cases closed in 2013), health and hygiene (54 new cases in 2013 of which 49 closed, 5 back cases resolved in 2013).

In 2013, in addition to acting on reports received from citizens, the Veneto Ombudsperson started several investigations on his own initiative, following press reports. A specific instance involved the Magistrate for Water and Waterways after his office had sent out about 5,000 requests for backdated additional payments relative to the occupation of space on waterways: the case was resolved after the administration had drawn up a proposal for new special rules governing the issue of permits to occupy waterways, subsequently approved and implemented by decree after the financial stability bill.

Regarding the actions to promote a culture of familiarity with the Ombudsperson's role, the Office continued to work with the Human Rights Centre of the University of Padua and the National Coordinating Body of Ombudspersons, organising a series of peer-to-peer meetings on the role of the Ombudsperson and citizens' rights, which were attended by ombudspersons' offices, top and middle managers of local, provincial and regional authorities, teachers, education managers and members of civil society (see, in this Part, Sub-national Human Rights Structures, III).

VIII. Regional Commission for Equal Opportunities between Men and Women

The Commission was established by r.l. 30 December 1987, No. 62 and it is the regional consultative body on gender policies for the actual implementation of the principles of equality and equal opportunities enshrined in the Constitution and by the Regional Statute. Chair of the Commission is Simonetta Tregnago.

> The main function of the Commission is to carry out investigations and research into the condition of women in Veneto, with particular reference to issues involving employment, labour and professional training, and to disseminate information on these areas. At the same time, the Commission respects its commitment to being present on the ground and to developing new synergies with all the actors and forces involved to promote and support the realisation of equal opportunities in the social, political and economic life of the population of Veneto. It may offer opinions on the current state of implementation of laws and on bills, as well as drawing up proposals of its own. The Veneto Equal Opportunities Commission carries out its mission in contact with other Commissions at the local, regional and national level and maintains a constant exchange with all women's organisations in the Region.

The Commission undertook a number of initiatives in the Region in 2013 and published the results of research and joint study work undertaken with other bodies and organisations. Special mention is made of the following:

– *La "Mia" impresa. Nuovi lavori e nuove professioni. L'imprenditoria femminile in Veneto* ("My" company. New jobs and new professions. Female entrepreneurship in Veneto), inquiry promoted and carried out by the Commission and by Confartigianato Veneto (April 2013).

– *Il Tempo ritrovato: percorsi, idee e proposte di conciliazione in Veneto* (Time found again: routes, ideas and proposals for reconciliation in Veneto), inquiry promoted and carried out by the Commission jointly with the Fondazione Nord Est from Mestre (July 2013);

– *Violenza in famiglia: l'altra faccia della realtà* (Domestic violence: the other side of the fact), promoted by the Commission and conducted by the National Observatory on Domestic Violence (September 2013).

IX. Regional Observatory on Social Policies

As of January 2011 the Observatory was established to replace its predecessor, the *Integrated Network of Regional Observatories on Social Policies*.

The function of the Observatory on Social Policies is to activate an information-gathering, monitoring and evaluation system on the interventions and actions relating to regional social services and healthcare policies, in order to support decision-making and planning processes and to develop a regional social information system capable of ensuring a close connection with local information systems. This function is performed mainly through the organisation of events, training activities and consultancy on local social services and healthcare issues, but also through the development and management of databases and support activities for the regional social services headquarters. The Observatory's activities are organised according to the themes which were the object of attention by the observatories under the previous Integrated Network: minors, young people, families, senior citizens and people with disabilities, addictions and social exclusion, with a specific focus on the aspects concerning volunteering and European projects.

Among the many different activities involving the Observatory in 2013, the following are highlighted:

– the organisation of a seminar introducing and debating the issue of *Social inclusion and combating poverty against the backdrop European Funds programmes for the period 2014–2020*, held in Venice on 4 July 2013;

– the organisation of the 3rd Youth Meeting entitled "Il volo giova: dammi spazio. Noi giovani cittadini creativi" (Flying helps: give me space. We young and creative citizens), held in Villorba (TV) on 19 December 2013. The event, overseen by the Regional Councillor's Office for Social Policy, aimed to support young people by fostering the development of innovative career guidance programmes and entrepreneurship, the use of new technology to enhance professional skills and encouraging creative expression to bolster the talents of young adults.

The Observatory also contributed to the publication of the following reports:

– *Coinvolti di diritto*, a report on the "Daphne Project" *Involved by right*, run by the Bassano del Grappa (VI) local health authority No. 3 on behalf of the Region of Veneto, the aim of which is to establish new ways and opportunities for group listening to young boys and girls undergoing a course of treatment.

– La *Direzione del sociale nel welfare regionale* (Managing the social in regional welfare), a report designed to extend awareness of the outcomes of regional programmes of social services and healthcare in recent years.

– *Qualche dato sulle attività del servizio famiglia* (Some data on services for families), a report aiming to supply updated information on family planning clinics, health and protection centres, the protection of minors, adoptions, early childhood and other services for families.

X. Regional Observatory on Immigration

The Observatory is overseen by the Project Unit on Migratory Flows (the Councillor's office on migratory flows policies) and is managed by Veneto Lavoro. Its establishment was included in the three-year programme 2007–2009 comprising measures and initiatives in the field of immigration and confirmed by the adoption of the subsequent 2010–2012 plan, pursuant to art. 3 of r.l. 9/1990 (Measures in the immigration sector).

> The Observatory is defined as a technical-scientific instrument aiming to monitor, analyse and disseminate data and information on migratory flows and integration at the regional and national level. To this end, it: collaborates with the other regional observatories which are for one reason or another involved in the migration phenomenon; assures the proper functioning and constant input for databases, the monitoring of immigration dynamics, further study on various thematic aspects, housing conditions, the social and educational integration of minors and their development; it ensures an updated collection of specialised laws, proposing training sessions to increase knowledge of these laws and their correct implementation.

In September 2013, the Observatory published its tenth *Annual report on foreign immigration to Veneto*. The report presents a systematic analysis of data and trends in migratory flows in relation to certain aspects crucial for Veneto and the whole of Italy, such as the demographic changes, employment and unemployment figures, education, services to the person, policies to encourage repatriation, recent trends and changes to entry policies and the economic significance of immigration.

The data presented in this edition as concerns the resident population was conditioned by the outcome of the census of late 2011, which now constitutes the statistical reference point for the preparation of the report. According to this data, there were 457,328 foreigners resident in Veneto at the end of 2011, constituting 11.4% of all foreigners in Italy (4,029,145). Compared to the rest of Italy, the Region of Veneto has the second largest foreign population (after Lombardy). The foreigners resident in Veneto make up 9.4% of the total regional population, the fourth highest percentage after Emilia-Romagna, Umbria and Lombardy. The Provinces with the largest percentage of foreigners as compared to the overall population are Treviso (10.7%), Verona (10.5%) and Vicenza (10.4%). According to the projections based on ISTAT data, 9,751 foreigners were born in Veneto in 2012; 8,346 foreigners resident in Veneto acquired Italian citizenship, representing 13% of those granted citizenship in Italy as a whole (approximately 65,400). As of 1 January 2013, the largest numbers of residence permits in Veneto were held by foreigners from Morocco (15%), Albania (10%), China (9%) and Republic of Moldova (9%). As concerns 2012 arrivals in the Veneto Region, the five main Countries of origin were Morocco, Republic of Moldova, China, the United States and Serbia/Kosovo/Montenegro.

Part III

Italy in Dialogue with International Human Rights Institutions

The United Nations System

I. General Assembly

The General Assembly, which is the main deliberative body of the United Nations, comprises six Committees, each of which is made up of all 193 United Nations Member States. Human rights issues are handled mainly within the Third Committee (Social, Humanitarian and Cultural Committee). The responsibilities of this Committee include issues such as torture and other cruel, inhuman and degrading treatment or punishment; the advancement of women; the rights of refugees and displaced persons; the promotion and protection of the rights of children; the rights of indigenous peoples; the elimination of racism, racial discrimination, xenophobia and related intolerance; the right of peoples to self-determination; and social development.

On 2 April 2013 the General Assembly adopted the Arms Trade Treaty, with 154 votes in favour, 3 against and 23 abstentions. The treaty aims to establish common rules regulating the international arms trade as well as thwarting and repressing the illegal trade of so-called conventional weapons, i.e. battle tanks, combat aircraft, combat vehicles, artillery, helicopters, warships, missiles, and long-range rockets, but also small arms and light weapons such as guns, pistols and ammunition.

Moreover, in December 2013, the 68th General Assembly adopted 68 human rights resolutions which had been debated and approved by the Third Committee during the months of October and November. The following ones are specifically highlighted:

– *Protecting women human rights defenders* (A/RES/68/181). This is the first ever United Nations resolution recognising the role of women human rights defenders. The resolution specifically establishes that women human rights defenders must be granted unconditional access to national and international mechanisms protecting human rights and urges States to adopt specific laws and gender-sensitive policies which will protect them from any forms of retaliation.

– *National institutions for the promotion and protection of human rights* (A/RES/68/171). This resolution requests the United Nations Secretary General to explore the feasibility of enabling national human rights institutions compliant with the Paris Principles to participate in their own right and independently of the delegations of their member States in the United Nations mechanisms and processes.

– four resolutions pertaining to the human rights situation in the following Countries: Democratic People's Republic of Korea, Myanmar, Iran and Syria.

On 19 July 2013, H.E. Sebastiano Cardi was named as the new Permanent Representative of Italy to the United Nations in New York, replacing H.E. Cesare Maria Ragaglini; the First Counsellor of the Permanent Mission Emilia Gatto is responsible for following the activities of the Third Committee. The chart below shows the most significant interventions by the Italian delegation and government representatives in General Assembly meetings in 2013.

Date	Event	Statement
7 February 2013	51st session of the Commission for social development	Raffaele Tangorra, Director General for social integration and social policy, Ministry of Labour and Social Policy on the theme "Promoting empowerment of people in achieving poverty eradication, social integration and full employment and decent work for all"
7 February 2013	51st session of the Commission for social development	First Secretary Filippo Cinti on the theme "Review of relevant United Nations plans and programmes of action pertaining to the situation of social groups"
12 February 2013	Presentation of the Global Report on Trafficking in Persons	H.E. Ragaglini
5 March 2013	57th session of the United Nations Commission on the Status of Women	Elsa Fornero, Minister of Labour, Social Policies and Equal Opportunities
25 April 2013	GA thematic debate on the Peaceful Resolution of Conflicts in Africa	H.E. Ragaglini
14 May 2013	High-level Meeting of the General Assembly on the Global Plan of Action to Combat Trafficking in Persons	Deputy Permanent Representative of Italy, Antonio Bernardini
3 June 2013	Ceremony for the opening for signature of the Conventional Arms Trade Treaty	Bruno Archi, Deputy Minister for Foreign Affairs

27 June 2013	GA Plenary session on the Report of the Security Council & the Question of equitable representation and increase in its membership	H.E. Ragaglini
24 September 2013	Inaugural meeting of the high-level political forum on the theme "Building the future we want: from Rio+20 to the post-2015 development agenda"	Enrico Letta, Prime Minister
25 September 2013	Inaugural meeting of the 68th session of the General Assembly	Enrico Letta, Prime Minister
26 September 2013	High-level Meeting on the situation in Sahel	Enrico Letta, Prime Minister
4 October 2013	High-level Dialogue on "International Migration and Development"	Deputy Permanent Representative of Italy, Antonio Bernardini
7 November 2013	Debate on the reform of the Security Council	Deputy Permanent Representative of Italy, Antonio Bernardini
27 November 2013	GA Plenary meeting on the situation in Afghanistan	H.E. Sebastiano Cardi
26 November 2013	Third Committee	H.E. Sebastiano Cardi, presentation of the draft resolution "Strengthening the United Nations crime prevention and criminal justice programme, in particular its technical cooperation capacity"
12 December 2013	GA 10th Round of intergovernmental negotiations on the issue of fair representation and increase of the membership of the Security Council and others issues relating to the Council.	H.E. Cardi, speaking for the group "United for consensus"
19 December 2013	Special General Assembly Plenary Meeting on the Life and Memory of Nelson Mandela	Counsellor Emilia Gatto

Source: Italy's Permanent Mission to the United Nations in New York.

A. Resolutions on Human Rights: Italy's Voting Behaviour

As in the past, again in 2013 Italy's action in support of human rights prioritised the following thematic areas: promotion of the rule of law and strengthening of democracy; the fight against torture, xenophobia, racism and all forms of discrimination, with special attention to religious discrimination and intolerance; the rights and protection of children; the abolition of the death penalty; combating violence against women and female genital mutilation.

More in detail, Italy, following a practice consolidated over the years, presented the resolution *Strengthening the United Nations Crime Prevention and Criminal Justice Programme, in particular its technical cooperation capacity*, approved by consensus by the General Assembly (A/RES/68/193); in addition, Italy sponsored 34 resolutions (+ 1 compared to 2012) and was asked to pass an open vote on 14 resolutions (5 votes in favour, 7 against and 2 abstentions), the outcome of which is shown below.

Subject	Resolution	Main sponsor of the Resolution	Information regarding Italy	Outcome of the plenary vote
Social development	A/RES/68/130 Policies and programmes involving youth	Senegal	Co-sponsor of the resolution	Approved by consensus
	A/RES/68/131 Promoting social integration through social inclusion	Peru	Co-sponsor of the resolution	Approved by consensus
	A/RES/68/132 Literacy for life: Shaping future agendas	Mongolia	Co-sponsor of the resolution	Approved by consensus
	A/RES/68/133 Cooperatives in social development	Mongolia	Co-sponsor of the resolution	Approved by consensus
	A/RES/68/134 Follow-up to the Second World Assembly on Ageing	Fiji	Co-sponsor of the resolution	Approved by consensus
Advancement of women	A/RES/68/138 Convention on the Elimination of All Forms of Discrimination against Women	Norway	Co-sponsor of the resolution	Approved by consensus
	A/RES/68/139 Improvement of the situation of women in rural areas	Mongolia	Co-sponsor of the resolution	Approved by consensus

Subject	Resolution	Main sponsor of the Resolution	Information regarding Italy	Outcome of the plenary vote
Refugees, displaced persons and humanitarian issues	A/RES/68/141 Office of the United Nations High Commissioner for Refugees	Finland	Co-sponsor of the resolution	Approved by consensus
	A/RES/68/143 Assistance to refugees, returnees and displaced persons in Africa	Liberia	Co-sponsor of the resolution	Approved by consensus
Report of the Human Rights Council	A/RES/68/144 Report of the Human Rights Council	Cameroon	Voted against	94 in favour, 71 against, 23 abstentions
Promotion and protection of the rights of children	A/RES/68/146 The girl child	Malawi	Co-sponsor of the resolution	Approved by consensus
	A/RES/68/147 Rights of the child	Lithuania	Co-sponsor of the resolution	Approved by consensus
	A/RES/68/148 Child, early and forced marriage	Canada and Zambia	Co-sponsor of the resolution	Approved by consensus
Rights of indigenous peoples	A/RES/68/149 Rights of indigenous peoples	Bolivia	Co-sponsor of the resolution	Approved by consensus
Elimination of racism, racial discrimination, xenophobia and related intolerance	A/RES/68/150 Combating glorification of Nazism and other practices that contribute to fuelling contemporary forms of racism, racial discrimination, xenophobia and related intolerance	Russian Federation	Abstained	135 in favour, 4 against, 51 abstentions

Subject	Resolution	Main sponsor of the Resolution	Information regarding Italy	Outcome of the plenary vote
	A/RES/68/151 Global efforts for the total elimination of racism, racial discrimination, xenophobia and related intolerance and the comprehensive implementation of and follow-up to the Durban Declaration and Programme of Action	Fiji	Abstained	134 in favour, 11 against, 46 abstentions
The right of peoples to self-determination	A/RES/68/152 Use of mercenaries as a means of violating human rights and impeding the exercise of the right of peoples to self determination	Cuba	Voted against	128 in favour, 55 against, 8 abstentions
	A/RES/68/154 The right of the Palestinian people to self-determination	Egypt	Co-sponsor of the resolution Voted in favour	178 in favour, 7 against, 4 abstentions
Implementation of human rights instruments	A/RES/68/155 International Covenants on human rights	Finland	Co-sponsor of the resolution	Approved by consensus
	A/RES/68/156 Torture and other cruel, inhuman or degrading treatment or punishment	Denmark	Co-sponsor of the resolution	Approved by consensus

Subject	Resolution	Main sponsor of the Resolution	Information regarding Italy	Outcome of the plenary vote
Human rights questions, including alternative approaches for improving the effective enjoyment of human rights and fundamental freedoms	A/RES/68/157 The human right to safe drinking water and sanitation	Germany and Spain	Co-sponsor of the resolution	Approved by consensus
	A/RES/68/158 The right to development	Cuba	Voted in favour	158 in favour, 4 against, 28 abstentions
	A/RES/68/159 Human rights and cultural diversity	Cuba	Voted against	136 in favour, 54 against, no abstentions
	A/RES/68/161 Promotion of equitable geographical distribution in the membership of the human rights treaty bodies	Cuba	Voted against	135 in favour, 54 against, 1 abstention
	A/RES/68/162 Human rights and unilateral coercive measures	Cuba	Voted against	135 in favour, 55 against, no abstentions
	A/RES/68/163 The safety of journalists and the issue of impunity	Greece	Co-sponsor of the resolution	Approved by consensus
	A/RES/68/164 Strengthening the role of the United Nations in enhancing periodic and genuine elections and the promotion of democratization	United States of America	Co-sponsor of the resolution	Approved by consensus

Subject	Resolution	Main sponsor of the Resolution	Information regarding Italy	Outcome of the plenary vote
	A/RES/68/165 Right to the truth	Argentina	Co-sponsor of the resolution	Approved by consensus
	A/RES/68/166 International Convention for the Protection of All Persons from Enforced Disappearance	France	Co-sponsor of the resolution	Approved by consensus
	A/RES/68/168 Globalization and its impact on the full enjoyment of all human rights	Egypt	Voted against	136 in favour, 55 against, no abstentions
	A/RES/68/170 Freedom of religion or belief	Lithuania	Co-sponsor of the resolution	Approved by consensus
	A/RES/68/171 National institutions for the promotion and protection of human rights	Germany	Co-sponsor of the resolution	Approved by consensus
	A/RES/68/172 Effective promotion of the Declaration on the Rights of Persons Belonging to National or Ethnic, Religious and Linguistic Minorities	Austria	Co-sponsor of the resolution	Approved by consensus
	A/RES/68/241 United Nations Human Rights Training and Documentation Centre for South-West Asia and the Arab Region	Qatar	Voted in favour	132 in favour, 1 against, 1 abstention
	A/RES/68/173 Follow-up to the International Year of human rights learning	Cameroon	Co-sponsor of the resolution	Approved by consensus

Subject	Resolution	Main sponsor of the Resolution	Information regarding Italy	Outcome of the plenary vote
	A/RES/68/174 Subregional Centre for Human Rights and Democracy in Central Africa	Cameroon	Co-sponsor of the resolution	Approved by consensus
	A/RES/68/175 Promotion of a democratic and equitable international order	Cuba	Voted against	132 in favour, 52 against, 6 abstentions
	A/RES/68/177 The right to food	Cuba	Co-sponsor of the resolution	Approved by consensus
	A/RES/68/178 Protection of human rights and fundamental freedoms while countering terrorism	Mexico	Co-sponsor of the resolution	Approved by consensus
	A/RES/68/180 Protection of and assistance to internally displaced persons	Norway	Co-sponsor of the resolution	Approved by consensus
Human rights situations and reports by Special Rapporteurs and Representatives	A/RES/68/182 Situation of human rights in the Syrian Arab Republic	Saudi Arabia	Co-sponsor of the resolution; Voted in favour	127 in favour, 13 against, 47 abstentions
	A/RES/68/242 Situation of human rights in Myanmar	Lithuania	Co-sponsor of the resolution	Approved by consensus
	A/RES/68/183 Situation of human rights in the Democratic People's Republic of Korea	Lithuania	Co-sponsor of the resolution	Approved by consensus

Subject	Resolution	Main sponsor of the Resolution	Information regarding Italy	Outcome of the plenary vote
	A/RES/68/184 Situation of human rights in the Islamic Republic of Iran	Canada	Co-sponsor of the resolution; Voted in favour	86 in favour, 36 against, 61 abstentions
Criminal justice and prevention of crime	A/RES/68/192 Improving the coordination of efforts against trafficking in persons	Belarus	Co-sponsor of the resolution	Approved by consensus

Source: United Nations General Assembly.

II. Human Rights Council

The Human Rights Council is the subsidiary body of the General Assembly responsible for promoting worldwide respect of all human rights and fundamental freedoms for all, without distinction of any kind.

Established in 2006 under resolution 60/251, the Council is an inter-governmental body made up of 47 United Nations Member States elected by the General Assembly for an initial period of three years, extendable for not more than two consecutive terms. It meets in Geneva, usually in three ordinary sessions per year, for an overall period of at least ten working weeks. Furthermore, although it is a body of Government representatives, the Council is open to the contributions of nongovernmental organisations which enjoy advisory status with the ECOSOC, which may participate in the meetings and submit written documents.

The Council has established several different "mechanisms" for monitoring human rights (resolution A/HRC/RES/5/1 of June 2007), including: the Universal Periodic Review (UPR), the Special Procedures (which include mandates by Country and thematic mandates), the Advisory Committee and a Complaints Procedure.

In 2013 the following States were members of the Council (shown in brackets is the date their mandate expires):

– *African States* (13 seats): Angola (2013), Benin (2014); Botswana (2014); Burkina Faso (2014); Democratic Republic of the Congo; Ivory Coast (2015); Ethiopia (2015); Gabon (2015); Kenya (2015); Libya (2013); Mauritania (2013); Sierra Leone (2015); Uganda (2013).

– *Asian States* (13 seats): India (2014); Indonesia (2014); Japan (2015); Kazakhstan (2015); Kuwait (2014); Malaysia (2013); Maldives (2013); the

Philippines (2014); Qatar (2013); Republic of Korea (2015); Thailand (2013); United Arab Emirates (2015).

– *Latin American and Caribbean States* (8 seats): Argentina (2015); Brazil (2015); Chile (2014); Costa Rica (2014); Ecuador (2013); Guatemala (2013); Peru (2014); Venezuela (2015).

– *Western European and other States* (7 seats): Austria (2014); Germany (2015); Ireland (2015); Italy (2014); Spain (2013); Switzerland (2013); United States of America (2015).

– *Eastern European States* (6 seats): Czech Republic (2014); Estonia (2015); Montenegro (2015); Poland (2013); Republic of Moldova (2013); Romania (2014).

In the course of 2013, the Council held three ordinary sessions: the 22nd (25 February-22 March); the 23rd (27 May-14 June); the 24th (9–27 September) and three sessions of UPR: the 15th (21 January-1 February); the 16th (22 April-3 May); and the 17th (21 October-1 November).

Special note is made of the adoption, in the course of the 23rd ordinary session, of the resolution *Promotion of the right to peace*, under which the Council authorises a further session in 2014 of the inter-governmental working group responsible for negotiating the draft *United Nations Declaration on the human right to peace*. The resolution was approved with 30 votes in favour, 9 against and 8 abstentions: the African Group and the Latin American and Caribbean Group voted as one in its favour, as did the majority of Countries from the Asian Countries Group; votes against came from Austria, the Czech Republic, Estonia, Germany, Japan, Montenegro, the Republic of Korea, Spain and the United States; Italy abstained, as did India, Ireland, Kazakhstan, Poland, the Republic of Moldova, Romania and Switzerland.

In 2011 Italy was elected to the Human Rights Council for the second time for the three-year period June 2011-June 2014. On 2 September 2013, H.E. Maurizio Enrico Serra was appointed Permanent Representative of Italy to the International Organisations in Geneva, replacing H.E. Laura Mirachian; Italy was also represented in the Council by the Deputy Permanent Representative Amedeo Trambajolo, by the Counsellor Paolo Cuculi and by the First Secretary Marco Lapadura. Listed below are the main interventions by the Italian mission in 2013.

Date	Event	Statement
21 January-1 February 2013	15th session of UPR	Statements relative to the analysis of the human rights situation in the following States: Tonga, France, Mali, Romania, Bahamas, Botswana, Luxembourg, Barbados, Montenegro, United Arab Emirates and Serbia

Date	Event	Statement
25 February 2013	22nd session of the Human Rights Council	H.E. Laura Mirachian, during the High-level Panel on the XX Anniversary of the Vienna Declaration and Plan of Action
1 March 2013	22nd session of the Human Rights Council	Counsellor Paolo Cuculi, on the occasion of the interactive dialogue with the High Commissioner for Human Rights
1 March 2013	22nd session of the Human Rights Council	First secretary, Marco Lapadura, at the High-Level panel discussion on Mainstreaming Human Rights
5 March 2013	22nd session of the Human Rights Council	H.E. Laura Mirachian, at the interactive dialogue with the Special Rapporteur on Freedom of religion or belief
11 March 2013	22nd session of the Human Rights Council	H.E. Laura Mirachian, at the interactive dialogue with the Commission of Inquiry on Syria
20 March 2013	22nd session of the Human Rights Council	Counsellor Paolo Cuculi, at the general debate on technical assistance and capacity building
11 March 2013	22nd session of the Human Rights Council	H.E. Laura Mirachian, at the vote on the resolution "Combating intolerance, negative stereotyping and stigmatization of, and discrimination, incitement to violence and violence against, persons based on religion or belief (A/HRC/22/L.40)
22 April-3 May 2013	16th session of UPR	Statements made with reference to the analysis of the human rights situation in the following Countries: Burkina Faso, Turkmenistan, Cape Verde, Colombia, Tuvalu, Uzbekistan, Djibouti, Germany, Canada, Bangladesh, The Russian Federation, Azerbaijan, Cameroon, Cuba
9 September 2013	24th session of the Human Rights Council	H.E. Maurizio Enrico Serra, at the presentation of the Annual Report by the High Commissioner for Human Rights
10 September 2013	24th session of the Human Rights Council	First Secretary Marco Lapadura, at the interactive dialogue on children in armed conflict
11 September 2013	24th session of the Human Rights Council	First Secretary Marco Lapadura, at the discussion on the human rights of children of parents sentenced to the death penalty or executed

Date	Event	Statement
16 September 2013	24th session of the Human Rights Council	Deputy Permanent Representative Amedeo Trambajolo, at the interactive dialogue with the Commission of Inquiry on Syria
24 September 2013	24th session of the Human Rights Council	H.E. Maurizio Enrico Serra, at the High-level interactive dialogue on Somalia
25 September 2013	24th session of the Human Rights Council	H.E. Maurizio Enrico Serra, at the interactive dialogue on the human rights situation in Somalia
21 October-1 November 2013	17th session of UPR	Statements relative to the analysis of the human rights situation in the following Countries: Senegal, Saudi Arabia, Nigeria, China, Mexico, Malaysia, Jordan, the Central African Republic, Israel, Chad and Congo
26 November 2013	Forum on Minority issues	H.E. Maurizio Enrico Serra

Sources: Italy's Permanent mission to the United Nations in Geneva and *UN web TV*

A. Italy's Voting Behaviour at the Human Rights Council in 2013

In 2013, Italy participated in the three ordinary sessions of the Human Rights Council as a Member State (hence, with the right to vote).

Over the whole year, the Human Rights Council adopted 95 resolutions (+1 compared to 2012), distributed as follows: 34 resolutions during the 22nd session (25 February-22 March); 26 during the 23rd session (27 May-14 June); 35 during the 24th session (9–27 September). Of these resolutions, 67 (or 71%) were adopted with the consensus of all Member States, whereas for 28 of them (29%), it was necessary to use majority voting, thus revealing a certain level of disagreement.

The paragraphs below aim to analyse Italy's behaviour in the Human Rights Council in 2013, with special attention to two specific aspects: Italy's diplomatic efforts in the negotiation and presentation of the resolutions, and its voting behaviour.

On the first count, it can be seen that over half of the resolutions adopted by the Council were negotiated with the direct participation (sponsoring) or diplomatic support (co-sponsoring) of Italy. Indeed, of the 95 resolutions adopted, Italy sponsored 4 (as compared to 1 in 2012) and co-sponsored 48 (44 in 2012, constituting 47% of the total). Two of the 4 resolutions sponsored by Italy were of a thematic nature and referred, respectively, to the contributions of national parliaments to the Universal Periodic Review and to the World Programme for Human Rights Education. The other two resolutions were "country-specific" and concerned the human rights situation in Syria and technical assistance to Somalia in the field of human rights.

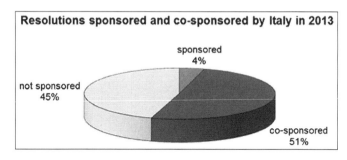

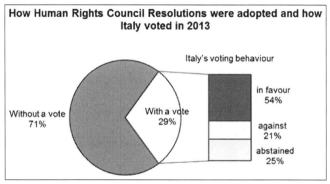

As concerns Italy's voting behaviour, it proved "winning" in 15 of the 28 votes called; whereas 6 resolutions which Italy had voted against were adopted by a majority vote; Italy abstained 7 times.

More in detail, Italy supported resolutions sponsored by Countries belonging to all the regional groups represented in the Council: of its 15 votes in favour, 2 referred to resolutions presented by Countries from the Western Group (USA and Ireland), 1 by the Eastern European Group (Hungary), 6 by the Asian Group (Pakistan, Bahrain, Palestine, Qatar and Iran), 1 by the Latin American Group (joint resolution from Ecuador, Costa Rica and Peru), and five 'yes' votes were given in favour of transversal resolutions sponsored by Countries belonging to two or more regional groups. Resolutions voted against by Italy were presented by Cuba (4 out of 6), Iran (1) and jointly by South Africa and Gabon (1). Finally, the abstentions were distributed over three regional groups: the African Group (3: South Africa, Gabon and Tunisia), the Asia Group (2: Pakistan, Bahrain and Palestine) and the Latin American Group (2: Cuba and Brazil).

The chart below summarises the data relative to both aspects examined above and also shows that, out of the resolutions sponsored or co-sponsored by Italy, 85% were adopted by the Council by consensus, and 15% by a majority vote.

Chart summarising Italy's behaviour at the Human Rights Council in 2013

	Adopted by the Council by consensus	Adopted by the Council with a majority vote			Tot.
		Italy: voted in favour	Italy: voted against	Italy: abstained	
Resolutions sponsored by Italy	3	1	-	-	4
Resolutions co-sponsored by Italy	41	7	-	-	48
Resolutions not sponsored by Italy	23	7	6	7	43
Tot.	67	15	6	7	95

Human Rights Council: resolutions sponsored by Italy in 2013

Resolution	Other sponsors of the resolution	Outcome of the voting process
A/HRC/RES/22/15 Contribution of parliaments to the work of the Human Rights Council and its universal periodic review	Ecuador, Argentina, Maldives, Morocco, Romania, Spain	Adopted without a vote
A/HRC/RES/24/15 World Programme for Human Rights Education	Costa Rica, Morocco, Philippine, Senegal, Slovenia, Switzerland	Adopted without a vote
A/HRC/RES/24/22 The continuing grave deterioration of the human rights and humanitarian situation in the Syrian Arab Republic	USA, France, Germany, Jordan, Kuwait, Morocco, Qatar, Saudi Arabia, Turkey, United Kingdom	40 in favour, 1 against, 6 abstentions
A/HRC/RES/24/30 Assistance to Somalia in the field of human rights	Somalia, United Kingdom, Australia, Austria, Djibouti, Ethiopia, Norway, Qatar, Sweden, Turkey, United Arab Emirates, USA, Yemen	Adopted without a vote

Sources: United Nations, Human Rights Council

Human Rights Council: resolutions co-sponsored by Italy in 2013

Resolution	State(s) presenting the resolution	Outcome of the voting process
22nd Session (25 February-22 March)		
A/HRC/RES/22/1 Promoting reconciliation and accountability in Sri Lanka	USA	25 in favour, 13 against, 8 abstentions
A/HRC/RES/22/3 The work and employment of persons with disabilities	Mexico, New Zealand	Adopted without a vote
A/HRC/RES/22/4 Rights of persons belonging to national or ethnic, religious and linguistic minorities	Austria	Adopted without a vote
A/HRC/RES/22/5 Question of the realization in all Countries of economic, social and cultural rights	Portugal	Adopted without a vote
A/HRC/RES/22/6 Protecting human rights defenders	Norway	Adopted without a vote
A/HRC/RES/22/7 Birth registration and the right of everyone to recognition everywhere as a person before the law	Mexico, Turkey	Adopted without a vote
A/HRC/RES/22/10 Promotion and protection of human rights in the context of peaceful protests	Switzerland, Costa Rica, Turkey	Adopted without a vote
A/HRC/RES/22/11 Panel on the human rights of children of parents sentenced to the death penalty or executed	Belgium	Adopted without a vote
A/HRC/RES/22/18 Assistance to the Republic of Mali in the field of human rights	Gabon	Adopted without a vote
A/HRC/RES/22/19 Technical assistance for Libya in the field of human rights	Libya, Morocco	Adopted without a vote
A/HRC/RES/22/21 Torture and other cruel, inhuman or degrading treatment or punishment: rehabilitation of torture victims	Denmark	Adopted without a vote
A/HRC/RES/22/22 Prevention of genocide	Armenia	Adopted without a vote

Resolution	State(s) presenting the resolution	Outcome of the voting process
A/HRC/RES/22/23 Situation of human rights in the Islamic Republic of Iran	Sweden, Panama, Moldavia, Macedonia, USA	26 in favour, 2 against, 17 abstentions
A/HRC/RES/22/24 Situation of human rights in the Syrian Arab Republic	Morocco, Jordan, Kuwait, Qatar, Saudi Arabia, Tunisia, United Arab Emirates	41 in favour, 1 against, 5 abstentions
A/HRC/RES/22/34 Education as a tool to prevent racism, racial discrimination, xenophobia and related intolerance	Brazil, Mozambique, Portugal, Colombia, Honduras, Romania	46 in favour, 0 against, 1 abstention
23rd Session (27 May-14 June)		
A/HRC/RES/23/1 The deteriorating situation of human rights in the Syrian Arab Republic, and the recent killings in Al-Qusayr	Qatar, Turkey, USA	36 in favour, 1 against, 8 abstentions
A/HRC/RES/23/2 The role of freedom of opinion and expression in women's empowerment	Montenegro, USA	Adopted without a vote
A/HRC/RES/23/4 The right to education: follow-up to Human Rights Council resolution 8/4	Portugal	Adopted without a vote
A/HRC/RES/23/5 Trafficking in persons, especially women and children: efforts to combat human trafficking in supply chains of businesses	Germany, Philippines	Adopted without a vote
A/HRC/RES/23/6 Independence and impartiality of the judiciary, jurors and assessors, and the independence of lawyers	Hungary	Adopted without a vote
A/HRC/RES/23/7 Elimination of discrimination against women	Colombia, Mexico	Adopted without a vote
A/HRC/RES/23/8 Mandate of the Special Rapporteur on the human rights of internally displaced persons	Austria	Adopted without a vote
A/HRC/RES/23/9 The negative impact of corruption on the enjoyment of human rights	Morocco	Adopted without a vote

Resolution	State(s) presenting the resolution	Outcome of the voting process
A/HRC/RES/23/19 National policies and human rights	Ecuador, Peru	Adopted without a vote
A/HRC/RES/23/22 Technical assistance to Côte d'Ivoire in the field of human rights	Gabon	Adopted without a vote
A/HRC/RES/23/23 Strengthening of technical cooperation and consultative services in Guinea	Gabon	Adopted without a vote
A/HRC/RES/23/26 The deterioration of the situation of human rights in the Syrian Arab Republic, and the need to grant immediate access to the commission of inquiry	Qatar	37 in favour, 1 against, 9 abstentions
24th Session (9–27 September)		
A/HRC/RES/24/1 Promoting human rights through sport and the Olympic ideal	Russian Federation	Adopted without a vote
A/HRC/RES/24/2 Local government and human rights	Republic of Korea	Adopted without a vote
A/HRC/RES/24/3 Special Rapporteur on contemporary forms of slavery, including its causes and consequences	United Kingdom	Adopted without a vote
A/HRC/RES/24/5 The rights to freedom of peaceful assembly and of association	Mexico, USA	Adopted without a vote
A/HRC/RES/24/6 The right of everyone to the enjoyment of the highest attainable standard of physical and mental health	Brazil	Adopted without a vote
A/HRC/RES/24/7 Arbitrary detention	France	Adopted without a vote
A/HRC/RES/24/8 Equal political participation	Czech Republic	Adopted without a vote
A/HRC/RES/24/11 Preventable mortality and morbidity of children under 5 years of age as a human rights concern	Ireland, Botswana	Adopted without a vote
A/HRC/RES/24/12 Human rights in the administration of justice, including juvenile justice	Austria	Adopted without a vote

Resolution	State(s) presenting the resolution	Outcome of the voting process
A/HRC/RES/24/16 The role of prevention in the promotion and protection of human rights	Ukraine	Adopted without a vote
A/HRC/RES/24/17 Conscientious objection to military service	Costa Rica, Croatia, Poland	Adopted without a vote
A/HRC/RES/24/18 The human right to safe drinking water and sanitation	Germany, Spain	Adopted without a vote
A/HRC/RES/24/19 Regional arrangements for the promotion and protection of human rights	Belgium	Adopted without a vote
A/HRC/RES/24/21 Civil society space: creating and maintaining, in law and in practice, a safe and enabling environment	Ireland, Japan, Tunisia	Adopted without a vote
A/HRC/RES/24/23 Strengthening efforts to prevent and eliminate child, early and forced marriage: challenges, achievements, best practices and implementation gaps	Sierra Leone	Adopted without a vote
A/HRC/RES/24/24 Cooperation with the United Nations, its representatives and mechanisms in the field of human rights	Hungary	31 in favour, 1 against, 15 abstentions
A/HRC/RES/24/27 Technical assistance and capacity-building for human rights in the Democratic Republic of the Congo	Gabon	Adopted without a vote
A/HRC/RES/24/29 Advisory services and technical assistance for Cambodia	Japan	Adopted without a vote
A/HRC/RES/24/31 Enhancement of technical cooperation and capacity-building in the field of human rights	Thailand	Adopted without a vote
A/HRC/RES/24/32 Technical assistance and capacity-building for Yemen in the field of human rights	Netherlands, Yemen	Adopted without a vote
A/HRC/RES/24/34 Technical assistance to the Central African Republic in the field of human rights	Gabon	Adopted without a vote

Sources: United Nations, Human Rights Council

Human Rights Council: resolutions not sponsored by Italy in 2013

Resolution	State(s) presenting the resolution	Outcome of the voting process	Information regarding Italy
22ⁿᵈ Session (25 February-22 March)			
A/HRC/RES/22/2 Composition of the staff of the Office of the High Commissioner for Human Rights	Cuba	31 in favour, 15 against, 1 abstention	Voted against
A/HRC/RES/22/8 Protection of human rights and fundamental freedoms while countering terrorism: mandate of the Special Rapporteur on the promotion and protection of human rights and fundamental freedoms while countering terrorism	Mexico	Adopted without a vote	-
A/HRC/RES/22/9 The right to food	Cuba	Adopted without a vote	-
A/HRC/RES/22/12 The negative impact of the non-repatriation of funds of illicit origin to the Countries of origin on the enjoyment of human rights, and the importance of improving international cooperation	Tunisia, Gabon	32 in favour, 2 against, 13 abstentions	Abstained
A/HRC/RES/22/13 The situation of human rights in the Democratic People's Republic of Korea	Ireland, Japan	Adopted without a vote	-
A/HRC/RES/22/14 Situation of human rights in Myanmar	Ireland	Adopted without a vote	-
A/HRC/RES/22/16 Promotion and protection of human rights in post-disaster and post-conflict situations	Uruguay	Adopted without a vote	-

Resolution	State(s) presenting the resolution	Outcome of the voting process	Information regarding Italy
A/HRC/RES/22/17 Human rights in the occupied Syrian Golan	Pakistan	29 in favour, 1 against, 17 abstentions	Abstained
A/HRC/RES/22/20 Freedom of religion or belief	Ireland	Adopted without a vote	-
A/HRC/RES/22/25 Follow-up to the report of the United Nations Independent International Fact-Finding Mission on the Gaza Conflict	Pakistan, Bahrein, Palestine	43 in favour, 1 against, 3 abstentions	Voted in favour
A/HRC/RES/22/26 Israeli settlements in the Occupied Palestinian Territory, Including East Jerusalem, and in the occupied Syrian Golan	Pakistan, Bahrein, Palestine	44 in favour, 1 against, 2 abstentions	Abstained
A/HRC/RES/22/27 Right of the Palestinian people to self-determination	Pakistan, Bahrein, Palestine	46 in favour, 1 against, 0 abstentions	Voted in favour
A/HRC/RES/22/28 Human Rights situation in the Occupied Palestinian Territory, including East Jerusalem	Pakistan, Bahrein, Palestine	46 in favour, 1 against, 0 abstentions	Voted in favour
A/HRC/RES/22/29 Follow-up to the report of the independent international fact-finding mission to investigate the implications of Israeli settlements on the civil, political, economic, social and cultural rights of the Palestinian people throughout the Occupied Palestinian Territory, including East Jerusalem	Pakistan, Bahrein, Palestine	45 in favour, 1 against, 0 abstentions	Voted in favour
A/HRC/RES/22/30 Intergovernmental Working Group on the Effective Implementation of the Durban Declaration and Programme of Action	South Africa, Gabon	34 in favour, 1 against, 12 abstentions	Abstained

Resolution	State(s) presenting the resolution	Outcome of the voting process	Information regarding Italy
A/HRC/RES/22/31 Combating intolerance, negative stereotyping and stigmatization of, and discrimination, incitement to violence and violence against, persons based on religion or belief	Pakistan	Adopted without a vote	-
A/HRC/RES/22/32 Rights of the child: the right of the child to the enjoyment of the highest attainable standard of health	Ireland, Uruguay	Adopted without a vote	-
A/HRC/RES/22/33 Open-ended intergovernmental working group to consider the possibility of elaborating an international regulatory framework on the regulation, monitoring and oversight of the activities of private military and security companies	South Africa, Gabon	31 in favour, 11 against, 5 abstentions	Voted against
23rd Session (27 May-14 June)			
A/HRC/RES/23/3 Enhancement of international cooperation in the field of human rights	Iran	Adopted without a vote	-
A/HRC/RES/23/10 Promotion of the enjoyment of the cultural rights of everyone and respect for cultural diversity	Cuba	Adopted without a vote	-
A/HRC/RES/23/11 The effects of foreign debt and other related international financial obligations of States on the full enjoyment of all human rights, particularly economic, social and cultural rights	Cuba	30 in favour, 15 against, 2 abstentions	Voted against
A/HRC/RES/23/12 Human rights and international solidarity	Cuba	32 in favour, 15 against, 0 abstentions	Voted against
A/HRC/RES/23/13 Attacks and discrimination against persons with albinism	Gabon	Adopted without a vote	-

Resolution	State(s) presenting the resolution	Outcome of the voting process	Information regarding Italy
A/HRC/RES/23/14 Access to medicines in the context of the right of everyone to the enjoyment of the highest attainable standard of physical and mental health	Brazil	31 in favour, 0 against, 16 abstentions	Abstained
A/HRC/RES/23/15 Situation of human rights in Belarus	Ireland	26 in favour, 3 against, 18 abstentions	Voted in favour
A/HRC/RES/23/16 Promotion of the right to peace	Cuba	30 in favour, 9 against, 8 abstentions	Abstained
A/HRC/RES/23/17 National institutions for the promotion and protection of human rights	Australia	Adopted without a vote	-
A/HRC/RES/23/18 Technical assistance to the Central African Republic in the field of human rights	Gabon	Adopted without a vote	-
A/HRC/RES/23/20 Human rights of migrants	Mexico	Adopted without a vote	-
A/HRC/RES/23/21 Situation of human rights in Eritrea	Djibouti, Nigeria, Somalia	Adopted without a vote	-
A/HRC/RES/23/24 Technical assistance and capacity-building for South Sudan in the field of human rights	Gabon	Adopted without a vote	-
A/HRC/RES/23/25 Accelerating efforts to eliminate all forms of violence against women: preventing and responding to rape and other forms of sexual violence	Canada	Adopted without a vote	-
24th Session (9–27 September)			
A/HRC/RES/24/4 The right to development	Iran	46 in favour, 1 against, 0 abstentions	Voted in favour

Resolution	State(s) presenting the resolution	Outcome of the voting process	Information regarding Italy
A/HRC/RES/24/9 Human rights and indigenous peoples: mandate of the Special Rapporteur on the rights of indigenous peoples	Mexico, Guatemala	Adopted without a vote	-
A/HRC/RES/24/10 Human rights and indigenous peoples	Mexico, Guatemala	Adopted without a vote	-
A/HRC/RES/24/13 The use of mercenaries as a means of violating human rights and impeding the exercise of the right of peoples to self-determination	Cuba	31 in favour, 15 against, 1 abstention	Voted against
A/HRC/RES/24/14 Human rights and unilateral coercive measures	Iran	31 in favour, 15 against, 1 abstention	Voted against
A/HRC/RES/24/20 The human rights of older persons	Argentina, Brazil	Adopted without a vote	-
A/HRC/RES/24/25 The Social Forum	Cuba	Adopted without a vote	-
A/HRC/RES/24/26 From rhetoric to reality: a global call for concrete action against racism, racial discrimination, xenophobia and related intolerance	South Africa, Gabon	32 in favour, 2 against, 13 abstentions	Abstained
A/HRC/RES/24/28 Technical assistance for the Sudan in the field of human rights	Gabon	Adopted without a vote	-
A/HRC/RES/24/33 Technical cooperation for the prevention of attacks against persons with albinism	Gabon	Adopted without a vote	-
A/HRC/RES/24/35 Impact of arms transfers on human rights in armed conflict	Ecuador, Costa Rica, Peru	42 in favour, 1 against, 4 abstentions	Voted in favour

Sources: United Nations, Human Rights Council

B. Universal Periodic Review

With the 13th session of the UPR (21 May-4 June 2012), the Human Rights Council began the second cycle of review of all 193 United Nations Member States (2012–2016), which will focus first of all on ascertaining the level of implementation of the recommendations made during the first review cycle, as well as on the development of the overall situation of human rights in the individual Countries.

Italy underwent its Universal Periodic Review in 2010 (7th session) and will be reviewed again in 2014, during the 20th session of the UPR. During the previous review, 92 recommendations were made to Italy, of which it fully accepted 78, partially rejected 2 and fully rejected 12. Detailed information on the outcome of the first Universal Periodic Review for Italy is contained in the 2011 edition of the *Italian Yearbook of Human Rights* (pp. 169–173).

C. Special Procedures

In 2013, the Human Rights Council activated a new thematic Special Procedure (Independent Expert on the enjoyment of all human rights by elderly people) and two new Country mandates (Mali and the Central African Republic). Consequently, all told, there were 37 thematic Special Procedure and 14 Country mandates in operation at the Council.

Compared to the 7 reports from the same number of Special Procedures in 2010, the 5 in 2011 and the 2 in 2012, Italy was mentioned only in the report by the Special Rapporteur on the human rights of migrants. In 2013, moreover, two visits to Italy were made, by the Special Rapporteur on human trafficking and the Special Rapporteur on freedom of expression respectively.

1) *Report by the Special Rapporteur on the human rights of migrants, François Crépeau, on his mission to Italy* (30 September-8 October 2012. Doc. A/HRC/23/46/Add.3). During his mission, the Special Rapporteur visited Rome ("Ponte Galeria" Centre for Identification and Expulsion – CIE), Florence, Palermo, Trapani ("Milo" CIE), Bari ("Palese" CIE) and Castel Volturno, and was able to meet with Government and institutional figures, representatives of international organisations and civil society as well as migrants themselves, some of whom in an irregular situation (see *2013 Yearbook*, pp. 182–183). The Special Rapporteur recognises that Italy has developed a broad framework of laws and policies directed towards managing irregular migration and border management; however, much remains to be done in order to ensure full respect of the human rights of migrants in Italy. On these issues, the report includes the following recommendations.

A) *Normative and institutional framework for the protection of the human rights of migrants*. The Special Rapporteur invites Italy to:

– create a national institution for human rights in line with the Paris Principles, vested with the authority to investigate all issues relating to human rights, including those of migrants, regardless of their administrative status;

– establish a fully independent national preventive mechanism in accordance with the Optional Protocol to the Convention against Torture, which is mandated to visit all places where migrants may be deprived of their freedom;

– develop a national system of data collection, analysis and dissemination regarding immigration policies and practices, which should be used as a foundation for rights-based policy-making;

– ratify the International Convention on the Protection of the Rights of All Migrant Workers and Members of Their Families.

B) *Border Management.* Italy is requested to:

– fully respect the human rights of migrants in relation to the implementation of all readmission agreements entered into;

– ensure that readmission and cooperation agreements, aimed at, *inter alia*, combatting irregular migration, include safeguards to fully respect the human rights of migrants as well as ensure adequate protection of vulnerable migrants, including asylum seekers and refugees, in particular as regards the principle of *non-refoulement*;

– establish a comprehensive mechanism for the identification of unaccompanied minors that includes not only medical exams but also a psychosocial and cultural approach, in order to best identify specific protection measures in the best interests of each child;

– revoke the declaration (ordinance of 24/09/2011) of Lampedusa as not being a safe place for the disembarkation of migrants rescued at sea in order to maintain an effective system of search and rescue at sea;

– set up information services (providing information on international and national protection mechanisms in all landing points).

C) *Bilateral agreements.* The Special Rapporteur recommends that Italy:

– ensure bilateral agreements are negotiated and subsequently published in full transparency, highlighting the human rights protection mechanisms integrated at all stages;

– ensure that migration cooperation with Libya does not lead to any migrant being returned to Libyan shores, either by Italian authorities, or by Libyan authorities with the technical or logistical support of their Italian counterparts;

– prohibit the practice of informal automatic "push-backs" to Greece;

– ensure that "quick return" agreements, such as those with Tunisia and Egypt, adequately safeguard the human rights of migrants, and ensure proper and systematic individual screening for protection concerns, as well as guarantee full access by international and civil society organizations.

D) *Detention*. In this area, the Special Rapporteur recommends Italy to:

– ensure that migrants are detained only when they present a danger for themselves or others, or would abscond from future proceedings, always for the shortest time possible, and that non-custodial measures are always considered first as alternatives to detention;

– ensure that all detained migrants have access to proper medical care, interpreters, adequate food and clothes, hygienic conditions, adequate space to move around and access to outdoor exercise;

– systematically inform detained migrants in writing, in a language they understand, of the reason for their detention, its duration, their right to contact their family, to have access to a lawyer (which should be free of charge) and consular services and the right to challenge their detention and to seek asylum;

– guarantee the full access by international organisations, including UNHCR and IOM, civil society organisations, doctors, journalists and lawyers to all areas where migrants are held or detained, at all stages of the procedure, including in temporary reception centres;

– develop comprehensive training programmes on international human rights law and international refugee law for the justices of the peace and all staff who work in such centres;

– reduce the maximum period of immigration detention for the purposes of identification to 6 months.

E) *Asylum seekers*. Italy is requested to:

– ensure that all detained persons who claim protection concerns are, without delay, adequately informed of their right to seek asylum, have access to registration of asylum claims and can communicate with UNHCR, lawyers and civil society organisations;

– ensure that all decision-makers within the Territorial Commissions are adequately trained in asylum and human rights law in order to appropriately determine asylum claims;

– ensure that those migrants awaiting a judicial decision on their request to suspend repatriation procedures, following a negative decision made by the competent territorial commission, not be repatriated before the aforementioned decision is made.

F) *Other concerns*. Finally, the Special Rapporteur asks Italy to:

– provide access to basic services to everyone living in the Italian territory, regardless of their immigration status, in accordance with international human rights standards;

– take all necessary measures to execute of the judgment of the European Court of Human Rights in the *Hirsi* case;

– fully implement the EU directive introducing minimum standards on sanctions and measures against employers of illegally-staying third country nationals (directive 2009/52/EC of 18 June 2009);

– effectively sanction landlords who exploit migrants by housing them in inappropriate and unsanitary conditions;

– use terminology that does not reinforce prejudices against migrants and refrain from using charged expressions such as "illegal migrant" or "clandestini";

– Support, both technically and financially, civil society organisations which offer services and support to migrants, regardless of their administrative status, and especially those which help migrants defend their rights.

The Italian Government has sent the office of the High Commissioner for Human Rights a report containing comments and observations on the recommendations made by the Special Rapporteur on the rights of migrants following his mission to Italy (Doc. A/HRC/23/46/Add.6, 21 May 2013).

Concerning the *normative and institutional framework for the protection of the human rights of migrants*, the Government points out that the members of Parliament who participated in the parliamentary discussion on the ratification of the Optional Protocol to the Convention Against Torture (l. 9 November 2012, No. 195) expressed the wish that the functions of "National Mechanism of Prevention" be performed by the proposed National Commission for the promotion and the protection of human rights.

As concerns *border management*, Italy highlights the fact that art. 403 of the Italian civil code is applicable to unaccompanied migrant minors, and allows the Public Prosecutor with the juvenile court to place foreign minors in a foster community, where protection and suitable education programmes are provided, according to their needs. These provisions are normally applied to all unaccompanied foreign minors who enter Italy, regardless of the means by which they do so. As of 2011, following the so-called "Arab Spring" and the "North Africa Emergency", specific measures were adopted for the protection of these minors, with the assistance of local administrations. Specifically, law l. 135/2012 established a specific national fund for the reception of unaccompanied foreign minors, to ensure the challenges of the 2012 humanitarian emergency were met and allow for normal management of future migrant flows. The fund for 2012 amounted to 5 million euros, shared between the Municipalities charged with reception of the unaccompanied foreign minors.

With references to the *detention* of migrants, Italy points out that all detainees have the right to contact their families, as well as their lawyers, when they are arrested or when they enter a detention centre. Foreign detainees also have the right to ask that the consular authorities of their Country be informed of their arrest, as well as having the right to make phone calls and to be assisted by an interpreter during interviews or visits. The permanent presence of lawyers at the CIEs is guaranteed: if the detainee cooperates in the identification process, his or her stay in the Centre is short. Moreover, the Italian system generally ensures judicial review of the following measures:

– expulsion orders issued by the Prefect: this measure can be appealed before the appropriate local justice of peace, who has 20 days to decide from the date the appeal is lodged;

– preventive detention ordered by the Chief of Police: this measure is validated by a decree from the appropriate local justice of peace, who makes a decision within 48 hours of notification of the measure, which must be effected within 48 hours of the measure being applied to the person concerned. The validation order can be appealed at the Supreme Court;

– expulsion order issued by the Chief of Police: this measure is validated (after checking the formal and substantial requirements have been met) by a decree from the appropriate local justice of peace within 48 hours of notification, which must be effected within 48 hours of the order being served to the person concerned. The validation order can be appealed at the Supreme Court.

As concerns further developments of the *Hirsi* case, Italy reiterates the fact that the April 2012 agreement ("Processo verbale") lays the basis for renewed cooperation between the two Countries, with clear reference to respect of the human rights of migrants, also during the stay of irregular migrants in Libyan reception centres. At the same time, all individuals intercepted at sea are currently taken to specific centres in Italy in order to evaluate their individual situations, in line with all guarantees offered by the European Convention on Human Rights. Following the meeting on 7 March 2013, the Committee of Ministers of the Council of Europe expressed its satisfaction with the measures taken, and considered that Italy had respected the provisions of the judgment.

Finally, Italy noted that the EU directive introducing minimum standards on sanctions and measures against employers of illegally-staying third country nationals was implemented under lgs.d. 16 July 2012, No. 109. On the question of sanctions, Italy remarks that the phenomenon of so-called "caporalato" (gangmaster system) has been tackled not only by the aforementioned legislative decree, but also by more substantial legal provisions implemented by l.d. 13 August 2011, No. 138 (Further urgent measures for financial stabilisation and development), which introduced a new type of offence into the criminal code: "illegal intermediation and exploitation of labour" (art. 603-bis of the criminal code). The new article reads "whoever carries out an organised intermediation activity, recruiting labour or organising work involving exploitation, by means of violence, threats, or intimidation, taking advantage of the state of necessity or needs of the workers, shall be punished with a prison sentence of five to eight years and a fine of €1,000–2,000 for each worker recruited".

2) *Visit of the Special Rapporteur on the trafficking in persons, especially women and children, Joy Ngozi Ezeilo* (12–20 September 2013). During her mission to Italy, the Special Rapporteur visited Rome, Venice, Turin, Palermo, Naples, Caserta and Castel Volturno, and met with local and national officials, representatives of non-governmental organisations and a number of victims originating from Africa, Europe, Asia and Latin America. The Special Rapporteur observed that trafficking to Italy is continually on the rise, more so since the increase in migratory flows caused by the so-called "Arab Spring". More in detail, trafficking for sexual exploitation, which involves mainly women from Nigeria and eastern Europe, is the most widespread and best documented form of exploitation, although not the only one requiring attention from the authorities. Consequently, although she recognised that Italy does on the whole have sufficient anti-trafficking legislation, at the close of her mission the Special Rapporteur urged the Italian Government to strengthen and better coordinate measures against the trafficking of persons, especially by developing mechanisms for permanent monitoring and evaluation of the situation, so as to improve the impact of these measures and the protection of victims. Her observations will be contained in a report that the Special Rapporteur is due to present to the Human Rights Council in June 2014.

3) *Visit of the Special Rapporteur on the freedom of opinion and expression, Frank La Rue* (11–18 November 2013). The aim of his mission was to understand and assess, in a spirit of cooperation and dialogue, the situation on the right to freedom of opinion and expression in Italy and the measures taken for its realisation. The Special Rapporteur was particularly interested in analysing media-related regulations, especially those in respect of oversight and ownership, as well as issues related to privacy and hate speech. In the course of his visit, the Special Rapporteur met with members of the Government (including the Minister for Integration, Cécile Kyenge, and the Deputy Minister for Foreign Affairs, Marta Dassù), members of Parliament, of the Judiciary, representatives of civil

society, lawyers and journalists. At the end of his visit, and in advance of the conclusions of a more substantial report which he is to present to the United Nations Human Rights Council in June 2014, the Special Rapporteur made some preliminary observations and recommendations, urging the Italian Government to make the national media system more democratic, by distributing concessions of broadcasting frequencies fairly and ensuring that the elections of the board members of the regulatory bodies are transparent. Of the many recommendations made, those relative to the following areas are highlighted.

– *National Human Rights Institution.* The Special Rapporteur, in expressing his support of the bill for the establishment of a human rights commission presented in parliament in February, encourages such institution being established without further delays and in accordance with the Paris Principles.

– *Access to information law.* The Special Rapporteur considers current legislation on access to information (Transparency decree of 14 March 2013) should extend further to increase the transparency and credibility of all state institutions. Moreover, access to information laws should also be accompanied with the establishment of an independent state authority to guarantee the exercise of this right and the effectiveness of this law.

– *Decriminalisation of defamation.* Commenting on the bill to amend the defamation law (act C.925), approved by the Chamber of Deputies in October and currently being examined by the Senate, the Special Rapporteur recommends total decriminalisation of the offence of defamation and that it is reclassified as a civil offence, considering that a criminal action, even if it does not provide for a prison sentence to be handed down, can still have an intimidator effect on journalists. In connection with this, the Special Rapporteur recalls resolution 1577 (2007) of the Council of Europe Parliamentary Assembly, which, in order to safeguard freedom of expression, recommends complete decriminalisation of defamation. Following this resolution, defamation, libel and slander have been reclassified as civil offences in many European Countries.

– *Hate speech.* According to art. 20 of the International Covenant on Civil and Political Rights hate speech against any group must not be tolerated in a democratic State. The Special Rapporteur expressed particular concern over hate speech towards migrants and other minorities during election campaigns: a phenomenon which is becoming ever more frequent in many European Countries, also as a consequence of the financial crisis. The Special Rapporteur expresses his full support for the efforts made by the Italian Government to combat this situation, also through awareness-raising programmes, including information and education campaigns which can contribute to eradicating prejudice and ignorance, often the root causes of these unacceptable attitudes and behaviours.

The Special Rapporteur also welcomes the proposed bill on homophobia and transphobia, however he believes that further amendments should be made in order to eliminate all exceptions for institutions or particular groups. Moreover he encourages Parliament to consider introducing a law on other forms of hate speech, such as incitements to violence against women or persons with disabilities.

– *Transparency in media ownership and control.* Recalling the recommendations made in 2005 by the European Commission for democracy through the Council of Europe (the so-called Venice Commission), the Special Rapporteur renews the request to implement a legislative reform which would introduce the explicit incompatibility between holding elected or Government offices and ownership of media. This reform should also establish an obligation to disclose the full identity of the ownership of the media and the mechanisms on decision-making and control therein. This information should be made accessible to the public by the Communications Regulatory Body (AGCOM), as should information on the sources of revenue of the media.

The Anti-Trust body should also be the subject of legislative reform, so that Italy can overcome the excessive concentration of media and the possible establishment of monopolies, which limit diversity and plurality of freedom of expression and challenge democracy.

– *AGCOM.* The Special Rapporteur is concerned by the role of AGCOM in establishing penalties with regard to intellectual property, as this should be under the purview of Parliament. Indeed, while AGCOM may by law apply some limitations on on-line contents, the taking-down of an on-line content should be decided by the courts on a case-by-case basis.

– *Public broadcasting service.* While reiterating his support for the existence of a public service alongside private broadcasting, the Special Rapporteur nonetheless emphasises the necessity of ensuring the independence of the public service. The fact that two out of the nine board members of the RAI are appointed by the Government, and that the concession on the frequencies used by RAI, as well as the public service itself, is granted by the Ministry of Economic Development, can have a serious impact on the independence of the public system. For this reason, the Special Rapporteur recommends that the RAI should be established as an independent body of the State, be administered as a public asset, and that the appointment of members of the board be conducted in a transparent manner.

– *Protection of journalists.* During his visit, the Special Rapporteur heard some accounts from journalists who had been threatened, intimidated or attacked in the exercise of their profession: in many cases, these attacks went unpunished. The Special Rapporteur therefore calls upon Parliament to enact legislation that would establish the crime of intimidation, threats, harassment and acts of violence against journalists and social communicators.

The table below shows the visits made by Special Rapporteurs in recent years, those agreed (but not yet carried out) and those merely requested by Special Rapporteurs.

Visits carried out and reports	Agreed visits	Requested visits
Special Rapporteur on the independence of judges and lawyers (11–14 March 2002). Preliminary Report: E/CN.4/2002/72/Add.3	Independent expert on extreme poverty and human rights (dates to be confirmed)	Special Rapporteur on the independence of judges and lawyers (visit requested in July 2013)
Special Rapporteur on the human rights of migrants (7–18 June 2004). Report: E/CN.4/2005/85/Add.3		
Special Rapporteur on the right to freedom of opinion and expression (20–29 October 2004). Report: E/CN.4/2005/64/Add.1		
Special Rapporteur on contemporary forms of racism (9–13 October 2006). Report: A/HRC/4/19/Add.4		
Working group on arbitrary detention (3–14 November 2008). Report: A/HRC/10/21/Add.5		
Special Rapporteur on violence against women (15–26 January 2012) Report: A/HRC/20/16/Add.2		
Special Rapporteur on the rights of Migrants (30 September-8 October 2012). Report: A/HRC/23/46/Add.3		
Special Rapporteur on trafficking in persons (12–20 September 2013) Report to be presented in June 2014		
Special Rapporteur on freedom of opinion and expression (11–18 November 2013) Report to be presented in June 2014		

Source: United Nations Human Rights Council.

Finally, on 18 July 2013 Italy was sent a joint note by the Special Rapporteur on the human rights of migrants, the Special Rapporteur on torture and the Special Rapporteur on the independence of judges and lawyers, urging the Italian authorities to undertake all measures necessary to allow the return to Italy of the Kazakh citizen Alma Shalabayeva and her six-year-old daughter, who were deported to Kazakhstan on 31 May 2013. According to the United Nations experts, the circumstances of the deportation gave rise to the appearance that this was in fact an extraordinary rendition; the actions of the Italian authorities had violated guarantees of due process and deprived Ms. Shalabayeva of her right to appeal against deportation and to apply for asylum. Moreover, the Italian authorities also appeared to have ignored concerns that Ms. Shalabayeva might be at risk of being persecuted, tortured or subjected to other forms of ill-treatment upon her forcible return to Kazakhstan due to her husband's political activities. On the other hand, the experts were pleased that the Italian authorities had decided to officially revoke the deportation order and they welcomed the announcement that investigations were under way to determine responsibility for the illegal expulsion; they also reminded the Italian authorities that they have an obligation, under international law, to provide for an effective remedy to the victims of the violation of human rights. Finally, they appealed to the Italian and Kazakh authorities to reach a diplomatic agreement to facilitate the rapid return to Italy of Ms. Shalabayeva and her daughter.

III. High Commissioner for Human Rights (OHCHR)

The Office was established by the General Assembly in December 1993 with resolution 48/141.

The High Commissioner has a very broad mandate which includes the prevention of violations of human rights, ensuring the respect of all human rights, coordinating all United Nations activities involving human rights and strengthening national systems for protecting human rights and the rule of law. In this context, one of the crucial strategic activities for the High Commissioner's Office is supporting the introduction and development of independent human rights commissions at the national level.

In order to fulfil its mandate, the Office of the High Commissioner has consolidated its presence "on the ground", establishing 10 regional offices and the same number of national offices, sending its own experts on integrated United Nations peace missions or planning independent fact-finding operations, as well as mainstreaming the human rights component in United Nations teams' activities at Country or Programme level, and in those of specialised agencies of the United Nations (such as UNDP). In 2013, the High Commissioner for Human Rights was Navanethem Pillay (South Africa), who has held the post since 2008. On 15 March 2013, the Italian Flavia Pansieri was appointed Deputy High Commissioner for Human Rights.

On 4 October 2013, Italy was sent a note by the Office of the High Commissioner concerning the tragic shipwreck off Lampedusa on 3 October, which caused the death of hundreds of refugees and migrants, mainly from Eritrea. After expressing grief over the victims, the High Commissioner's Office stated its appreciation for the Italian authorities' efforts to handle the issue according to international human rights law and with respect for the dignity of all human beings, with particular reference to the national day of mourning declared by the Government. These efforts are important and mark a significant and long-awaited change in the attitude of the Italian authorities. The High Commissioner's Office also requested the Italian authorities and the international community, especially the European Union, to redouble its efforts to avoid such tragedies happening again and to tackle the root causes of the problem by really improving the human rights situation in the Countries of origin of the migrants so that people no longer feel the need to risk their lives by undertaking extremely perilous journeys.

The High Commissioner's Office is funded one-third by the ordinary budget of the United Nations, approved by the General Assembly every two years; the remaining two thirds of the budget comes from voluntary contributions, mostly from States, but also from international organisations, foundations, commercial enterprises and private citizens.

In 2013, Italy contributed to the budget of the High Commissioner's Office with funds for about 68,000 dollars (ranking 42nd among donors), about 25,000 dollars less than the previous year, when it ranked 40th among donors (see graph below).

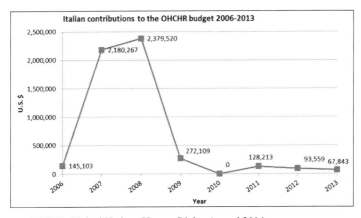

Source: OHCHR, United Nations Human Rights Appeal 2014.

IV. High Commissioner for Refugees (UNHCR)

This Office was established by the United Nations General Assembly on 14 December 1950, with resolution A/RES/428(V).

The mandate of the Agency is to coordinate international action for the protection of refugees and the resolution of their problems all over the world. Its primary mission is the protection of the rights and wellbeing of refugees and to ensure that all of them can exercise their right to request asylum and seek safe refuge in another State, with the option to return voluntarily to their home country, integrate locally or to resettle into a third country. The remit of the UNHCR also includes assistance to stateless persons.

In 2013 the High Commissioner for Refugees was António Guterres (Portugal), elected by the General Assembly for the first time in 2005 and re-elected in 2010 for a second five-year mandate.

The UNHCR has had its own office in Rome since 1953. The Italian office participates in the procedures to determine refugee status in Italy and performs other duties regarding international protection, training, dissemination of information on refugees and asylum-seekers in Italy and in the various crisis areas all over the world, raising public awareness and fund-raising with Governments, companies and from individual donors. Since 2006, the Italian UNHCR Office has become a Regional Office, with responsibilities for Albania, Cyprus, Greece, Malta, Portugal, San Marino and the Holy See in addition to Italy. In 2013 the position of UNHCR Spokesperson in Italy, covered until 2012 by Laura Boldrini, was filled by Laurens Jolles (the Netherlands), Regional UNHCR Representative for Italy and Southern Europe.

In January 2013, the UNHCR published the paper "Italia Paese di Protezione? (Is Italy a Country offering protection?)", which highlights the persistent gaps in the national system for protecting, receiving and integrating asylum-seekers and refugees. Based on this analysis, the UNHCR drew up some recommendations for the improvement of the Italian system.

– *Access to Italian territory*. In order to assist in the respect of the principle of *non-refoulement*, the UNHCR requests Italy to include suitable clauses for the protection of asylum-seekers and refugees in any agreements made to combat irregular immigration, in particular in its agreement with Libya. Border control mechanisms should ensure timely information about the possibility of lodging an asylum claim is provided, before any measures are taken to remove the person. Specifically, the support and information services to be provided pursuant to the Consolidated Law on immigration should be made available to all people potentially in need of some form of international protection, not merely to those who have already expressed their intention to seek asylum, and the services should be extended to the migrant landing areas in Apulia, Calabria, Sicily and Sardinia.

– *Procedures*. In order to improve the current system, UNHCR requests the Italian authorities to consider the possibility of establishing an independent administrative authority which would take responsibility for the procedure of recognising international protection. Further, provisions should be introduced allowing increases in the numbers and size of the Territorial Commissions based on the number of requests lodged. Finally, the Regulations implementing lgs.d. 25/2008 on the asylum-granting process should be adopted.

– *Holding and repatriation*. The UNHCR welcomes the fact that Italian law does not mandate the holding of asylum-seekers, except in special cases; however, it feels further guarantees should be introduced enabling people already held or detained to gain access to the procedure. Concern is also expressed over the extension of the maximum duration of the holding period for migrants to eighteen months, without providing for any enhancement of guarantees of respect for the rights of people held, nor an improvement in the conditions in which they are held. Strengthening of the measures for assisted voluntary return would also be desirable.

– *Reception*. The UNHCR considers a reorganisation of the reception system necessary to harmonise the very different reception conditions and standards, currently provided by several different types of structures. However, the assistance and services provided to asylum-seekers and refugees should be tailored to their distinct needs, ensuring adequate support to the former while awaiting the decision on their status, whereas refugees need measures to facilitate their integration into Italian society. In this context, SPRAR system should be strengthened and oriented towards specialisation in the latter type of reception. UNHCR calls upon the Italian Government to increase its current reception capacity and to strengthen its existing monitoring and quality control of reception conditions.

– *Integration*. With a view to assisting the integration of those granted international protection, UNHCR calls on Italy to review and amend its current legal and administrative processes in order to remove bureaucratic obstacles, including those regarding registration of residency and recognition of educational qualifications, which have a negative impact on the process of socio-economic integration of refugees. Beneficiaries of international protection should also be facilitated in the granting of a European Union residency permit for those staying long-term.

– *Institutional communications*. UNHCR calls on politicians and representatives of the institutions to use terminology reflecting greater understanding of migrant flows in their communications, and to adopt affirmative actions for the dissemination of proper information, in order to avoid the spread of common use of denigratory or discriminatory expressions such as the word "clandestino" when referring to asylum-seekers, refugees and migrants.

– *Citizenship*. In order to foster the full integration of refugees into Italian society, and while awaiting the possible full-scale overhaul of citizenship laws, the process for their naturalisation should be further facilitated, as provided by art. 35 of the Geneva Convention.

– *Statelessness*. UNHCR calls on Italy to show greater commitment to tackling the issue of statelessness and take steps to avoid future cases of stateless people by adopting the 1961 Convention on the Reduction of Statelessness. Moreover, the procedure for recognising people as stateless should be regulated in a clear and transparent manner. Finally, Italy should adopt measures to prevent statelessness and facilitate access to Italian citizenship for members of the Roma and Sinti communities, particularly for children born in Italy.

– *Governance*. The "emergency measures" approach to granting asylum which has to date been prevalent in Italy should be replaced by systematic planning of interventions, supported by sufficient funding and multi-level governance, which should include the participation of the relevant ministries, the Regions, local authorities and civil society. Consequently, UNHCR calls on Italy to consider setting up a steering committee charged with rationalising and optimising the resources dedicated to the various sectors of the system, ensuring adequate standards and coordinating measures to foster the integration of beneficiaries of international protection, both socially and into the labour market.

In July 2013, the UNHCR published the document "Recommendations on important aspects of refugee protection in Italy", with a view to further strengthening Italian asylum policies and practices and aligning the handling of refugees' rights with international and European standards. The paper presents 40 recommendations, many of which are updates or extensions of recommendations already contained in the January 2013 paper; they refer in particular to: access to Italian territory and the principle of *non-refoulement*; protection of unaccompanied minors; access to the asylum procedure; quality of the asylum procedure in Italy; reception conditions for asylum-seekers; local integration of refugees; and UNHCR's work for refugees elsewhere in the world.

According to data provided by UNHCR, in January 2013 there were 71,264 people coming under the agency's responsibility resident in Italy (-1,497 compared to January 2012), of whom 64,779 refugees (+6,719 compared to 2012), 6,015 asylum-seekers (-7,510) and 470 stateless persons (-706).

In 2013, particularly following the numerous arrivals of boats crossing the Mediterranean, 27,800 asylum claims were lodged in Italy (+60% compared to 2012, but well below the peak of 34,100 claims reached in 2011, the year of the so-called "Arab Spring" in north African nations), a figure which places Italy seventh in the ranking of the 44 industrialised nations with the highest number of asylum seekers (with about 5% of all claims). Nigeria is the Country of origin of the highest number of asylum-seekers in Italy (3,500 claims recorded, more than double those of 2012), followed by Pakistan (3,300 claims), Somalia (2,900 claims, four times those of 2012) and Eritrea (2,200, triple the 2012 number).

Further data are needed to gain better understanding of the capacity of each Country to accept asylum-seekers: the number of asylum claims in proportion to national population and wealth, expressed in terms of GDP per capita. With reference to the first indicator, between 2009 and 2013 Malta and Sweden received, on average, the highest number of asylum claims in proportion to their population: 20.2 and 19.2 claims per 1,000 inhabitants respectively. Italy is in 21st place, with 1.8 claims per 1,000 inhabitants. With reference to the second indicator, between 2009 and 2013, Germany and France were on average the Countries receiving the highest number of asylum claims: 7.5 and 7.3 claims per dollar of GDP per capita. Italy is in seventh place, with 3.6 claims per dollar of GDP per capita.

In 2013, Italy contributed to the UNHCR budget with an allocation of approximately 9.3 million dollars, representing a decrease of about 3.4 million dollars compared to the previous year (see graph below).

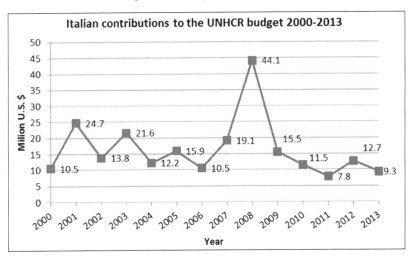

V. Human Rights Treaty Bodies

Over the years, the United Nations have created an organic International Bill of Human Rights, whose core is made up of the nine conventions listed below: the Convention for the Elimination of All Forms of Racial Discrimination (ICERD, 1965); the Covenant on Civil and Political Rights (ICCPR, 1966); the Covenant on Economic, Social and Cultural Rights (ICESCR, 1966); the Convention on the Elimination of All Forms of Discrimination against Women (CEDAW, 1969); the Convention against Torture and other Cruel, Inhuman or Degrading Treatment or Punishment (CAT, 1984); the Convention on the Rights of the Child (CRC, 1989); the Convention on the Protection of the Rights of all Migrant Workers and Members of Their Families (ICRMW, 1990); the Convention on the Rights of Persons with Disabilities (CRPD, 2006); the Convention for the Protection of All Persons from Enforced Disappearance (CPED, 2006).

Italy has ratified seven conventions and their related optional protocols (as shown in the chart below). It has signed but not yet ratified the CPED (in 2007), the Optional Protocol to ICESCR (in 2009) and the Optional Protocol to the CRC on the communications procedure (in 2012); it has not yet signed the ICRMW. On 3 April 2013 Italy deposited the instrument of ratification of the Optional Protocol to the CAT (signed in 2003) with the Secretariat-General of the United Nations.

Convention	Ratification Law	Declarations/ Reservations	Recognition of competence of specific Committees
ICERD	l. 13 October 1975, No. 654	Yes (art. 4)	Individual communications (art. 14): Yes
ICESCR	l. 25 October 1977, No. 881	No	-
ICCPR	l. 25 October 1977, No. 881	Yes (art. 15.1 and 19.3)	Inter-State communications (art. 41): Yes
OP – 1	l. 25 October 1977, No. 881	Yes (art. 5.2)	-
OP – 2	l. 9 December 1994, No. 734	No	-
CEDAW	l. 14 March 1985, No. 132	Yes (general)	-
OP	Deposit date of ratification instrument: 22/09/2000	No	Inquiry procedure (art. 8 and 9): Yes

CAT	l. 3 November 1988, No. 498	No	Individual communications (art. 22): Yes Inter-State communications (art. 21): Yes Inquiry procedure (art. 20): Yes
CRC	l. 27 May 1991, No. 176	No	-
OP – AC	l. 11 March 2002, No. 46	Binding declaration in accordance with art. 3: 17 years old	-
OP – SC	l. 11 March 2002, No. 46	No	-
CRPD	l. 3 March 2009, No. 18	No	-
OP	l. 3 March 2009, No. 18	No	Inquiry procedure (art. 6 and 7): No

Legend:
OP = Optional Protocol
OP – AC = Optional Protocol to the Convention on the Rights of the Child on the Involvement of Children in Armed Conflict
OP – SC = Optional Protocol to the Convention on the Rights of the Child on the Sale of Children, Child Prostitution and Child Pornography.

Besides enunciating fundamental rights therein, the United Nations have set up control mechanisms for each treaty, the so-called Committees or Treaty Bodies, each comprising from 10 to 23 independent experts, selected on the basis of their high moral character and recognised expertise in the field of human rights.

In 2013, Alessio Bruni was a member of the Committee against Torture; Bianca Maria Pomeranzi was on the Committee on the Elimination of Discrimination against Women; and Maria Rita Parsi member of the Committee on the Rights of the Child.

The principal duty of the Committees is to examine the periodic reports on the implementation in States Parties of the terms of the internationally binding rules, which the States Parties are under obligation to submit regularly (normally every 4 or 5 years). In addition to this procedure, some Committees can monitor implementation through three further mechanisms: by conducting country enquiries (in the field); by examining inter-state communications and by examining individual complaints. Finally, the Committees publish their interpretation of the contents of provisions on human rights, the so-called

General comments (for further detail on these functions, see *2011 Yearbook*, p. 180).

Italy is subject to monitoring by seven Committees, as shown in the table below. In 2013, Italy presented a follow-up report to the Committee for the Elimination of Racial Discrimination; no concluding observations were made.

Italy's cooperation with United Nations Treaty Bodies

Committee	Total number of reports	Latest report	Latest concluding observations	Reporting status
CERD	18	July 2011	March 2012	XIX and XX joint report: to be submitted in February 2015
CESCR	5	August 2012	-	V report: submitted and awaiting discussion
CCPR	5	March 2004	April 2006	VI report: overdue since October 2009
CEDAW	6	December 2009	August 2011	VII report: to be submitted in July 2015
CAT	4	May 2004	July 2007	VI report: overdue since July 2011
CRC	4	January 2009	October 2011	V and VI joint report: to be presented in April 2017
OP – AC	2	January 2009	October 2011	Information on the implementation of the Protocol to be included in the V and VI joint report
OP – SC	2	January 2009	October 2011	Information on the implementation of the Protocol to be included in the V and VI joint report
CRPD	1	November 2012	-	I report: submitted and awaiting discussion

A. Committee on Economic, Social and Cultural Rights

In 2013 the Committee held two sessions: the 50th (29 April-17 May) and the 51st (4–29 November). During the 50th session, reports from Azerbaijan, Denmark, Iran, Jamaica, Japan, Ruanda and Togo were considered; during the 51st, those of Albania, Austria, Belarus, Belgium, Bosnia Herzegovina, Djibuti, Egypt, Gabon, Kuwait and Norway. No General comments were adopted during the year.

Italy presented (but has not yet discussed) its latest report in August 2012 (see *2013 Yearbook*, pp. 191–197).

B. Human Rights Committee (civil and political rights)

In 2013 the Committee held three sessions: the 107th (11–28 March), the 108th (8–26 July) and the 109th (14 October-1 November). The 107th session examined the reports from Angola, China (Hong Kong), China (Macau), Paraguay, Peru and Belize (without there being any report for the latter); the 108th session the reports from Albania, the Czech Republic, Finland, Indonesia, Tajikistan and Ukraine; the 109th the reports from Bolivia, Djibouti, Mauritania, Mozambique and Uruguay. No General comments were adopted in 2013.

The last periodic report on Italy was discussed by the Committee in October 2005, during its 85th session (see *2011 Yearbook*, pp. 184–186). Italy should have submitted its sixth report in October 2009, but as of 31 December 2013, it had not yet discharged its duty in this respect.

C. Committee against Torture

In 2013 the Committee held two sessions: the 50th (6–31 May) and the 51st (28 October-22 November). During the 50th session, the reports from Bolivia, Estonia, Guatemala, Japan, Kenya, Mauritania, the Netherlands, the Netherlands (Antilles), the Netherlands (Aruba) and the United Kingdom were examined; during the 51st, those from Andorra, Belgium, Burkina Faso, Kyrgyzstan, Latvia, Mozambique, Poland, Portugal and Uzbekistan. No General comments were adopted during the year.

Italy's last periodic report was discussed by the Committee in May 2007, during its 38th session (see *2011 Yearbook*, pp. 187–188). Italy should have submitted its sixth report in July 2011, but as of 31 December 2013, it had not yet discharged its duty in this respect. This report will have to supply detailed answers to the list of issues that the Committee prepared in the course of its 43rd session (November 2009) and forwarded to the Italian Government in January 2010 (see doc. CAT/C/ITA/Q/6).

D. Committee on the Elimination of Racial Discrimination

In 2013 the Committee held two sessions: the 82nd (11 February-1 March) and the 83rd (12–30 August). During the 82nd session, reports from

Algeria, the Dominican Republic, Kyrgyzstan, Mauritius, New Zealand, the Russian Federation and Slovakia were considered; in the 83rd those of Belarus, Burkina Faso, Chad, Chile, Cyprus, Jamaica, Sweden and Venezuela. General recommendation No. 35 was also adopted, concerning combating racist hate speech.

Italy's latest periodic report was considered by the Committee on March 2012 in the course of the 80th session (see the *2013 Yearbook*, pp. 198–201). On that occasion, the Committee asked the Italian Government to provide detailed information within a year as to how it intended to follow up the recommendations concerning the human rights of Roma, Sinti and travellers contained in the concluding observations. The Committee specifically recommended that Italy should put an end to the practice of forced evictions; provide adequate alternative accommodation to the Roma and Sinti communities; avoid locating Roma and Sinti in camps situated far from residential areas and without access to basic social, healthcare and educational facilities; provide effective remedy for the negative consequences brought about by the implementation of the "nomad emergency decree".

In response to this request, on 9 July 2013 Italy presented its follow-up report (doc. CERD/C/ITA/CO/16–18/ADD.1). In this report, the Government states that its "National Strategy for the Inclusion of Roma, Sinti and travellers Communities", adopted in February 2012, aimed to definitively overcome the emergency phase, which characterised past years. To this end, the Government has established an inter-ministerial steering committee comprising the Ministry for Integration, the Ministry of Labour and Social Policies, the Ministry of the Interior, the Ministry of Health, the Ministry of Education, Universities and Research and the Ministry of Justice, as well as a system of multi-level governance which includes the National Anti-Racial Discrimination Office, local and regional bodies, representatives of civil society and of the Roma, Sinti and travellers' communities. Moreover, the implementation of the Strategy involves:

– establishing of four thematic working groups on housing, education, labour and health;

– establishing further working groups to collect data which will be essential to making proper political choices and to studying the disparate legal status of Roma without papers who arrived in Italy following the conflicts in the Balkans (*de facto* stateless persons), in order to identify possible legislative paths to be undertaken;

– ongoing monitoring of national and EU funding, to ensure the viability of the aforementioned objectives.

The National Strategy also requires rethinking the "camp system", that is to say, large-scale settlements located on the fringes of urban areas. It is estimated that about 40,000 people live in such camps in Italy, mainly in the Municipalities of Turin, Genoa, Milan, Brescia, Pavia, Padua, Bologna, Reggio Emilia, Rome, Naples, Bari and Foggia. In recent years, however, there has been an increase in best practice implemented by local administrations, proving that the local dimension makes integration processes feasible. Inclusive residential solutions can only be realised if they are accompanied by social policies: the move from "camp" to "home" (or to the "community" or so-called "micro-area") needs promoting in the context of a comprehensive programme which is not limited to the mere building and assigning of housing.

Finally, the National Strategy has allowed amendments to law l. 431/1998 on the system for rent control. During the XVI legislature, there was much parliamentary activity concerning housing policies, particularly on the introduction of measures to help disadvantaged people gain access to social housing (art. 11 of l.d. 112/2008, "Piano casa" – housing plan). In 2009, the Government also introduced the National Plan for Residential Housing, with the objective of guaranteeing the respect of the minimum standards in residential housing at the national level. The National Strategy mentions a vast array of possible housing options which Municipalities can adopt, such as: social housing, support for the purchase or rent of private housing, renting of houses and farms which are publicly owned.

E. Committee on the Elimination of Discrimination against Women

In 2013 the Committee held three sessions: the 54th (11 February-1 March), 55th (8–26 July) and 56th (30 September-18 October). At the 54th session, reports from Angola, Austria, Cyprus, Greece, Hungary, Pakistan, former Yugoslav Republic of Macedonia were considered; at the 55th those of Afghanistan, Bosnia Herzegovina, Cape Verde, Cuba, the Democratic Republic of Congo, the Dominican Republic, Serbia, the United Kingdom, the United Kingdom (Crown Dependencies) and the United Kingdom (Overseas Territories); at the 56th those of Andorra, Benin, Cambodia, Colombia, Republic of Moldova, the Seychelles and Tajikistan. Two General recommendations were also adopted, No. 29 on the economic consequences of marriage, family relations and their dissolution (art. 16 of the Convention against all Forms of Discrimination against Women), and No. 30 on the role of women in conflict prevention, conflict and post-conflict situations.

Italy's latest report was discussed by the Committee in July 2011, during its 49th session (see the *2012 Yearbook*, pp. 191–194). Italy is due to submit its seventh report in July 2015.

F. Committee on the Rights of the Child

In 2013 the Committee held three sessions: the 62nd (14 January-1 February), 63rd (27 May-14 June) and 64th (16 September-4 October). Reports considered during the 62nd session were from Guinea, Guyana, Malta, Niue and Uzbekistan; at the 63rd those of Armenia, Guinea-Bissau, Israel, Rwanda, Slovenia and Uzbekistan; at the 64th the reports from China, China (Hong Kong), China (Macau), Kuwait, Lithuania, Luxembourg, Monaco, Sao Tome and Principe, and Tuvalu. General comment No. 14 was also adopted on the right of the child to have his or her best interests taken as a primary consideration (art. 3, para. 1 of the Convention on the Rights of the Child).

Italy's latest periodic report was discussed by the Committee in September 2011, during the 58th session (see *2012 Yearbook*, pp. 195–199). Italy is due to present its joint fifth and sixth report in 2017.

G. Committee on the Rights of Persons with Disabilities

In 2013 the Committee held two sessions, the 9th (15–19 April) and the 10th (2–13 September), during which concluding observations were adopted concerning Paraguay (9th session), Australia, Austria and El Salvador (10th). No General comments were adopted in 2013.

Italy presented, but has not yet discussed, its first periodic report in November 2012 (see *2013 Yearbook*, pp. 202–212).

H. Committee on Migrant Workers

In 2013 the Committee held two sessions, the 18th (15–26 April) and 19th (9–13 September), during which concluding observations were adopted concerning Azerbaijan, Bolivia, Colombia (18th session), Burkina Faso and Morocco (19th session). General comment No. 2 was also adopted, on the rights of migrant workers in an irregular situation and members of their families.

Italy has not ratified the Convention on the Protection of the Rights of all Migrant Workers and Members of their Families and, consequently, is not subject to monitoring by the Committee.

I. Committee on Enforced Disappearances

In 2013 the Committee held two meetings relating to organisational issues, the 4th (8–19 April) and the 5th (4–15 November), during which concluding observations were adopted concerning France, Uruguay (4th session), Argentina and Spain (5th session).

Italy has not ratified the Convention for the Protection of All Persons from Enforced Disappearance and, consequently, is not subject to monitoring by the Committee.

VI. Specialised United Nations Agencies, Programmes and Funds

A. *International Labour Organisation (ILO)*

Established by the Treaty of Versailles in 1919, the ILO became the first specialised agency of the United Nations in 1946.

The ILO is devoted to promoting decent and productive work for men and women in conditions of freedom, equality, safety and dignity. Its chief objectives are: to promote rights at work, to encourage decent employment opportunities, to enhance social protection and to strengthen dialogue on work-related issues. The ILO is the only United Nations agency which has a tripartite structure: representatives of governments, employers and workers jointly elaborate the policies and programmes of the Organisation. 185 States are members of the ILO.

Since its foundation, the ILO has adopted 189 conventions. Of these, the ILO has identified 8 which it defines as "fundamental" or "core" (No. 29 on Forced Labour, 1930; No. 87 on Freedom of Association and Protection of the Right to Organise, 1948; No. 98 on the Right to Organise and Collective Bargaining, 1949; No. 100 on Equal Remuneration for Men and Women Workers for Work of Equal Value, 1951; No. 105 on the Abolition of Forced Labour, 1957; No. 111 on the Elimination of All Forms of Discrimination in Employment, Occupation, Vocational Training and Terms and Conditions of Employment, 1958; No. 138 on the Minimum Age for Admission to Employment or Work, 1973; and No. 182 on the Elimination of the Worst Forms of Child Labour, 1999) and 4 defined as "priority" (or "governance": No. 81 on Labour Inspection, 1947; No. 122 on Employment Policy, 1964; No. 129 on Labour Inspection [Agriculture], 1969; and No. 144 on Tripartite Consultation [International Labour Standards], 1976).

Italy has been a member of the ILO since 1919 (it is one of the founding members); it withdrew from the Organisation in 1937 but joined again permanently in 1945. The ILO is present in Italy with its offices in Rome, which have been operating since 1920, and the International Training Centre, established in Turin in 1965.

Italy has ratified 113 conventions adopted by the ILO (of which 82 in force and 31 denounced), including the 8 fundamental ones, the 4 priority ones and 101 of the 177 technical conventions: in 2013 it ratified two technical conventions: Convention No. 189 on Domestic Workers and the Convention on Maritime Labour.

The complete list, updated to December 2013, of ILO conventions and of Italy's acceptance status (ratification, signature, no initiative is available on-line at: www.italianhumanrightsyearbook.eu, in the section "attachments".

In order to monitor the application of conventions ratified by States, in 1926 the ILO established the *Committee of Experts on the Application of Conventions and Recommendations*, a body made up of twenty eminent jurists and social professionals, who are independent of Governments and appointed on individual merits. The monitoring mechanism requires each Member State to submit periodic reports on the steps they have taken, in law and in practice, to apply each of the conventions it has ratified. At the same time, Governments are required to submit copies of their reports to employers' and workers' organisations, which are entitled to make comments and supply further information. Government reports are initially examined by the Committee of Experts, which can make two different kinds of comments: *observations* and *direct requests*. The observations contain comments on fundamental questions raised by the application of a particular convention by a State, and are published in the Committee's annual report. On the other hand, direct requests relate to more technical requests or requests for further information; they are not published in the report but are communicated directly to the Governments concerned.

Upon conclusion of its considerations, the Committee presents an annual report to the *International Labour Conference*, the most representative body of the ILO, comprising representatives from all the ILO Member States and including all its observations and recommendations, which are carefully examined by the *Conference Committee on the Application of Standards*, a tripartite standing committee made up of Government, employer and worker delegates. This Committee selects a number of observations from the report for more in-depth discussion. The Governments referred to in these comments are invited to respond before the Conference Committee to provide information on the situation in question. In many cases, the Conference Committee adopts conclusions recommending that Governments take specific steps to remedy a problem or to invite the ILO to come on a mission to their Country or to request technical assistance.

In 2013 Italy received 7 direct requests, the same number as in 2012 and 2 observations from the Committee of Experts on the Application of Conventions and Recommendations, again the same number as in 2012.

The Committee's direct requests were made in order to obtain further information on Italy's legislative, administrative and political instruments connected with the implementation of the following conventions: No. 29 – Forced Labour; No. 97 – Migrant Labour (revised); No. 100 – Equal Remuneration; No. 111 – Discrimination (employment and occupation);

No. 143 – Migrant Labour (Supplementary Provisions); No. 152 – Safety and Health in Ports; No. 175 – Part-Time Work.

The observations were related to the following Conventions: No. 111 – Discrimination (employment and occupation); No. 143 – Migrant Workers (Supplementary provisions).

Convention No. 111 on Discrimination (employment and occupation)

– *Gender discrimination, pregnancy and maternity.* The Committee makes reference to the practice of "blank resignation" consisting of making workers sign, at the moment of their employment, an undated resignation letter, to be used in future by the employer as he or she sees fit. This practice affects mainly female workers when they get pregnant. The Government claims that law 28 June 2012, No. 92 (Provisions for labour market reforms in a growth perspective) included measures regulating this practice: resignations of pregnant women and female workers with children under three years old must be upheld by labour inspectors before they become effective. However, the Committee notes that, according to statistics supplied by the Italian Government, the labour inspectorate approved 17,681 resignations in 2011 and 19,187 in 2012, representing a 9% increase in a period of one year. The vast majority of these resignations were from women aged between 26 and 35 years old; the main reason for resignation was the impossibility of reconciling family responsibilities and work obligations, because of the lack of child support services or of support from the workers' parents.

Considering the significant increase in the number of violations of the laws protecting pregnancy and maternity in the workplace, the Committee requested the Government to adopt further tangible measures to tackle the issue of termination without a just cause of pregnant women and working mothers, as well as forestalling and eliminating all forms of discrimination against women based on pregnancy and maternity.

– *Equality of opportunities and treatment without any distinction based on race or nationality.* The Committee calls on the Government to supply further information on the activities of the National Anti-Racial Discrimination Office and to ensure that the measures adopted to tackle the issue of discrimination based on race and nationality are closely monitored in order to improve their effectiveness. Particular attention should be devoted to evaluating the consequences of the economic and financial crisis, and the impact of the austerity measures adopted on the employment levels of workers from minority groups and migrant workers.

– *Roma, Sinti and travellers.* The Committee requests the Government to step up its action to eliminate discrimination and foster the social inclusion of Roma, Sinti and travellers. Specifically, the Committee called on the Government to supply information on: the impact of the National Strategy for the inclusion of Roma, Sinti and travellers, with particular reference to their access to education, training and employment opportunities; the impact of the activities carried out under the Dosta! Campaign; the results of the research project on the integration of Roma, Sinti and travellers carried out by ISTAT and the Department for Equal Opportunities.

Convention No. 143 on Migrant Workers (Supplementary Provisions)

– Art. 2–7: conditions of irregular migrants; multilateral and bilateral cooperation. Over the last five years, the Committee has frequently referred to the seriously vulnerable conditions of irregular migrant workers, who are particularly at risk of violation of their fundamental human rights. While recognising the breadth and complexity of the issue, and the efforts made by the Government to tackle the issue of irregular immigration, particularly during the current time of economic crisis, the Committee calls on the Government to continue to adopt all measures necessary to promote forms of cooperation at the national (by involving workers' and employers' associations), bilateral, multilateral and regional level, so as to take on this task with the utmost respect for the human rights of migrant workers and to prosecute and punish those who plan and carry out secret movement of migrants.

– Art. 1 and 9: minimum standards of protection; access to justice. The Committee highlights the fact that, following routine inspections carried out in 2011 by local and regional labour office managers, specifically in the areas of agriculture, construction and industry, over 2,000 workers were found to be in an irregular situation. Further, the Committee observes that section 1(1)(b) of the lgs.d. 109/2012 includes provisions for the issue of a residence permit of six months on humanitarian grounds for foreign citizens who, while working under "working conditions of particular exploitation", make official complaints or cooperate in the criminal proceedings against their employer. This residence permit can be extended for a year or for the time necessary to complete the criminal proceedings. The Government claims that the irregular situation of migrant workers does not deprive them of their rights in terms of pay, social security contributions, working hours, health and safety in the workplace, and the principle of non-discrimination. However the trade unions CGIL, CISL and UIL complain that they are not granted access to the reception centres nor to the centres for asylum-seekers, where migrants in irregular situations are held: this circumstance prevents them from helping migrant workers and supplying information to them. On this point, the Committee stresses that access to justice, including sufficient access to forms of support and consultancy, is a fundamental right which must be guaranteed to all migrant workers. The Committee therefore calls on the Government to: give specific clarification on the area of application of the expression "working conditions of particular exploitation", as per art. 1(1)(b) of the

lgs.d. 109/2012; provide information on the means of access to justice for migrant workers in an irregular situation, so that they can claim legal retribution for the violation of their rights deriving from cessation of employment, including unpaid or underpaid salaries, social security and other benefits; supply data concerning the number of migrant workers in an irregular situation who have presented administrative or legal claims of violations of their fundamental human rights, so as to be able to evaluate the effectiveness of current mechanisms; supply information as to how adequate legal support is provided to migrant workers in an irregular situation, including inside the detention centres; to continue to supply information on inspections carried out in the construction and agriculture sectors, with the aim of identifying instances of illegal employment of migrants.

– *Art. 10 and 12: domestic policies on equality of opportunities and treatment of migrants in Italy in a regular situation.* The Committee notes that the Government has adopted the "Plan for safe integration – identity and dialogue", and opened a number of local help desks for immigrants, which play an important role in promoting and supporting the training courses which foreign citizens undertake to attend as part of their integration agreement. The Government also refers to activities and projects carried out in the framework of the long-term plan adopted by the Central Office for immigration and asylum policies at the Ministry of the Interior for the period 2007–2013. However, the Committee observes that no information has been supplied as to the impact and outcomes of these programmes. The Government also supplies information on a series of measures aimed at fostering the integration of migrant workers and raising public awareness on migrant-related issues, including: the "Migrant integration portal", which offers a number of services to migrant workers, through a public-private partnership working on integration issues; a handbook entitled "Immigration: how, where, when – the integration handbook", designed for people who have not yet reached Italy; the Co.In project, designed to help migrant workers integrate into society and Italian society to become aware of the reciprocal benefits of integration. Measures have also been introduced to improve the approach of the media to immigration, including the publication of a handbook on migration and the mass media. However the Committee observes that, according to the trade unions CGIL, CISL and UIL, migrant workers continue to occupy the lowest levels of income (occupied by 27.5% of Italians and 55.9% of migrant workers) and are also the hardest hit by unemployment. These data are moreover confirmed by the "Third Annual Report on Migrant Workers in the Italian Labour Market", published by the Ministry of Labour and Social Policies, according to which the wage gap between Italian workers and immigrants has increased substantially in recent years. Consequently, the Committee calls on the Government to continue to supply information on the developments of domestic policies regarding equality of opportunities and treatment of migrant workers, including the forms of cooperation undertaken with employers' and employees' associations; to illustrate the impact of measures adopted to implement such policies, including the long-term plan 2007–2013, as well as any obstacles encountered; to supply detailed information on the measures adopted to tackle the wage gap between Italian workers and immigrants, particularly in the sectors where the gap is highest.

During 2013, none of these observations was selected by the Conference Committee on the Application of Standards for more in-depth discussions.

The overall budget of the ILO is structured through three main funding sources: the regular budget, voluntary contributions in addition to the regular budget (the Regular Budget Supplementary Account) and the extra-budgetary resources for technical cooperation. As in previous years, in 2012 Italy contributed 5% of the regular budget of the ILO, an amount equivalent to approximately 18.1 million Swiss Francs. In the two-year period 2012–2013, Italy made a further voluntary contribution to the regular budget equivalent to approximately 612,000 dollars (data updated to 31 December 2013); in the two-year period 2010–2011, the contribution was 300,000 dollars, and in 2008–2009 it was approximately 1.5 million dollars), making Italy one of the six donor Countries, along with Belgium, Denmark, Germany, the Netherlands and Norway. Finally, in 2013 Italy contributed to the ILO's resources for technical cooperation, allocating approximately 231,000 dollars (in 2012 the amount was 840,000 dollars; see graph below).

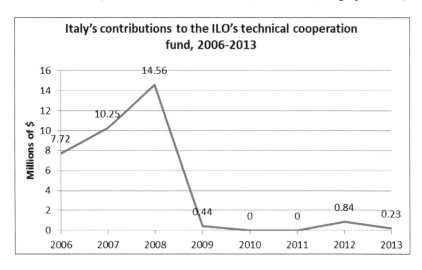

Source: ILO Development Cooperation Dashboard

B. United Nations Educational, Scientific and Cultural Organisation (UNESCO)

The human rights which fall under the responsibility of UNESCO are the right to education, the right to benefit from scientific progress, the right to participate freely in cultural life and the right to information, including freedom of opinion and expression. In connection with these, the right to freedom of thought, conscience and religion, the right to seek, receive and impart information and ideas through any instrument and across borders, the right to protection of the moral and material interests resulting from any scientific, literary or artistic production are pertinent, as are the right to freedom of assembly and association.

Italy has been a Member State of UNESCO since 1948. Since its inception, UNESCO has adopted 28 Conventions, of which Italy has ratified 20.

The complete list, updated to December 2013, of UNESCO conventions and of Italy's acceptance status (ratification, signature, no initiative is available online at: www.italianhumanrightsyearbook.eu, in the section "attachments".

On 27 September 2013, H.E. Vincenza Lomonaco was appointed to the post of Italy's Permanent Representative to UNESCO, replacing H.E. Maurizio Enrico Serra. Besides being a member of the Executive Council, Italy was represented in 2013 on the Legal Committee, on the Conciliation and Good Offices Commission which is responsible for the settlement of any disputes which may arise between States Parties to the Convention against Discrimination in Education (member: Francesco Margiotta-Broglio), on the Intergovernmental Oceanographic Commission and in the Committee for the Protection of Cultural Property in case of Armed Conflict.

In the education area, in 1991 the 26th General Conference of UNESCO established the International Programme for University Cooperation (IUC). The Programme is working to foster the creation of a network of centres of excellence (UNESCO Chairs) which will implement advanced teaching and research programmes in fields related to UNESCO policies, with special reference to the areas of peace, human rights, democracy and intercultural dialogue. There are over 780 UNESCO Chairs worldwide: in 2013 Italy had 20 Chairs (+ 4 compared to 2012), 3 of which are specifically devoted to human rights and include these words in their name: the Chair in "Human Rights, Democracy and Peace", established in 1999 at the University of Padua (Chair: Antonio Papisca); Chair in "Human Rights and Ethics of International Cooperation" established in 2003 at the University of Bergamo (Chair: Stefania Gandolfi); and the Chair in "Bioethics and Human Rights", established in 2009 at the

"Regina Apostolorum" Pontificial Athenaeum, European University of Rome (Chair: Alberto García).

There are two committees on bioethics operating in UNESCO: the International Bioethics Committee (IBC) and the Intergovernmental Bioethics Committee (IGBC).

The IBC was established in 1993, particularly thanks to the efforts of Director-General of UNESCO at that time, and it is a body made up of 36 independent experts coming from different geographical and disciplinary backgrounds. Its mission is to follow progress in life science and its applications in order to ensure respect for human dignity and human rights and to promote reflection on the ethical and legal issues raised by research in the life sciences and their applications. To this end, over the years it has published a number of recommendations and other documents, the most significant of which is the Universal Declaration on Bioethics and Human Rights, adopted by the UNESCO General Conference in 2005. The Committee convenes once a year upon invitation from the UNESCO Director-General. The 2013 session (twentieth) was held in Seoul from June 19–21 and debated the issue of non-discrimination and non-stigmatisation, as set forth in art. 11 of the Declaration. In 2013 the Chairperson of the Committee was Stefano Semplici, full professor of Moral Philosophy at Rome "Tor Vergata" University and member of the Committee since 2008.

The IGBC was created in 1998 pursuant to art. 11 of the IBC Statute. It is comprised of 36 Member States who are elected by the UNESCO General Conference, and meets at least once every two years to examine the proposals and recommendations of the IBC and to forward these proposals, accompanied by its own opinions, to the other UNESCO Member States. The IGBC held its eighth session from 5 to 16 September 2013, during which it examined the *Report of the IBC on Traditional Medicine Systems and their Ethical Implications*, adopted by the IBC in February 2013, and the *Draft Report of the IBC on the Principle of Non-discrimination and Non-stigmatisation* debated during the 20th session of the IBC.

Italy was not a member of the IGBC in 2013.

As in past years, Italy contributed to about 4.5% of UNESCO's regular budget (which covers ongoing expenses for personnel and the main activities of the Organisation), a sum equivalent to approximately 14.4 million dollars, placing it seventh among the main contributors to the Organisation. Moreover, Italy ranked fifth in 2013 (after Japan, the European Union, Sweden and Spain) in terms of voluntary contributions (which fund multi-year cooperation programmes managed by UNESCO), with a contribution of approximately 6 million dollars (-2.4 million dollars compared to 2012 and -5.4 million compared to 2011).

UNESCO Machinery

In 2013, Italy presented its periodic report on the implementation of the International Convention against Doping in Sport at the fourth Conference of the States Parties to the Convention (Paris, 19–20 September).

The Conference found that, in general, the measures adopted by Italy to combat doping in sport are compliant with the provisions of the Convention in 79% of cases. More in detail, a high level of conformity is found with reference to the following articles: art. 8 (restricting the availability and use in sport of prohibited substances and methods); art. 11 (financial measures); art. 12 (measures to facilitate doping control); art. 13 (cooperation between anti-doping organisations and sports organisations); art. 16 (international cooperation in doping control); art. 19 (general education and training principles); art. 20 (professional codes of conduct); art. 21 (involvement of athletes and athlete support personnel); art. 24 (promotion of research in anti-doping); art. 25 (nature of anti-doping research); art. 27 (sport science research). On the other hand, lower than average compliancy was found relative to the following articles: art. 9 (measures against athlete support personnel); art. 10 (nutritional supplements); art. 22 (sports organisations and ongoing education and training on anti-doping); art. 23 (cooperation in education and training); art. 26 (sharing the results of anti-doping research).

C. *The Food and Agriculture Organisation of the United Nations (FAO)*

The FAO was established in 1945 in Ville de Quebec, Canada and has its headquarters in Rome. José Graziano da Silva (Brazil) has been the Director-General of the Organisation since 1 January 2012. Italy is currently appointed to the Council, with a three-year term that started on 1 December 2011. The Organisation budget for the two-year period 2014–2015 is 2.4 billion dollars, plus approximately 1.4 billion dollars in voluntary contributions.

As of December 2013, Italy was the sixth largest contributors to the FAO, with approximately 13 million dollars. In addition, Italy works with the FAO on the Cooperation Programme FAO/Italy, the main components of which, funded by Italian voluntary contributions are: the Traditional Programme; the Italian Trust Fund for Food Security and the Decentralised Cooperation Programme.

D. *The World Health Organisation (WHO)*

The primary objective of the Organisation, established in 1948, is the attainment by all peoples of the highest possible level of health, understood not as the absence of disease but as a state of complete physical, mental and social well-being.

In Italy there are two offices of the WHO (Rome and Venice) and currently 27 accredited collaborating centres. The latter, specialised institutions which receive no funding from the WHO, are identified by the Director General of the WHO and are part of a worldwide network to support the Organisation in various medical and scientific fields. In Italy their activity is coordinated by the Ministry of Health.

E. The United Nations Development Programme (UNDP)

The United Nations Development Programme (UNDP) was established by the General Assembly in 1965 and has the role of central agency for the coordination and funding of development cooperation of the United Nations system.

UNDP action pursues the general objective of "human development", understood as not only economic growth but also as social development, based on gender equality and respect for human rights. UNDP conducts research and analysis, preparing studies and reports. Of the most significant, worth noting are the Annual Report on Human Development and the report on the state of achievement of the Millennium Development Goals.

F. The United Nations Environment Programme (UNEP)

The UNEP's mission is to coordinate and facilitate the realisation of a global partnership for development projects and environmental protection activities so that nations and peoples may improve their quality of life without jeopardising that of future generations.

The current Director General is Achim Steiner. The Permanent Representative to the UNEP and also head of the Italian Embassy mission in Nairobi is H.E. Mauro Massoni.

G. The United Nations Human Settlements Programme (UN-HABITAT)

The mission of UN-HABITAT, the United Nations Human Settlements Programme, is to promote sustainable urbanisation in social and environmental terms, for the ultimate purpose of guaranteeing everyone the right to decent housing. The current Director General is Joan Clos (Spain). The Permanent Representative to UN-HABITAT and also the head of the Italian Embassy mission in Nairobi is H.E. Mauro Massoni.

UN-HABITAT works closely with local authorities, including Municipalities, Provinces and Regions, mainly due to the special relationship formed with UNACLA, the United Nations Advisory Committee on the Local Authorities. The latter consists of mayors and representatives of umbrella organisations of local authorities chosen by the Director General of UN-HABITAT on the basis of their expertise and commitment in implementing the UN agenda on human settlements. The only local authority in Italy which is part of UNACLA is the City Council of Naples.

H. The United Nations Children's Fund (UNICEF)

UNICEF in the permanent United Nations Fund mandated to protect and promote the rights of boys, girls and adolescents with the aim of improving their living conditions. Anthony Lake (USA) has been the Executive Director since 1 May 2010.

Italy hosts the UNICEF Research Centre at the Istituto degli Innocenti in Florence. Moreover, the Italian Committee for UNICEF, a non-governmental organisation whose activity is regulated by a cooperation agreement signed with UNICEF International, has been operating in Italy since 1974. Chairperson of the Committee is Giacomo Guerrera, who has held the post since November 2011.

As concerns Italy's contribution to the Fund in 2013, UNICEF's ranking of donor Countries places in Italy in 18th place.

VII. International Organisations with Permanent Observer Status at the General Assembly

Of the 20 inter-governmental organisations of a universal or regional nature that have permanent observer status at the UN General Assembly and maintain permanent representation offices at the United Nations headquarters in New York, one of the most active in issues related to human rights is the International Organisation for Migration.

A. The International Organisation for Migration (IOM)

Established in 1951, the IOM is the major inter-governmental organisation which deals with migrant issues. Its mission is to promote orderly migration based on respect for human dignity; to this end, it collaborates with Governments and civil society.

The IOM Coordination Centre for the Mediterranean Countries is based in Rome and the main activities of the IOM offices in Italy concern: providing information services on immigration; guidance on migration for work purposes and social integration; combating trafficking in human beings and providing assistance to victims; reuniting families; projects designed to help prevent the spread of HIV and promote consideration of the health implications of migration; migration and development projects and appreciation of the African diaspora in Italy; supporting voluntary return and reintegration in their area of origin for vulnerable migrants, citizens from other Countries resident in Italy and foreigners in an irregular position.

The IOM is present in Sicily, Apulia and Calabria in the places where migrants land and in the migrant centres, where it provides information on the procedures and potential risks of staying in Italy without regular permits. It also carries out monitoring activities inside the structures. Together with the UNHCR, Save the Children and the Italian Red Cross, the IOM is part of the Praesidium project, funded by the Italian Ministry of the Interior. Finally, the Organisation is also active in Italy in a series of other projects such as "Equi-Health", which aims to improve access to health services for immigrants and vulnerable ethnic minorities, and the "Progetto Anatolè – Il Sole che sorge" (the Rising Sun), providing psycho-social support to all those asylum seekers who arrive daily in Bari airport but come under the so-called "Dublin Regulation" category, and have neither the means nor the resources to remain on Italian soil.

Council of Europe

Founded on 5 May 1949, the Council of Europe (CoE, 47 Member States) is the first and most advanced system of promotion and protection of human rights at the regional level. Major bodies of the Council of Europe are the Committee of Ministers and the Parliamentary Assembly. In 1994 the Congress of Local and Regional Authorities was established as an advisory body. The European Court of Human Rights works organically within the institutional framework of the Organisation.

The main legal instrument adopted by the CoE is the European Convention for the Protection of Human Rights and Fundamental Freedoms (ECHR, 1950) which established the European Court of Human Rights in Strasbourg (ECtHR); the Convention has been accompanied over the years by 14 protocols (2 new Protocols were adopted in 2013, but they have not entered into force yet). Other essential legal instruments are the European Social Charter (1961, a revised version was adopted in 1996), the European Convention for the Prevention of Torture and Inhuman or Degrading Treatment or Punishment (1987), the Framework Convention for the Protection of National Minorities (1995), the European Convention on the Exercise of Children's Rights (1996), the Convention on Human Rights and Biomedicine (Oviedo Convention, 1997), the Criminal Law and the Civilian Law Conventions on Corruption (1999) and the Convention on Action against Trafficking in Human Beings (2005), the Convention on the Protection of Children against Sexual Exploitation and Sexual Abuse (Lanzarote Convention, 2007) and the Convention on Preventing and Combating Violence against Women and Domestic Violence (Istanbul Convention, 2011).

For each of these conventions a system has been put in place for the monitoring of the current state of their implementation by the States that ratified them. Within the General Secretariat of the CoE, the Directorate-General for Human Rights and Rule of Law oversees the dynamic application of various treaties and its follow-up mechanisms, providing assistance and support to the bodies of the Council of Europe and the Member States and organises programmes, and training and awareness initiatives.

The Permanent Representative of Italy to the Council of Europe is Amb. Manuel Jacoangeli. Since 2012 an Italian expert, Claudia Luciani, has led the Democratic Governance, Culture and Diversity Directorate.

In 2013 Italy contributed to the activities of the Council of Europe for an overall total of 35,477,291 euros, of which 27,346,590 euros for the ordinary budget (in 2012 the total contribution was 35,188,649 euros of which 27,105,624 for the ordinary budget). In 2013, voluntary contributions paid by Italy amounted to 501,947.79 euros (506,337.21 euros in 2012).

The following pages will illustrate, with reference to Italy, the activities of the Parliamentary Assembly and the Committee of Ministers; of five bodies established by a treaty: the European Court of Human Rights, the Committee for the Prevention of Torture, the European Committee of Social Rights, the Advisory Committee on the Framework Convention for the Protection of National Minorities, the Group of Experts on Action against Trafficking in Human Beings; of four bodies established by the Committee of Ministers: Commissioner for Human Rights, the European Commission against Racism and Intolerance, the European Commission for Democracy through Law, the Group of States against Corruption.

I. Parliamentary Assembly

In the Parliamentary Assembly of the Council of Europe (PACE), made up of delegations from the national Parliaments of the Member States of the CoE, 18 members of the Senate and the Chamber of Deputies sit for Italy; there are an equal number of alternate members.

The following are the members and the alternate members (a) of PACE after the Italian political elections of 24 and 25 February 2013 (for the members of the previous legislature and their roles in parliamentary committees, see *2013 Yearbook*, p. 234): Sandro Gozi, Francesco Maria Giro, Vincenzo Santangelo, Ferdinando Aiello (a), Francesco Maria Amoruso (a), Anna Ascani (a), Deborah Bergamini, Anna Maria Bernini, Teresa Bertuzzi, Alessandro Bratti, Nunzia Catalfo, Elena Centemero, Massimo Cervellini (a), Lorenzo Cesa, Khalid Chaouki (a), Vannino Chiti, Eleonora Cimbro (a), Paolo Corsini, Celeste Costantino, Jonny Crosio, Luca D'Alessandro (a), Cristina De Pietro (a), Manlio Di Stefano, Claudio Fazzone (a), Giuseppe Galati (a), Adele Gambaro, Carlo Lucherini (a), Emanuela Munerato (a), Michele Nicoletti, Luis Alberto Orellana (a), Laura Puppato (a), Lia Quartapelle Procopio (a), Andrea Rigoni, Milena Santerini (a), Maria Edera Spadoni (a), Francesco Verducci (a).

The President of the Italian delegation is Sandro Gozi, who is also one of the 20 Vice-Presidents. Deborah Bergamini is Chair of the Sub-Committee on Media and Information Society (Committee on Culture, Science, Education and Media).

The Assembly is a forum for discussion on the main issues underlying the mandate of the Council of Europe and has an advisory role in relation to all international conventions developed in this context. It elects the judges of the

European Court of Human Rights, the Commissioner for Human Rights, the Secretary-General of the Council and his Deputy.

In 2013, the PACE adopted two resolutions which refer specifically to Italy.

Resolution 1914 on *Ensuring the viability of the Strasbourg Court: structural deficiencies in States Parties*, was adopted on 22 January 2013 on the basis of a report submitted to the Committee on Legal Affairs and Human Rights (*rapporteur*: Kivalov). In it, the Parliamentary Assembly deplores the fact that the ECtHR is still overloaded with a large number of repetitive cases revealing widespread dysfunctions in national legal systems. Having already underlined the issue in previous resolutions (for example resolution 1787/2011), the PACE confirms that Italy is among the Countries facing major structural problems which lead to delays in the execution of the Court's judgments (alongside Bulgaria, Greece, the Republic of Moldova, Poland, Romania, the Russian Federation, Turkey and Ukraine). With a view to improving this state of affairs, the Assembly calls on States Parties to: strengthen their efforts to execute fully and rapidly the Court's judgments and amend legislation according to standards stemming from the case-law of the Court; put in place effective domestic remedies, primarily in areas affected by structural problems; take comprehensive measures with a view to raising awareness of the Convention standards as interpreted by the Court; strengthen national authorities' cooperation with civil society, bar associations, experts and national human rights institutions; strengthen legal guarantees of independence of the Court's judges and secure their immunity. In addition, having reaffirmed the importance of national parliaments in monitoring the effective implementation of the Convention standards at national level, the Assembly: reiterates its call on States Parties to put into practice the basic principles for parliamentary supervision in this field; invites Parliaments to ensure that their committees monitoring compliance with human rights obligations are actively involved in the execution of the Court's pilot judgments and other judgments revealing structural problems; and invites the members of the Assembly, in their capacity as national parliamentarians, to question their governments regularly regarding the state of execution of the Court's judgments.

Resolution 1920 on *the State of media freedom in Europe* was adopted on 24 January 2013 on the basis of a report submitted to the Committee on Culture, Science, Education and Media (*rapporteur*: Johansson). In it, the PACE stresses that freedom of expression and information constitutes a cornerstone of good governance and democracy. Guaranteeing freedom of expression and information is therefore a fundamental obligation of each Member State under article 10 ECHR. In that respect,

the Assembly condemns the numerous attacks and threats against journalists in some CoE Countries and expresses its concern over certain
laws on freedom of expression, freedom of the press and defamation
currently in force in Turkey, Hungary and Belarus. On the same issue,
the resolution refers specifically to the fourteen-month prison sentence
imposed on journalist Alessandro Sallusti in 2012 for libel in print in
the "Cocilovo case" in Italy (see *2013 Yearbook*, p. 289). In that regard,
the Assembly asked the Venice Commission to prepare an opinion on
whether the Italian laws on defamation are in line with article 10 ECHR.
The Commission's opinion on the matter was adopted in December
2013 (see, in this Part, Council of Europe, IX). In general, the Assembly
calls on all States to revoke or amend provisions criminalising defamation and to abolish imprisonment sentences for the same in line with
CoE standards.

Finally, regarding independent public service broadcasting, in *resolution 1920*, the Assembly notes with concern recent reports about political pressure on public service broadcasters in Hungary, Italy, Romania,
Serbia, Spain and Ukraine and invites the European Broadcasting Union
to co-operate with the CoE in this regard. It reminds member States of the
indicators for media in a democracy: "public service broadcasters must
be protected against political interference in their daily management and
their editorial work; senior management positions should be refused to
people with clear party political affiliations; public service broadcasters
should establish in-house codes of conduct for journalistic work and to
ensure editorial independence from political influence".

In 2013, moreover, a report on the arrival of mixed migratory flows to Italian
coastal areas, prepared by British MP Christopher Chope, was presented to
the Committee on Migration, Refugees and Displaced Persons. On the basis of this report, a draft resolution was adopted unanimously by the same
Parliamentary Committee on 2 October 2013. The document will be submitted for debate in plenary session in 2014. The draft resolution states that,
despite experience with extraordinary migration flows to Italy following the
"Arab Spring" (almost 63,000 migrants reached the Country in 2011), Italy
has, once again, shown that it is ill-prepared to deal with such phenomena, as
shown by the management of a new surge of mixed migration caused by the
ongoing crisis in Syria. The resolution therefore recommends that the Italian
authorities should develop a consistent policy to manage these types of situations efficiently, to ensure that the conditions in reception and detention
centres meet international standards and that persons seek asylum in Italy,
as their first Country of arrival, in order to prevent asylum forum shopping
elsewhere in Europe (a practice whereby international asylum seekers lodge
asylum applications in several EU Member Countries and then choose the
Country offering the best conditions for reception).

Regarding the activities of the Italian members of the PACE in 2013, the reports to be noted were submitted to the various committees in the first half of the year under review mainly by parliamentarians appointed during the previous parliamentary term: report by Pietro Marcenaro to the Committee on Political Affairs and Democracy on *The situation in the Middle East* (10 June); report by Luca Volonté to the Monitoring Committee on *Post-monitoring dialogue with Bulgaria* (4 January), and to the Committee on Political Affairs and Democracy on the themes of *Violence against religious communities* (4 April) and *Evaluation of the partnership for democracy in respect of the Parliament of Morocco* (10 June); reports by Andrea Rigoni to the Committee on Migration, Refugees and Displaced Persons on *Management of mixed migration and asylum challenges beyond the European Union's eastern border* (8 April) and to the Committee on Equality and Non-Discrimination on *Parental leave as a way to foster gender equality* (13 May).

II. Committee of Ministers

On the subject of human rights, the Committee of Ministers (CM) relies on the work of the Steering Committee for Human Rights, an inter-governmental body composed of representatives of the 47 Member States which performs, among other things, standard-setting and follow-up.

The CM adopts recommendations regarding the Member States and on matters for which a common policy is agreed upon – in accordance with its role in the implementation of the European Social Charter (art. 29) – with the aim of asking some States to adapt their laws and public policies with the provisions contained in the Charter. In addition, it is ultimately responsible for monitoring the Framework Convention on National Minorities (art. 26). In this context, it adopts specific resolutions by Country based on the opinions of the Advisory Committee of the Framework Convention.

With regard to its role in relation to the European Court of Human Rights, the CM has the function of supervising the execution of judgments of the Court, ensuring that Member States act in accordance with the rulings issued by the same. The Committee terminates each case by adopting a final resolution. Finally, the CM may apply to the Court for a ruling on issues related to difficulties of interpretation of the judgments of the Court itself which would impede their implementation and if it believes that a Member State is refusing to comply with a final judgment, it may refer the issue to the Court.

In 2013, the CM adopted three conclusive resolutions on the implementation of judgments of the ECtHR for Italy: CM/ResDH(2013)32 on the case *Abbate against Italy*; CM/ResDH(2013)63 on three cases against Italy (Capitani and Campanella, Paleari, Pozzi); and CM/

ResDH(2013)188 on four cases against Italy (Sergi, Bassani and Colombo, Ruffolo, Andrenelli).

With reference to the judgments still to be executed against Italy, the Committee of Ministers adopted five decisions.

On 7 March 2013, during the 1164th session, the CM adopted a decision (CM/Del/Dec(2013)1164/14) with reference to the case *Hirsi Jamaa and others* (see *2013 Yearbook*, p. 243). In this, the Committee noted, as regards individual measures, the repeated requests from the Italian to the Libyan authorities to obtain assurances against possible ill-treatment in Libya or the applicants' arbitrary repatriation to Somalia and Eritrea, as required by the Court's judgment. Secondly, the CM noted that the Italian authorities had not been able to obtain the assurances due to objective difficulties arising from developments in Libya. It also noted that the Italian authorities expressed their intention to continue their contacts with the Libyan authorities and to also consider other possible actions in response to potential requests made by the applicants' representatives. The Committee noted, as regards general measures, the Government's repeated assurances that the ordinary Convention-compliant guarantees contained in Italian laws and regulations as regards the treatment of refugees and asylum seekers were applicable, under all circumstances. The CM noted the Italian Government's indication that, in the light of the measures taken and the assurances and commitments made, Italy considered that it had complied with its obligations with reference to the measures indicated by the ECtHR. In addition, the Committee noted the recent developments aimed at overcoming the legal obstacles to the payment of just satisfaction to the applicants' representatives and expressed their expectation that payment, together with default interest, would be made without further delay. Finally, the CM invited the authorities to submit a comprehensive, consolidated action report with a view to allowing a conclusive assessment of the case.

During the same session, the CM adopted a decision on the *Sneersone and Kampanella* case (CM/Del/Dec(2013)1164/15) (see *2012 Yearbook*, p. 356). In this, it recalled that in this case, the ECtHR found that the mere existence of the order for the return of the minor involved to Italy, irrespective of its actual enforcement, amounted to an interference with the applicants' right to respect of their family life, due to the adverse psychological effects it causes to the child. In that respect, the CM noted that the Public Attorney's Office at the juvenile court has brought proceedings to set aside the return order and that the Italian authorities have assured that the order will not be enforced. The Committee further noted that, after a stay of the proceedings ordered due to the parents' failure to appear at the first hearing, the father was located by the judicial authorities and the proceedings for setting aside the return order were resumed. The first applicant (the mother of the child) has the possibility to exercise her right to participate therein personally or by representation. The CM therefore invites the Italian authorities to continue their efforts to ensure that these proceedings are brought to a swift conclusion and to inform the Committee of Ministers of the progress achieved in the adoption of the individual measures in this case.

On 6 June 2013, during its 1172th session, the CM adopted a decision on a number of judgments concerning Italy, among which, the cases *Gaglione and others*, the *Ceteroni* group, the *Luordo* group and the *Mostacciuolo* group (CM/Del/OJ/DH(2013)1172/14). In this, the Committee notes with satisfaction that the Italian authorities reiterated their determination to adopt the necessary measures to eradicate the structural problem of the excessive length of judicial proceedings in Italy and to put an end to the recurring delays in the payment of the compensation awarded under the "Pinto" law. As concerns the first of the two above-mentioned problems (excessive length of judicial proceedings), the CM notes that most of the reforms announced to the Committee for the civil proceedings have been adopted. The CM welcomes the information provided by the Italian authorities, while requesting precise and updated data for a full assessment of the situation and underlines, in that regard, that the long-term success of the strategy adopted hinges upon the setting-up at domestic level of a monitoring mechanism for the reforms allowing the authorities to measure their impact and to rapidly adopt the additional and/or corrective measures which might be required. In this respect, the CM invites the authorities to finalise a consolidated action plan enabling the Committee to assess the ongoing progress. As regards the second issue (dysfunctions of the "Pinto remedy"), the CM notes with interest that as a result of the new provisions set forth by the budget law for 2013, the funds allocated for the payments to be made under the "Pinto" law have not been reduced. At the same time, however, the authorities are invited to provide information on the lifting of the budgetary limitations on the payment of the compensation awarded under the "Pinto" law and on the earmarking of necessary funds for the payment of the arrears. Stressing in this regard the urgency to stop the flow of repetitive applications before the ECtHR caused by the deficiencies in the "Pinto" remedy, the CM calls upon the authorities to adopt these measures without further delay.

During the same session the CM adopted a decision (CM/Del/OJ/DH(2013)1172/15) on the *Sulejmanovic* case. In this the CM recalls the requests submitted in 2012 at its 1150th meeting (see *2013 Yearbook*, p. 242) to submit further information on the additional total capacity forecasted in Italian prisons, on how this total capacity is calculated and on the monitoring of detention conditions carried out, particularly in relation to prison overcrowding and the impact of the measures adopted so far. The CM underlines that in this context the importance of the existence, both in theory and practice, of effective domestic remedies had already been pointed out. The Committee notes in this respect that the ECtHR delivered the pilot judgment on the case *Torreggiani and others* (see Part IV, Italy in the Case-law of the European Court of Human Rights, I, A) which sets a deadline of one year from when the judgment becomes final for the authorities to grant an effective domestic remedy capable of affording adequate and sufficient redress in cases of overcrowding in prisons. Given that this judgment became final on 27 May 2013, the CM encourages the authorities to deploy all the efforts necessary to submitting an action plan, together with a calendar, for the setting up of such a remedy before the 27 May 2014 and also to submit the further information requested by the Committee on prison conditions in Italy.

On 26 September 2013, during its 1179th session, the CM adopted a decision (CM/Del/OJ/DH(2013)1179/10) on the *Cirillo* case (see Part IV, Italy in the Case-law of the European Court of Human Rights, I, A and *2013 Yearbook*, p. 375). In this, the Committee notes with interest the measures adopted by the Italian authorities to secure the applicant adequate medical care and invites the authorities to provide information on the arrangements made to ensure that the applicant receives such medical care on a regular basis. In addition, the CM notes the direct link established by the ECtHR in this case between the lack of regular access to medical care and the structural problem of prison overcrowding in Italy and underlines the complexity of the issues related to the medical care in a prison environment characterised by structural overcrowding. The Committee notes also that the group of cases *Scoppola* (see *2013 Yearbook*, p. 375) concerns issues related to material prison conditions incompatible with the health condition of prisoners suffering from serious pathologies and to the impossibility of providing the required medical care to them in a prison environment. In this group of cases, the Committee notes that Italian authorities have provided to the Committee a revised version of the action plan and decides to continue monitoring the issues raised by the *Cirillo* case and by the *Scoppola* group of cases in accordance with the enhanced supervision track.

On 11 September 2013, in addition, the CM adopted resolution CM/ResCSS(2013)9 on the application of the European Code of Social Security by Italy (in relation to the period from 1 July 2011 to 30 June 2012). In this, the Committee finds that the law and practice in Italy continue to give full effect to the parts of the Code that have been accepted by Italy. Nonetheless, the CM invites the Government of Italy to submit further information and statistical data on the current situation concerning the social security institutions and services in the Country in order to enable better understanding of the direction which the Italian social security system is taking under the pressure of austerity policies adopted by the Italian Government to respond to the economic and financial crisis. In particular, such data would serve to verify that the new lean organisational model of the INPS (National Social Welfare Institution) is not achieved at the expense of quality and accessibility of its services provided to the population. The CM moreover requests the most recent statistics on the dynamics of poverty in Italy, including pensioners and children with the active population, and on the minimum amounts of social benefits payable at the established poverty threshold.

Finally, on 16 December 2013, in the context of the Landscape award of the CoE, attributed this year to the Szprotawa river valley in Poland, the CM decided to attribute a special mention for strengthening democracy to the rebirth of the Alto Belice Corleonese in Sicily (CM/Del/Dec(2013)1187/7.2E). The reason given for the award is that the "rebirth" of the area was obtained through the recovery of land confiscated from mafia organisations, in particular thanks to the contribution of the association *Libera*.

III. European Court of Human Rights

The European Court of Human Rights (ECtHR), the first international court specifically designed for the protection of human rights in a particular region of the world, guarantees the respect of the commitments laid down in the ECHR and its protocols by Member States of the CoE.

In 2013, the Committee of Ministers of the Council of Europe adopted two new Protocols to the Convention, both of which are still pending the necessary ratification for their entry into force.

The first of these, Protocol 15, introduces in the Preamble of the ECHR a reference to the principle of subsidiarity and the doctrine of state margin of appreciation which constitute key references for the effectiveness of the ECtHR. The Protocol, moreover, amends the text of the ECHR in various aspects, providing for: a reduction in the age limit for judges, from 70 to 65 years; the removal of the parties' right to object the relinquishment of a case to the Grand Chamber (art. 30 ECHR); the reduction from six to four months of the time limit within which an application may be made to the Court following the date of a final domestic decision. Finally, Protocol 15 deletes one of the safeguard clauses outlined in article 35(3)(b) which states that a case must be declared inadmissible unless the applicant has suffered "significant disadvantage", and provided that the case has not been duly considered by a domestic tribunal.

The second protocol adopted by the Committee of Ministers, Protocol 16, introduces a system similar to reference for a preliminary ruling provided for by the Court of Justice of the European Union, allowing the highest courts of a State Party to the Convention to suspend their domestic proceedings and request the Grand Chamber to give advisory opinions on the interpretation or application of the Convention or its protocols. A panel of five judges from the Grand Chamber shall decide whether to accept the request and shall give reasons for any refusal to accept it. Advisory opinions submitted by the Grand Chamber shall not, however, be binding. At the time of ratification, each State Party shall, by means of a declaration, indicate the domestic courts that it designates to request advisory opinions from the Grand Chamber.

The Italian judge who now sits at the Court, specifically in the II Section, is Guido Raimondi, elected by the PACE in January 2010. Of the 670 members of the Registry, which provides legal and administrative support to the Court in exercising its functions, 17 are Italian.

The statistical data provided by the Court and updated in December 2013 reports that the total number of complaints pending against Italy amounts to 14,379, equivalent to about 14.4% of the total (only Russia is worse off with 16,813 (16.8%) pending complaints). In 2013, the Court received 3,184 valid applications by individuals who complained of a violation of the rights enshrined in the ECHR by Italy (3,253 in 2012 and 4,714 in 2011). During the same period, 2,872 applications were declared inadmissible or struck from the register, while 39 led to the delivery of a decision on the merits (relative to 78 applications), 34 of which identified at least one violation of the Convention; 62 were communicated to the State in view of a hearing on their merits. The ECtHR also received 18 requests for temporary measures pursuant to article 39 of the rules of Court, mostly regarding the suspension of deportation proceedings for as many applicants, none of which was granted by the ECtHR.

The ECtHR judgments that had most resonance during 2013 were the two pilot judgments adopted in the cases *Torreggiani and others against Italy* (application 4357/09, 46882/09, 55400/09; 57875/09, 61535/09, 35315/10, 37818/10, judgment of 8 January 2013) and *M.C. and others against Italy* (application 5376/11, judgment of 3 September 2013). An analysis of Court's judgments concerning Italy during 2013 is presented in Part IV, Italy in the Case-law of the European Court of Human Rights.

IV. Committee for the Prevention of Torture

The European Committee for the Prevention of Torture and Inhuman or Degrading Treatment or Punishment (CPT) was established by the 1987 Convention of the same name, conceived as complementary to the regulations under art. 3 ECHR which sets forth an absolute ban on torture. The CPT is a body composed of independent experts and has one member for each State Party to the Convention for the Prevention of Torture. The members of the Committee are elected by the Committee of Ministers. The independent expert for Italy is Ms Andreana Esposito, who has held the position since 20 December 2011 and whose term expires in December 2015.

During 2013, the CPT visited 16 Countries: Armenia, Azerbaijan, Belgium, Cyprus, Germany, Greece, Hungary, Latvia, Montenegro, Poland, Portugal, Russian Federation, San Marino, Slovak Republic, Turkey and Ukraine. The Committee has published 19 reports concerning previous visits to Bosnia-Herzegovina, Estonia, Georgia, Greenland, Iceland, Italy (2 reports), Latvia, Malta, Monaco, Portugal (2), Russian Federation (2), Slovenia, Spain (2), Turkey and Ukraine.

The CPT has made ten visits to Italy to date, the most recent in 2012. A request for publication of the two most recent reports, concerning the ninth and tenth visits, was made by the Italian authorities on 19 November 2013. Each report was then published, together with the relevant observations made by the Italian Government on the issues raised therein. In the following paragraphs an analysis is made of the main recommendations formulated by the CPT in relation to both visits.

The *ninth visit* took place between 14 and 18 June 2010. The Committee's report (CPT/Inf(2013)30) contains a first report, dated 3 December 2010, and a supplementary report, adopted on 14 April 2011. The document containing the Italian Government's observations on the visit (CPT/Inf(2013)31) is also made up of two reports, one dated 5 April 2011 and a supplementary report, submitted on 13 October 2011.

This was an *ad hoc* visit "required in the circumstances" as set out in article 7 of the Convention for the Prevention of Torture. The visit focused specifically on three issues which are particularly relevant as regards the situation of persons deprived of their liberty in Italy: 1) the prevention of suicide and self-harm in the prison context; 2) the transfer of responsibility for prison health care to regional health-care authorities and 3) the accountability for ill-treatment by law enforcement officials and prison staff including through an examination of the effectiveness of the investigations (this issue is dealt with in the supplementary report). The CPT's delegation visited numerous detention centres including prisons, health care units, courthouses, Police and Carabinieri stations. During the visit the delegation met public prosecutors, members of Parliament as well as the Ombudsman for detainees for the Lazio Region and various representatives of NGOs.

A number of recommendations, observations and requests for additional information on the dialogue between the CPT and the authorities were formulated in the reports compiled following this visit. The Committee's main considerations are listed by issue below.

In relation to the first of the three issues (*prevention of suicide and self-harm*), the CPT recommends that the Italian authorities introduce a standard screening algorithm to assess the risk of suicide in prisons, in particular to ensure that drug and/or alcohol dependence are adequately taken into account as factors potentially heightening the risk of suicide. Furthermore, information on an inmate at risk of suicide or self-harm should be transmitted in full and promptly to all those who have a role in caring for the prisoner, including when he or she is transferred to another establishment. All prison staff should be trained in recognising behaviour indicating suicide risk, and on using basic resuscitation skills. As for the division of roles between medical and custodial staff in the management of the risk of suicide or self-harm, the CPT recommends that their respective roles be better defined and strengthened in this regard. Staff entrusted with the supervision of prisoners presenting a suicide risk should receive specific training on interpersonal communication skills. Concerning the detention environment, the Committee recommends that persons who present a major suicide risk are placed in a cell which does not contain any ligature points or other means which might facilitate an attempt to commit suicide and that when necessary, appropriate "suicide-proof" clothing is provided to inmates. The same reasoning is applied in relation to the presence of gas canisters in prison cells for cooking purposes and which can be used by prisoners to self-harm or to attempt suicide. Alternative cooking arrangements should be made in such cases. Moreover, the CPT recommends that the necessary steps be taken to ensure that persons presenting an acute risk of suicide are immediately transferred to an acute mental health unit for appropriate care. Effective access to psychological or psychiatric care for all prisoners who request it should be ensured. According to the Committee, the Italian authorities should analyse the high suicide rate and its causes and introduce alternative suicide prevention measures – instead of isolation – such as physical activity, opportunities for socialising, contact with the outside world and addiction treatment. Further, measures should be taken to ensure that prevention efforts are adequately coordinated, through meetings of the multidisciplinary team and through an adequate level of input from specialist staff such as psychiatrists and educators. Finally, in relation to measures taken in the event of death or self-harm in custody, the CPT recommends that the Italian authorities introduce a clear and comprehensive procedure for the identification of the causes of death of detained persons and clear criteria on the classification of deaths as suicides. Every death should be the subject of a thorough investigation to ascertain, the cause of death, the facts leading up to it, and whether the death might have been prevented.

An autopsy should also be carried out and the prison staff should be informed of the outcome.

In relation to the second of the three issues analysed during the visit (*transfer of responsibility for prison health care from the Ministry of Justice to the regional health-care authorities*), the CPT recommends that the authorities take the necessary steps to ensure that these arrangements do not undermine other important aspects of prison life, such as the provision of an appropriate regime and sufficient numbers of staff present on the wings. The Committee underlines that access to health care provided by specialists visiting prisons should be managed in a transparent, non-discriminatory manner and that records drawn up after a medical examination of a prisoner should contain a full account of statements made by the prisoner concerned, including any allegations of ill-treatment made by him/her and if the prisoner refuses to reveal the cause of any signs of violence or, alternatively, gives reasons other than ill-treatment. According to the Committee, when detained persons are found to show signs of injury, doctors should be required to bring the record of such injuries to the attention of the relevant prosecutor immediately. Prison doctors moreover, should not sit on prisoner disciplinary panels. Finally, Italian authorities should take appropriate measures to ensure that all aspects of the work of health-care services are duly monitored, including by effecting joint inspections by the Ministry of Health and the Ministry of Justice.

The third issue (*accountability for ill-treatment of detained persons*) shall be dealt with in a separate report, once the Committee has taken the necessary time to analyse the extensive documentation on the issue provided by the Italian authorities. In its report, the CPT refers specifically to three cases of alleged ill-treatment, reported anonymously. Among the numerous recommendations and observations provided in the report, it is worth noting the following, which are grouped by issue.

In relation to the *effectiveness of investigations in the event of allegations or signs of ill-treatment in police custody or in prison*, the Committee invites the competent authorities to take the necessary measures to ensure that, whenever a person is brought before a court and alleges ill-treatment or presents visible signs consistent with ill-treatment, such allegations or visible signs are recorded in writing, a forensic examination is immediately ordered, and the issue is the subject of a proper investigation. In addition, the CPT recommends that the Italian authorities reinforce their concrete initiatives so as to promote a working environment, where people are detained, within which it is regarded as unprofessional to resort to ill-treatment and, consequently, the decision to report any ill-treatment by colleagues is perceived as the right thing to do. This requires the introduction of a clear reporting procedure as well as the adoption of whistle-blower protective measures.

In relation to *the procedural safeguards against ill-treatment during detention by law enforcement agencies*, the CPT invites authorities to ensure that lawyers can provides assistance during custody effectively and that all persons deprived of their liberty can have access to a lawyer during the period immediately following their deprivation of liberty (and at all events before appearing in court). Moreover, the Committee recommends that the Italian authorities take immediate steps to ensure that in law enforcement establishments as well as at courthouse detention facilities, all medical examinations of detained persons are conducted outside the hearing and, unless the doctor concerned requests otherwise, out of the sight of law enforcement officials. Specific legal provisions should also be adopted governing the right of persons detained by law enforcement agencies to have access to a doctor of their own choice (at their own expense). In addition, the staff at all law enforcement establishments, as well as at courthouse detention facilities, should maintain custody/detention registers meticulously. The CPT further recommends the introduction of an effective policy on the use of CCTV, which includes security features needed to counter any manipulation of recordings. Moreover, detention facilities of all law enforcement agencies should be effectively examined by the relevant judicial/prosecutorial authorities and the possibility of inspections being carried out by other independent bodies should also be considered.

In relation to the *prevention of ill-treatment in prisons*, the Committee invites authorities to take the necessary steps to ensure that all prisoners are able to have access to a lawyer and that sufficient contacts with the outside world should be facilitated; this is especially important when the prisoner's state of health is uncertain. The CPT further recommends the establishment of a national, independent inspectorate mandated and adequately resourced to visit all places where people are deprived of their liberty and to receive any complaints from such persons. In general, the Committee recommends that the Italian authorities ensure that whenever a person is injured while under the supervision of public officials, the case is considered by the relevant authorities as one indicative of ill-treatment. The necessary measures should be taken to raise awareness among law enforcement, prison, medical and other staff at every hierarchical level of the important duty incumbent on them of reporting ill-treatment to the competent authorities. On the same issue, the Committee invites the Italian authorities to consider setting up a specialised service to deal with allegations of ill-treatment by law enforcement and/or prison officials.

In the *final comments to the ninth report on Italy*, the CPT underlines that criminal sanctions imposed on only a small proportion of the persons involved in the acts committed in the Bolzaneto Barracks and Diaz School cases during the Genoa G8 Summit of 2001, casts doubt on the effectiveness of the system of protection from ill-treatment by law enforcement and prison officials and that Italian authorities should increase their efforts to introduce the crime of torture into the criminal code, in accordance with the Country's binding obligations under international law. This recommendation was further reiterated at the beginning of the subsequent Committee report, summarised in the following pages.

The CPT's *tenth visit* to Italy took place from 13 to 25 May 2012. The Committee's report (CPT/Inf(2013)32) on this visit was adopted in November 2012 and published on 19 November 2013 together with the Italian Government's observations and responses to the comments and requests for information formulated by the Committee (CPT/Inf(2013)33).

During the visit the delegation visited nine State Police Headquarters and Carabinieri stations, the Bologna CIE, eight prisons and three psychiatric hospitals. The Committee met the Minister of Justice, the Minister of Health and other ministry officials, as well as representatives of the Carabinieri, the Guardia di Finanza (Finance Police) and representatives of NGOs. A summary list of the principal recommendations formulated by the CPT, grouped by investigation theme, follows.

In relation to the *conditions of detention for persons in custody* there are numerous recommendations concerning the problem of ill-treatment. In this respect, the CPT recommends that a formal message emanating from the relevant authorities be delivered to all law enforcement officials, (particularly in the Milan area), reminding them that they should be respectful of the rights of persons in their custody and that the physical ill-treatment of such persons will be the subject of severe sanctions. In this respect, the CPT recommends that the Italian authorities take the necessary steps to ensure that the physical ill-treatment becomes prosecutable *ex officio*, irrespective of the prognosis of recovery, applying therefore the necessary amendments to the criminal code. The Committee further requests that steps be taken by all relevant authorities to ensure that, whenever injuries are recorded by a doctor which are consistent with allegations of ill-treatment made by a detained person, the record is systematically brought to the attention of the relevant prosecutor.

On the issue of the *safeguards against ill-treatment by law enforcement officials*, the CPT reiterates basically all the recommendations of the previous report (see above). It underlines the importance of ensuring that persons who have been deprived of their liberty are fully informed of their rights as from the very outset of their deprivation of liberty, and also, that the persons concerned should be requested to sign a statement attesting that they have been informed of their rights in a language which they understand.

On the issue of *conditions of detention*, the Committee requests that the Italian authorities take immediate steps to improve the material conditions in detention cells at the Florence Questura, which were deemed particularly poor, and to ensure that in all law enforcement establishments, persons detained overnight are provided with a clean mattress and clean blankets and that all persons who are held in custody for 24 hours or more are offered adequate washing facilities. In addition, the authorities should ensure that all custody cells in Italy have adequate access to natural light and that the persons concerned are offered outdoor exercise every day.

On the theme of *detention of foreign nationals under aliens legislation* the CPT recommends that immediate steps be taken at the Bologna CIE to ensure that foreign nationals are provided with board games and a television set and have frequent access to the existing sports facilities. In this respect, the Committee recommends that the Italian authorities redouble their efforts to provide foreign nationals held at the Bologna CIE with a range of purposeful and developed activities. In relation to the health care situation in the CIEs, apart from the recommendation on the systematic transmission to the relevant prosecutor of information on injuries which is indicative of ill-treatment in all CIEs, the CPT recommends that steps be taken to ensure that the confidentiality of medical data is fully respected at the Bologna CIE. In addition, a proper legal basis and clear procedures should be established as regards the isolation of immigration detainees for reasons of good order or security in CIEs in Italy.

As for the *conditions in prisons*, the Committee recommends that the Italian authorities pursue vigorously their endeavours to combat prison overcrowding, in particular through increased application of non-custodial measures during the period before any imposition of a sentence. Various recommendations from the Committee of Ministers of the CoE are cited as guidelines to resolve this issue. On the issue of ill-treatment, the CPT's recommendations concentrate in particular on the Vicenza prison. In this vein, the CPT requests the appropriate authorities to deliver a clear message to the staff of Vicenza Prison that all forms of ill-treatment will be duly punished; and that the authorities inform the outside bodies responsible for monitoring the situation at Vicenza Prison of the allegations received by the delegation during the visit. In line with the previous recommendations regarding detained persons in the custody of law enforcement officials, the authorities must take the necessary steps to ensure that in Vicenza prison, and in all prisons in Italy, whenever injuries are recorded by a doctor which are consistent with allegations of ill-treatment made by a detained person, the record is systematically brought to the attention of the relevant prosecutor.

In relation to the *conditions of detention of the general prison population*, the Committee recommends that material conditions of detention be improved in a majority of the prisons visited, particularly at Palermo-Ucciardone. In addition, the CPT recommends that the Italian authorities take steps to reduce cell occupancy levels in all of the prisons visited so as to provide for at least 4 m² of living space per prisoner in multi-occupancy cells; for this purpose, the area taken up by in-cell sanitary facilities should not be taken into account. Further, any cells providing less than 8 m² of living space should be used for single occupancy only. As recommended for the CIE, finally, the CPT calls upon the Italian authorities to redouble their efforts to improve the programme of activities, work and vocational training opportunities for prisoners.

On the issue of *prisoners subjected to the "41-bis" regime at Terni Prison*, the CPT calls upon the Italian authorities to review the current "41-bis" detention regime (a system of maximum security imposed on those convicted of mafia-related crimes), specifically in order to provide these prisoners with a wider range of purposeful activities. The Committee calls upon the Italian authorities to allow these prisoners to spend at least four hours per day outside their cells together with the other inmates of the same living unit, granted the right to accumulate unused visit entitlements and allowed to make at least one telephone call per month, irrespective of whether or not they receive a visit during the same month. Furthermore, having seen that all "41-bis" prisoners at the prison visited were subjected to CCTV surveillance inside their cells, the CPT recommends the use of CCTV surveillance only in the few cases where such measure is deemed appropriate based on an accurate individual risk assessment, and ensuring that detainees are guaranteed reasonable privacy.

On the issue of *health care services*, the Committee recommends immediate steps be taken to improve the state of hygiene in the Palermo-Ucciardone and Bari prisons. In these two prisons, the budget for specialist consultations should be increased and the organisation of escorts of prison officers to transport prisoners to outside specialists should be improved. In addition, steps should be taken to improve facilities in cells accommodating prisoners suffering from physical disabilities, such as providing mobility-impaired and paraplegic prisoners with specialised hospital beds. The Committee further recommends that steps be taken by the relevant authorities to ensure that agents responsible for the care of this particular type of prisoners receive appropriate training. In general, the CPT invites all relevant authorities to ensure that a dedicated register for the recording of injuries observed on prisoners is kept in all Italian prisons and recommends the Department of Prison Administration (DAP) to take immediate steps, in co-operation with the relevant regional health authorities, to ensure that the principle of medical confidentiality is fully respected in all prisons.

Among the other recommendations provided in the report, the CPT recommends that the current legislation and practice are revised to ensure that prisoners facing *disciplinary charges* are allowed to call witnesses on their behalf and to cross-examine evidence given against them. They should also be allowed to have a lawyer present during hearings before the disciplinary commission and receive a copy of the disciplinary decision, informing them about the reasons for the decision and the avenues for lodging an appeal. The authorities should ensure that appeals against disciplinary sanctions are also examined on the merits by supervisory judges and that the practice of involving prison doctors as members of disciplinary commissions are abolished. The Committee requests a review, in light of CoE standards, of the role of health-care staff in relation to disciplinary matters and the relevant criminal legislation concerning the possible imposition of daytime solitary confinement on prisoners sentenced to life-imprisonment (as part of the sentence). The principle requiring this amendment to the law is that a person should be kept in prison as a punishment, not to receive further punishment.

In relation to the *situation in psychiatric establishments*, the CPT urges all relevant regional and national authorities to implement a reform of the existing psychiatric services as a matter of priority and ensure that patients are provided with a therapeutic environment and individualised treatment programme based on a multidisciplinary approach. A clearly defined policy on seclusion should be established and a specific register should be established in every psychiatric structure to record all instances of seclusion. Furthermore, every patient subject to seclusion should be continuously supervised by a qualified member of health-care staff. According to the CPT's assessment, when an involuntary patient held in a psychiatric structure dies, an autopsy should follow, unless a medical authority independent of the hospital decides otherwise. Moreover, the relevant authorities should institute a practice of carrying out a thorough inquiry into every death of a psychiatric patient, in particular with a view to ascertaining whether there are lessons to be learned as regards operating procedures. The Committee also recommends the necessary steps to be taken to ensure that, in the context of judicial review procedures, court decisions are not taken only on the basis of the assessment provided by the forensic patient's treating doctor. Moreover, steps should be taken by the relevant authorities to ensure that nursing staff at the Milazzo Psychiatric Service for Diagnosis and Care (SPDC) are provided with adequate training and guidance to enable them to manage agitated and/

or violent patients in an appropriate manner and to diversify the treatment made available to patients allowing for therapeutic alternatives to pharmacotherapy. In addition, the CPT recommends that a clearly defined policy on measures of containment is established and effectively implemented in practice in all psychiatric structures in Italy. Finally, the CPT reiterates its recommendation that steps be taken by the relevant authorities (including at the legislative level) to ensure that, in the context of initial TSO (compulsory psychiatric admission) certain procedures are followed, including: ensuring that the formal decision to place a person in a SPDC (Psychiatric Service for Diagnosis and Care) is always based on the opinion of at least one psychiatrist; that doctors draw up detailed medical certificates; as far as possible, a patient's treating psychiatrist should try to avoid drawing up the statutory detailed initial or "co-validation" certificate relating to the involuntary admission of his or her patient to an SPDC; that patients should as a rule be heard in person by the competent guardianship judge, preferably on the hospital premises.

V. European Committee of Social Rights

The European Committee of Social Rights (ECSR) was established pursuant to art. 25 of the European Social Charter of 1961 in order to determine whether the legislation and practice of States Parties comply with the provisions of the European Social Charter, its Protocols and the European Social Charter (revised) (ESC-R). Currently, the Committee is composed of 15 independent experts elected by the Committee of Ministers for a period of six years, renewable only once. Since 10 November 2010 Giuseppe Palmisano has been a part of the Committee, and will remain in office until 31 December 2016.

Italy ratified the European Social Charter in 1965 and the revised European Social Charter in 1999, accepting 97 of its 98 numbered paragraphs. The only provision not accepted is article 25 ESC-R, which protects the right of workers in the event of the insolvency of their employer. As of 2012, Italy has not presented the Committee with the first report on this provision of the revised Charter, as envisaged by CM decision 821/4.1c of 13 December 2002. Between 1967 and 2012, the Government submitted 20 reports on the application of the Charter of 1961 and 12 on the application of the revised Charter.

The latest *conclusions* on Italy were published on 29 January 2014. The document refers to the twelfth report due, as per the provisions of the Committee, by 31 October 2012 but presented, in parts, between 6 December 2012 and 5 February 2013. Between April and May 2013, the Committee addressed two letters to the Italian Government to request supplementary information in relation to art. 23 ESC-R and art. 13(2) ESC-R respectively. The Italian authorities have submitted a reply to the first of the two letters only, on 19 June 2013. Comments on the Italian Government's report made by the Working Group "Social Charter" of the Human Rights Committee of the Conference of International Non-Governmental Organisations to the Council of Europe, the Italian LGBT network and by ILGA-Europe were considered when drawing up the report. The *Conclusions 2013* relates to the provisions of the Charter accepted by Italy in relation to the thematic group "Health, social security and social protection" (articles 3, 11, 12, 13, 14, 23 and 30 ESC-R). The reference period for the Committee's analysis goes from 1 January 2008 to 31 December 2011.

Overall, the final document of the Committee refers to the Italian situation in relation to 19 articles and numbered paragraphs of the revised Charter, providing 8 conclusions on compliance (occasionally asking for the submission of additional information) and 7 in regard to noncompliance. In relation to four provisions (articles 3.3, 3.4, 11.1 and 13.2 ESC-R), the Committee postpones its assessment to the next report, asking the Italian Government for the specific data needed to assess the status of implementation of the articles in question.

Paragraph outline of the Conclusions 2013 on Italy

Article of the ESC-R	Conclusions of conformity	Conclusions of non-conformity	Request for further information
art. 3 ESC-R (right to safe and healthy working conditions)	para. 2 (safety and health regulations)	para. 1 (national occupational safety and health policy)	para. 3 (enforcement of safety and health regulations) 4 (occupational health services)
art. 11 ESC-R (right to protection of health)	para. 2 (advisory and educational facilities) 3 (prevention of diseases and accidents)		para. 1 (removal of the causes of ill-health)
art. 12 ESC-R (right to social security)	para. 2 (maintenance of a social security system at a satisfactory level at least equal to that necessary for the ratification of the European Code of Social Security)	para. 1 (existence of a social security system) 3 (development of the social security system) 4 (social security of persons moving between States)	

art. 13 ESC-R (right to social and medical assistance)	para. 3 (prevention, abolition or alleviation of need) 4 (specific emergency assistance for non-residents)	para. 1 (adequate assistance for every person in need)	para. 2 (non-discrimination in the exercise of social and political rights)
art. 14 ESC-R (right to benefit from social services)	para. 1 (promotion or provision of social services) 2 (public participation in the establishment and maintenance of social services)		
art. 23 ESC-R (right of elderly persons to social protection)		*Whole article (composed just by one paragraph)*	
art. 30 ESC-R (right to be protected against poverty and social exclusion)		*Whole article (composed just by one paragraph)*	

In relation to article 3 ESC-R (the right to safe and healthy working conditions), the Committee concludes that the situation in Italy is in compliance with para. 2 (safety and health regulations). Nevertheless, it requests more detailed and up-to date information on changes in legislation and regulations during the reference period and asks for information on the implementation of a number of EU directives in this area. To assess whether temporary workers, interim workers and workers on fixed-term contracts actually do have the same level of protection as employees on permanent contracts, the Committee asks for the next report to include examples of the way in which the particular nature of the employment of these categories of worker is taken into account. The situation in Italy, however, is deemed not in conformity with para. 1 (national occupational safety and health policy), as there is no appropriate occupational safety and health policy in the Country and there is no adequate system to organise occupational risk prevention. In relation to para. 3 (enforcement of safety and health regulations), the Committee laments the lack of necessary information for an effective evaluation of the situation and requests this information in the next report. It draws the Government's attention to the fact that unless this information is set out in the next report, it will lack the requisite information to establish whether the situation in Italy is in conformity with the provisions of the European Social Charter. In particular, in relation to the number of occupational accidents and diseases, the Committee requested explanations on the major discrepancies between the data on fatal work accidents supplied by the Italian authorities and those published by Eurostat. The Committee also requests that the next report contain information on the declaratory obligations and monitoring processes for work accidents and vocational diseases. In relation to the activities of the Labour Inspectorate, the Committee requests information in the next report on the rate of workers covered by the inspection visits carried out and on the number of labour inspectors working, their functions and powers to establish violations, make orders and impose sanctions in cases of violations of the specific regulations on health and safety at work as well as the consequences of the criminal offences recorded and the number of criminal sentences passed on cases referred to the public prosecutor's office. The Committee adopted a similar opinion on para. 4 (occupational health services). In this regard the Committee asked for information on the proportion of undertakings equipped with occupational health services or sharing them in practice and on existing strategies, in consultation with employers' and workers' organisations, to improve access to occupational health services for independent and home-based workers.

In relation to art. 11 ESC-R (right to protection of health), the Committee found that the situation in Italy is in conformity with para. 2 and 3 although, in this case also, it requests further information from the authorities on the subject. In relation to para. 2 (advisory and educational facilities), the Committee asks for updated information in the next report on all the activities carried out by the public health services or other bodies to promote good health and prevent disease, as well as on screening programmes available throughout the Country. It also asks for confirmation that free and regular consultation and screening for pregnant women exists across the Country. In relation to para. 3 (prevention of diseases and accidents), the information requested by the Committee concerns the state of implementation of existing regulations to reduce environmental hazards, improving the quality of air and water, food safety, noise and asbestos pollution. In relation to para. 1 (removal of the causes of ill-health), the Committee decided to temporarily postpone its conclusions while awaiting the decision which it will adopt on a collective complaint against Italy presented by the International Planned Parenthood Federation, declared admissible in October 2012 (complaint No. 87/2012, see *2013 Yearbook*, p. 255). In that complaint, currently under examination by the Committee, the applicant organisation claims that section 9 of act No. 194/1978, which governs the conscientious objection of medical practitioners and other health personnel in relation to the voluntary termination of pregnancy violates, specifically, article 11 ESC-R and the first paragraph in particular.

In relation to article 12 ESC-R (right to social security), the Committee considers that the situation in Italy is in conformity with para. 2 (maintenance of a social security system at a satisfactory level at least equal to that necessary for the ratification of the European Code of Social Security). On the contrary, the situation in Italy is deemed not in conformity with para. 1 (existence of a social security system), para. 3 (development of the social security system) and para. 4 (social security of persons moving between States). In particular, for the first paragraph, the Committee concludes that the information provided in the report does not establish that the minimum level of sickness benefit and pension benefit are adequate. In relation to para. 3, the situation is deemed to be in non-conformity because it has not been established that measures were taken to raise the system of social security to a higher level. In relation to para. 4, the Committee adopts the conclusion that the situation is in non-conformity on the grounds that neither equal treatment with regard to social security rights nor the retention of accrued benefits are guaranteed to nationals of all other States Parties to the European Social Charter: Albania, Andorra, Armenia, Azerbaijan, Georgia, the Republic of Moldova, Ukraine and the Russian Federation.

In relation to article 13 ESC-R (right to social and medical assistance), the situation in Italy was found to be in conformity with para. 3 (prevention, abolition or alleviation of need) and with para. 4 (specific emergency assistance for non-residents). On the contrary, the Committee adopts a conclusion of non-conformity for para. 1 (adequate assistance for every person in need) on the grounds that social assistance is not provided for everybody in need and because the general level of assistance appears inadequate. In relation to para. 2 (non-discrimination in the exercise of social and political rights), the Committee notes that the situation in Italy was deemed to be in conformity with the provisions of the European Social Charter in the last five evaluation cycles. Nevertheless, pending receipt of confirmation from the Italian Government that no restrictions apply, in law or in practice, to the social and political rights of beneficiaries of social assistance, the Committee defers its conclusion. In the absence of the required information, there will not be adequate reason to conclude that the situation in Italy in this regard is in conformity with the provisions of the revised European Social Charter.

In relation to article 14 ESC-R (right to benefit from social services), the Committee concludes that the situation in Italy is in conformity with both paragraphs of the article. Nevertheless, in relation to para. 1

(promotion or provision of social services), the Committee requests further information concerning the overall organisation and functioning of social services and the total number of persons employed by these services. In relation to para. 2 also (public participation in the establishment and maintenance of social services), further information is requested. Specifically the Committee invites the authorities to provide details of the number of people using social services provided by voluntary organisations, the number of such organisations registered, their geographical distribution, the number of salaried persons and volunteers working for them and the amounts and sources of their funding. The Committee also asks for information in the next report on the practical and financial support (such as tax benefits) offered to voluntary organisations by the State. The Committee requests information on the initiatives taken to promote representation of specific user-groups in bodies where the public authorities are also represented, and action to promote consultation of users on questions concerning organisation of the various social services and the aid they provide. If the necessary information is not provided in the next report there will be nothing to show that Italy is in conformity with the Charter.

In relation to article 23 ESC-R (the right of elderly persons to social protection), the Committee concludes that Italy is in non-conformity because the information provided in the report does not show that there is an adequate legal framework to combat age discrimination outside employment.

Also in relation to article 30 ESC-R (right to be protected against poverty and social exclusion) the Committee concludes that the situation in Italy is not in conformity with the Charter because the information contained in the report presented by the Italian authorities does not show that there is an overall and coordinated approach to combating poverty and social exclusion. In fact, there is discriminatory treatment of migrant Roma and Sinti with regard to citizen participation. The assessment underlying this conclusion of non-conformity also contains a follow-up to collective complaint No. 58/2009 on the case *COHRE v. Italy*, decision on the merits, 25 June 2010 (see *2011 Yearbook*, pp. 218–219). In the case in question, the Committee had established, *inter alia*, that restrictions on the possibilities for migrant Roma and Sinti to participate in civic decision-making processes in their own cities lead to discriminatory treatment with regard to the right to vote or other forms of citizen participation and, thus, is a cause of marginalisation and social exclusion, in breach of article E ESC-R (non-discrimination) taken in conjunction with article 30 ESC-R. The information presented in the Italian Government's report does not lead the Committee to take a different view of the situation.

The thirteenth report on the implementation of the European Social Charter (revised), whose presentation to the Committee is scheduled by 31 October 2013, refers to the provisions accepted by Italy in relation to the thematic group "Labour rights". It will therefore concern articles 2 ESC-R (right to just conditions of work), 4 ESC-R (right to a fair remuneration), 5 ESC-R (right to organise), 6 ESC-R (right to bargain collectively), 21 ESC-R (right to information and consultation), 22 ESC-R (right to take part in the determination and improvement of the working conditions and working environment), 26 ESC-R (right to dignity at work), 28 ESC-R (right of workers' representatives to protection in the undertaking and facilities to be accorded to them) and 29 ESC-R (right to information and consultation in collective redundancy procedures). Observations of the ECSR concerning this report will be published at the end of December, in the *Conclusions 2014*.

As regards the collective complaints procedure established with the Additional Protocol of 1995, in 2013 three complaints were presented against Italy. The first (No. 91/2013), presented by the Confederazione Generale Italiana del Lavoro (CGIL – Italian labour trade union), invites the ECSR to declare article 9 of law No. 194 of 1978, which governs the conscientious objection of medical practitioners in relation to the termination of pregnancy, to be in violation of article 11 ESC-R (right to health), 1 (right to work), 2 (right to just conditions of work), 3 (right to safe and healthy working conditions), 26 (right of dignity at work) and E (non-discrimination). According to the CGIL, in fact, the absence of a legal framework combined with the high number of objecting medical practitioners in hospitals in Italy not only undermines the right of women to have access to procedures for the termination of pregnancy, contrary to the European Social Charter, but also discriminates against non-objecting medical personal who would be obliged to bear the burden of guaranteeing that right (on the same issue, though leading to different profiles of incompatibility, refer to complaint No. 87/2012 against Italy, *2013 Yearbook*, p. 132). In relation to the complaints procedure in 2013, on 30 May the Italian Government presented its observations on both the admissibility and the merits of the complaint.

The second collective complaint presented against Italy in 2013 was submitted to the Committee by the international NGO Association for the Protection of All Children (Approach). The complaint (No. 94/2013), in particular, complains of a violation of article 17 (right of children and young persons to social, legal and economic protection) of the ESC-R on account of the absence of legislation in Italy to explicitly prohibit the use of corporal punishment or other cruel, inhuman or degrading punishment of children and young persons. In this case it is interesting to note how, even though in a previous collective complaint against Italy (*OMCT v. Italy*, No. 19/2003) the Committee had not found this absence of such legislation to be in violation of the European Social Charter, the international NGO justifies reviewing the issue in light of the Committee's new more restrained legal orientation. In relation to the complaint, judged admissible in July 2013, the Italian Government presented its observations on the decision on the merits on 26 September 2013.

The third complaint (No. 102/2013) against Italy was submitted on 2 August 2013 by the Associazione nazionale giudici di pace (the National Association of Justices of the Peace). This complaint, on the grounds of the lack of adequate legislation governing the social security and welfare protection for this category of honorary judges in Italy, including in the event of illness, accident, maternity or unpaid holidays, alleges a violation of art. 12(4)(b) ESC-R which provides that States Parties must guarantee "the granting, maintenance and resumption of social security rights by such means as the accumulation of insurance or employment periods completed under the legislation of each of the Parties".

VI. Commissioner for Human Rights

The Commissioner for Human Rights is an independent non-judicial institution created by the Committee of Ministers' resolution (99)50 of 7 May 1999. Nils Muižnieks (Latvia) is the present Commissioner for Human Rights of the Council of Europe (in office since 1st April 2012).

In 2013 the Commissioner published reports concerning two visits which took place in 2012 (to the Czech Republic and to the former Yugoslav Republic of Macedonia) and seven visits which took place in 2013 (to Azerbaijan, Estonia, the Russian Federation, Greece, Moldova, Spain and Turkey). In the same year visits were made to Albania, Armenia, Bosnia and Herzegovina and Denmark. It is also worth noting a five-day mission lead by the Commissioner to Turkey, Bulgaria and Germany in order to assess the Syrian refugee crisis.

The Commissioner made five visits to Italy. The most recent visit occurred from 3 to 6 July 2012. The purpose of the visit was to re-examine a series of critical issues relating in particular to the excessive length of legal proceedings and to the protection of the rights of Roma, Sinti, migrants and asylum-seekers. The resulting report was published on 18 September 2012 (CommDH (2012)26) (see *2013 Yearbook*, pp. 256–260). Previous visits took place: from 10 to 17 June 2005 (report published on 14 December 2005 – CommDH (2005)9); from 19 to 20 June 2008 (report published on 28 July 2008 – CommDH (2008)18), from 13 to 15 January 2009 (report published on 16 April 2009 – CommDH (2009)16) and from 26 to 27 May 2011 (report published on 7 September 2011).

On 12 November 2013, the Commissioner sent a letter to the mayor of Rome, Ignazio Marino, in order to draw his attention to two issues raised in the above-mentioned 2012 report: the segregation of Roma and Sinti on the one hand, and the living conditions and integration of beneficiaries of international or humanitarian protection on the other.

On the first issue, after reiterating his concern for the living conditions of Roma and Sinti in so-called "authorised" camps (or segregated camps) which he visited in 2012, the Commissioner expressed his concern about the existence of legislation adopted by the former municipal administration of Rome at the beginning of the year concerning the criteria for assigning social housing. According to these criteria, in fact, persons living in formal camps are not considered as living in "greatly disadvantaged housing conditions", and are therefore not eligible for prioritisation for the assignment of social housing. An additional source of concern was the fact that, under this legislation, these segregated camps shall be considered permanent structures. In this respect, the Commissioner called on the Mayor of Rome to ensure the possibility for Roma and Sinti living in these camps to have access to social housing on an equal footing with the rest of the population.

Again in relation to these communities, the Commissioner notes with concern the forced eviction of Roma families from the informal camp of Salviati and their relocation to the formal camp of Castel Romano against their will and without any genuine prior consultation with the inhabitants. The Commissioner underlines that international standards on the right to adequate housing, which are binding to Italy, establish that evictions should only take place as a last resort and following appropriate procedural safeguards, including genuine consultation with those affected. Forced evictions and segregated camps must therefore be relegated to the past and ordinary housing solutions must found for Roma and Sinti in Italy in accordance with Italy's National Strategy for the Inclusion of Roma and Sinti, adopted by the Council of Ministers in February 2012 (see *2013 Yearbook*, pp. 99 and 257).

On the *situation of beneficiaries of international protection*, the Commissioner expressed his appreciation of the commitment shown by the municipal government, in particular he welcomed the personal visit made by the Mayor of Rome to "Salaam Palace" (an abandoned university building in which hundreds of refugees are living) and information that the situation concerning residence registration had improved considerably. The latter was one of the issues raised by the Commissioner during his 2012 visit. At the same time, nonetheless, the Commissioner expressed concern after he was informed by certain NGOs that the number of persons living in Salaam Palace had notably increased (from around 800 in 2012 to 1,250), and that the sanitary conditions had further deteriorated. The Commissioner therefore invited the Mayor to keep him informed of developments concerning the solutions adopted to improve the situation for these people.

On 4 December 2013, Rita Cutini, Municipal Counsellor for Social Affairs of the City of Rome responded with a letter to the issues raised by the Commissioner for Human Rights. The letter highlights the various steps forward taken by the Municipal Government in fully implementing the Strategy for the Inclusion of Roma and Sinti. Among the measures mentioned, is a new plan which should lead to an expansion of the reception network in cities and the launch of the above-mentioned National Strategy through the organisation of four working tables on employment, housing, education and health. In relation to the relocation of the Via Salviati camp, mentioned in the letter, the Counsellor indicates how the measures adopted are in accordance with UNAR guidelines.

In relation to the issue of beneficiaries of international protection, the reply letter illustrates the municipal government's commitment in that regard. Actions specifically highlighted are the decision to receive survivors of the Lampedusa shipwreck (3 October 2013) and the 2000% increase in the available accommodation provided by the Protection System for Asylum Seekers and Refugees (SPRAR).

Among the other activities carried out by the Commissioner for Human Rights, it is worth mentioning the online publication of the *Human Rights Comments*, a sort of blog in which the Commissioner examines and comments briefly on the human rights situation in Europe. Over the year in question, 10 comments were published (27 in 2011 and 13 in 2012). Four of these contain specific references to the human rights situation in Italy:

Governments should act in the best interest of stateless children (15 January 2013); the Commissioner analyses the situation of stateless children in Europe stressing that statelessness is not disappearing with time, but being transmitted over generations and that the best interest of the child is to have citizenship. In this respect, the Commissioner encourages Governments of Member States of the CoE to act more vigorously to break this cycle by targeting measures to end statelessness, especially, by ensuring that all children are registered in birth registry books immediately after their birth, by granting citizenship automatically at birth to children born in their territory who would otherwise be stateless, and by collecting disaggregated statelessness data on a regular basis to determine effective public policies. In the presentation of the situation of stateless persons in Europe, Italy is mentioned on account of the presence in the Country of around 15,000 Roma coming from the Former Yugoslavia who are denied citizenship in Italy and in other Countries (so-called "*de facto* statelessness", see *2012 Yearbook*, p. 35).

Europe must combat racist extremism and uphold human rights (13 May 2013); the Commissioner tackles the issue of the worrying intensification of activities of racist extremist organisations in Europe and proposes a series of measures which Governments should adopt in order to counter the phenomenon of racist violence from a human rights based approach. These organisations are considered as posing a serious threat to the rule of law and to human rights. Italy is mentioned, alongside Hungary and Serbia as an example of a Country in which the political presence of racist extremist parties in Parliament lends legitimacy and credibility to political extremism that is often linked to racist and other hate crimes, in particular against migrants, Muslims and vulnerable social groups such as Roma.

Child labour in Europe: a persisting challenge (20 August 2013); the Commissioner dedicates this comment to the issue of child labour in Europe and highlights the existence of strong indications that child labour remains a serious problem and that it might be growing in the wake of the economic crisis, in particular following the adoption of austerity measures in many European Countries. In this respect, Governments need to monitor this situation and to use the UN Convention on the Rights of the Child and the European Social Charter as guidance for preventive and remedial action. Italy figures among the Countries for which data is available on child labour. The Commissioner mentions a study of 2013 which indicates that 5.2% of children younger than 16 are working.

Time for accountability in CIA torture cases (11 September 2013); upon the twelfth anniversary of the terrorist attacks of 11 September 2001, the Commissioner uses the occasion to commemorate the victims of these attacks and to reflect on the anti-terrorist measures adopted by the USA and Europe. According to the Commissioner, by allowing unlawful detentions and interrogation techniques amounting to torture, the response of the West caused further suffering and violated human rights law. In particular, emphasis is placed on the abuse of state secret privilege by Governments involved in CIA operations carried out in Europe between 2002 and 2006 which hampered judiciary and parliamentary initiatives aimed at establishing the truth and ensuring accountability for their complicity in the unlawful programme of "extraordinary renditions". The only Country to have handed down sentences against people involved in the CIA programme is Italy. The criminal court convicted *in absentia*, twenty-three US citizens, all but one CIA agents, as well as five Italian secret service agents for the kidnapping and rendition to Egypt of a Muslim cleric, Hassan Mustafa Osama Nasr, also known as Abu Omar, from the streets of Milan in 2003.

Finally, it is worth noting the adoption by the Commissioner of an opinion on the legislation of the Russian Federation on non-commercial organisations (CommDH(2013)15) and the publication of two issue papers on the following issues: *Safeguarding human rights in times of economic crisis* and *The right to leave a Country*.

VII. European Commission against Racism and Intolerance

The European Commission against Racism and Intolerance (ECRI), established in 1993, is a monitoring body of the Council of Europe specialised in combating any form of racism, xenophobia, anti-semitism and intolerance in a human rights perspective. The members of ECRI remain in office for five years. They are selected for their moral authority and their recognised experience in the field of combating racism, xenophobia, anti-semitism and intolerance; they act on an individual basis and independently. The Commission is composed by a member and, if a Government so wishes, a deputy member for each State of the Council of Europe. The expert in respect of Italy during 2013 has been Vitaliano Esposito (actual member, the mandate of Antonio Mura, deputy member, ended in January 2013). The External Relations Officers of the Commission Secretariat, part of the Directorate-General Human Rights and the Rule of Law of the Council of Europe, is Stefano Valenti.

In the course of 2013, the Commission published reports on the fourth monitoring cycle concerning the Russian Federation, Finland, Ireland, Liechtenstein, Malta, Republic of Moldova, Netherlands, Portugal, San Marino. In addition, the ECRI presented conclusions on its priority recommendations in respect of the following Countries: Albania, Austria, Estonia, Former Yugoslav Republic of Macedonia, France, Georgia, Poland and United Kingdom. In 2013 the fifth monitoring cycle began, with visits made by the Commission to Belgium, Germany, the Slovak Republic, Romania, Slovenia and Switzerland.

In relation to Italy, the fourth monitoring cycle concluded in February 2012, with the publication of report (CRI(2012)2), concerning the visit made by the Commission during the month of November 2010 (see *2012 Yearbook*, pp. 253–262). The three previous reports by the ECRI on Italy are as follows: report on the first monitoring cycle (CRI(98)48), adopted and published on 15 June 1998; report on the second monitoring cycle (CRI(2002)4), adopted on 21 June 2001 and published on 23 April 2002; and report on the third monitoring cycle (CRI(2006)19), adopted on 16 December 2005 and published on 16 May 2006 (see *2011 Yearbook*, pp. 224–226).

VIII. Advisory Committee on the Framework Convention for the Protection of National Minorities

The Committee is a monitoring body instituted pursuant to art. 26 of the Council of Europe Framework Convention for the Protection of National Minorities. It is composed of 18 independent experts with recognised expertise in the field of the protection of national minorities. They shall serve on the Committee in their individual capacity, for a period of four years. Since 2012 Italian expert, Francesco Palermo, has been a member of the Advisory Committee.

The Advisory Committee serves to assist the CM in evaluating the implementation of the Framework-Convention in States Parties, through the examination of periodic State Reports. The results of this evaluation are expressed in a detailed opinion which serves as a basis for the preparation of the CMs conclusive resolutions on the Country in question. Follow-up meetings are generally organised by the Advisory Committee with a view to bringing together all actors – governmental and non-governmental – interested in the implementation of the Convention and to examine ways of implementing the results of the monitoring procedure.

Italy has participated to three full monitoring cycles. The first cycle opened with the presentation of the Italian Government's report (ACFC/SR(1999)007) on 3 May 1999; the opinion of the Committee (ACFC/IF/OP/I(2002)007) was adopted on 14 September 2001 and the final resolution by the Committee of Ministers (ResCMN(2002)10) on 3 July 2002. The second cycle opened with the presentation of the Italian report (ACFC/INF/OPII (2004)006) on 14 May 2004; the relative opinion (ACFC/INF/OP/II (2005)003) dates back to 24 February 2005, and the consequent resolution by the CM (ResCMN(2006)5) to 14 June 2006. The third monitoring cycle opened with presentation of the Italian Government report (ACFC/SR/III(2009)011) on 21 December 2009 (see *2011 Yearbook*, pp. 227–228). The Advisory Committee's opinion (ACFC/OP/III(2010)008) was adopted on 15 October 2010 (see *2012 Yearbook*, pp. 263–269), while the final resolution of the Committee of Ministers (ResCMN(2012)10) was adopted on 4 July 2012 (see *2013 Yearbook*, pp. 244–246). The presentation of the fourth report by the Italian Government on the implementation of the Framework Convention is due on 1 March 2014.

In 2013, as part of the respective monitoring cycles, the Advisory Committee of the Framework Convention carried out visits to Latvia, Lithuania, Montenegro, the Netherlands, Poland and Serbia. In addition, the Committee adopted and published its own *opinion* on the situation of national minorities in Kosovo; it adopted, but has not yet published, in line with the principle of confidentiality, *opinions* on Bosnia-Herzegovina, Latvia and Montenegro and published opinions on Azerbaijan, Ireland and Ukraine, adopted during the previous year.

IX. European Commission for Democracy through Law

The Commission, also known as the *Venice Commission*, is the Council of Europe's advisory body on constitutional issues; it was established in 1990 and receives financial support by a law of the Region of Veneto.

The Commission is composed of independent experts with extensive experience in the area of democratic institutions or excellence in the legal and political domains. Members are designated for four years by the participating Countries which, as well as the 47 Member States of the CoE, include Algeria, Brazil, Chile, South Korea, Israel, Kazakhstan, Kyrgyzstan, Morocco, Mexico, Peru, United States and Tunisia. Belarus is an associate member, while Argentina, Canada, Japan, the Holy See and Uruguay participate in the work of the Commission as observer Countries. The European Commission, Palestinian National Authority and South Africa have a special co-operation status.

Since 2009, Gianni Buquicchio has been the President of the *Venice Commission*. There are two further substitute members for Italy in the Commission: Sergio Bartole and Guido Neppi Modona.

One of the Commission's activities is the production of reports on topics within its mandate and promoting seminars on specific Countries and issues. Moreover, on request from the Parliamentary Assembly of the Council of Europe, it can adopt opinions on specific issues.

In the course of 2013, the *Venice Commission* adopted 30 opinions relating to the adoption of laws or bills of constitutional importance in the following Countries: Armenia, Azerbaijan, Bosnia-Herzegovina, Egypt, former Yugoslav Republic of Macedonia, the Russian Federation, Georgia (5), Iceland, Italy, Kyrgyzstan, Mexico, Montenegro, the Principality of Monaco, Republic of Moldova, Serbia (2), Tajikistan, Tunisia (2), Hungary, Ukraine (6). An opinion was also adopted on the issue of the prohibition of so-called "Propaganda of homosexuality" in the light of recent legislation in some Council of Europe Member States.

The *opinion* mentioned on Italy (CDL-AD(2013)038) was adopted by the Commission on 7 December 2013 during its 97th session following a request by the Parliamentary Assembly in its resolution 1920 (2013) on the *State of media freedom in Europe* (see, in this Part, Council of Europe, I). Following the request made by the PACE, the scope of the Commission's opinion was to assess whether Italian laws on defamation are in line with European standards in that regard. As the request of the Parliamentary Assembly was made with reference to the 14-month prison sentence imposed on newspaper editor Alessandro Sallusti for press defamation, the recommendations contained in the *Venice Commission*'s analysis place particular emphasis on defamation through the media.

The analysis is divided into two parts. The first part recalls the main European standards and ECtHR case-law concerning defamation and freedom of the press with particular reference to the following issues: the right to freedom of expression as an essential foundation of democratic society, the right to protection of one's reputation, the public's right to receive information, differentiation between statements of fact and value judgments, nature and severity of sanctions including the "chilling effect" of sanctions. In this respect, the Commission reaffirms the Council of Europe's approach concerning sanctions for defamation expressed in the *2004 Declaration on freedom of political debate in the media*. According to CoE standards, defamation or insult by the media should not lead to imprisonment, unless the seriousness of the violation of the rights or reputation of others makes it a strictly necessary and proportionate penalty, especially where other fundamental rights have been seriously violated through defamatory or insulting statements in the media, such as hate speech.

The second part of the opinion focuses on the existing legislative framework in Italy, made up of the "Law of the press" (No. 47/1948), from articles 57–58-bis, 278, 290, 290-bis, 291, 594–599 of the criminal code, and on eventual amendments to the framework with the adoption of bill No. 925. This latter was approved by the Chamber of Deputies on 17 October 2013 and is currently pending review by the Senate. The Commission's analysis also examines the case-law of the courts in matters of defamation and freedom of expression in Italy (see, in this Part, Organisation for Security and Cooperation in Europe, III).

After analysing the above-mentioned legislative framework and case-law in Italy in light of European standards, the *Venice Commission* adopted a series of conclusions. In general, it acknowledges that criminal defamation provisions currently in force in the Italian legislation do not fully meet the CoE standards on freedom of expression, notably due to the severity of sanctions and the absence of an upper limit for the financial penalties applicable for defamation published in the media. In this respect, nonetheless, the bill 925 represents a welcome effort to improve, modernise and bring the Italian legal framework on defamation into conformity with the ECHR requirements. In particular, the bill demonstrate a clear commitment by the Italian legislator to achieve a more appropriate balance between the safeguards required by the protection of reputation and the unhindered exercise of freedom of expression, including freedom of the press. As regards the system of sanctions, in particular, the abolition of the prison sanction for defamation, set out in the bill, is a significant step forward, demonstrating a clear commitment to giving a constructive response to the recent judgments of the Strasbourg Court against Italy – Italy was condemned for the severity of its criminal sanctions for defamation – (the reference is to the cases *Belpietro v. Italy*, judgment of 24 September 2013 and *Ricci v. Italy*, judgment of 8 October 2013, see Part IV, Italy in the Case-law of the European Court of Human Rights, II, C). Another positive aspect of the bill in this respect is the limiting of the use of criminal provisions by strengthening the right to reply and rectifications.

According to the Commission, while the wording of articles 595 (defamation) and 596 (excluding the defence of justification) of the Italian criminal code raises issues under the ECHR, the interpretation and application of these two provisions appear to have been corrected and brought more in line with European standards. Nonetheless, the defence of truth, the defences of public interest and responsible journalism, already widely recognised in domestic case-law in Italy, should be explicitly introduced into the legal framework, hence, articles 595 and 596 of the bill should be reconsidered in light of the aforementioned case-law and the specific recommendations provided in this document.

The Commission's opinion also underscores that making the requirement of proportionality of sanctions and the criterion of the economic condition of the journalist more explicit in the defamation provisions would, alongside the general proportionality principle in the Italian legal system, help avoid the application of excessive fines and ensure the proportionality of damage awards. Also, the introduction of a temporary ban (from 1 to 6 months) on the exercise of the journalistic profession for repeated defamation should be reconsidered, according to the opinion. This measure may lead to media self-censorship and may have a chilling effect on investigative journalism, thereby limiting the vital role of the press as a "public watchdog" which is essential in a democratic society.

In addition, the Commission reaffirms that political debate as well as fair and responsible criticism against public figures as part of the public interest debate should enjoy the highest protection. In this respect, it recommends that the Italian authorities abolish article 595(4) of the criminal code, according to which increased sanctions will be applied when defamation targets a political, administrative or judicial agency, and, to revise articles 278 of the criminal code (offences against the honour or prestige of the President of the Republic), 290-bis of the criminal code (equation to the President of the Republic of those who act in his stead) and 291 of the criminal code (defamation of the Italian nation).

In conclusion, the *Venice Commission* recommends that the Italian authorities quickly conclude the adoption of bill 925, keeping in consideration the recommendations made by the Commission in this opinion on the existing legislation.

X. Group of Experts on Action against Trafficking in Human Beings

The Group of Experts (GRETA) was formed in line with art. 36 of the Council of Europe Convention on Action against Trafficking in Human Beings and is charged, together with a Committee made up of the representatives in the CM of the States Parties to the Convention (Committee of the Parties), with monitoring the implementation of the obligations contained in the Convention.

The Group is made up of 15 independent experts known for their recognised competence in the fields of human rights, assistance and protection of victims of trafficking in human beings or having professional experience in the areas covered by the Convention. The monitoring procedure is divided into 4-year rounds. The Group of Experts starts the dialogue with the Party under evaluation by sending out a questionnaire, which may be followed by requests for further information. If the Group of Experts deems it necessary, additional information may be requested from civil society organisations or gathered by organising a visit to the Country concerned. The draft report is sent to the relevant Government for comments. On receiving them, GRETA prepares its final report and conclusions and transmits it to the Party concerned and to the Committee of the Parties, which can adopt recommendations on the basis of the contents of the document. Each Party to the Convention appoints a contact person to co-operate with GRETA, distributing the questionnaire to the different national bodies concerned, co-ordinating their replies and submitting a consolidated version of the replies to the questionnaire to GRETA.

The first evaluation round covers the period 2010–2013. During the year under review, the Group of Experts adopted and published its first evaluation reports on the state of implementation of the Convention in: Belgium, Bosnia-Herzegovina, France, Ireland, Latvia, Malta, Norway, Poland, Portugal and Spain.

The first evaluation visit by GRETA to Italy took place from 2 to 6 December 2013. The GRETA delegation held consultations with officials from the Department for Equal Opportunities, the Ministry of the Interior, the Ministry of Justice, the Ministry of Labour and Social Policies, the Ministry of Foreign Affairs, the Carabinieri, the National Anti-Mafia Directorate, the Financial Police and the National Institute of Statistics (ISTAT). Furthermore, the delegation travelled to Bari, L'Aquila, Lecce, Martinsicuro (Teramo), Naples, Padua and Venice where it met representatives of various law enforcement agencies, the Labour Inspectorate and regional and municipal officials involved in action against human trafficking and for the protection of children. In addition, meetings were held with members of civil society organisations, religious organisations, trade unions, lawyers, academics and representatives of the International Organisation for Migration and the Office of the United Nations High Commissioner for Refugees. In the course of the visit, the GRETA delegation visited shelters for victims of trafficking, a drop-in centre and the Ponte Galeria Identification and Expulsion Centre (CIE).

On the basis of the information gathered during the visit and the reply from the Italian authorities to GRETA's questionnaire, GRETA will prepare a draft report on the implementation of the Convention by Italy and suggestions for further action. This draft report will be transmitted to the Italian authorities for comments, which will be considered by GRETA when establishing its final report. GRETA's final report will be made public, together with potential comments from the Italian authorities.

XI. Group of States against Corruption

The Group of States against Corruption (GRECO) was established in 1999 in order to monitor the compliance of CoE Member States with the anti-corruption standards and rules of the Organisation. These benchmarks are contained in the legal instruments adopted by the Council of Europe on actions against corruption – the Criminal Law Convention on Corruption with its Additional Protocol and the Civil Law Convention on Corruption – as well as the recommendations and resolutions adopted by the Committee of Ministers (in particular resolution (97)24 on the 20 Guiding Principles for the Fight against Corruption).

The Group comprises 49 States (47 Member States of the CoE plus Belarus and the United States). GRECO's main objective is to improve the capacity of its members to fight corruption by monitoring their compliance with Council of Europe anti-corruption standards through a dynamic process of mutual evaluation and peer pressure. It helps to identify shortcomings in national anti-corruption policies, prompting the necessary legislative, institutional and practical reforms. GRECO also provides a platform for sharing best practices in the prevention and detection of corruption. GRECO's monitoring system occurs in periodical cycles and involves: a "horizontal" evaluation procedure in which all members are active and ends with the preparation of recommendations on the legislative and institutional reforms required; there is then a separate "compliance" procedure to assess the measures taken by the Member States to implement these recommendations.

On 13 June 2013, Italy deposited the instruments for ratification of the Criminal Law Convention and the Civil Law Convention of the Council of Europe, after the respective ratification and implementation laws (110/2012 and 112/2012) had been adopted by the Italian Parliament on 28 June 2012.

Italy became a member of GRECO on 30 June 2007. To date the Country has undergone three evaluation rounds. The first and second rounds were dealt with jointly by GRECO and concerned the following themes: independence, specialisation and means available to national bodies engaged in the prevention and fight against corruption, extent and scope of immunities, corruption proceeds, public administration and corruption, legal persons and corruption. The evaluation report (Greco Eval I/II Rep (2008) 2E) was adopted on 2 July 2009; the corresponding compliance report (Greco RC-I/II (2011) 1E) was adopted on 27 May 2011 following GRECO's reception of the report on the measures adopted by Italy in relation to the recommendations made in the first report (see *2012 Yearbook*, pp. 270–271). The third round took place in 2011 and concerned the following themes: incriminations and funding of political parties. The evaluation reports (Greco Eval III Rep (2011) 7E Theme I; Greco Eval III Rep (2011) Theme II) were adopted and published on 23 March 2012.

On 1 July 2013, GRECO published an addendum to the compliance report (Greco RC-I/II (2011) 1E Addendum) which definitively concludes the first and second evaluation rounds on Italy. In this document, GRECO concludes that out of the 22 recommendations issued to Italy in the first compliance report, 17 recommendations have been implemented in a satisfactory manner, 3 recommendations have been partially implemented, and 2 recommendations concerning respectively the adoption of a code of conduct for all public officials and the need to review and strengthen the accounting requirements for all forms of company and to ensure that the corresponding penalties are effective, have not been implemented. In general, nonetheless, GRECO concludes that, pending an evaluation over time of the effectiveness of the measures adopted, Italy deserves recognition for the commitment it has demonstrated in recent years to strengthen its anti-corruption system, in particular by improving transparency and accountability in public administration and by better targeting areas of public concern, including, *inter alia*, the regulation of public tenders and contracts, conflicts of interest and whistleblower protection. Likewise, GRECO welcomes the establishment of an institutional framework to adopt, implement, monitor and evaluate anticorruption policies and the designation of the Commission for the Evaluation, Transparency and Integrity of Public Administration as the national anti-corruption authority.

European Union

I. European Parliament

The European Parliament (EP), together with the Commission and the Council of the European Union, exercises a fundamental role in the promotion and implementation of the Union's human rights policies.

Among the permanent EP Committees closely concerned with human rights issues, figures the Sub-Committee on Human Rights (Italian member: Pino Arlacchi) within the Committee on Foreign Affairs (Vice Chairman: Fiorello Provera, other Italian members: Pino Arlacchi, Luigi Ciriaco De Mita, Pier Antonio Panzeri).

Other Committees closely related to human rights issues are the Committee on Civil Liberties, Justice and Legal Affairs (Vice Chairman, Salvatore Iacolino; other Italian members: Sonia Alfano, Roberta Angelilli, Rita Borsellino, Mario Borghezio, Salvatore Caronna, Clemente Mastella); the Committee on Constitutional Affairs (Chair: Carlo Casini; other Italian members: Alfredo Antoniozzi, Roberto Gualtieri); the Committee for Legal Affairs (Vice chairman: Raffaele Baldassarre; other Italian members: Luigi Berlinguer, Giuseppe Gargani, Francesco Enrico Speroni), the Committee on Employment and Social Affairs (Italian members: Mara Bizzotto, Andrea Cozzolino, Licia Ronzulli, Andrea Zanoni), the Committee on the Environment, Public Health and Food Safety (Italian members: Paolo Bartolozzi, Sergio Berlato, Franco Bonanini, Elisabetta Gardini, Mario Pirillo, Oreste Rossi, Salvatore Tatarella); the Committee on Development (Vice Chair: Iva Zanicchi); the Committee on Women's Rights and Gender Equality (Vice Chair: Barbara Matera) and the Committee on Petitions, which is presented below.

In 2013, the Sakharov Prize for Freedom of Thought was awarded to Malala Yousafzai, a Pakistani activist for female education.

Among the Parliament's opinions and resolutions which in 2013 directly concerned Italy are: the resolution of 23 October 2013 on *Migratory flows in the Mediterranean, with particular attention to the tragic events off Lampedusa* (P7_TA-PROV(2013)0448) and the resolution of 10 October 2013 on *Alleged transportation and illegal detention of prisoners in European Countries by the CIA* (P7_TA-PROV(2013)0418) with which, whereas on the one hand, the Parliament encourages the Italian authorities to continue their efforts to obtain justice regarding human rights violations by the CIA on Italian territory, on the other hand, it invites Italy to reply to the follow-up letters sent by the UN Special Procedures, requesting additional information on global practices with regards to secret detention in relation to countering terrorism.

Committee on Petitions

The Committee on Petitions' task is to examine petitions presented by citizens (a fundamental right enshrined in the CFREU in art. 44, as well as in articles 24 and 227 TFEU) and to work to resolve possible infringements of the rights conferred on them by EU law. Chair of the Committee is Erminia Mazzoni.

The report on the Committee's activities in 2012 was published in September 2013. It notes that in 2012 the European Parliament received 1,986 petitions, of which 1,406 considered inadmissible. As for the previous year, the petitions focused mainly on: fundamental rights (500), the environment (279), the internal market (143). The Countries specifically mentioned with the greatest number of petitions were Spain (298), Germany (249) and Italy (170) respectively, while petitions directed at the European Union institutions as a whole came in first position (542).

Concerning Italy in particular, the report on the activities of the Committee on Petitions 2012 summarises the issues which emerged during the fact-finding mission led by a delegation of MEPs from 29 to 30 October 2012 in the Lazio and Campania Regions. The delegation expressed its disapproval of the policies pursued in the Lazio Region regarding waste management, in particular in relation to the excessive reliance placed upon landfills. The delegation also expressed deep concern at the apparent inability of the regional and provincial authorities to work in a more transparent and coherent manner with Municipalities and civil society, towards establishing a workable waste strategy. Nevertheless, members recognised that the approach of the current Minister of the Environment is positive and deserves support from the European Parliament.

Amongst other recommendations, the delegation urged Italian authorities to engage in a constructive dialogue with petitioners and civil society, recalling the right of citizens to be publicly consulted. The delegation also recommended that the military withdraw from every aspect of waste policy and that powers given to the Special Commissioner, by using the instrument of emergency legislation, be revoked immediately.

II. European Commission

The European Commission has a central role in the development and implementation of European Union policies, including human rights policies, both within the Union and in relation to third Countries.

Of the 27 Commissioners, particularly important to the issue of human rights are the Vice-President and Commissioner for Justice, Fundamental Rights and Citizenship, Viviane Reding; Vice-President Catherine Ashton, who is also the High Representative of the European Union for Foreign Affairs and Security Policy; the Commissioner for Home Affairs, Cecilia Malmstrom; the Commissioner for Employment, Social Affairs and Inclusion, Làszlò Andor and the Commissioner for International Cooperation, Humanitarian Aid and Crisis Response, Kristalina Georgieva.

A vital financial resource for European Union human rights activities world-wide is the European Instrument for the Promotion of Democracy and Human Rights (EIDHR) which, among other things, supports the activities of the European Inter-university Centre for Human Rights and Democratisation (EIUC), in particular for the European Master in Human Rights and Democratisation. Particularly significant sources of funding for human rights are the programmes *Fundamental Rights and Citizenship* and *Daphne*.

Concerning Italy in particular, it is worth noting the visit of 9 October 2013 to Lampedusa by European Commission President José Manuel Barroso and Commissioner for Home Affairs Cecilia Malmström in light of the tragic events which on 3 October saw the deaths at sea of 366 migrants in their attempts to reach the Sicilian island.

Additional information on the Commission's activities is provided in the section on EU legislation in 2013 (see Part I, International Human Rights Law, IV, B).

III. Council of the European Union

Within the Council there are the Human Rights Working Group (COHOM), the Working Party on Fundamental Rights, Citizens' Rights and Free Movement of Persons (FREMP) and the Working Group of Public International Law (COJUR), within which a sub-group devoted to the International Criminal Court operates (COJUR-ICC).

On 24 June 2013, the Council of the European Union adopted two new sets of Guidelines in the area of human rights dealing with the following issues: the promotion and protection of the enjoyment of all human rights by lesbian, gay, bisexual, transgender and intersex (LGBTI) persons; the promotion and protection of freedom of religion or belief. With the latter set of Guidelines, the EU reaffirms its determination to promote, in its external human rights policy, freedom of religion or belief in a timely, consistent and coherent manner. The guidelines reassert that the EU is impartial and is not aligned with any specific religion or belief and give clear political guidelines to officials of EU institutions and EU Member States, to be used in contacts with third countries and with international and civil society organisations, in order to prevent violations of freedom of religion or belief and to react effectively to violations wherever they occur. EU action on freedom of religion or belief will be based on the following overriding principles: the universal character of freedom of religion or belief; freedom of religion or belief is an individual right which can be exercised in community with others; recognition of the primary role of States in ensuring freedom of religion or belief; the connection with the defence of other human rights and with other EU guidelines on human rights. Among the latter, the EU Guidelines on Death Penalty, adopted in 1998 and revised in 2008, were further updated in 2013.

In 2013 no activities concerning or linked to the human rights situation in Italy were recorded.

IV. Court of Justice of the European Union

Following the entry into force of the Treaty of Lisbon, the Charter of Nice became legally binding and the Court of Justice thus plays a more vital role in the promotion of human rights in the implementation of EU law. Italian members of the Court currently include Antonio Tizzano, as a judge, and Paolo Mengozzi, as an Advocate-General.

According to data provided by the CJEU, in 2013 Italy was ranked 2nd for the number of requests for a preliminary ruling (art. 267 TFUE) submitted to the Court (62 out of 450), preceded only by Germany.

For the case-law of the CJEU regarding Italy in 2013, see Part IV, Italy in the Case-law of the Court of Justice of the European Union.

V. European External Action Service

The European External Action Service (EEAS) assists the High Representative of the Union for Foreign Affairs and Security Policy in upholding the CFSP/CSDP and ensuring the consistency of EU external actions in her functions both as President of the Foreign Affairs Council and as Vice-President of the Commission.

No significant activities concerning Italy in 2013.

VI. Special Representative for Human Rights

Appointed by EU Council decision 2012/440/CFSP of 25 July 2012, the mandate of the European Union Special Representative for Human Rights involves enhancing dialogue with all relevant stakeholders concerning EU human rights policy, including international organisations, States as well as civil society organisations. Stavros Lambrinidis was appointed on 1 September 2012 as the first incumbent.

No significant activities concerning Italy in 2013.

VII. Fundamental Rights Agency

The European Union Agency for Fundamental Rights (FRA), an advisory body set up in 2007, is the main technical instrument for the EU, charged with supporting European and national institutions in the promotion and protection of human rights. Director of the Agency is Morten Kjaerum (Denmark). Since July 2012 Italy has been represented in the Management Board of the FRA by Lorenza Violini; Stefano Rodotà was a member of the Scientific Committee until May 2013.

The FRA's research work is done mainly by collecting and making comparative analyses of data on the situation of fundamental rights in the 28 Member States of the EU, including Italy. In this respect, below is a summary of some of the FRA reports made in 2013. After an introduction to each report, there are some remarks on the most significant data which emerged concerning Italy:

– *Inequalities and multiple discrimination in access to and quality healthcare* (March 2013). Based on legal analysis and fieldwork research conducted in Austria, Italy, Sweden, United Kingdom and Czech Republic, this report highlights the barriers and the individual experiences of multiple discrimination in accessing healthcare services. Among the main results, the findings suggest that health systems can create barriers which hinder access to or alter the quality of health care services for persons with combined protected characteristics, such as sex, disability and ethnic origin.

In relation to Italy, the report highlights how, contrary to discrimination on the grounds of racial or ethnic origin, sex and disability, there is no legislation in place to protect individuals from age discrimination in regard to healthcare in Italy. According to the FRA, moreover, as Italy is one of the few European Countries to cover multiple discrimination by law, the implementation of these regulations in health care is still quite limited.

– *Fundamental rights at Europe's Southern sea borders* (March 2013). This report examines the treatment of citizens from third Countries at EU external borders, covering sea border surveillance and disembarkation procedures, as well as general issues such as training of border guards. In particular, the report analyses the situation of the four Member States most affected by this type of migration, namely Greece, Italy, Malta and Spain, and concludes that only a comprehensive approach including all States, organisations and other parties involved can succeed in putting an end to the high death toll at sea.

According to the report, in numerical terms, Italy is the Country with the highest number of arrivals by sea. This figure decreased significantly between 2009 and 2010 on account of the Italian-Libyan agreements to control immigration, but increased exponentially in 2011 in conjunction with the uprisings in Tunisia and Libya. The report recalls the ECtHR judgment against Italy in the *Hirsi case* on several occasions to demonstrate an example of the inviolability of the principle of *non-refoulement* in sea rescue operations. In relation to the humanitarian aid provided to the migrants upon their arrival, the report highlights the emergency approach adopted in Italy, a Country which since 2002 has seen a succession of legislation aimed at decreeing a state of emergency in all, or parts of the peninsula. Alongside this, nonetheless, the report underscores the promising *Praesidium* experiment, a reception project to assist and inform migrants arriving by sea to Italy, in which the Italian authorities work in partnership with international organisations (the IOM, the UNHCR), the Italian Red Cross and civil society organisations (Save the Children).

– *EU LGBT survey* – *European Union lesbian, gay, bisexual and transgender survey* (May 2013). The survey findings, which gathered over 93,000 testimonies, show that in Europe today LGBT persons very often feel that they cannot freely express themselves in their daily lives: at school, at work or in public. Many hide their identity and live in isolation or even in fear. Others suffer discrimination, and even violence, when they openly express their sexual orientation or their sexual identity.

Italy, along with seven other EU Member States, has adopted specific LGBT action plans or integrated the issues of sexual orientation and gender identity in national human rights action plans. In relation to the survey findings linked to discrimination and violence perceived and suffered by LGBT persons in Italy, the data reflects that Italy is essentially within the European average. In particular, the report demonstrates how, in Italy, in the year preceding the survey: 54% of respondents said that they had felt discriminated against or harassed on the grounds of sexual orientation (EU average 47%); one in five respondents who were employed and/or looking for a job felt discriminated against in these situations (EU average 32%); 93% of respondents recall negative comments or conduct because a schoolmate was perceived to be LGBT (EU average 91%); 69% said they often or always hid or disguised that they were LGBT during their schooling before the age of 18 (EU average 67%).

– *Legal capacity of persons with intellectual disabilities and persons with mental health problems* (July 2013) Some 80 million persons with disabilities live in the European Union. The report findings show that many have had their legal capacity restricted or removed, hindering their ability to live independently and make decisions on their own lives.

As for Italy, the report shows how the causes leading to legal incapacitation for a person with an intellectual disability are, in some cases, defined in quite broad terms (civil code, art. 404). Italy, together with Greece and Slovenia, is among the Countries in which the court delivers a single judgment, deciding that the person's legal capacity is restricted and that he or she will be placed under a protective measure. The question of incapacity and the need to institute a guardianship measure, or to appoint a representative is then assessed in parallel. Aside from specifically designating those who may legitimately apply for protective measures for the benefit of persons with an intellectual disability, the legislative framework in Italy explicitly states the need for the judge to consult with the person concerned, as well as the possibility to express their wishes about designating a future guardian in the event of their future incapacity. Finally, as regards the right to appeal the deprivation of legal capacity, Italy is among those Countries in which the legislation allows the person under guardianship to submit a request to appeal the decision.

– *Discrimination and hate crime against Jews in EU Member States: experiences and perceptions of anti-Semitism* (November 2013). This survey collects comparable data on Jewish people's experiences and perceptions of anti-Semitism, hate-motivated crime and discrimination in Belgium, France, Germany, Hungary, Italy, Latvia, Sweden and the United Kingdom, Countries that together are estimated to be home to some 90% of the EU's Jewish population.

With particular reference to Italy, the survey reveals how 60% of respondents consider anti-Semitism to be a problem in Italy (compared to an EU of 66%). Moreover, in the 12 months before the survey, 16% of all respondents declared that they had experienced one or more incidents involving verbal insults, harassment or physical violence because they are Jewish, while 39% are worried about becoming a victim of such incidents in the near future. In relation to reporting hate-motivated crimes, 77% of victims did not report the incident to the authorities, while 43% declared that they are not aware of the legislation that protects Jewish people from discrimination (compared to an average of 28%).

VIII. European Ombudsman

The European Ombudsman, an institution established in 1992 by the Treaty of Maastricht and provided for in art. 24 and 228 TFEU, examines the complaints lodged by European citizens about maladministration in the institutions and bodies of the European Union. Elected by the EP, the Ombudsman performs his duties with complete independence. Nikiforos P. Diamandouros, holder of this position since April 2003, was succeeded in October 2013 by Emily O'Reilly, previously the national Ombudsperson of the Republic of Ireland.

According to the European Ombudsman's report on his activities in 2012, published on 27 May 2013, over the time frame in question, the Ombudsman's office received 740 complaints, of which 118 from Italy. Again in 2012 it opened 465 investigations (+18% compared to 2011) and closed 390 of them (+23%). In that same year, the Ombudsman opened 10 enquiries of his own initiative while 3 enquiries were submitted by national or regional Ombudsmen on issues concerning EU law and its interpretation. Of the latter, two were presented by the regional Ombudspersons of Marche and Veneto concerning, respectively, the freedom of movement of workers and health insurance.

IX. European Data Protection Supervisor

Established by regulation 45/2001, the European Data Protection Supervisor (EDPS) is responsible for ensuring the right to the protection of individual privacy in the handling of personal data by EU institutions and bodies, as laid out in articles 7–8 of the Nice Charter. The EDPS is an independent supervisory authority elected by the Parliament and the Council of the EU. The current Supervisor is Peter Hustnix, whose mandate was renewed for a further five years in 2009. Giovanni Buttarelli, previously Secretary General to the Italian Data Protection Authority, is Assistant Supervisor.

Organisation for Security and Cooperation in Europe

Through a multi-dimensional approach to security, the OSCE (57 participating States) operates in the fields of conflict prevention, crisis management and post-conflict rehabilitation. Among its specific bodies and mechanisms worth noting are the Office for Democratic Institutions and Human Rights (ODIHR), the High Commissioner on National Minorities, the Representative on Freedom of the Media and the Special Representative and Co-ordinator for Combating Trafficking in Human Beings. Since 1 July 2011, Lamberto Zannier from the Italian diplomatic service is the Secretary General of the OSCE.

The permanent representative of Italy to the OSCE is Ambassador Filippo Formica. 13 members of the Italian Chamber of Deputies and Senate sit in the OSCE Parliamentary Assembly. Head of the Italian parliamentary delegation and President of the Assembly until March 2013, Riccardo Migliori was succeeded by Paolo Roman in the first post following the latest elections in Italy.

Italy is among the main contributor to the OSCE. In 2013, the Italian contribution to the budget was 14.75 million euros (10% of the budget), which was equal to those of France, Germany and the UK. Italy also made a contribution of approximately 1 million euro, also in 2013, to supplement the remuneration of Italian officials seconded to OSCE to participate in electoral observation missions, and help finance OSCE extra-budgetary projects.

I. Office for Democratic Institutions and Human Rights (ODIHR)

The ODIHR is the OSCE's main body charged with assisting Member States in the implementation of their human dimension commitments. Director of the Office since 2008 has been Ambassador Janez Lenarčič (Slovenia).

During 2013, ODIHR activities in Italy concerned mainly training and awareness-raising initiatives to combat hate crimes. Among the most relevant are the signing, on 29 May 2013, of a memorandum of understanding with the Ministry of the Interior to implement the TAHCLE programme in Italy, having as its goal the training against hate crimes for Italian law enforcement.

As for activities linked to election observation missions, following an invitation from the Permanent Mission of Italy to the OSCE, the ODIHR, between 7 and 10 January 2013, undertook a Needs Assessment Mission (NAM) to observe the 24 and 25 February 2013 parliamentary elections. The main conclusions of the assessment mission were: the realisation that the majority of Italian interlocutors expressed confidence in the electoral process in Italy and the ability of the election administration to organise elections professionally. Nevertheless, in addition to this observation, the NAM reveals that most interlocutors recognised that further improvements could be made to the electoral process, in particular to the legal framework and elements of the electoral system, campaign finance provisions, media coverage, and complaints and appeals mechanisms. On this basis and given that the interlocutors would welcome a potential observation activity for these elections, the NAM recommends the deployment of a Limited Election Observation Mission (LEOM) to Italy. For reasons linked to the absence of funding, however, the mission has not been deployed.

Finally, *Hate Crimes in the OSCE region-Incidents and Responses: Annual Report for 2012* is particularly important. This report, compiled from data and information supplied to the ODIHR by the Governments of the Member States, by civil society and by other international organisations, shows how this issue is still a serious problem in the OSCE region, both due to the large number of incidents and the gravity of these incidents. As for Italy in 2012, there were 71 cases reported to the police (compared to 68 in 2011 and 56 in 2010), 10 of which proceeded to judgment.

II. High Commissioner on National Minorities

The Office of the High Commissioner on National Minorities is the OSCE institution which is charged with identifying and seeking to resolve situations of ethnic tension in the OSCE region. In addition to serving as an instrument for preventing conflict, it can also promote rapid solutions such as to halt processes of escalation of violence. Since 20 August 2013, the position of High Commissioner has been held by Astrid Thors (Finland), who succeeded Knut Vollebaeck (Norway), holder of the office since 2007.

During 2013 there are no records of activities linked to or concerning Italy.

III. OSCE Representative on Freedom of the Media

Established in 1997 with a view to ensuring a high level of compliance with the rules and standards on freedom of expression and freedom of the media accepted by the OSCE participating States, the Representative on Freedom of the Media acts as an early warning instrument in cases of violation of freedom of expression, with particular attention to any obstacles or impediments to the activities of journalists. This position has been held since March 2010 by Dunja Mijatovic (Bosnia and Herzegovina).

During 2013, Italy was more than once the subject of remarks made by the OSCE Representative both in relation to the crime of defamation and concerning incidents of intimidation experienced by Italian journalists. As for the latter, in a press release on 10 April 2013, the Representative condemned the sending of a parcel bomb to the Turin-based headquarters of the daily newspaper La Stampa. Recalling how all threats to media outlets represent direct threats to media freedom, the Representative welcomed the immediate launch of an investigation into this matter, as well as the decisive condemnation of the events by all major Italian political parties. The string of cases in which journalists have been attacked and intimidated in Italy is worrying, concluded Dunja Mijatovic, and must be promptly addressed by the Italian authorities, who should spare no effort in fighting these cases.

In relation to the crime of defamation, on 27 May 2013 the Representative expressed concern over prison sentences handed down by the Court of Milan to three journalists at the Italian weekly news magazine Panorama on defamation charges of a magistrate. According to the Representative, in fact, imprisonment for libel is not only disproportionate and incompatible with the democratic standards which apply in the OSCE region, it also has a severe chilling effect that undermines the effectiveness of the media community as a whole.

Finally, once again in her efforts to promote the decriminalisation of defamation in the OSCE region, on 12 November 2013, in a letter addressed to the Italian Foreign Minister Emma Bonino, the Representative expressed some critical remarks in relation to the existing draft legislation on defamation issued by the Chamber of Deputies on 17 October 2013, and currently under discussion in the Senate. As previously occurred with the draft law on wiretapping (see *2012 Yearbook*, p. 287), the main observations and recommendations made by the OSCE Representative were presented to the Italian authorities in the form of a legal analysis of the draft measures in question, compiled, on request of the Representative, by Boyko Boev, Senior legal officer of *article 19*, a UK-based NGO. The positive aspects brought to light by the legal analysis of the draft legislation, which seeks to introduce amendments to the criminal code, to the civil code of procedure and to law No. 47/1948 (known as the "Press Act"), include the following: the abolishment of prison sanctions for insult and defamation and their replacement with fines; the adoption of measures against malicious complainants; allowing for media who have published a reply or rectification to be absolved from criminal sanctions; journalists are absolved from responsibility if the director of the newspaper has failed to publish a denial or correction; the limitation of liability of directors for defamation; higher level of responsibility for defamation of political, administrative or judicial agency, a representative of the latter or a collegial authority is abolished; it now ensures clarity on the owners and editor-in-chief of online newspapers.

On the other hand, the negative aspects revealed in the analysis are as follows: criminal liability for insult and defamation is retained; excessive fines are established and increases the pre-existing ones; penalty of prohibition from exercising the profession of journalist is retained; the statute of limitation period for filing a civil action for damages is unnecessarily long; the criteria for determination of compensation award for defamation are problematic; criminal liability for article 278 of the criminal code is maintained (offences against the honour or prestige of the President of the Republic); 290 (defamation of the Republic, constitutional institutions and armed forces) and 291 (defamation of the Italian nation).

IV. Special Representative and Co-ordinator for Combating Trafficking in Human Beings

The OSCE Office of the Special Representative and Co-ordinator for Combating Trafficking in Human Beings was set up with the purpose of assisting States in the implementation of commitments and in the full usage of recommendations proposed by the 2003 OSCE Action plan. It has also the mandate to ensure co-ordination of OSCE efforts in combating trafficking in human beings. The position of Special Representative has since January 2009 been held by Maria Grazia Giammarinaro.

The Special Representative visited Italy between 17 and 18 June and between 15 and 19 July 2013. During her numerous meetings with Government and Parliamentary authorities, representatives of the judiciary and actors of civil society, the Representative acknowledged Italy's long standing commitment to anti-trafficking action (since the early 1990s), and highlighted the innovative aspects of the Italian legislative framework, defined by its measures for unconditional access to assistance for victims, regardless of co-operation with law enforcement or judicial authorities.

As regards the most critical aspects of the Italian system, the OSCE Representative highlighted two issues concerning immigration laws: firstly, concerning the crime of illegal immigration as an obstacle to the emergence of the trafficking phenomenon, to the extent that this places the victim in a situation where they can be blackmailed and increases their vulnerability; the second, concerns the link between a work contract and residency status which tends to increase the victims' state of precariousness. Among the recommendations to Italian authorities following the official visit, the Special Representative called on the Italian authorities to re-launch co-ordination at the government level, and to establish a National Rapporteur on trafficking. According to the Special Representative, aside from the immediate need to enhance the security framework by ensuring social inclusion, political consultation with civil society on the issues of anti-trafficking, the emergence of the phenomenon and providing assistance to victims must be renewed also.

Finally, the Representative visited Italy on 8 February 2013 for a seminar in Rome on trafficking in human beings from the Southern Mediterranean shores to Europe. Giulio Terzi and Riccardo Migliori, the then respective Italian foreign minister and President of the OSCE Parliamentary Assembly participated in the event which was held in the Chamber of Deputies.

International Humanitarian and Criminal Law

I. Adapting to International Humanitarian and Criminal Law

Italy is party to all the main international conventions on the law of armed conflict and international criminal law.

In terms of its commitments to disarmament and non proliferation, in 2013 Italy ratified with law No. 118, on 4 October 2013, the Arms Trade Treaty, adopted in New York by the United Nations General Assembly on 2 April 2013. The goal of the Treaty, which will come into force following the deposit of the fiftieth ratification instrument, is to better regulate the international trade in conventional arms. The Treaty, aside from providing for a series of restrictions and restraints for States Parties in the areas of exporting, importing, transit and intermediation in the arms sector, in fact, establishes a monitoring system based on periodic reports, a Secretariat and a Conference of the States Parties.

Still in connection with the arms sector, the obligation to present periodic reports on the state of implementation of the provisions of the various conventions is particularly important. In this respect, in the course of 2013 Italy presented the annual report provided for in the Oslo Convention banning cluster mines (30 April 2013); the annual report for the Convention on Anti-Personnel Mines; the report requested by the Convention on Prohibitions or Restrictions on the Use of Certain Conventional Weapons (3 April 2013) and the Protocol to the CCW on Explosive Remnants of War.

II. The Italian Contribution to Peace-keeping and Other International Missions

In 2013, with two legislative decrees converted into law by Parliament (l.d. 28 December 2012, No. 227 converted by law 1 February 2013 No. 12 and l.d. 10 October 2013, No. 114, converted by law 9 December 2013, No. 135), Italy financed the extension of the participation of Italian military and civilian personnel in international missions. As for 2012, Italy did not extend participation in Syria, whereas it began operations in Mali, Iraq and Niger.

The following list shows the military and police missions in which Italy participated with its own forces in the course of 2013.

Country/Geographic Area of Intervention	Italy's Mission and Activities
Afghanistan	*International Security Assistance Force* (ISAF) (military, police and financial police component)
	EUPOL AFGHANISTAN (military and police component)
Afghanistan and other States	Participation of officers from the Guardia di Finanza (Financial Police) to the Joint Multimodal Operational Units (JMOUs) unità di coordinamento interforze denominate *Joint Multimodal Operational Units* (JMOUs) in Afghanistan, United Arab Emirates and Kosovo
Albania	Activity in support of the Albanian armed forces
Bosnia-Herzegovina	Integrated Police Unit (IPU) in the framework of the European Union ALTHEA operation
	Participation of officers from the *Arma dei Carabinieri*, the State Police and of one member of the judiciary in the European Union Police Mission (EUPM)
Cyprus	United Nations Peacekeeping Force in Cyprus (UNFICYP)
United Arab Emirates/ Bahrein/Qatar/Tampa, USA	Employment of military personnel in support of the missions in Afghanistan
Georgia	European Union Monitoring Mission in Georgia – EUMM Georgia (from 1 March 2012 to 31 December 2012)
Iraq	Participation of a member of the judiciary to the European Union integrated mission on the rule of law for Iraq – EUJUST LEX-Iraq
Kosovo/Balkans	Multinational Specialised Unit (MSU), European Union Rule of Law Mission in Kosovo (EULEX Kosovo) (military, police and financial police component), Security Force Training Plan in Kosovo
	Operation Joint Enterprise (NATO)
	Cooperation programmes of Italian police forces in Albania and in the Countries of the Balkan area
	Participation of State Police officers to the United Nations Mission in Kosovo (UNMIK)

Lebanon	United Nations Interim Force in Lebanon (UNIFIL), which includes the use of naval units in the UNIFIL Maritime Task Force
Libya	Assistance, support and training activities in Libya, according to resolutions 2009 (2011), 2016 (2011) and 2022 (2011), adopted by the United Nations Security Council on, respectively, 16 September, 27 October and 2 December 2011 (military and financial police component)
	Participation to the *European Union Border Assistance Mission in Libya* (EUBAM Libya) (military and police component) (from 1 October 2013)
Mali	Participation to European Union mission – EUTM Mali
	Participation to the *United Nations Multidimensional Integrated Stabilisation Mission in Mali* (MINUSMA), according to resolution 2100 (2013) of the United Nations Security Council
Eastern Mediterranean	Participation to Mission Active Endeavour in the Mediterranean (NATO)
Niger	Participation to European Union Mission – EUCAP Sahel Niger
Somalia/Indian Ocean	European Union ATALANTA military mission
	NATO operation Ocean Shield to combat piracy
	Participation to the *European Union Training Mission* (EUTM SOMALIA) and to EUCAP Nestor, as well as to further European initiatives for the *Regional maritime capacity building* of the Horn of Africa and in the Western Indian Ocean
South Sudan	Participation with military personnel to the *United Nations Mission in South Sudan* (UNMISS), according to resolution 1996 (2011) of the United Nations Security Council
Sudan	*United Nations/African Union Mission in Darfur* (UNAMID)
Occupied Palestinian Territories	Participation with military personnel to the mission Temporary International Presence in Hebron (TIPH2)
	Participation of State Police officers and of a member of the judiciary to the European Union Police Mission for the Palestinian Territories (EUPOL COPPS)
Occupied Palestinian Territories/ Egypt	*European Union Border Assistance Mission in Rafah* (EUBAM Rafah)

Part IV

National and International Case-law

Human Rights in Italian Case-law

During 2013, the Italian courts, including the Constitutional Court, have made extensive reference in their jurisprudence to sources of international human rights law, in particular the ECHR. The latter's provisions are used as "interposed parameter" of constitutionality as set forth in article 117(1) of the Constitution ("Legislative powers shall be vested in the State and the Regions in compliance with the Constitution and with the constraints deriving from EU legislation and international obligations"). This is now an established fact and acknowledged by all courts. The present survey does not purport to be exhaustive. Whereas judgments here presented address a wide range of issues relevant to human rights, the section does not purport to be a comprehensive and systematic overview of the huge Italian case-law. The aim is, more modestly, to report those judgments that appear either to consolidate a given jurisprudence or open new paths of human rights protection, with particular regard to the rulings that refer to the international legal standards, in particular the ECHR.

In this regard it is noticeable that reference to the CFREU is still rather episodic, despite the Charter provisions largely coincide with the ECHR. Indeed, a ruling of the Supreme Court (civil division, 22 May 2013, No. 12531) has address the issue the other way round. The Supreme Court has confirmed that only in exceptional circumstances and in relation to cases of direct and specific infringement of fundamental rights, a EU law provision may be challenged before the Constitutional Court for contrast with the inviolable rights of the person guaranteed by the Constitution or by the ECHR. In this case, the claim concerned a EU regulation restricting the access of European companies to the import-export of bananas that negatively affected an Italian trader. The restrictions on the freedom of enterprise, which had already been considered lawful by the ECJ as aimed at the legitimate goal of regulating the market, did not appear to the Court of Cassation to justify a claim of unconstitutionality for breaching of the EU treaties, nor the Court accepted the petitioner's request to disapply the norm for non-conformity to EU law.

I. Dignity of the Person and Principles of Biolaw

A. Gender Reassignment and Termination of the Marriage

The Court of Cassation (judg. 14329/2013) heard a petition against a decision of the civil registrar of a Municipality who, after duly amending the records relating to a person who had a sex change, had also noted the "cessation of the civil effects" of the marriage contracted by the concerned person, in the absence of any judicial decision on the point taken at the request of the spouses. The Court observes that, in the light of the applicable law, and in particular of article 4 of the law 14 April 1982, No. 164 ("The judgment of rectification of attribution of sex [...] involves the termination of the marriage"), the upshot is that the change of gender of a spouse constitutes a case of "forced divorce". This, however, raises, according to the Supreme Court, an issue of compatibility between the mentioned art. 4 and the Constitution's arts. 2 and 29, and of arts. 8 and 12 of the ECHR (arts. 3 and 24 of the Constitution are also relevant). In this case, the change of sex of one of the spouses automatically impinged upon the marriage via the sex change judgment, without taking into any account the willingness of the couple to continue in wedlock, and interfering heavily on the spouses' private and family life. The Supreme Court cites some recent rulings of the constitutional courts of Austria and Germany, that found it unconstitutional to record a sex change before a court had declared the dissolution of the marriage, or to pronounce the divorce before proceeding with the action for having the change of sex recorded. Also the ECrHR, in a case involving Finland (*H. v. Finland*, 13 November 2012), found it compatible with articles 8 and 12 ECHR the national law provisions requiring the prior consent of the spouse to proceed with the sex change recording of the other spouse. Worth noting that the Finnish case is much less dramatic than the other two (as well as the Italian case), because in Finland same sex civil unions were legally recognised, so the sex change just transformed the "marriage" into "civil partnership". Eventually, the Supreme Court raised the question of constitutionality of article 4 of law 164/1982 in relation to articles 2, 3, 24 and 29 of the Constitution, as well as of article 117(1), as for the envisageable breach of articles 8 and 12 ECHR as interposed norms.

B. Informed Consent

The Court of Cassation has ruled in a case for damages initiated by a patient against a number of doctors and the hospital where she had undergone in 1999 a laparohysterectomy intervention. The operation, which has obviously resulted in a permanent loss for the patient, had been conducted appropriately and with the consent of the patient, but on the basis of a misdiagnosis, which had detected the presence of a cancer that supposedly could be eradicated by removing the uterus; later however it appeared that the cancerous mass could have been treated with a less invasive procedure. Both in first instance and on appeal, the contractual and tort claims were rejected. The Supreme Court (civil division, Sec. III, judg. 19 February 2013, No. 4030) eventually allowed the woman's application. The Court of Cassation noted that, considering the sequence of errors from diagnosis to the planning of the surgery as a whole negligence, it follows that the consent given by the patient was not actually "informed" and that the hospital managers and the personnel were liable for a degree of negligence that could not be considered slight, but rather gross. The removal of the uterus was decided without waiting for a more accurate evaluation of the extent of the cancer. Not to have put the patient in a condition to express a fully free and informed consent constituted a violation of her fundamental rights as protected, in particular, in articles 2, 13 and 29 of the Italian Constitution.

C. Infringement of Human Rights, Including the Right to Life, and the Right to an Effective Remedy

In the case decided by the criminal division of the Court of Cassation, section III, judgment 4 June 2013, No. 29735, the Supreme Court clarifies its jurisprudence on compensation for non-pecuniary damage in favour of the family of the deceased as a result of a car accident. The issue brought to the Court concerned, among other things, the share of non-pecuniary damages that the person responsible for an accident should correspond to the grandparents of the person he had killed by negligence. Citing some previous judgments of the Court of Cassation, the applicant sought to argue that only the grandparents living with the dead person were entitled to compensation for moral damages; since this was not the case in the instant situation (the grandparents did not live with the victim), the claim for non-pecuniary damages had to be dismissed. The Court distanced itself from the decisions cited by the claimant, clarifying that matters of this kind must be treated on a case-by-case basis and that the absence of cohabitation might very well be offset by other equally significant forms of relationship between grandparents and grandson that justify the granting to them of the compensation for the non-pecuniary damage resulting from the violent decease of their grandchild. Otherwise reasoning would be in contrast with the dignity of the individual and with the protection of the family (articles 2 and 29 of the Constitution), the latter not to be understood as a strictly "nuclear" entity.

The issue of the right to an effective remedy in the event of a breach of a fundamental right was mentioned also in the judgment pronounced on the so-called "Mondadori award" case (Court of Cassation, judgment 17 September 2013, No. 21255). The Court *inter alia* stated that: "the right to an effective protection of one's rights is, ultimately, the right to benefit from appropriate tools to ensure the complete satisfaction of one's interests, since the constitutional provision on the (inviolable) right to access to a court must be interpreted not only in line with the reasoning indicated by the Constitutional Court (indeed, the Constitutional Court, although evoking it here and there, has never explicitly stated, so far, that the fundamental right to jurisdictional protection includes, besides the principles of due process, the effective protection of the substantive right claimed in court), but also in the light of the more general context represented by the international order [...], in which the proliferation of references to the right to effective remedy emerging from several provisions like article 8 of the Universal Declaration of Human Rights, article 13 of the ECHR and article 47 of the CFREU, and now the Treaty of the European Constitution [*sic*], is evidence that the judicial protection is not only understood as a right of access to a court or to a specific judicial procedure, but also, in a more substantial way, as a right to have appropriately ensured one's underlying need for protection."

D. Adoption and the Right to Know One's Origins

The Juvenile Court of Catanzaro challenged the constitutionality of article 28(7) of law 4 May 1983, No. 184 (Right of the child to a family), as replaced by article 177(2) of the lgs.d. 30 June 2003, No. 196 (Code of personal data protection), in so far as it excludes the possibility of authorising an adopted person to access information about his or her origins if his or her mother opted not to be identified in the birth certificate of the child. The mentioned law provides that the secret about the mother's identity expires a hundred years after the formation of the birth certificate. In the meantime the child can be provided information about his birth, but nothing that may identify the mother. The aim of the Italian law is to protect the right of the mother to oblivion, even in the face of the child's will to know his or her origins. The point had been dealt with by the ECtHR in the *Godelli v. Italy* case in 2012 (see *2013 Yearbook*, p. 371). The ECtHR found that Italy infringed article 8 ECHR; this judgment requires the Italian Constitutional Court to review its previous jurisprudence, namely judgment 425/2005. In this decision the Court maintained the constitutionality of the contested provision. In 2013, in the case 278/2013, the Constitutional Court reversed its previous jurisprudence and declared article 28(7) unconstitutional in so far as it crystallises in a definitive and irreversible way the mother's choice to hide her identity. The judges considered that the legislature, in order to safeguard the rights of the adopted child to the family and to the personal identity, should establish a procedure which allows a court to ascertain the mother's persistent unwillingness to disclose her identity to the child, once the latter is turned adult and asks to know all details about his or her birth.

II Asylum and International Protection

A. *Recognition of International Protection*

Also in 2013 the Supreme Court, competent to adjudicate applications against court judgments concerning the claims against the decision of Asylum Territorial Commissions, has consistently applied its jurisprudence according to which, when required to grant one of the many forms of protection prescribed by the law (namely lgs.d. 19 November 2008, No. 25, transposing the pertinent EU directive), the Italian judge must carefully tailor the measure to the specific case. The options the legislation provides include not only the recognition of refugee status in accordance with the 1951 Geneva Convention, but also the subsidiary protection, covering situations of grave danger the claimant may be confronted with not related to an individual persecution, but to circumstances that threaten his or her life, such as an armed conflict affecting the Country of origin. Moreover, a third form of international protection, the so-called humanitarian protection, can be attributed in connection with unspecified forms of vulnerability. The courts, therefore, in order to dismiss an application against the negative decision of an Asylum Territorial Commission should not simply ascertain that the requirement for refugee protection were not met; it has also the duty to verify whether the conditions for subsidiary of humanitarian protection occur (see, for example, Court of Cassation, civil division, Sec. VI, orders 23 May 2013, No. 12751 and 10 January 2013, No. 563).

Accordingly, in several decisions the Court of Cassation endorsed its established case-law (explicitly supported also by some laws) according to which, in the event the applicant for international protection may not be able to provide reliable evidence of the persecution of which he is the victim or of the serious danger to which he or she would be exposed if repatriated, it is the duty of the court to verify case by case the existence of reasons justifying the international protection – namely, to grant subsidiary or humanitarian protection when the conditions for the recognition of refugee status lack (see also *2013 Yearbook*, pp. 303–304). According to the decision 26887/2013 of the Court of Cassation, civil division, the Court of Appeal of Rome, that had denied any protection to an individual who feared persecution in the Country of origin by a paternal uncle who had already brutally murdered the applicant's mother, is duty barred to verify: a) the objective credibility and plausibility of the applicant's statements; b) the effective capacity by the local police authority to prevent life threatening and other harms affecting the applicant; c) how serious and spread are violent practices described by the applicant and to which extent the inaction of state authorities is among the causes of such situation; d) to which extent social conflicts such as those referred to by the applicant are actually left to traditional authorities and procedures that do not comply with human rights principles.

Similarly, the Court of Cassation, civil division, Sec. VI, ord. 18 November 2013, No. 25873, found that for the protection seeker, a Nigerian woman, the threat of a forced marriage was a threat to her rights sufficiently severe as to require the court to examine more carefully the case, going beyond the cautios and reticent statements of the woman and assuming, even *motu proprio*, more information about the general practice of forced marriage.

> On this regard see also: Court of Cassation, civil division, Sec. VI, ord. 24 October 2013, No. 24064 (the applicant, who had been convicted in Cameroon for crimes that led back to practices of "witchcraft", complained about the inhuman conditions in which she would be detained: both issues – persecutory motives of the conviction and prison conditions – must be actively investigated by the Italian courts); Court of Cassation, civil division, Sec. VI, ord. 24 October 2013, No. 24066 (an Afghan citizen who had worked as an airport officer, frequently threatened by armed factions: the Supreme Court found that the requirements were met for subsidiary protection); Court of Cassation, civil division, Sec. VI, ord. 28 May 2013, No. 13172 (even if dated back to 2003–04, the evidence of civilians' insecurity in Darfur provided by the applicant could easily be updated by the court of appeals required to review the case – note that the application for international protection had been rejected by the Asylum Territorial Commission and by the first instance tribunal only on the grounds that the information submitted about the armed conflict in Darfur was outdated); Court of Cassation, civil division, Sec. VI, ord. 4 April 2013, No. 8281 (the threats received by the applicant, a christian Nigerian, at the workplace, were not due to mere differences concerning labour union policies, but could be traced back to the inter-religious conflict that the State authorities are manifestly unable to handle).

The duty of the courts to play an active role in checking – also on the basis of information provided by reports of qualified non-governmental organisations – has been reiterated in the judgments issued to review the decisions of the Asylum Territorial Commissions. See, among others, Court of Trieste, judgment 20 November 2013, No. 1386, concerning a request of asylum submitted by an Afghan Shiite Muslim. The Tribunal of Rome (Sec. I, judg. 21 October 2013, No. 20908) grounded its decision to grant subsidiary protection to a Nigerian Catholic on news reports of the Nigerian press as well as on the information provided in the website "safe journey" of the Italian Ministry of Foreign Affairs. The Nigerian situation and the threats addressed to the applicant by members of the terrorist group Boko Haram are on the background of a judgment of the Court of Trieste (on 9 October 2013): the petitioner was granted subsidiary protection.

To be a member of an organisation for the rights of homosexuals and other LGBTI individuals in Nigeria, justifies, according to the Court of Naples, the recognition of refugee status, despite the contrary opinion of the Asylum Territorial Commission (Court of Naples, Sec. I, ord. 25 October 2013). The Court especially considered the harsh criminal legislation in force in Nigeria on homosexual conducts as well as the social stigma that is associated with it.

An Iranian citizen who, in his Country, was convicted to the punishment of flogging in public for having drunk some wine is entitled to subsidiary protection; the Italian court noted the disproportionate nature of the punishment – also in light of the fact that the Iranian criminal code prescribes the death penalty after three violations of the rule against the consumption of alcoholic beverages (Court of Trieste, judgment of 12 November 2013).

An Afghani citizen, member of a political party, who was threatened by a rival local politician belonging to a minority party at the national level, was not recognised as entitled neither to refugee status nor to subsidiary protection; nevertheless the Court of Trieste granted him humanitarian protection (judgment of 15 October 2013). The same Court of Trieste, however, while not considering reliable the statements of a Pakistani applicant who claimed to be persecuted by some Sunni terrorist organisations in the Country because of his conversion to Shiism, nevertheless decided to grant the applicant the humanitarian protection, in consideration of the objective risk for anyone professing the Shia posed by Sunni extremist organisations in Pakistan (judgment of 15 October 2013). The severity of the armed conflict in Darfur is a reason for granting subsidiary protection, according to the Tribunal of Rome (section I, judgment of 14 October, 2013, No. 20425).

Being the target of coercive measures carried out by the Russian military authorities during the short occupation of Georgia in the summer of 2008 does not justify humanitarian or subsidiary protection to a Georgian woman (Court of Cassation, civil division, Sec. VI, ord. 24 June 2013, No. 15757). The Supreme Court deems appropriate the investigation carried out by the ordinary court to check the statements of the applicant, a political activist of the Ivory Coast; the investigation disclosed that the applicant lacked the requirements for international or humanitarian protection (Court of Cassation, civil division, Sec. VI, judg. 18 April 2013, No. 9500). Similarly, the Supreme Court agreed with the lower courts and the Asylum Territorial Commission not to recognise any link between the alleged risk to the life in which the applicant would incur in returning to Nigeria and the conflict that affects the area of the Niger Delta (Court of Cassation, civil division, Sec. VI, ord. 9 January 2013, No. 359).

> The Supreme Court has also ruled on whether the murdering of his wife – a crime for which the applicant, an Albanian citizen, was convicted in Italy – could be seen as a reason to grant him humanitarian protection, as in Albania the man would be exposed to the revenge of the woman's family members, bound to retaliate by the local customary law – the Kanun. The Asylum Territorial Commission and the court of first instance had ruled that the risk of facing revenge was not a situation that required a form of humanitarian or international protection. The Supreme Court endorsed this finding. In particular, it shared the view that the Kanun's provisions are nowadays effectively countered by the consolidation of the rule of law in all Albanian territories and by the diffusion in those areas more at risk, of initiatives at the institutional and civil society levels aimed at curbing the vengeance system. This fact – and neither the seriousness of the offence committed by the applicant, nor the lack of recognition of the harsh situation brought about by the revenge system imposed by the Kanun – leads to conclude that the requirements are not met for granting international or humanitarian protection (Court of Cassation, civil division, Sec. VI, ord. 17 May 2013, No. 12134).

B. *Statelessness*

In judgment 8 November 2013, No. 25212, the civil division of the Court of Cassation, Sec. I, addressed a problem of implementation of the Convention on Statelessness of 28 September 1954 (ratified in Italy by law 306/1962) involving a Cuban citizen who, by virtue of a law of that Country, having been continuously in Italy for more than eleven months, had lost his residence in Cuba and a number of rights in the field of private law and public law (including inheritance rights of real estate ownership). The claim to be recognised as a stateless person had been rejected by the Court of Florence, on the grounds that formally the person was not stripped of his Cuban citizenship. The very significant limitations related to the status of "emigrant", however, led the Supreme Court to prefer a substantive reading of the notion of citizenship. Such interpretation is indeed supported by the letter of the 1954 Convention, according to which, in the words of the Court of Cassation, "a stateless person is one who lives in a Country of which he is not a citizen coming from another Country of which has lost formally or *substantially* the citizenship" (*italics added*).

III. Discrimination

A. *Equal Opportunities in Access to Public Offices*

During 2013, the Regional Administrative Tribunal of Lazio (TAR Rome, Sec. II-bis, judg. 21 January 2013, No. 633; Sec. II, judg. 11 September 2013, No. 8206) quashed the decisions adopted by the mayors of Civitavecchia and Colleferro that had included in the executive council of the respective Municipalities only one woman or had replaced with a man the only woman councillor. The court held – particularly in the first of the cases cited – a close examination of international and EU provisions on non-discrimination, to conclude in favour of the applicants (women's associations and some individual women). The TAR, among other things, did not accept the local administration's request to raise a reference for a preliminary ruling to the ECJ, arguing that the principle of non-discrimination on the basis of sex is deeply rooted in EU law (article 2 TEU, 19 TFEU, articles 21 and 23 CFREU). In the Italian Constitution, the principle of equal opportunities is recognised as immediately applicable also in the framework of administrative discretionary powers, both for national and local public bodies. Indeed, municipal and provincial statutes, pursuant to article 6 of lgs.d. 18 August 2000, No. 267, as amended, most recently by the law 23 November 2012, No. 215, should ensure equal opportunities between men and women and provide for the presence of both men and women in all executive and consultative bodies of local government units, as well as in institutions and companies controlled by the public sector.

B. *Discrimination Towards the Roma*

The Civil Cassation's joint sections (judg. 22 April 2013, No. 9687) upheld the judgment issued in 2011 by the Council of State that annulled a number of exceptional measures taken by the Government to counter the alleged "Roma emergency" (see *2012 Yearbook*, p. 313): the administrative court did not exceed its competence.

IV. Rights of Persons with Disabilities

A. *Attendance Allowances and Immigrants*

The Constitutional Court has intervened once again on the provisions of the Finance act for 2001, which had introduced a number of restrictions on immigrants' access to social benefits (see, for example, *2012 Yearbook*, p. 323). In particular, this law had stated that the allowances provided to family members of persons with severe disabilities (l. 11 February 1980, No. 18) could be granted only to immigrants holding a "residence card", that is a EU long term residence permit. This document can be requested if some conditions are met, in particular a sufficient income, an adequate housing and at least five years of regular staying in Italy. This provision is indeed an exception to the principle laid down in article 41 of lgs.d. 286/1998 (the Consolidated immigration act), which states that "foreigners who hold a residence card or residence permit of a duration of not less than one year, as well as their children therein registered, shall be equated to Italian citizens as for the enjoyment of the social assistance benefits, including economic allowances." The Constitutional Court, in line with its previous rulings, found the discriminatory character of the attacked provisions, as they unreasonably distinguish between different categories of immigrants, in violation of articles 2, 3 and 29 of the Constitution, and of article 117(1) Const., taken in conjunction with article 14 ECHR. The norms indeed are more favourable to those who less need social benefits. The financial benefit in question must be conceived as a fundamental right in so far as it is needed to cope with the discomfort the severe disability affecting a family member. The judgment 40/2013 of the Constitutional Court therefore ruled that article 80(19) of law of 23 December 2000, No. 388 is unconstitutional.

It is worth noting that according to the Court some welfare measures exceed the scope of social security benefits to which every individual should be able to access, and therefore may reasonably be allocated only to those immigrants who are more rooted in Italy: this is the case of the benefit set forth in article 3(6) of the law 8 August 1995, No. 335 (see Constitutional Court, judgment 197/2013).

B. Discrimination in Schools

The parents of a child with Down syndrome have lodged an application before the Court of Catanzaro for a finding of discriminatory conduct on the basis of article 3 of law 67/2006 and article 44 of lgs.d. 286/1998. The facts date back to 2011, and refer to the conduct of a school director who, talking with the classmates of the boy while the latter was not in class, asked them not to inform him about the school trips that the school was planning, in order not to allow him to participate since, in light of his disability, he could not profit from those activities. The children however did not agree to the director's request and indeed in the following days and weeks a huge mobilisation took place within and outside the school, with the involvement of local and national media, in support of the child that was allegedly discriminated against, so that the school director's plan completely failed. Eventually, the director was also suspended from office for a few months as a disciplinary sanction. The suit for discriminatory conduct was aimed at obtaining a reparation for the non-pecuniary damages suffered by the child with Down syndrome and his family. The

Court noted that the anti-discrimination procedure's goal is that of impos-ing an immediate halt to the illegal conduct and impose to the author of the discriminatory conduct the payment of compensations; in this case, however, the reaction of the classmates and of the local civil society was such as to prevent any act of discrimination from taking place. There was therefore only an "attempted discrimination", and the disciplinary sanc-tion inflicted appeared largely appropriate to stigmatise the fact. The ap-plication was therefor dismissed as inadmissible (Tribunal of Catanzaro, Sec. I, judg. 15 January 2013).

> In the judgment, 21166/2013, the Supreme Court discussed the claim –
> rejected by the trial court – submitted by a parent to obtain restitution from
> the Municipality of residence of approximately 20,000 euros he spent over
> some years to accompany to school his son, physically impaired, since he was
> 5 years old: these costs, according to the applicant, should have been fully cov-
> ered by the local administration. A number of provisions in the Constitution
> and in international instruments affirm precisely the right to education of all
> children, including those who have some form of disability. The Supreme
> Court endorses the claim. It rejects the assertion of the Court of Appeal ac-
> cording to which the principles of the Constitution and of the international
> instruments on non-discrimination and free education are merely program-
> matic. On the contrary, they have largely prescriptive value, so that an act
> setting low quality standard in education, the exclusion of certain categories
> of persons from access to school, or the duty to pay education fees for those
> in economic distress, etc., would be unconstitutional. This however does not
> mean that the State should provide for free all services associated with the
> right to achieve free primary education, such as those of school transport.
> Access to such services can be made conditional to a financial contribution
> from the families that are in a position to pay for it. The State has to imple-
> ment the "reasonable accommodation" that the Convention on the Rights of
> Persons with Disabilities foresees as a tool for the fulfilment of fundamental
> rights (Constitutional Court, judgment 21166/2013).

C. Special Leave for Family Members of Persons with Severe Disabilities

The Constitutional Court (judgment 203/2013) has significantly rec-ognised the unconstitutionality of article 42(5) of lgs.d. 26 March 2001, No. 151 (Consolidated act on the protection and support of motherhood and fatherhood, as last amended in 2011), insofar as it does not provide that the special leave of up to two years provided for an employee who in-tends to take care of a person with severe disabilities with which he or she lives can only be granted to the spouse, a parent, a child or a sibling of the person with disability (and in this order). The Court's outcome is that any relative or any person related by affinity, up to the third degree of kinship, who lives together with the person in need, is entitled to such a leave, provided no closer family member is in a position to do so. The Court takes note of the fact that the contested rule was enacted to allow the care of children with disabilities without forcing them to abandon the domestic environment; the same rule however may apply to any other individual in need of care, including the elderly. Hence the opportunity to expand the scope of the norm, albeit in a moderate fashion: the limit of the third degree of kinship or affinity is the same as provided by law 104/1992 on the paid leave to provide care to a family member with severe disabilities. It should be noted that the Constitutional Court based this decision, among other things, also on article 118(5) of the Constitution, recognising how the commented rule was implementing the principle of subsidiarity.

> Some judgments of the Council of State reaffirmed the orientation consolidated in previous years (see *2013 Yearbook*, p. 319) that although the contribution for hospitalisation in nursing home for persons with severe disability or non self-sufficient over-65 years old must be paid by the competent public authority (generally the Municipality) having exclusive regard to the personal income of the beneficiary, as it is a strictly individual right, the family of the latter nevertheless is required to disclose to the Municipality's welfare officers their equivalent economic situation indicator (ISEE), since the contribution (perhaps merely symbolic) of the family to the costs of the extra-home care service is required to compensate the removal of the non-independent person from the home context (Council of State, judgment 3574/2013).

D. Right to Assistance and Support Teacher

The TAR Abruzzo (judgment 744/2013) issued a detailed ruling on an appeal in which the parents of a child with Down syndrome challenged the decision of the school authority to provide the child with a support teacher for only nine hours a week; the claimants maintained that their child was entitled to avail himself of a support teacher during all hours of attendance of the kindergarten. The claim was based, among other things, on the provisions of the Convention on the Rights of Persons with Disabilities as well as on the jurisprudence of the Constitutional Court, namely judgment 80/2010 (see *2011 Yearbook*, p. 270). The TAR noted that the right to the allocation of a specialised teacher derogating to the staffing plan set by the Ministry does not automatically imply the right of the disabled person to be assigned the support teacher for the full school time. The teacher cannot be considered as assigned exclusively to a specific student, but as a teacher sharing the educational function of the school's faculty. The provision is not meant to provide a personal teacher to the child with disabilities, but to encourage his or her integration into the group of peers and a way of enriching and empowering the child. Therefore, on the one hand, there is no automatic duty to enable a one-to-one tuition between the child with disabilities and the support teacher;

on the other hand, the TAR observed, the opposite is not true either, that the specific needs of the child should not deserve consideration when they oppose the staff organisation. Since the allocation of hours of support teaching was made by the school without carrying out the complex process of assessing the needs of the child, without having prepared an individual educational plan, and therefore without any real justification, the measure taken is annulled.

> In line with the judgment just summarised, see also Council of State, Sec. V, judg. 2 May 2013, No. 2391; TAR Molise, judg. 263/2013. See also, in connection with the right of a student with a disability to benefit both of a support teacher (a task of the school administration) and of an assistant to the person (a task under the responsibility of the provincial government), the Council of State's judgments, Nos. 2391/2013; 3950/2013 and 3954/2013.

E. Specific Learning Disorders

The TAR Campania (Regional Administrative Tribunal of Naples, Sec. IV, judgment 6 March 2013, No. 1254) ruled on a case concerning law 8 October 2010, No. 170 (New rules on specific learning disorders in school). The case involved a girl who, following the school teachers' advice, was examined at a specialised centre and found to have a learning disability. Despite the parents' request to appoint a support teacher to help the child, no specific measure was adopted by the school and the child eventually flunked the year. The TAR, to which the parents reported the case, sanctioned the school administration for failing to implement measures to support the disabled schoolgirl. It was not permissible in a case of this kind, in which the presence of a learning disability was well known to the school authorities, to require the parents to apply for special support measures by exhibiting medical certificates or ad hoc instances; instead it was a duty of the school to take action in order to identify any suspected cases of learning disorder, to request their diagnostic assessment by a public health service and to adopt the appropriate individualised educational measures.

V. Social Rights

A. Right to Health and Right to Work

The ruling 85/2013 of the Constitutional Court dealt with a complex legal case related to the industrial and environmental crisis of "Ilva Taranto", the largest steel plant of Italy, that has repeatedly suspended its activity because of a series of court's orders aimed to prevent the harmful consequences of the industrial processes on the health of workers and of the inhabitants of Taranto. The industrial and financial crisis of the group and the criminal investigation involving the owners of the company made the situation even more complex. The Constitutional Court judgment, requested by the judge for preliminary investigations and the Court of Taranto, focused on the reasonableness of the balance of interests made in the d.l. December 2012, No. 207, articles 1 and 3, between on one hand the right to work of Ilva employees, and on the other the right to health of the same workers and of the inhabitants of Taranto. According to the judicial bodies that have raised the constitutionality issue, the decree – that may be qualified as an ad-hoc law as expressly tailored to face the Ilva crisis –, gave overriding importance to preserving the productive capacity of the corporate group, largely neglecting the public health, although the right to health features prominently in article 32 of the Italian Constitution and is also mentioned in the CFREU (articles 3 and 35).

The Constitutional Court has carried out an extensive analysis of the content of the contested decree-law and found that the claim of unconstitutionality made by the referring court was ill-founded. Among other things, the Court noted that the decision to grant Ilva, identified as an asset of strategic interest, a green light to continue production despite the judicial seizure of the industrial site, was justified by the urgent need to safeguard the employment and the production capacity of an industry of key importance for the Country. The Constitutional Court found that the constraints imposed on the company for resuming the production in full compliance, for the next 36 months, with the parameters established by the special environmental permission issued by the Government, parameters that are even stricter than those recommended by the EU, appeared likely to ensure that the industrial activity is not achieved at the expense of the environment and of human health. The directions imposed on the Ilva management by the decree-law in question did not negatively affect the investigation on the criminal implications of the whole story. Indeed the decree was an interference in the autonomous functions of the judiciary that had stopped any industrial activity of Ilva. Nevertheless the decree-law was justified by the need to face urgently and promptly a social and ecological emergency that also the judiciary aimed to address. The decree's provisions, on the one hand, did not undermine the criminal case and, on the other hand, did not result in a resumption of activities dangerous for the environment and for human health, since the strict environmental standards imposed by the decree-law are such as to reasonably exclude that outcome.

B. *Corporate Social Responsibility*

The Council of State ruled on the legal relevance of the SA 8000/2008 certification (an international social accountability standard) on the occasion of a complex dispute regarding the assignment by contract by a

Municipality of some services to a company that had not submitted, as required by the tender document as a *sine-qua-non* condition, the above certification. The so-called SA 8000/2008 is an international standard certification created and administered by the Council of Economic Priorities Accreditation Agency, in order to assess some aspects of business management for the promotion of corporate social responsibility. Monitored aspects include respect of human rights standards, labour rights and trade unions' rights, disciplinary practices, rules preventing the exploitation of child labour, on health and safety in the workplace, etc.; standards are largely set in accordance with international legal instruments such as the ILO conventions, the Universal Declaration of Human Rights and the various international human rights conventions. The Regional Administrative Tribunal of Veneto had considered legitimate to exclude a company from the tender list because, although it could show that its business practice was mostly in compliance with the SA 8000/2008 standards, including the adoption of a code of ethics, it had not completed the certification process at the time of the bid. The Council of State (judgement 12 November 2013, No. 5375), differently interpreting the legislative decree No. 163/2006, ruled instead that the public authority can condition the participation of companies in a tender to the possession of some substantive requirements in the field of corporate social responsibility, but this cannot include the holding of a specific certification document. To comply with the Italian legislation (which largely reflects the international labour standards) and to have adopted a code of conduct inspired by the same principles used by the SA 8000/2008 certification, should be considered sufficient to meet the tender conditions. The Council of State acknowledged that in order to get an international certification document a company had undergone some stringent audit and assessment procedures; the international certification, however, cannot be given the value of a legal proof, since compliance with the relevant norms can be proved also in other ways.

C. House Assigned, After Separation, to one of the Spouses Free of Charge

A chamber of the Supreme Court has dealt with a particularly complex issue and, with an interim decision, has referred it to the joint sections of the Court of Cassation. The case concerned two parents who, in order to help their son and his spouse, had loaned gratuitously a flat to the couple, without establishing a term. Later on, however, the two – who in the meantime had a baby – started a separation procedure and a court assigned the apartment to the woman, together with the custody of the child. The question facing the Court of Cassation is whether the loan still exists, considering that it was originally meant to benefit the son of the landlords or his family, and not the new family composed by the ex-wife and the baby. One would also ask whether the parents have a right to have back the apartment and loan it, for instance, to another child. The Cassation found that the jurisprudence on this point was not consistent, hence the referral to the joint sections.

VI. Laws Affecting Individual Rights with Retroactive Effect

The Constitutional Court (judgment 308/2013, 17 December 2013) examined the constitutionality of a law of the Region of Sardinia, which intervened in the field of urban planning and landscape and environmental protection in the light of its own jurisprudence and of the ECtHR case-law concerning the retroactive effects of a law. The case can be summarised as follows. A regional law adopted in October 2012 gave an authoritative interpretation of a provision of a previous act, the lgs.d. 22 January 2004, No. 42 (Code of cultural heritage and landscape), establishing, in particular, that the "zone of respect" of 300 meters from the shore line (a no building area) did not apply to "wetlands", while it continued to apply to lakes and artificial basins. The regional law was enacted a few months after that a decision of the Council of State had found that a building area has illegally developed precisely in Sardinia near a wetland. One of the immediate consequences of the regional law of 2012 was to prevent the concerned local administration from giving effect to that judgment. The Constitutional Court recalled its previous decisions 78/2012 (see *2013 Yearbook*, p. 322) and 170/2013, as well as the jurisprudence of the ECtHR (among others: *Maggio v. Italy* – see *2012 Yearbook*, p. 347 – *Arras and Others v. Italy* – see *2013 Yearbook*, p. 369) and stated that only overriding reasons of general interest may justify an interference of the legislative power in the judiciary in order to influence the outcome of judicial proceedings. The regional law of 2012 is therefore found unconstitutional.

A situation similar to that just considered, again triggered by a law allegedly providing an authoritative interpretation of previous legislation, but actually creating a new norm with retroactive effects, was dealt with by the Constitutional Court in judgment 103/2013. The retroactive effects of a law adopted in 2010 were that those who had purchased a home that failed to comply with the rules on acoustic pollution were barred from seeking compensation from the property developer. This created a discrimination with respect to those who before the entry into force of the new legislation managed to suit for damages the building company and obtained reparation (violation of article 3 of the Constitution). The Court noted that the 2010 law could not qualify as an authoritative interpretation of an existing norm, but was instead a fully innovative provision with retroactive effect; effects of this kind can be justified – unless they are in criminal matters – only in extraordinary circumstances that were not present in the case: indeed, the rule was intended merely to extend the deadline for setting new standards on acoustic pollution that the State should have adopted in 2004.

In this context can also be mentioned the Constitutional Court's judgment 92/2013: the Court quashed as unconstitutional the provisions of the law 30 September 2003, No. 269 the effect of which was to recognise to the car service centres where vehicles seized by the police or the judiciary where deposited lower fees. The Court concludes for the unconstitutionality of the new law for violation of article 3 of the Constitution because of its retroactive effect. The judiciary task in this and in many other similar cases is, in the Court's words, "to prevent that a widespread urgency of containing public expenses always and almost ineluctably results in a limitation of the rights or a compression of interests of individuals and groups."

The Constitutional Court, ruling on a number of constitutionality issues raised in relation to a 2012 law that abolished the system of legally established national forensic tariffs, with effects that the referring judges deemed to be retroactive because the new regime was applicable also to proceedings ongoing at the time of the adoption of the reform (see *2013 Yearbook*, pp. 320–322), denied that the contested norms were retroactive at all. According to settled case-law, the amount owed to a lawyer regards the full legal service provided to a client, not any single legal step. The Constitutional Court therefore rejected the allegation that the 2012 law retroactively affected the lawyer's rights and therefore impaired the right of access to the court (this right indeed seems to be enhanced by a general lowering of lawyer's fees).

The Supreme Court has adopted a number of decisions that replicate the contrast between the jurisprudence of the ECtHR and that of the Constitutional Court regarding the retroactive application of rules that provided for the transition from the retributive to the contributive pension scheme and extended it also to Italian citizens who had worked in Switzerland, although the issue was still being litigated in various judicial proceedings (see *2013 Yearbook*, pp. 320–321). The Supreme Court has concluded for the applicability of the rules in question, which the Constitutional Court had found constitutionally sound (see, e.g., Court of Cassation, civil division, judgments Nos. 22449/2013, 22549/2013, 22550/2013, 22551/2013, 22620/2013, 22740/2013, 23779/2013, 22877/2013, 22874/2013 and 23703/2013).

The ECtHR *Arras* jurisprudence (see *2013 Yearbook*, p. 369) has reverberated in 2013 on a number of judgments of the Supreme Court. The Court of Cassation reiterated in several judgments (see, for example, civil division,

Sec. Labour, judg. 27 September 2013, No. 22269) that a national court cannot ignore the decisions taken by ECtHR in cases similar to those submitted to it and, though the hermeneutic outcome might diverge, since the Strasbourg Court's judgments do not set any precedent, it must give reasons as to why it departed from the ECtHR ruling. The case ruled by the Court of Cassation involved a retiree of an Italian bank, the Banco di Napoli, who had benefited from a favourable treatment in accordance to legislation subsequently repealed, with retroactive effect, by a 2004 act. Despite the fact that the ECtHR had found that the State was responsible for violating the right to a fair trial, in so far as the legislation in practice imposed the courts to settle in a given way the pending cases on the recognition of pension benefits, the new, less favourable, regulatory framework, according to the Supreme Court, cannot affect the legal situation of those whose position had been already confirmed by a final judgment. On the contrary, it can legitimately have an impact (a negative one) on the situation of those whose claim was not settled with a final judgment by a national court. This view is maintained by the Court of Cassation despite the infringement of article 6 ECHR that it seems to carry out.

Law 15 July 2011, No. 111, conversion of the d.l. 6 July 2011, No. 98 (Urgent measures of financial stabilisation) was criticised by the Constitutional Court insofar as it included retroactive provisions in the matter of bankruptcy proceedings (article 2752(1) of the civil code). The reform gave a priority to the tax and other debts owned by the State, compared to any private creditor; this inevitably had an impact on a number of bankruptcy proceedings that were in progress at the moment the law was enacted. Moreover, the goal pursued was not to protect a general interest, but rather to ensure the interest of the State as a creditor. The law therefore infringes article 3 of the Constitution as well as its article 117(1), having article 6 ECHR as "interposed parameter".

VII. Immigration

A. *Crime of Illegal Immigration*

The Supreme Court has confirmed the applicability of the provision of the Consolidated immigration act which punishes as a criminal offence the irregular entry or stay of a migrant in the Italian territory (lgs.d. 286/1998, article 10-*bis*). The case concerned the ruling of a justice of the peace (*giudice di pace*) who, noticing that an irregular migrant had never been attained by an expulsion order, acquitted her of the said offence in question (see also, among others, the judgments of the Court of Cassation, criminal division, Nos. 42417/2013, 27610/2013, 27614/2013, 27616/2013, 27617/2013, 27618/2013, 27620/2013, 27623/2013, 30308/2013, 30309/2013, 30310/2013, 30311/2013, 30312/2013, 35587/2013, 35589/2013, 35590/2013, 42401/2013). As the Supreme Court pointed out, not only the Constitutional Court confirmed the legitimacy of the rule that criminalised the irregular entry or stay in Italy of a migrant (see judgment 250/2010 in *2011 Yearbook*, p. 278), but also the ECJ in its case-law has acknowledged the compatibility of national laws that punish as a crime a migrant's illegal entry into the territory of a EU State with the relevant EU directives (mentioned ECJ rulings are: ECJ, Section I, judgment 6 December 2012, *Sagor*, case C-430/11; ECJ, Section III, order 21 March 2013, *Mbaye*, case C-522/11, ECJ, Grand Chamber, judgment 6 December 2011, *Achughbabian*, case C-329/11). Moreover, the current Italian legislation excludes the applicability of the criminal penalty (a fine of 5,000 to 10,000 euros) if an administrative sanction had already been imposed, that is the expulsion of the irregular migrant (if the expulsion was already implemented, the court must indeed acquit the individual). It is also worth mentioning that the national rules found incompatible with the EU Return Directive – directive 2008/115 – were only those in articles 14 (5-ter) and (5-quater) of legislative decree No. 286/1998 as they read prior to the reform of decree-law 23 June 2011, No. 89, converted into law 2 August 2011, No. 129; as for the application of such provisions, which punish the non-fulfilment of the obligation to leave the territory of the State imposed to an alien who was not possible to repatriate, see Court of Cassation, criminal division, Sec. I, judg. 2 July 2013, No. 35581.

B. Expulsions, Refoulement

The joint sections of the Court of Cassation ruled on a controversial issue of interpretation stemmed from an alleged gap in the Consolidated immigration act which, insofar as the articles dealing with the pushing back of aliens not eligible for entry into Italy (articles 10 and 19 of lgs.d. 286/1998) did not specify which court is competent to hear a challenge to the decision rejecting the entry permit. In some cases, individuals who had been refused the right to cross the border to Italy had challenged the decision issued by the Police before the administrative courts; in other cases a claim against the same kind of decision was addressed to the ordinary civil courts. The Supreme Court has resolved the jurisdiction issue stating that, since the measure interferes with the enjoyment of fundamental rights, including the right to be recognised as a refugee, it is the judge of rights – that is, the ordinary courts – to be competent (as it is uncontroversially the case for claims under article 13 of lgs.d. 286/1998 concerning orders of expulsion) (Court of Cassation, civil division, joint sections, order 10 June 2013, No. 14502; see also Court of Cassation, civil division, joint sections, judgment 17 June 2013, No. 15115). The Court noted that to be legitimate, a refoulement carried out at the State border must establish, albeit *prima facie*, the lack of any circumstances that may lead to the recognition of political asylum or of any other form of international protection. This assessment, of course, should not affect the subsequent determination of the Asylum Territorial Commission, based on a more thorough and complete scrutiny. The judgment of the Supreme Court cited, in particular, the case *Hirsi Jamaa and Others v. Italy* of the ECtHR, which restated the obligation to fully respect the article 3 ECHR absolute prohibition of torture and inhuman treatment while performing refoulement procedures. Any application lodged before the Regional Administrative Tribunals must therefore be transferred to the ordinary courts.

It should be mentioned in this connection also the judgment of the joint sections of the Court of Cassation, civil division, 10 June 2013, No. 14501, which has made it clear that the damages cases occasioned by a delay in the adoption of administrative measures (in the case at issue it was the issuing of the permit to stay to a Congolese refugee due since 2004, a document he needed in order to travel abroad and accept a job offer), if they relate to disputes arisen before the entry into force of law 18 June 2009, No. 69 (the act that added article 2-bis to the law 241/1990), shall be brought either to the administrative tribunals or to an ordinary court according to the subjacent individual legal entitlements; when a measure such as the issuance of a permit to stay is involved, since it is likely to impact upon several rights of the individual, the proper forum is the ordinary judiciary, and not the Administrative Regional Tribunals (TAR). After the 2009 reform, however, TARs have exclusive competence for claims for damages related to excessive delay of an immigration procedure due to negligence or wilful misconduct: see article 133 of legislative decree 104/2010 (Code of administrative procedure).

> The Supreme Court has reasserted that the lodging of an application for international protection (even if reiterated after a previous rejection, provided it is based on some new elements) automatically suspends the execution of a deportation order. Any further validation made by the justice of the peace is therefore unlawful (Court of Cassation, civil division, section VI, order 20 June 2013, No. 15512).

> The Council of State (Section III, judgment 11 October 2013, No. 4984; see also Section III, judgment 29 July 2013, No. 3980) ruled that the special residence permit issued to an alien who applied for international protection only covered the duration of the proceedings before the Asylum Territorial Commission and did not extend to further proceedings in the ordinary courts. Therefore, the individual who is given an expulsion order and had impugned rejection of his or her application for international protection (asylum, subsidiary protection or humanitarian protection) is not entitled to obtain a residence permit. If particularly serious reasons exist, though, he may only ask the Prefecture to be allowed to stay in Italy, held in a "centre of custody and assistance", for up to sixty days (article 17(2) of presidential decree 303/2004).

The Constitutional Court (judgment 202/2013) has ruled on the legitimacy of a provision of the Consolidated immigration act which qualified as illegal the permanence in Italy of aliens who were convicted – although only at first instance – for an offence included in a long list of cases considered of particular social alarm; according to this provision, the strictly automatic application of this mechanism can be mitigated by the police authorities, who may consider in a discretionary way the actual and specific social dangerousness of the individual against the existence of family and personal ties in Italy, but only as regards foreigners who had entered to Italy or had remained in the State under a procedure of family reunification (article 5(5) of the Consolidated act on immigration). According to the Court, it was not reasonable to limit the use of the discretionary power to balance the prospective dangerousness of the person with his or her right to private and family life (to use the words in article 8 ECHR), only to individuals who had undertaken a family reunification procedure; indeed, people with significant family ties in Italy might well have entered the Country or stayed therein for a considerable length of time without having had the need or the interest to resort to the family reunification procedure. The mentioned provision of the Consolidated immigration act should therefore be meant to include the duty of the police to take into account the nature and duration of the family and personal ties, both in Italy and in the Country of origin, as well as the length of stay in Italy, of any person who, having been convicted for one of the mentioned offences, applies for having his or her the permit to stay renewed. Despite the conviction, a permit to stay may always be issued on the basis of either the lack of dangerousness or the existence of compelling family ties in Italy.

It is worth mentioning also the judgment of the Supreme Court in which it clarified that, in cases where there are consistent grounds to fear that an alien once deported to the Country of origin may incur unfair criminal proceedings or inhumane conditions of detention (the case at stake concerned a Turkish citizen who had lived in Italy for twenty years and was known to the Turkish authorities as an active member of a revolutionary communist faction), the person's not appearing at trial and his decision to abscond, probably to avoid contacts with the Turkish authorities, could not prevent the grant of humanitarian protection. The latter measure is required to respect the State's obligation to proscribe torture and inhuman treatment under article 3 ECHR; the humanitarian protection therefore is by no means conditioned by the individual's reciprocal conduct towards the Italian State, nor could it be denied by invoking an alleged non-cooperation with the judicial authorities (Court of Cassation, civil division, Sec. VI, judg. 20 September 2013, No. 21667).

In ruling on the legitimacy of an expulsion decree, courts are required to verify that no reasons exist to justify the granting of international protection to the concerned individual, taking into account all circumstances including those that had not emerged or raised during the procedure before the Asylum Territorial Commission (Court of Cassation, civil division, Sec. VI, judg. 20 February 2013, No. 4230).

C. Duration of Detention in Centres for Identification and Expulsion, and Damages for Unlawful Detention

Some judgments of local courts have ruled on claims for damages submitted by migrants unduly detained in the Italian Centres for identification and expulsion (CIE). In the case decided by the Tribunal of Rome, Section II, 15 March 2013, judgment No. 5764, the applicant had been restricted in the CIE of Rome for about two months despite the deportation order issued by the Police had not been validated by the competent justice of the peace. The determination of the non-pecuniary damage for undue detention in the CIE was equated to that for wrongful imprisonment: 235.82 euros per day.

The Supreme Court (civil division, orders 11451/2013 and 11452/2013) has stated that any extensions of the detention of an alien in a CIE, required in order to identify the person going to be expelled, are only those strictly defined by law (article 14(5) of lgs.d. 286/1998); for this reason, the order given by a justice of the peace allowing for an extension of the permanence in a CIE for an additional 90-day period is unlawful, since the law provides for periods of no more than 60 days each, that in case may be repeated up to a maximum detention term of 180 days in total.

D. Social Rights of Immigrants

A number of judgments of the Constitutional Court of 2013 scrutinised some laws enacted by Italian Regions or Autonomous Provinces which had introduced restrictions to the enjoyment of certain social benefits based on the duration of residence or "permanent abode" in the respective Region or Autonomous Province.

In the judgment 2/2013, the Court declared unconstitutional the provisions of the law of the Autonomous Province of Bolzano 28 October 2011, No. 12 (on the integration of foreign nationals of both sexes) on the grounds that it had conditioned the access of non-EU citizens to social assistance benefits being "of economic nature" to their residence and permanent abode in the Province of Bolzano for at least five continuous years; the duration of residence or permanent abode is also a condition for accessing other services the exceeds the core benefits prescribed by law. The Constitutional Court, while acknowledging that the requirement of the residence in a given territory is an acceptable criterion to justify whether or not an individual is entitled to the social benefits provided by a sub-state government entity, noted that measures such as those set forth in the provincial law at issue did not respect the principles of reasonableness and equality enshrined in article 3 of the Italian Constitution. More specifically, the Court found that there was no correlation between the length of an individual's residence in the territory and his or her incurring in the situations of need or hardship that require the social measures set out in the law (reference is made to judgment 40/2011 of the Constitutional Court: see also *2012 Yearbook*, pp. 322–324); moreover, it is not possible to desume that immigrants permanently living in the Province although for less than five years should not need such social support measures. The fact that the public funds for social benefits have shrunk cannot justify unreasonable restrictions. Similarly, it is not constitutionally founded to condition the attribution to non-EU immigrants of provincial allowances to attend schools and universities located outside the Province of Bolzano to their residence in the same Province for at least five years, nor to subordinate their entitlement to receive financial support to attend foreign language courses to their residence in the Province for at least one year.

The law of the Autonomous Province of Bolzano was also found partially unconstitutional by the Court in so far as, for the family reunification purposes, it extended the same requirements of housing condition, including hygienic and health standards, and of minimum annual income established for local residents to non-EU citizens, superseding the standards set forth in the State legislation. Indeed, the matter of migration is attributed by article 117(2) of the Italian Constitution to the national law. For the same reason, the provisions of the law of the Autonomous Province of Bolzano that implement, independently from what was done under State law, the EU directive on the admission of third country researchers in the EU Member States, are also declared unconstitutional.

A similar decision was adopted by the Constitutional Court in its judgment 222/2013. The Court ruled that some provisions of the law of the Friuli-Venezia Giulia Autonomous Region 30 November 2011, No. 16 on the entitlement to social benefits, was illegitimate in so far as it limited the access to foreigners to certain social allowances to conditions such as the residence in the Italian territory for at least five years (in addition to holding a residence permit of the duration of at least one year, a condition set by the lgs.d. 286/1998 – the Consolidated immigration act); in so doing, the law introduced an unreasonable and discriminatory restriction, in breach of article 3 of the Constitution, as far as it is likely to deprive immigrants of the benefits of the regional funds to combat poverty and social distress and on the right to education. The distinction between residents and non-residents, however, was found a plausible and not unreasonable ground in relation to other social benefits provided by the same regional law, namely those supporting new births and providing allowances in the form of contributions to rental costs, access to subsidised housing, issuing of "family cards", to families who had suffered dramatic income contractions. In all these cases, the services offered were exceeding the basic need level that must be granted to anyone, and could be reasonably conditioned by the regional legislator to those potential beneficiaries having a strong link with the territory.

In the same vein also judgment 4/2013 of the Constitutional Court addressed a law of the Region Calabria aimed at supporting people with disabilities (r.l. 20 December 2011, No. 44). The law limited the access to some benefits it provided for non self-sufficient persons only to non-EU citizens awarded a regular residence card (more correctly: the EU long-term residence permit). According to the Court, once shown that the permanence of an individual within the State is not merely temporary and episodic, and that it has given rise to the awarding of a residence permit, the person should be granted access to the social measures in question, without requiring a residence permit of a special type.

> Concerning access to social measures such as attendance allowance, pensions or disability allowance, to be paid without discrimination between temporary residents and long-term residents, see also the judgments of the Court of Cassation, Nos. 10460/2013, 26380/2013.

> The Court of Appeal of Brescia was seized in connection with a court decision sanctioning as discriminatory the decision of a municipal government which attributed a cash support to the rental costs of families in hardship, provided their members were Italian citizens. Following the first instance ruling the Municipality was ordered to reopen the call to all residents. Furthermore, the Municipality, to comply with the judgment, had required the families already awarded the cash support to partially restitute the money, so as to reconstitute the fund now to be shared also with the families of the immigrants. This decision was however found by the Court of Appeal a prohibited form of retaliation: the City Hall was eventually ordered to restore the social fund by different means (Court of Appeal, Brescia, judg. 31 January 2013).

VIII. Right to Privacy, Right to Property

A. *Right to Privacy and the So-called "Redditometro"*

The Tribunal of Naples – Pozzuoli section (ord. 20 February 2013, No. 250; judg. 24 September 2013, No. 10508) found that the ministerial decree of 24 December 2012, No. 65648 issued by the Ministry of Finance to implement article 38(4) of d.p.r. 29 September 1973, No. 600 as amended by article 22(1) of the d.l. 31 May 2010, No. 78, which put into place the so-called "redditometro", namely the instrument that should guide the Italian Revenue Agency in its activities to combat tax evasion, is contrary to a number of laws and principles concerning the privacy of the individual. In order to detect tax evasion or tax avoidance, the ministerial decree provided the Italian Revenue Agency with the possibility to obtain information about a wide range of behaviours considered relevant to the assessment of inconsistencies between, on the one hand, the level of expenditures and the standard of living of individuals and families, and, on the other, their tax return. According to this decree, the Italian Revenue Agency could then gain knowledge of aspects of taxpayers' private and family life which, in the opinion of the Court, belong to the scope of the notion of privacy: medical expenses, education choices, eating or consumption habits possibly linked to the intimate life of each member of the family. The Court also challenges the suitability of the so-called "redditometro" to effectively identify inconsistencies between the expenditure incurred by a family and its fiscal situation. As a matter of fact, the Court notes, the instrument uses statistical data that in some cases end up rendering low-income earners more suspect than high-income ones. For these reasons, the Court ordered the Italian Revenue Agency not to collect or store data connected to the implementation of the relevant ministerial decree.

B. Right to Property, "Indirect Expropriation", Fair Compensation

Among the numerous rulings concerning "indirect expropriations" that, also in 2013, Italian courts have issued, it is possible to mention the decision of the Regional Administrative Tribunal of Campania (TAR Naples, Sec. IV, judg. 18 September 2013, No. 4348). In the circumstance, in 1980 the City of Naples had begun the construction of a viaduct without finalising the expropriation of the land interested by the public works. Despite the failure to complete the viaduct, the transfer of the land ownership to the City of Naples was finally decided by a court ruling in 2002. The Regional Administrative Tribunal, while recognising that the procedure of indirect expropriation or "inverted accession" originating from national case-law is contrary to the right to the peaceful enjoyment of property enshrined in article 1 Protocol I ECHR and, by now, also to Italian law, concludes that neither the ECtHR case-law nor the national law that has subsequently regulated the matter can overturn a final judgment.

From its part, the Supreme Court (see, among others, Court of Cassation, civil division, Sec. II, judg. 14 January 2013, No. 705; civil division, Sec. I, 28 January 2013, No. 1804) has reiterated the incompatibility between the procedure of indirect expropriation established by national legal precedents and the ECHR standards. The law that in 2011 reformed d.p.r. 327/2001 (Consolidated act on expropriations) has re-established, with partially retrospective effects, lawfulness of the procedure (see *2013 Yearbook*, pp. 329–330). Similarly, see also Council of State, judg. 2279/2013 and 2481/2013; TAR Catanzaro, judg. 678/2013; TAR Campania, judg. 1985/2013, 3879/2013; TAR Basilicata, judg. 132/2013.

IX. Children's Rights

A. *Ex Officio Initiation of Child Neglect Proceedings*

Among a number of measures introduced in order to bring elements of the adversarial system in juvenile court proceedings, article 10(1) of l. 4 May 1993, No. 184, as amended by l. 28 March 2001, No. 149, establishes that the judicial procedure for the recognition of a child state of neglect, being the first step of the proceedings that can lead to the child adoption, may be initiated exclusively by the Public Prosecutor of the Juvenile Court (the Juvenile Court, however, may take *ex officio* measures limiting or cancelling parental authority in case the welfare of a child is in serious danger). In this regard, the Juvenile Court of Trieste raises the issue of constitutionality on account of the fact that, having omitted to grant the President of the Juvenile Court or his delegate the possibility to institute a child neglect proceedings, the contested provision limits the right of the child to protection and welfare, which can also be implemented through access to adoption procedures.

According to the referring court, the contested norm violates articles 2, 31 and 32 of the Italian Constitution, as well as various provisions of international instruments (Convention on the Rights of Children and article 24 CFREU) devoted to the protection and promotion of children welfare. Even the Council of Europe Convention on the Exercise of Children's Rights (ratified by Italy with l. 20 March 2003, No. 77) urges States to grant judicial authority the power to act on its own motion in proceedings affecting a child. Above all, according to the referring court, the monopoly of the initiative entrusted to the Public Prosecutor in the matter implies that some situations deserving the intervention of the judicial authority, if undetected by the Prosecutor, cannot be promptly and speedily tackled. The Constitutional Court (order 136/2013) rejects the considerations of the referring court. As a matter of fact, the contested provision is functional to the choice made by the Italian legislature to extend the principles of the adversarial system to juvenile proceedings. In such a system, the judge must strictly conform to its role of impartial third party with respect to instances coming from private individuals or, indeed, from the Public Prosecutor of the Juvenile Court, which is the sole judicial body entrusted with the power of initiate legal proceedings in the field of child protection. Any wilful inertia of the Prosecutor cannot be compensated for by measures that frustrate the choices made by the legislature concerning the criminal law policy.

B. Privacy and Minors

The Supreme Court (civil division, Sec. I, judg. 6 December 2013, No. 27381) upheld the legitimacy of the measures adopted in 2005 by the Italian Data Protection Authority, which had imposed a penalty on the weekly magazine "Chi" for having published, in an article concerning the alleged extramarital affairs of the then director general of RAI (the Italian public service broadcaster), photos – only partially altered – of the face of the man's younger daughter, other family members and the family home, located in a small town. The editor of the magazine had challenged the decision of the Authority, claiming, among other things, that the then director general had on a previous occasion given interviews on his family members and authorised the publication of their photos, including minors. Referring to the International Convention on the Rights of the Child and to the Charter of Treviso on Children and Information which states that "the child involved as an author, victim or witness in news that, if disseminated, could adversely affect its growth, must be guaranteed absolute anonymity", the Supreme Court rejected the appellant's argument. The Court, indeed, concluded that the use of the RAI former manager's previously expressed consent to publish photos of his child for an article about his family in order to disseminate images of that child to complement an article about the RAI manager's alleged extramarital affair had violated the child's right to privacy.

C. Adoptability and Adoption in Special Cases

The Supreme Court, while acknowledging the very delicate nature of the situation (the child concerned had been placed since the age of two months in a foster family which has sheltered also the child's two brothers), considers that the proceedings for the "adoption in special cases" provided for in article 44 of law 184/1983 (Provision regarding the adoption and foster placement of children) cannot be initiated at the request of the foster family. The Court, indeed, noted that such a residual form of adoption can be activated only upon verification that no spouses are available for regular preadoptive placement. According to the Court, despite the initiation of the procedure for the declaration of adoptability and the placement – after many months – in the new foster family represent a definite trauma to the child, the rationale behind the system created by l. 184/1983 dictates that the declaration of adoptability, which may well result in the placement of the child in a family that is not the one she/he has been living with so far, cannot be disregarded. The system, of course, should be implemented with due consideration for the child's best interest. It is then up to the judge to assess whether the risks stemming from the child's transfer to the second family do not outweigh the positive effects of the new and definitive placement (Court of Cassation, civil division, Sec. I, judg. 27 September 2013, No. 22292).

The Supreme Court ruled on the case in which a mother contested the fact that her daughter had been declared to be adoptable. In the appellant's opinion, who had been considered unable to provide her daughter with essential care, the adoption of such a measure had been significantly justified by her mental disability. This would have led to a violation of both the right of the daughter to be raised by her biological mother, well recognised in international law as well, and the rights of the mother as a person with disabilities. The Supreme Court (judgment 28230/2013) states that, when the adoption of minors is concerned, the primary need of the child to live with and be raised by, as far as possible, her/his biological parents imposes particular rigor in the assessment of the state of adoptability, which may not in itself be based on the parent disability. Indeed, as provided for in the United Nations Convention on the Rights of Persons with Disabilities, the Supreme Court observes that the existence of a disability may not in itself justify the end of a parenthood relationship. This unless, despite all efforts undertaken by the State to provide appropriate supports, the existence of such disability irreversibly compromise the parents' capacity to raise and educate their children, thus resulting in a total inability to care for them. Taking into account that, when deciding the initiation of the procedure for the declaration of adoptability, the judge had showed due consideration for the above concerns, the Court of Cassation upheld the contested decision.

D. Unaccompanied Foreign Children

In 2013, the case-law on unaccompanied foreign minors – and in particular the possibility of renewing the residence permit once turned 18 years old – has consolidated. First of all, it is undisputed that l. 2 August 2011, No. 129 has reinstated the distinction between "unaccompanied" children and children under guardianship or in foster care: while for the first category the participation in a two years social and civil integration project is a condition for converting the permit of stay issued for their minor age; for the other, the conversion is always possible upon the approval of the Foreign Minors Office of the Directorate General of Immigration and Integration Policies, Ministry of Labour and Social Policies. For those who entered Italy under the regime created by l. 94/2009 – the law that had introduced the requirements of three years of presence in Italy and two years in a social and civil integration project as a condition for converting the permit of stay applicable to all minors, including those under guardianship or in foster care – administrative judges, after a few variations, agrees to exclude the retroactive effect of such provisions. The above-mentioned 2009 law, therefore, cannot be applied to those who could not materially meet the above-mentioned requirements, because older than 15 at their entry (see, for example, TAR Lazio Rome, Sec. II, judg. 4 June 2013, No. 5562; Council of State, Sec. III, judg. 17 January 2013, Nos. 269 and 270; Council of State, Sec. III, judg. 13 September 2013, No. 4545).

X. Fair Trial and Pinto Law

A. *Excessive Length of Proceedings*

Article 55 of law 7 August 2012, No. 134 has substantially innovated the procedure for the determination of damages suffered as a result of the excessive length of proceedings established by law 89/2001 (the so-called "Pinto act"). In a number of occasions in 2013, courts of first instance raised issues of constitutionality concerning these new provisions. In particular, the Court of appeal of Reggio Calabria challenged the constitutionality of article 2-bis(3) of law 89/2001 which states that "the amount of compensation, notwithstanding paragraph 1, cannot in any case exceed the amount in controversy or, if lower, that of the right established by the court". The judge, indeed, observes that in a case where the individual seeking compensation is the one who has lost the case in the main proceedings, the "amount of the right established by the court" which determines the compensation cannot but be null since the individual had lost the case. The amendments enacted, therefore, surreptitiously introduce a provision that seems contrary to the principle enshrined in article 6 ECHR and in the original rationale of the Pinto act as well, namely that both disputing parties, either the one who win and that who lose, are entitled to the right to have their case adjudicated in a reasonable length of time. In other words, while the party who lose the case could still obtain a legal finding recognising the violation of its rights, it could not obtain any compensation. This circumstance would evidently make the interest to raise the issue void and, ultimately, deny that party's right to a trial within a reasonable time. It goes without saying that the Pinto act and both the Italian and the ECtHR the case-law, rule out the possibility that the right at issue may be violated when the excessive length of the proceeding depends on the abusive behaviour or recklessness the party invoking it. The issue of constitutionality, considered not manifestly unfounded, is currently under review of the Constitutional Court (Court of Appeal, Reggio Calabria, 8 April 2013).

Cases of alleged misapplication of the Pinto act by appellate courts have been, sometimes quite systematically and extensively, dealt with by the Supreme Court in hundreds of judgments. The particular attention devoted by the Supreme Court to the issue was probably due to the fact that a number of claims tended to consider the jurisdiction of the ECtHR within the framework of EU law rather than in the context of the rules of international law of the ECHR (see, Court of Cassation, civil division, Sec. VI, judg., 4 December 2013, No. 27102).

The Supreme Court stated that only private entities (including non-governmental organisations) can take advantage of the guarantees provided by l. 89/2001 – as it is for the individual complaint procedure before the ECHR. Public bodies, and in general, any entity or branch of the public administration which, as such, holds or exercises a public power are then excluded (Court of Cassation, judgments Nos. 1007/2013, 27046/2013).

The equitable compensation cannot be determined taking into account the number of years of the proceedings prior to 1973, namely the year Italy had accessed the international procedure before the Commission-Court of Human Rights (Court of Cassation, judgment 26442/2013).

In its judgment 3740/2013, the Supreme Court (civil division) reaffirmed that in the cases of claims brought pursuant to l. 89/2001, after the entry into force of lgs.d. 104/2010 (that is on September 16th 2010), the requests for fair compensation may only be submitted if during the relevant proceedings the claimant had filed an interim drawing motion (*istanza di prelievo*). The period of time elapsed before the submission of the requested motion shall not be considered in determining the duration of the excessive length of the administrative proceedings. Before 16 September 2010, the presentation of the interim drawing motion was also required (by virtue of a law of 2008) but, from the standpoint of mainstream jurisprudence, the duration of the proceedings prior to its submission had to be taken into consideration by the judge for the determination of damages suffered as a result of the excessive length of proceedings (see, for example, Court of Cassation, civil division, Sec. VI, judg. 22 October 2013, No. 23887).

If, before the closing of the relevant proceedings, the individual concerned dies and is replaced by the heir, the latter's right to damages for the excessive length of the proceedings must be determined with due consideration to what is due to him as heir and what is due to him on a personal basis. The duration of the proceedings should therefore be broken into two. On the one hand, the successor may obtain compensation as heir if, at the moment of the death of the individual concerned, the proceedings had already exceeded the reasonable length; the amount of the compensation will then depends on the extent of that delay. On the other hand, once the successor has personally entered into the relevant proceedings, an additional compensation is due only if a further delay exceeding the average duration occurs (see, for example, Court of Cassation, civil division, Sec. VI, judg. 22 October 2013, No. 23879).

Many claims filed before the Supreme Court contested the amount of the compensation awarded. The standards of 750 euros payable for each of the first three years exceeding the reasonable length of the proceeding and 1,000 euros for each successive year, and the minimum limit of 500 euros per year of unreasonable length for administrative proceedings or when the amount in controversy is limited, are confirmed: see, for example, Court of Cassation, civil division, judgments Nos. 26192/2013; 26471/2013; 26644/2013; 26650/2013; 26844/2013; 26865/2013; 26866/2013; 26867/2013; 26896/2013; 26899/2013; 26453/2013. At any rate, when applying the standards used to determine the payable sum, the judge must always consider the specific circumstances of the case (see, for example, Court of Cassation, civil division, judgments 26196/2013; 26197/2013; 26198/2013; 26437/2013; 26898/2013). Such standards, indeed, may never be used to reduce the compensation to the extent that it become merely symbolic: Court of Cassation, civil division, Sec. VI, judg. 4 December 2013, No. 27106; see, also, Court of Cassation, civil division, Ord. 7654/2013 and judgments 27103/2013; 27104/2013.

If the claim for reparation is granted, the payment of non-pecuniary damages as a consequence for the violation of the right to a reasonably rapid trial is, save exceptional circumstances, always due. The amount of damages must be determined by the judge who has to treat them as part of the disposable income in the bankruptcy estate (Court of Cassation, civil division, judgments 26444/2013; 26997/2013; 26996/2013; 26998/2013; 26999/2013; 27087/2013; 27088/2013; 27089/2013; 27090/2013; 27091/2013; 27092/2013).

Also the determination of the costs of the proceedings to be included for the purposes of the fair compensation cannot be merely symbolic; moreover, the principle according to which in a proceeding where the State resists a claim filed by an individual each of the parties has to pay its litigation costs does not apply (see, for example, Court of Cassation, civil division, Sec. V, judg. 14 November 2013, No. 25577).

The Supreme Court also reiterates that the proceeding instituted to obtain compensation for the excessive length of a trial itself may be subject to appeal for unreasonable length (see, for example, judgments 22885/2013, 24411/2013; 24840/2013; 26071/2013; 26701/2013; 26702/2013; 26703/2013; 26704/2013; 26705/2013; 26706/2013; 26707/2013). If such proceeding also includes an appeal before the Supreme Court, its ordinary duration cannot exceed two years, including one year before the Court of Appeal (Court of Cassation, civil division, judgments 8561/2013, 26200/2013, see also Court of Cassation, civil division, Sec. VI, judg. 19 December 2013, Nos. 28499 and 28500). Moreover, what may be compensated under the Pinto act is the excessive length of the overall proceedings and not of its single phases (Court of Cassation, civil division, Sec. VI, judg. 19 December 2013, No. 28495). Furthermore, while taking into account the general criteria concerning the ordinary duration of proceedings at first instance, on appeal and before the Court of Cassation, the decision on the compensation must look at the process in its entirety (Court of Cassation, civil division, judg. 14786/2013; civil division, Sec. VI, judg. 19 December 2013, No. 28483). According to the ECtHR, the fact that under Italian law the amount of compensation is calculated only on the part of the proceedings that exceeded the average duration, and not on the entire length of the proceedings, does not exceed the acceptable margin of appreciation States enjoy when implementing its jurisprudence (Court of Cassation, civil division, judg. 28326/2013).

Compensation under the Pinto Act is not due – and this was judged to be compatible with the ECHR – if the unreasonably lengthy criminal proceedings had actually ended up in a positive way for the applicant who, because of the delay, was acquitted by prescription (see, for example, Court of Cassation, civil division, judgments 25288/2013; 27956/2013; 14777/2013); as the prejudice stemming from the excessive length of proceeding is always presumed, the applicant should not prove it (Court of Cassation, civil division, judg. 27856/2013; see also judg. 26476/2013); due to its scantiness, the damage for a proceedings which exceeded the limit of reasonable duration of a few months is, save exceptional circumstances, not payable (Court of Cassation, civil division, judg. 26181/2013: in this case, the Pinto procedure lasted five months beyond the two years standard).

The Court of Cassation, civil division, Sec. VI, judg. 19 December 2013, No. 28486 confirms that a proceedings ends once a final court decision has been adopted, which may well include the decision to definitely discontinue the proceedings, but not the simple stay of proceedings. The time-limit to file a claim under the Pinto act shall be calculated from the adoption of the final decision.

B. Incompatibility Between a Civil Servant's Functions and the Exercise of a Legal Profession

Some judgments delivered by the joint sections of the Supreme Court (Nos. 11833/2013, 27266/2013, 27267/2013, 27270/2013, 27272/2013) concerned a problem, pending also before the ECtHR, linked to the implementation of law 339/2003. This law introduces an incompatibility – to be settled over a three years period – between the status of civil servant and the exercise of a legal profession. The provision is justified – despite the general trend towards the liberalisation of professions and the principles of the EU which appear to push in the opposite direction – on account of the peculiarities of the legal profession which may lead to an inevitable conflict with the duty of loyalty imposed on civil servants under article 98 Constitution. In case the individual concerned fails to exercise the choice between the two professions, according to the current legislation, the removal from the bar is ordered by the board of the local bar association. The order may then be appealed before the Italian National Lawyers' Counsel. The applicants contested the fact that the decision on their exclusion from the bar was adopted by bodies lacking the necessary independence. The Supreme Court, firstly, rejects the arguments aimed at obtaining a suspension of the proceedings pending the decision of the ECtHR. Indeed, whatever the judgment of the Strasbourg Court may be, it could not have the effect to overturn a national decision which has become final.

As to the alleged violation of the principles of due process and the impartiality of court, the Supreme Court states that the Italian National Lawyers' Counsel presents all the characters of a judicial authorities (albeit special), with the guarantees of independence and impartiality, and operating in a proceeding in which the right of defence is fully respected.

XI. Torture, Prison Conditions, Rights of Detainees

In a number of Constitutional Court judgments, issues of constitutionality have been raised in connection to criminal laws and norms regulating the penitentiary system considered to have at least partly contributed to the dramatic situation of prison overcrowding, namely the situation in connection of which the ECtHR in the case *Torreggiani* (2013) had issued a pilot judgment condemning Italy for the systematic violation of the prohibition of degrading treatment against detainees (see, in this Part, Italy in the Case-law of the European Court of Human Rights, I, A).

In judgment 279/2013, the Constitutional Court examined the issues of unconstitutionality raised by the judges responsible for the execution of sentences of Venice and Milan both regarding article 147 of the criminal code. While this provision provides for an exhaustive lists of cases in which the judge may order the postponement of the punishment for the offender, it does not include, among the reasons justifying such postponement, the need to protect the convict from the degrading treatment connected with the situation of overcrowding of the prison in which he should serve the sentence. The referring courts, in essence, claimed that article 147 of the criminal code should be understood as closure rule allowing the postponement of a sentence at the time when the prison in which it is to be served is in a position to accommodate the convicted under conditions that do not conflict with the sense of humanity. Indeed, the assumption is that the "internal" measures that the prison administration may take to improve the management of space and to practically implement the measures ordered by the judiciary aimed at preventing detainees to be subject to degrading treatment will not be sufficient to reverse the situation stigmatised by the ECtHR in the case *Torreggiani*. It is therefore necessary to establish, through an expansive ruling modifying the content of article 147 of the criminal code, the postponement of the sentence as a measure of last resort, namely to be applied only after the prudent assessment of the judge.

The Constitutional Court, while acknowledging the structural inadequacy of the Italian prison system, declared the claim inadmissible due to the range of legislative solutions that, alongside the measure focused on article 147 of the criminal code proposed by the referring judges, may be adopted to alleviate prison overcrowding. Among others, the Court recall the possibility to broaden the use of home detention or to recur to other punitive or control measures different from those currently provided for, which are to be considered as alternative forms of enforcement of the sentence. In the Court's opinion, therefore, the referring judges claims were aimed at obtaining an expansive ruling that it could not issue. The Court, however, does not miss the chance to reiterate that the legislative inertia regarding the problem of prison overcrowding is not tolerable.

In judgment 135/2013, the Constitutional Court considered a jurisdictional dispute between two branches of the State, namely between the judges responsible for the execution of sentences (Judiciary) and the prison administration (Ministry of Justice). The dispute at the origin of the proceedings before the Constitutional Court is connected with a decision adopted by the Rome judge responsible for the execution of sentences that authorised an inmate subjected to the "41-bis" detention regime to watch two television programmes, "Rai Sport" and "Rai Storia" (a sport and history programme respectively). Without challenging the order of the judge, the Ministry of Justice, however, ordered not to execute it (the order will be performed only several months later). The case is indicative of a trend underscored also by the ECtHR in *Torreggiani*, namely the tendency of the prison administration to not implement in timely manner the decisions of the supervision judge issued in relation to objections filed by prisoners seeking order to uphold their rights, and to impose its discretionary choices over the judicial decisions. The Constitutional Court then found that the Ministry was not entitled to order the non-execution of the order issued by the supervision judge.

The possible implications of the *Torreggiani* and *Sulejmanovic* jurisprudence (see *2013 Yearbook*, p. 242; and, in this Part, Italy in the Case-law of the European Court of Human Rights, I, A) as well as of the number of concerns raised by international organisations on the conditions of Italian prisons are dealt with by the criminal division of the Court of Cassation (Sec. I, judg. 10 January 2013, No. 42894). Considering that the constitutionality of the norms governing the special detention regime for members of mafia organisations has been repeatedly confirmed by the Constitutional Court, the Court of Cassation rejects the claim of unconstitutionality and for the violation of the principle of human dignity raised by the applicant against article 41-bis, l. 354/1975 (penitentiary system).

The issue of torture was dealt by the criminal division of the Court of Cassation in the judgment concerning the appeal presented by the Public Prosecutor against the decision of the appellate court in the criminal case involving abuses inflicted on demonstrators during the G8 Summit in Genoa in 2001. Held in the Nino Bixio and Bolzaneto barracks, in that occasion protesters had been subjected to inhuman treatment and act of torture. Among other things, the Prosecutor asked the Court of Cassation to raise the issue of constitutionality of the norms of the criminal code on the statute of limitations (article 157) on account that they do not provide for the imprescriptibility of conducts corresponding to the notion of torture. The Supreme Court rejects the request noting, first of all, that the Constitutional Court could not substitute for the legislature in regulating a subject which under the Italian Constitution must be regulated by law (article 25). The issue, moreover, is irrelevant in relation to the proceedings at hand. As a matter of fact, any reform providing for the imprescriptibility of conducts corresponding to the notion of torture could only operate prospectively and would thus not be applicable to the current proceedings (Court of Cassation, criminal division, Sec. V, judg. 8 May 2013, No. 37088).

Again in 2013, a certain number of cases concerning the so called "ergastolo ostativo" ("obstructive" life sentence) were discussed. This is a situation whereby detainees, convicted for some serious crimes, mostly linked to the mafia, including those sentenced to life imprisonment, are not allowed to any benefit (work outside the prison, temporary licences, probation and other alternative measures), unless they cooperate with the judiciary (article 4 bis, l. 354/1975; see *2013 Yearbook*, p. 348). With judgment 40044/2013, the criminal division of the Court of Cassation rejects the claim of unconstitutionality of the relevant norm. The Court, in particular, observing that the contested legislation provide the condemned the choice to cooperate or not, excludes that it can constitute a treatment contrary to human dignity or to the rehabilitative function assigned to the criminal sanction.

XII. Criminal Matters

A. Piracy and Extraterritorial Jurisdiction

The Supreme Court has upheld a decision issued on appeal against a decision of the Juvenile Court which sentenced a number of Somali citizens, underage at the time of the relevant fact, to eight years in prison for crimes such as piracy and attempted kidnapping committed while attacking an Italian ship in the Gulf of Aden in 2011. Pirates had almost managed to take possession of the merchant ship named "Montecristo", when they were caught by British and United States military ships participating, together with the Italian navy, to the NATO operation "Ocean Shield". The latter, led and organised under the aegis of the United Nations, replaced the previous operation "Atalanta" managed by the EU. The issues raised before the Court of Cassation concerned both the jurisdiction of the Italian court to decide the case (it was argued that, considering that some of the pirates have never climbed on board of the Italian navy, the transfer to the Italian authorities of one of the pirates by the commander of the British military unit that had captured him on board of the "pirates' ship", was illegitimate), and the amendment of charges. While, initially, the indictees were charged with the crime of piracy with the purpose of international terrorism, the conviction referred, among other things, to the crime of kidnapping, without mentioning to international terrorism purpose. According to the appellants, moreover, lacking any request to initiate a proceedings from the Italian Ministry of Justice, the qualification of the facts as ordinary crimes should have had as consequence the lack of jurisdiction of the Italian courts over the case of the young pirate who did not leave the "pirates' ship". The Supreme Court observed that, under international law as well as under the Italian naval code, the jurisdiction over acts of piracy could be exercised over facts constituting such an offence committed on the high seas on board of Italian ships. The individuals who somehow contribute to the offence committed on board of an Italian ship are nonetheless subject to the Italian jurisdiction even if they did not physically boarded the ship flying the Italy's flag. Moreover, the possibility for the naval units belonging to others State participating to operations "Atalanta" and "Ocean Shield" to transfer those caught at high seas (or at the Somali territorial sea) to the State exercising jurisdiction is provided for in the agreements made to regulate these operations as well as in the Italian laws implementing such agreements. The latters, among other things, exclude that a request from the Ministry of Justice is a necessary condition in order to investigate or prosecute crimes committed against Italian citizens or goods in the area of said operations. About the discrepancy between the indictment issued against the defendants (which included the purpose of international terrorism) and the conviction, the Supreme Court excludes a limitation of the right of defence. In particular, as the issue had been extensively dealt with during the proceedings of first instance and on appeal, the Court concludes that the standards of fair trial enshrined in articles 6 ECHR and 111 of the Italian Constitution have been fully respected (Court of Cassation, criminal division, Sec. II, judg. 4 February 2013, No. 26825).

B. Extradition and the Risk of Ill-treatment

The Supreme Court, in relation to an extradition request made by the Brazilian Government for a Dutch national who had to serve 17 years as remaining prison term for the crime of drug trafficking, rejected the request and asked for a re-assessment of the case. In the Court's opinion, taking into account the situation of Brazilian prisons, it was not possible to exclude that the potential extradite would there be subject to inhuman treatment. In particular, the Court observed that "numerous non-governmental sources, such as [...] Amnesty International and Human Rights Watch, report that the situation of Brazilian prisons has long since been endemically characterised, especially in some districts – including that of Espirito Santo which is specifically relevant in this process – from patterns of violence and abuse against detainees perpetrated, on the one hand, by criminal bands which are well-known and tolerated by prison authorities, on the other, by prison guards. Moreover, the situation is worsened by the structural decay and inadequacy of prison buildings that is the cause of prison overcrowding and deficiencies in health and sanitation conditions, both of which have led to the spread of serious infectious diseases" (Court of Cassation, criminal division, Sec. VI, judg. 15 October 2013, No. 46212).

According to the Supreme Court, the extradition request for a Turkish citizen who, in his Country, has been accused of fraud and other related offences, is a member of an opposition party and is the recipient of a form of subsidiary protection in Italy, cannot be granted. In the Court of Cassation's opinion, the assessment of the judge of first instance, which detects a risk of inhuman treatment under the prison and criminal system of Turkey, is consistent with the assessment made the Territorial Commission for the recognition of international protection. For this reasons, the Court decides not to quash it (Court of Cassation, criminal division, Sec. VI, judg., 18 December 2013, No. 3746).

The extradition to Egypt should be rejected also if the individual concerned has to serve there a sentence of three years' imprisonment for the crimes of money laundering and fraud. This, primarily, on account of the current instability of the African Country, and in light of the fact that the potential extradite belongs to the Coptic minority, namely a religious group against which it is most likely that persecution may take place (Court of Cassation, criminal division, Sec. VI, judg. 6 March 2013, No. 10905).

In some of its judgments, the Court of Cassation excludes that Ukraine may be considered a Country where there is a risk of inhuman treatment for those who have been extradited there to serve a term of imprisonment (see, among others, Court of Cassation, criminal division, Sec. VI, judg. 21 October 2013, No. 47561; criminal division, Sec. VI, judg. 5 April 2013, No. 17605).

Similarly, the Court of Cassation considers that the extradition to Spain of individuals therein convicted or on trial for acts of terrorism (in the case at hand it was an alleged aider and abettor of groups of Basque terrorism) does not create a risk of inhuman treatment such as to prevent the execution of extradition.

On an extradition request to the United States, the Court of Cassation (criminal division, Sec. VI, judg. 27 February 2013, Nos. 15017 and 15018) specifies, among other things, that extradition is legitimate even if, under the law of California, the offence of which the person to be extradited was accused is punished with imprisonment with hard labor, and notwithstanding the fact that the prohibition of forced labor is enshrined in article 4 ECHR. According to the Court of Cassation, it is the Ministry of Justice's task to obtain assurances from the United States about the non-application of such treatment to the person concerned. Similarly, the fact that in the American criminal system the determination of the sentence is calculated differently from the Italian one, and that in such a system the maximum prison sentence is relatively indeterminate, does not per se justify the dismissal of an extradition request on account that it violates article 25 of the Italian Constitution and article 7 ECHR. Again, an extradition request cannot be dismissed simply because under the American legislation the crime of bank fraud is punished much harsher than under Italian law (Court of Cassation, criminal division, Sec. VI, judg. 28 March 2013, No. 15927).

The extradition to Spain of a person suspected of having taken part in some events promoted by organisations acting for the independence of the Basque Country and charged with crimes of terrorism can be granted. The Court of Cassation (criminal division, judg. 18241/2013) excludes that the Spanish criminal legislation on terrorism can be described as "vague" and rejects the argument according to which individuals entering the Spanish penal system may be at risk of inhuman treatment or torture.

C. Life Sentence and the Scoppola Case-law: Duty to Comply with the Judgments of the ECtHR

In 2013, the Constitutional Court ruled on the implications of the 2009 *Scoppola (2)* case-law of the ECtHR (see *2013 Yearbook*, pp. 347–349). The joint sections of the Court of Cassation raised the issue of constitutionality of article 7(1) of the l.d. 24 November 2000, No. 341 (Urgent provisions for the effectiveness and efficiency of the administration of justice), converted, with amendments, into l. 19 January 2001, No. 4. With retroactive effect, such provision provided that, if the accused had chosen to undergo the summary procedure, the sentence of life imprisonment with daytime isolation could be commuted to ordinary life imprisonment, while that of ordinary life imprisonment could be substituted with thirty years imprisonment. The previous law (l. 479/1999), on the contrary, without making any distinction between the two types of life imprisonment sentences, provided that life imprisonment ought to be substituted by a thirty years prison term. In the judgment in the case *Scoppola (2)*, the ECtHR found that the 2000 reform could not be considered an act of authentic interpretation. Rather, recognising its innovative character, the newly introduced norm adversely affected the situation of those who had requested to be tried under summary procedure while the 1999 law was in force trusting to avoid any form of life imprisonment (and not simply a life sentence with daytime isolation). For these reasons, Italy was condemned for the violation of article 7 ECHR.

In relation to similar cases that are analogous to *Scoppola (2)*, other individuals sentenced to life imprisonment requested the retroactive application of the rule more favourable to them. Their requests, however, were invariably dismissed for the prevalence of the principle of finality of criminal judgment. The Supreme Court asks the Constitutional Court to extend, in general terms, the conclusions reached by the ECtHR in the case *Scoppola (2)*. The Constitutional Court, more specifically, is called to declare the unconstitutionality of the provisions of article 7(1) of the 2000 decree-law mentioned above having an unduly and adversely retroactive effect.

The issue is dealt with by the Constitutional Court in judgment 210/2013 (subsequently confirmed by judgment 235/2013).

During the proceedings, the State Attorney has contested the admissibility of the issue of constitutionality arguing that, with the entry into force of the Lisbon Treaty, the Italian norms found to be in conflict with ECHR provisions enjoying an equivalent protection in the CFREU (in this case, article 7 ECHR and article 49(1) CFREU) must be set aside directly by national courts on the ground that they are contrary to EU law, without the need to wait for a decision of the Constitutional Court. The Constitutional Court, recalling its settled case-law on the issue (in particular, judgments Nos. 80/2011 and 303/2011, see *2012 Yearbook*, pp. 300–303) dismisses the argument and confirms its competence to decide on the matter. On the one hand, the Court noted, the European Union has not become part to the ECHR yet; on the other, article 6(2) TEU, envisaging such accession, does not in any way interfere on the relationship between the national and ECHR legal orders.

On the merits, the Court extensively elaborates on the legal effects of ECtHR judgments which, especially when qualified as pilot sentences, cannot be confined to the individual case. Despite the judgment in the case *Scoppola (2)* is not a pilot sentence (the judgment itself excludes it), it implicitly encourages the State to adopt general measures aimed at extending to all individuals facing the same situation as Scoppola the more favourable treatment imposed by the Strasbourg Court's ruling, namely the substitution of the sentence of life imprisonment with the lighter sentence of thirty years prison term. In conclusion, the Constitutional Court finds that article 7(1) of the above mentioned 2000 decree-law has to be declared unconstitutional every time it produces a situation which is identical to the one found to be in violation of the principle enshrined in article 7 ECHR (and in the Italian as well), according to which the criminal law that is more favourable to the offender must entail retroactive effect. Indeed, in such circumstances, even the principle of legal certainty, which is at the basis of the principle of finality of judgments, should not prevail. It will be therefore up to the judge responsible for the execution of sentences, whenever it detects a situation which is equivalent to the case *Scoppola (2)* decided by the ECtHR, not to apply the part of article 7(1) recognised unconstitutional. In such circumstances, the judge will have to apply the more favourable legislation in force before the 2000 reform. On the contrary, the ordinary judge could not disregard a final judgment if the criminal proceedings which resulted in a final sentence is, according to a Strasbourg Court's ruling, tainted by a violation of the principle of fair trial (article 6 ECHR), namely procedural rules that can be remedied by the reopening of the proceedings. In these particular cases, indeed, only a judgment of the European Court of Human Rights permit, on a case-by-case basis, to challenge a final judgment.

D. *Preventive Custody and Mafia-related Crimes*

With judgment 57/2013, the Constitutional Court dealt with another aspect of article 273(3) of the criminal procedure code. The relevant provision, by virtue of an amendment introduced in 2009, provided that, when the evidence of guilt for a number of particularly serious offences is remarkably strong, the imposition of the remand in custody is mandatory. In such cases, indeed, both the dangerousness of the offender and the need to cope with it with the imposition of measures affecting the personal freedom are taken for granted. The absolute nature of such presumption of dangerousness, and the related automatic imposition of remand in custody, had already been found to be in breach of constitutional principles in a number of previous decisions of the Constitutional Court (in particular, judgments 265/2010 and 164/2011), although with reference to another illegal conducts. Judgment 57/2013 then extends the finding of unconstitutionality also to article 273(3) of the criminal procedure code which refers to crimes committed through the modalities proscribed by article 416-bis of the criminal code (that is through "mafia methods") or crimes aiming at facilitating mafia-like organisations such as those indicated in article 416-bis (these offences are referred to by the reference to article 51-bis of the code of criminal procedure). The Court considers that the commission of these offences does not necessarily imply that their author is a member of a mafia-like organisation, circumstance which would conversely justify the mandatory application of the remand in custody. Therefore, the Constitutional Court observes, the judge must be granted the possibility to rebut the absolute presumption of dangerousness provided by the contested provision. While, according to the latter, the dangerousness of the accused can be preempted only by the remand in custody, it should be recognised that, in the light of the specific circumstances of the case, different precautionary measures other than the preventive custody in prison may be imposed.

E. Crime of Racist Propaganda, Negationism

According to the Tribunal of Rome (Sec. VI, judg. 12 November 2013, No. 18931), the offence punishable by law 13 October 1975, No. 64 (as amended by law 24 February 2006, No. 85), consisting of making propaganda of ideas based on racial superiority (a norm introduced to implement of the 1965 United Nations Convention against Racial Discrimination), is not committed if statements denying the existence of the Holocaust are made at school during conversations with individual students or colleagues. The case referred to some phrases aimed at minimizing the Shoah pronounced (in 2008) by a high school professor in Rome. The first one during a conversation with a student (of Jewish origin), outside of class, which have also been heard from another student; the second one, during a class council in which the experience of a study trip to Auschwitz was commented: the teacher in question complained that similar trips were not arranged to visit "sinkholes" (foibe). Considering the limited audience and the fact that the views expressed were not even aimed at conveying the idea of racial superiority, the court concludes that in both episodes the opinions expressed did not constitute forms of "propaganda". Moreover, the court also adds that the holocaust denial theories were expressed through a completely impersonal language so that, it seems to understand, they could not express or spread racial hatred. The teacher (who, by a disciplinary measure, had been suspended from teaching for a few months) is therefore acquitted of all charges.

The offence of racist propaganda was also dealt with by the Supreme Court. The Court of Cassation, in particular, stated that the crime of criminal conspiracy aimed at the propaganda of ideas based on racial or ethnic superiority may be committed also by creating and maintaining a blog on the Internet, through which not only texts and materials were shared, but rallies and fundraising activities were organised; contacts among members maintained; and anti-racist activists reported (Court of Cassation, criminal division, sec. III, judg. 24 April 2013, No. 33179). The Court of Cassation, therefore, confirmed the remand in custody issued against those suspected of the crime under art. 3(3) of l. 654/1975, which prohibits the participation, promotion and management of organisations aiming at incitement to discrimination and racial violence. The virtual community of the blog is therefore treated as a "real" association. The fact that the blog in question was the Italian version of a blog operating also in other Countries and hosted by an overseas server is irrelevant.

On the use of the aggravating circumstance of racial discrimination motive provided by l. 122/1993 in order to impose the precautionary measure of house arrest on two individuals accused of personal injury against two immigrants from the Maghreb, the Supreme Court clarified that such aggravating circumstance is applicable whenever, regardless of the motive of the crime itself, the use of a crime for racial hatred ends is evident. The fact of having associated the assault with phrases such as "nigger" is sufficient to characterise as discriminatory – and therefore deserving an aggravated punishment – the illegal conduct (Court of Cassation, criminal division, Sec. V, judg. 4 February 2013, No. 30525). The aggravating circumstance can be applied even if the racist expressions are not perceived by third parties (Court of Cassation, criminal division, Sec. V, judg. 15 May 15 2013, No. 25870).

F. Racist Expressions and Sport Events

The Court of Cassation (criminal division, Sec. III, judg. 2 October 2013, No. 12351) upheld the ban from sporting events imposed on some fans of the Pro Patria from Busto Arsizio that, during a friendly football match with the team of AC Milan, had staged noisy demonstrations of hostility towards blacks opponents players. The prohibitive measures had been taken by the head of local police (Questore) and validated by a court pursuant to law 401/1989, which provides for the right of the law enforcement authorities to limit the access to locations hosting sport events to, among others, persons accused of having violated l. 205/1993 (known as the "Mancino law"). The latter punishes, in particular, anyone who in public meetings manifest or flaunt emblems or symbols of organisations, associations, movements or groups whose purpose is incitement to hatred or racial discrimination. In the notion of "manifestation" may also fall the chorus used in Busto Arsizio systematically addressing with "buuh" black players. Given the context, the Supreme Court agrees with the court of first instance in considering that such chorus could not but be perceived on the outside as expressions of hate and discrimination based on race.

The Supreme Court confirmed the sentence pronounced against a person who went to an hockey match in South Tyrol exhibiting a T-shirt with the image of Benito Mussolini and some Fascist phrases. Indeed, the offence under article 2(2) of the Mancino Law (l. 205/1993) requires no more than accessing location hosting sport events with emblems or symbols of racist groups or associations. Neither the actual membership in such organisation or groups nor the specific intent of making propaganda of the ideology to which symbols refer to are relevant (Court of Cassation, criminal division, sec. III, judg. 4 June 2013, No. 39860).

G. *Parliamentary Immunity and Defamatory Opinions*

The issue of the conflict between the right to expression and the protection of the reputation of the person subject to public statements was dealt by Italian courts within a number of cases involving personalities from the political arena. The Constitutional Court, in particular, on two occasions had to pronounce itself on claims raised by some judges for jurisdictional conflict between branches of State. The issues related to some decisions adopted by the Senate and the Chamber of Deputies qualifying as falling within the bounds of the political function of members of Parliament, and therefore no subject to civil or criminal jurisdiction, some statements on which the referring courts were proceeding for the offence of affront on the honour and prestige of the President of the Republic and for tort damages. In articles printed or posted on the Internet, two senators had publicly, and in any case outside the Parliament, expressed defamatory opinions on the President of the Republic and the founder of the NGO Emergency, Gino Strada. The Senate and the Chamber of Deputies had decided (respectively in 2009 and 2010) that the statements considered offensive were linked to the parliamentary activities of two senators, and were thus covered by immunity under article 68 of the Constitution. The Constitutional Court, in judgments 305/2013 and 313/2013 stated that, according to his own settled case-law, for the purposes of parliamentary immunity there should be a specific functional link between the statements publicly expressed outside the Parliament and the parliamentary activity of the author. According to the Court, such a link may be determined by a temporal contiguity, for which the statement may be simply regarded as a way to disseminate what had been said in Parliament shortly before, and a thematic correspondence between what is publicly expressed and what is the subject of the parliamentary activity. In both cases, the statements challenged in court had only tenuous links with bills, parliamentary questions and similar documents produced by the two politicians concerned. Therefore, the statement of absolute immunity issued by the Senate and the Chamber of Deputies should be considered an undue interference in the action of the judiciary. On the statements against the President of the Republic, the Constitutional Court is even doubtful about whether to consider them "opinions" on account of the fact that they seem unsupported by any consistent argument. The Constitutional Court therefore annulled the decisions adopted by the Senate and the Chamber of Deputies.

H. *Criminal Procedure Issues: Rights of Defence and Art. 41- bis of the Prison Regulations, Publicity of Hearings*

The Constitutional Court has been seized of the question of legality of a rule introduced by the so-called 2009 "security package" in order to strengthen one aspect of the system of maximum security imposed on those convicted of mafia-related crimes (article 41-bis (4-quater), letter b) of l. 26 July 1975, No. 354). The new provision introduces a "quantitative" limitation on the talks between prisoners and their lawyer: no more than three one hour visits and three phone calls of ten minutes each per week. The Court, referring to the case-law of the ECtHR, balances the undoubted restriction on the right of defence (article 24 of the Constitution) with the interest of preventing detainees from transmitting information to the criminal organisation they belong through contacts with their lawyers. The measure restricting communications introduced in 2009 equates the length of weekly talks between prisoners and lawyers with those organised between prisoners and family members. Only the latter are, however, heard and videotaped. The Constitutional Court (judgment 143/2013), however, did not find that, against the indisputable and relevant compression of the right to defence of the prisoner, the newly introduced measure have a decisive ability to neutralise any passage of information to the outside. The Court then declared it unconstitutional.

The Constitutional Court (judgment 214/2013) ruled on the claim of unconstitutionality raised by the joint criminal sections of the Court of Cassation regarding the follow-up of the ECtHR case-law in *Lorenzetti* (see *2013 Yearbook*, pp. 354 and 377). In that case, the ECtHR had found that article 315(3) of the Italian criminal procedure code violated article 6 ECHR (fair trial) on account of the fact that, in a case of reparation for wrongful imprisonment occurring at Court of Appeal, it did not envisage the possibility to hold, where requested by the individual concerned, public hearings. Although, in its claim, the Court of Cassation had required the intervention of the Constitutional Court on the issue essentially driven by the need to prevent the possible recurrence of *Lorenzetti*-like cases before the ECtHR, the Constitutional Court declared the claim inadmissible as during the relevant proceedings none of the parties involved had asked for the publicity of hearings. In the absence of any practical relevance of the issue in the pending proceeding, the Constitutional Court considers the request of the joint divisions as an attempt to obtain from the Constitutional Court an "additive" sentence manipulating an existing legal provision. The claim is therefore inadmissible.

Italy in the Case-law of the European Court of Human Rights

I. Pilot Judgments and Related Cases

In 2013 the European Court of Human Rights (ECtHR) delivered two pilot judgments concerning Italy. While the first, issued in the case *Torreggiani and others*, concerned the overcrowding of detention facilities, with the second, the ECtHR condemned Italy's failure to pay the supplementary part of a compensation allowance due to persons accidentally contaminated as a result of blood transfusions or the administration of blood derivatives (case *M.C. and others*).

A pilot judgment procedure is adopted when the ECtHR receives several applications which derive from a common dysfunction at the national level. The Court then can select one or more applications for priority treatment and extend its conclusions to all similar cases. In a pilot judgment procedure, the Court can indicate the type of remedial measures which the Contracting Party concerned is required to take at the domestic level as well as a specific timeframe to be followed. Pending the adoption of the remedial measures required, the examination of all similar applications may be adjourned.

A. *Prison Conditions, Torture, Expulsion*

In its judgment in the case *Torreggiani and others v. Italy* (Nos. 4357/09, 46882/09, 55400/09, 57875/09, 61535/09, 35315/10, 37818/10), the II Section of the ECtHR unanimously condemned Italy for the violation of article 3 ECHR (prohibition of torture and inhuman or degrading treatment) in connection with the situation of prison overcrowding. Having identified the latter as a structural problem at the origin of hundreds of cases pending before the Strasbourg Court, the judges decided to apply the pilot judgment procedure.

In the present case, the applicants, seven inmates serving sentences in Busto Arsizio and Piacenza prisons, complained that they had been subjected to treatments contrary to article 3 ECHR as they had to share for periods of two or three years, or even longer, a cell of nine square meters with two other prisoners. According to the applicants, moreover, the severe shortage of space had been exacerbated by the lack of hot water and, in some cases, of inadequate lighting in the cells. Before entering the merits of the complaint, the ECtHR rejected a number of preliminary issues raised by the Italian Government contesting the admissibility of the case. First of all, contrary to what Italy claimed, the Court observed that the fact that all the applicants but one were now free could not constitute a valid reason to deprive them of the quality of victim of an alleged breach of article 3 ECHR. With regard to the exception based on the non-exhaustion of domestic remedies, the ECtHR, while recognising that the Italian legislation provides prisoners with remedies through which contest the deficiencies in treatment, denied that such remedies were effective in practice. Indeed, the Court stressed that the enforcement of decisions of the judge responsible for the execution of sentences is left to the discretion of the prison authorities and, ultimately, depends on the availability of free cells. On the other hand, the Court noted, it is the very nature of the situation of Italian prison overcrowding which renders impossible to make a concrete improvement of prison conditions as well as to deprive any decision adopted in favour of detainees of its effectiveness.

With regard to the merits of the case, the ECtHR, applying its settled case-law on inhuman or degrading treatment against detainees and assisted by the standards of the Council of Europe Committee for the Prevention of Torture (CPT) on the issue, concluded that the applicants had been subjected to treatment in breach of article 3 ECHR. First of all, the Court found that the applicants' living space had not conformed to the standards deemed to be acceptable in terms of living space in cells (4 square meters per person). Moreover, the shortage of space to which the applicants had been subjected, a situation almost unavoidable due to the overcrowding in Italian prisons, had been exacerbated by other conditions such as the lack of hot water over long periods, and inadequate lighting and ventilation. In conclusion, while there was no indication of any intention to humiliate or debase the applicants, the Court considered that their conditions of detention had subjected them to hardship of an intensity exceeding the unavoidable level of suffering inherent in detention. There had therefore been a violation of article 3 of the Convention. The Court then held that Italy was to pay the applicants a total of nearly 100,000 euros in respect of non-pecuniary damage.

In accordance with the pilot judgments procedure, the Court, together with the finding of a violation in the specific case, indicated the general measures to be taken by the Italian Government to remedy the problem of overcrowding in prisons. Firstly, the ECtHR called on Italy to take action to reduce the number of inmates by using, among other things, alternative measures to detention wherever possible and minimizing the use of remand in custody. Secondly, the judges of the Court urged Italy to put in place an accessible and effective domestic remedy capable of bringing about a rapid end to the violation of the right not to be subjected to inhuman and degrading treatment, and affording adequate and sufficient redress for the violation suffered. Italy is now called to adopt the measures recommended by the ECtHR within one year from the date on which the present judgment became final, that is May 27, 2013 (the day the panel of five judges of the Grand Chamber rejected the request for referral submitted by Italy) (see also Part III, Council of Europe, II). Pending the adoption by domestic authorities of recommended measures, the examination of applications dealing solely with overcrowding in Italian prisons has been adjourned.

In 2013, the ECtHR examined a complaint dealing with the lack of adequate medical treatment afforded to a detainee affected by an acute disease. In the case *Cirillo* (No. 36276/10) the Court concluded that the failure of the Italian authorities to provide the applicant with a treatment appropriate to his health conditions constituted a violation of article 3 ECHR (see *2013 Yearbook*, p. 375).

Again in relation to the adequacy of medical treatment provided in detention, the Court declared inadmissible as manifestly ill-founded the cases *Prestieri v. Italy* (No. 66640/10) and *Tellissi v. Italy* (No. 15434/11). In both cases, the Court held that the Italian authorities had complied with the obligation to protect the physical integrity of detainees, thereby ensuring appropriate medical treatments according to their state of health. Not having significantly exceeded the unavoidable level of suffering inherent in detention, the treatments to which the applicants were subjected did not amount to a violation of article 3 ECHR. The Court had also rejected the second ground of incompatibility under article 3 ECHR raised in the *Tellissi* case on account of the shortage of personal space in the cell and the lack of services such as hot water, heating, lighting and hygiene equipment. Indeed, according to the Court, although for two periods of about one year the applicant had a personal space of just 3.6 square meters in a cell group (compared to 4 sq. m recommended by the CPT), the lack of space alone, not being less than 3 sq. m, did not in itself constitute a violation of article 3 ECHR. As for the additional shortcomings (hot water, electricity, hygiene materials), the Court did not consider them exceeding the threshold of severity required by article 3 ECHR.

The cases *Mohammed Hussein and others* (No. 27725/10), *Miruts Hagos* (No. 9053/10), *Mohammed Hassan and others* (Nos. 40524/10, 11746/13, 18764/11, 20355/12, 23696/12, 41993/10, 57531/10, 62865/12, 7903/13, 81839/12) and *Diirshi Hussein and others* (Nos. 2314 /10, 18324/10, 47851/10, 51377/10) all concerned the alleged incompatibility with article 3 ECHR of asylum seekers transfers from the Netherlands to Italy pursuant to the "Dublin Regulation." The applicants of the mentioned cases all came from the Horn of Africa. After having arrived in Italy and having there requested, and in some cases obtained, different forms of international protection, they moved to the Netherlands where they had lodged new asylum requests. In application of the Dublin Regulation (which, among other things, states that the State responsible for examining an application for asylum submitted by a national of a third Country is the State of first entry), however, the Dutch authorities, having identified Italy as the State responsible to deal with the applicants' asylum claims, rejected the applicants requests. The applicants then applied to the Strasbourg Court complaining that they had been subjected to degrading treatment during their stay in Italian reception centres, claiming also that their transfer to Italy would expose them to the risk of being subjected to treatment contrary to article 3 ECHR as well as to the risk of being expelled to their Countries of origin. The ECtHR rejected all allegations as manifestly ill-founded. First, the Court held that the applicants had not been subjected to any treatment contrary to article 3 ECHR while in Italy, a Country where, all in all, some of the applicants had obtained a residence permit and benefited from free health and social services. In addition, although characterised by some shortcomings, the Court excluded that the general situation of asylum seekers in Italy showed any systemic failings reaching the threshold of severity required by article 3 ECHR.

The same conclusion was reached by the Court in the cases *Halimi* and *Abubeker*, identical to the others but for the fact that the Country where the applicants had moved after arriving in Italy was Austria. The ECtHR relinquished its jurisdiction to the Grand Chamber in the case *Tarakhel and others v. Switzerland* (No. 29217/12). Relying, among others, on article 3 ECHR, the applicants (an Afghan couple and their five children) complained that, considering their particular family situation, their return in Italy would expose them to the risk of being subjected to inhuman treatment because of inadequate reception conditions for asylum seekers.

In 2013, the case *Riina v. Italy* (No. 43575/09) was communicated to the Italian Government. While the Court held inadmissible as manifestly ill-founded the general allegations concerning the incompatibility of the 41-bis detention regime with articles 3 ECHR (prohibition on inhuman and degrading treatment) and 8 ECHR (right to respect for private and family life), it considered appropriate to examine, under the same provisions, the compatibility with the ECHR of the constant surveillance of the applicant cell, including the toilets.

B. Fair Trial, Excessive Length of Proceedings

In the case *M. C. and others v. Italy* (No. 5376/11) the ECtHR condemned Italy for the violation of articles 6 ECHR (fair trial), 1 Protocol I ECHR (right to peaceful enjoyment of property) and 14 ECHR (prohibition of discrimination) for not having corresponded the annual reassessment of the supplementary allowance granted under law 201/1992 to individuals infected following blood transfusions.

In the present case, the ECtHR held that the Italian Government, through the adoption of a legislative measure of authentic interpretation (l.d. 78/2010) aiming at clarifying retroactively the scope of the law 201/1992, had infringed the principle of the rule of law and the right to a fair trial (article 6 ECHR) of the applicants, 162 Italian citizens infected by different virus following blood transfusions. As a matter of fact, the contested decree-law, specifying that the supplementary allowance (IIS) due to individuals infected following blood transfusions could not be re-assessed, had definitively set the terms of a debate that was still *sub iudice* in a way that was favourable to the State. Indeed, the new criteria established by l.d. 78/2010 not only determined the outcome of pending proceedings but also rendered ineffective the favourable decisions obtained by some of the applicants. Moreover, the Court noted, the applicants had been unable to obtain re-assessment of the IIS even after the Constitutional Court's judgment (293/2011) that had declared the unconstitutionality of the impugned l.d. 78/2010 to the extent that it introduced an unjustified difference between categories of citizens suffering from different diseases.

As for the violation of article 1 Protocol I ECHR (right to property), considering the above and the fact that the IIS represented more than 90% of the total amount of the allowance paid to the applicants, the Court found that the adoption of the d.l. 78/2010 had placed an excessive burden on the applicants so to render the interference with their right to the peaceful enjoyment of their possessions disproportionate. The Court concluded, unanimously, that there had also been a violation of article 14 ECHR (non-discrimination) in conjunction with article 1 Protocol I in the light of the fact that, despite the ruling of the Constitutional Court, the applicants were still victims of a discriminatory treatment.

Having determined that the violations of the Convention rights in the present case stemmed from the same underlying problem, that is the non-recognition by the competent authorities of the revaluation of the IIS even after the judgment of the Constitutional Court's judgment 293/2011, the ECtHR opted for the pilot judgment procedure. Within a period of six months from the date on which the Strasbourg Court's judgment became final, Italy was required to set a time-limit in which it undertook to guarantee the fulfilment of the entitlements in question to any person entitled to the compensation, irrespectively of whether or not the individual had brought proceedings to obtain it. Examination of non-communicated applications having the same subject-matter as the present case was adjourned for one year.

The incompatibility with the principle of due process of legislative initiatives that, despite being presented as "interpretative laws" of existing provisions, as a matter of fact interfered retroactively with matters that were still *sub iudice* was at issue in two other decisions adopted by the Court in 2013: *Casacchia and others, Natale and others* (both of 15 October). Both cases related to the dispute involving former employees of the Banco di Napoli which had already been dealt by the ECtHR in the case *Arras and other v. Italy* of 14 February 2012 (see *2013 Yearbook*, p. 369; see also, in this Part, Human Rights in Italian Case-law, I, F).

In the case *Anghel v. Italy* (No. 5968/09) the applicant complained that his right to appeal against the decision of the Bologna Youth Court which had refused to order the return of his son in Romania had been impaired by the delays attributable to the Italian authorities in granting him legal aid. The circumstances of the case can be summarised as follow. According to the applicant, a Romanian national, his former partner has wrongfully removed their son to Italy. In order to obtain the return of his son to his Country of origin, the applicant, in accordance with the Hague Convention on the Civil Aspects of International Child Abduction, lodged a petition before the competent authorities of Romania. The Bologna Youth Court, the Italian judicial authority assigned the case, rejected the applicant's request. Having then decided to contest this decision, due to a series of delays and faults in the Italian legal aid system the applicant had not been able to appeal. The ECtHR, first of all, observed that since a degree of appeal is provided for by the domestic law of a Contracting State, it is for the latter to guarantee litigants an effective right of access to court. In the present case, the Court stressed the delays on the part of the Italian authorities in providing the applicant information concerning the outcome of the proceedings, the available avenue for appeal and the list of lawyers available for legal aid. In addition, the Court noted, some information were found to be unclear, incomplete and sometimes even erroneous. In conclusion, the Court considered that the delays attributable to the Italian authorities in providing relevant and correct guidance, coupled with the lack of practical and effective representation, impaired the very essence of the applicant's right of access to court, thus resulting in a breach of article 6 ECHR.

In the case *Plesic v. Italy*, declared inadmissible as manifestly ill-founded, the applicant complained under article 6 ECHR for having both the Court of Appeal and the Court of Cassation held a hearing in the absence of the lawyer of her choice. The applicant, who was found guilty by the Court of first instance for circumvention of a person of unsound mind, had already obtained a postponement of the appeal for having fired, on the eve of the first hearing, her two defence lawyers. The appeal, already postponed twice (the first time for the renunciation of the mandate from the applicant's new legal counsel, and the second to allow the court-appointed lawyer to study the case), was then held in the presence of the sole court-appointed lawyer, even though the day before the applicant had announced her intention to revoke the mandate of the latter in favour of a new defence lawyer. Having the judgment of first instance been upheld on appeal, the applicant filed an appeal before the Court of Cassation. The hearing, which had dismissed the applicant's case, was held without the lawyer of the applicant who was absent because of a strike. Given the particular circumstances of the case, the ECtHR found that the decision of the Court of appeal to held the hearing even in the absence of the applicant legal counsel was justified by the need to ensure a speedy trial as well as a speedy processing of cases. Moreover, the presence of the court-appointed lawyer had in any case guaranteed the applicant an adequate defence. On the proceedings before the Court of Cassation, finally, the ECtHR noted that under Italian law the presence of the applicant's lawyer is not strictly necessary.

As in previous years, in 2013 the judgments of the European Court of Human Rights condemning Italy for the excessive length of domestic proceedings, including the unreasonable length of the "Pinto" procedures, are numerous. In a number of these rulings, the ECtHR also found a violation of articles 6 ECHR (execution of judgments) and 1 Protocol I ECHR (right to property) on account of the delay in paying the compensation awarded under the "Pinto" procedure. See, for example, judgments *Iannelli* (12 February), *Caruso* (April 2), *Galasso and others*, *Corrado and others*, *Gagliardi and others*, *Fiocca* (all of 16 July), *Limata and others* (10 December), *Mercuri* (October 22), *Ascierto Buffolino*, *Bencivenga and others* (both on 5 November), *Quattrone* (November 26, in this case, the ECtHR also found a violation of the principle of fair trial (article 6 ECHR) due to the lack of motivation in respect of the Court of Cassation order on the applicant to pay the costs related to the proceedings), *Maffei and De Nigris* (26 November).

II. Other Cases Decided by the Chambers and Committees of the Court

A. *Nulla Poena Sine Lege, Right to Liberty*

In *Varvara v. Italy* (No. 17475/09) the Strasbourg Court held that the imposition, despite the termination of criminal proceedings, of a penalty in the form of a confiscation order was contrary to article 7 ECHR (*nulla poena sine lege*). In the present case, the criminal proceeding against the applicant for unlawful land development was discontinued on the grounds that the prosecution of the offence had become time-barred. Despite this, however, pursuant to article 44 of the Building code, the national court of appeal ordered the confiscation of the applicant's land and buildings concerned by the unlawful development plan. Reaffirming its admissibility decision in the case *Sud Fondi and others* (No. 75909/01), the ECtHR observed that land confiscation could not be considered an administrative sanction as held by domestic courts. Rather, it amounts to a criminal penalty under article 7 ECHR. This Convention right, in particular, requires not only the existence of a legal basis for any offence and related penalty, but also implies the prohibition to impose a penalty without a finding of liability. In the present case, the Court observed, the confiscation had been imposed on the applicant despite the fact that prosecution of the offence in question had become time-barred and his liability had not been established in a verdict as to his guilt. There had then been a violation of article 7 ECHR. Moreover, as the penalty at issue was not provided by law and was then arbitrary, the Court found also a violation of the applicant's right to property (article 1 Protocol I ECHR).

> In the case *Previti v. Italy* (No. 1845/08) the applicant alleged, among other things, a violation of article 7 ECHR on account of the fact that he had not been able to benefit retrospectively from a more favourable law (l. 251/2005) shortening the limitation period for the offence of bribery. Considering that, under the ECHR, rules on limitation periods are classified as procedural laws and that the Italian legislature choice to exclude from the application of the new norm the proceedings that were still pending Cassation at the time of its entry into force was not arbitrary, the Court declared the case inadmissible as manifestly ill-founded.

> In 2013, the case *Contrada v. Italy* (No. 66655/13) was communicated to the parties. The applicant claimed a violation of article 7 ECHR (prohibition of non-retroactivity of criminal law) on account of the fact that the offence of aiding and abetting a mafia-type organisation he was found guilty of was the result of a development in the national case-law subsequent to the time the facts he was accused of had been committed.

> The *Azenabor* case (No. 25367/11) concerned the alleged violation of article 5 ECHR (right to liberty and security). The applicant, subjected to involuntary treatment by a measure adopted by the mayor and later confirmed by the guardianship judge, complained about the fact that the judge in charge of the decision neither visited her at the hospital to hear her opinion nor made any enquiry to ascertain her real conditions. The ECtHR, while stressing the importance for every guardianship judge to adopt all necessary measures to properly and concretely assess the situation of a person deprived of his/her liberty, declared the case inadmissible. Since the applicant did not appeal the contested decision the before the Court of Cassation, she failed to exhaust domestic remedies.

B. Property Rights, "Indirect Expropriations", Fair Compensation

In both the cases *De Luca v. Italy* (No. 43870/04) and *Pennino v. Italy* (No. 43892/04) the applicants had been unable to obtain the full recovery of a claim considered enforceable by a judicial decision against an insolvent local authority. The applicants, invoking article 1 Protocol I ECHR (right to the peaceful enjoyment of property), claimed that the prohibition provided by national law to initiate or pursue an enforcement procedure against the insolvent local authority had deprived them of the opportunity to collect debts considered certain and payable by a final judicial decision. Moreover, as the ban on enforcement proceedings against the Municipality was to remain in force until the approval of the statement of accounts, that is of a procedure the length of which was fully beyond their control, the applicants submitted that their right of access to a court guaranteed by article 6 ECHR had also been violated. The ECtHR found a violation of the applicants' right to property as a Municipality's lack of funds, and therefore an organ of the State, cannot justify a failure on its part to honour its obligations arising from a final judgment against it. Furthermore, while the ban on enforcement proceedings against the Municipality had pursued the legitimate aim of ensuring equal treatment of creditors, the Court found that the applicants had been deprived of their right of access to a court for an excessive length of time (art. 6 ECHR).

> The ECtHR found a violation of articles 6 ECHR and 1 Protocol I ECHR also in the case *Giuseppe Romano v. Italy*. The applicant, a former employee in a company, brought proceedings against it, seeking unpaid remuneration and seniority pay to which he considered himself entitled to. Apart from considering the length of the bankruptcy proceedings incompatible with the standards of article 6 ECHR, the ECtHR found that the applicant's right to property had been violated because of the time needed to recover the amounts claimed and the delay in obtaining awards made under the "Pinto" procedure.

In 2013, on more than one occasion, the ECtHR condemned Italy for the violation of the right to peaceful enjoyment of property in connection with cases of "indirect expropriation". In the cases *Ventura, Musella and Esposito, Gianquitti and others* (all of 22 January), *Rubortone, Rubortone and Caruso* (both 5 February) and *Stea and others* (12 March), the Strasburg Court observed the practice of Italian courts to consider, in application of the indirect expropriation procedure, the applicants to be deprived of their possession as of the completion of the public works. The Court, however, noted that in the absence of an act formalising the expropriation, the applicants could have had legal certainty concerning the deprivation of the land only from the date on which a finding of unlawfulness has become final and binding. Not considering the situation as "foreseeable" and therefore not compatible with the principle of lawfulness, the Court found that there had been a violation of the applicants' right to the peaceful enjoyment of their possessions (article 1 Protocol I ECHR). In all cases, but *Stea and others*, the Court also found a violation of article 6 ECHR in connection to the unreasonable length of proceedings. All applicants were afforded just satisfaction according to criteria determined by the Grand Chamber in the case *Guiso-Gallisay v. Italy* (22 December 2009).

Relying on article 1 Protocol I ECHR and 13 ECHR (right to an effective remedy), the applicants in a number of cases brought before the ECtHR complained about the excessive length of building restrictions applied to their land as well as the lack of an effective domestic remedy to challenge such restrictions (*Marino and others, Segesta s.as., Materazzo and others, Traina, Di Pietro and Caruso, Boadicea Property Services Co. Limited and others*). All cases were declared inadmissible for non-exhaustion of domestic remedies.

In the case *Contessa and others v. Italy*, which the ECtHR declared inadmissible as manifestly ill-founded, the applicants, relying on the town planning scheme, had bought a land for building purposes. The applicants, however, due to the failure on the part of the competent local authorities to adopt the plan for productive settlements and the entry into force of some environmentally protective restrictions, had been unable to obtain a building permit. The Court, considering that the applicants had their claim duly considered at the national level as well as the wide margin of appreciation States enjoy in urban planning, concluded that a fair balance between the demands of the general interest and the requirements of the protection of the individual's fundamental rights had been struck.

Worth noting, and not only in connection to property rights, is the case *Parrillo v. Italy* (No. 46470/11), communicated to the parties in May 2013 after being declared partly inadmissible. The applicant, in particular, complained that the prohibition under the Italian law on assisted reproduction technology (l. 40/2004) to donate the embryos she and her partner, now deceased, obtained through in vitro fertilisation for scientific research was a violation of her right to property and her right to respect for private life.

Finally, the only judgment on just satisfaction issued by the ECtHR in 2013 was on the case *Lanteri v. Italy* (No. 56578/00). The drastic reduction of this type of decisions compared to previous years (see *2013 Yearbook*, pp. 366–367; *2012 Yearbook*, p. 358; *2011 Yearbook*, p. 301) is due to the ECtHR's initiative to invite the Italian Government to reach friendly settlements in the framework of the 105 pending cases already communicated to the Parties, dealing exclusively with just satisfaction claims.

C. Freedom of Expression, Free Elections

The applicant in the case *Ricci v. Italy* (No. 30210/06) is the producer and presenter of a satirical television programme that in 1996 broadcasted some "off the air" footages of a State television channel in order to denounce the real nature of television. Given a suspended prison sentence of four months for fraudulent interception and disclosure of confidential communications, the applicant alleged a violation of his right to freedom of expression (article 10 ECHR) and, more specifically, of his right to inform the public about the real nature of television. The ECtHR, while not contesting the national court's finding that the social interest of the information broadcasted could not be regarded as of "paramount" interest so to excuse the applicant's behaviour, found that the applicant's right to freedom of expression had been violated on account of the nature and quantum of the sentence imposed. In particular, noting that under the Convention the imposition of a prison sentence for media-related crimes is justified only in exceptional circumstances, the ECtHR considered that, in the present case, the content of the video released was not likely to cause significant damage. In conclusion, considering the significant chilling effect of such a harsh sanction for all media operators, the Court found that the interference with the applicant's right to freedom of expression had not remained proportionate to the legitimate aims pursued.

The same conclusion was reached by the Court only a few weeks before in the case *Belpietro* (No. 42612/10) in which, however, the Court had to test the compatibility with the European standards on freedom of expression of the Italian legislation concerning the crime of defamation. The case concerned the then director of the newspaper "Il Giornale" who had been found guilty of defamation for having omitted to exercise his duty of supervision as provided for by article 57 of the Italian criminal code in relation to an article criticising members of the prosecuting authorities and the carabinieri in Palermo. As in the *Ricci* case, the Court did not consider the applicant's conviction in itself contrary to article 10 ECHR. Rather, it was the imposition of a prison sentence to a journalist found guilty of the crime of defamation to be contrary to ECHR standards. In the absence of exceptional circumstances capable of justifying such a heavy penalty, the Court considered that the imposition of a prison sentence (although suspended) for crimes related to the press was not proportionate to the legitimate aims pursued. The applicant is awarded 10,000 euros in respect of non-pecuniary damages.

In the case *Di Giovanni v. Italy*, the applicant is a judge alleging that the disciplinary measure she had been given by the National Council of the Judiciary (CSM) in relation to the content of an interview she gave to the newspaper "Libero" had violated her right to freedom of expression (article 10 ECHR). Indeed, following the applicant's statements concerning the alleged involvement of another judge in irregularities within a public competition to recruit judges and public prosecutors, she was sanctioned by the disciplinary board of the CSM with a warning for having failed in her duty of respect and discretion. In examining the case, the Court recalled that, while article 10 ECHR also apply to civil servants, the higher imperatives of justice and the importance of the judicial function in any democratic society require judges to exercise their freedom of expression with the utmost discretion whenever the authority and impartiality of the judiciary can be called into question. In the present case, considering the applicant's lack of prudence in issuing an interview concerning alleged serious irregularities in a competition for the recruitment of new judges, the ECtHR found that the disciplinary measure she had been given was not unjustified. Moreover, since the warning was the mildest among the disciplinary measures provided for by national law, the Court also found that it had been proportionate and that, consequently, there had been no violation of article 10 ECHR. As for the additional allegation made by the applicant on the lack of impartiality and independence of the disciplinary board of the CSM (alleged violation of article 6 ECHR), the Court dismissed it as manifestly ill-founded.

> In 2013 the case *Brambilla and others* (No. 22567/09) was communicated to the parties. The applicants are some journalists complaining about the violation of their right to freedom of expression and, in particular, of the right of access to journalist sources on account of their conviction for having intercepted police radio communications.

The case *Occhetto v. Italy* (No. 14507/07) concerned the right to free elections and, in particular, the free expression of the opinion of the people in the choice of the legislature (article 3 Protocol I ECHR). The applicant is an Italian politician who had stood for election to the European Parliament (EP). After having voluntarily signed an agreement with the co-founder of the political movement to which he belonged renouncing his entitlement to a seat, he wished to withdraw his renouncement. The decision of the State Council to consider his renouncement of his parliamentary seat as irrevocable had, according to the applicant, deprived the votes he had received of any useful effect and thus constituted a violation of article 3 Protocol I ECHR. Taking into account the wide margin of appreciation enjoyed by States in respect of the "passive" aspects of the rights guaranteed by the article invoked, the ECtHR did not, however, find any appearance of arbitrariness. Indeed, according to the Strasbourg Court, the refusal to accept the withdrawal of the applicant's renouncement had pursued the legitimate aims of guaranteeing legal certainty in the electoral process and the protection of the rights of others, in particular those of the person who had been proclaimed elected to the seat that could have been taken by the applicant. Moreover, in the opinion of the judges of the Court, the possible disappointment felt by voters who had voted for the applicant could not be directly attributed to the Italian authorities, but rather to the agreement voluntarily signed by the applicant. There being no appearance of violation of the right to free elections, the case is declared inadmissible.

D. Right to Private and Family Life, Right to Education

In the case *Lombardo v. Italy* (No. 25704/11), the Strasbourg Court found a violation of article 8 ECHR (right to private and family life) to the extent that Italy failed to effectively guarantee the applicant's right of contact with his daughter, in spite of a number of court decisions providing for his right of access. According to the ECtHR, in particular, national authorities had not adopted all measures at their disposal in order to guarantee contacts between the applicant and his daughter. Specifically, the Strasbourg Court observed that the national Juvenile Court had merely taken note of the difficulties which have arisen in the exercise of the applicant's right of access, delegating to social services the arrangement of visits. Indeed, according the ECtHR, all national authorities did was adopting automatic and stereotyped measures such as requesting additional information. This attitude, concluded the Court, had contributed to stabilise a situation which was detrimental to the applicant's right to build a stable relationship with his child. The applicant was awarded 15,000 euros in respect of non-pecuniary damages and 10,000 euros for costs and expenses.

A similar finding was issued by the ECtHR in the case *Santilli v. Italy* (No. 51930/10) also related to a separated father's inability to exercise access rights to his son. As national authorities had failed to adopt all the necessary measures in order to restore the applicant's rights to visit his child, the Court found a violation of article 8 ECHR (right to respect for family life). The applicant was awarded 10,000 euros in respect of non-pecuniary damage plus the refund of costs and expenses.

The cases *Cariello and others v. Italy* (No. 14064/07) and *D'Auria and Balsamo v. Italy* (No. 11625/07) both related to a case of telephone and environmental interceptions against some judges or third persons connected to them authorised as part of a criminal proceeding, subsequently filed, investigating the alleged corruption of some judges by members of the organised crime. Excerpts of the wiretapped conversations had subsequently appeared on a weekly newspaper. Invoking article 8 ECHR, the applicants challenged the legality of the telephone and environmental wiretaps arguing, in particular, that the judicial authorities had authorised them in the absence of sufficient evidence. They also argued that relevant domestic provisions on wiretapping were devoid of the necessary character of precision and predictability in relation to the cases, the places and the persons which may be intercepted. In both cases, the applicants further alleged a violation of article 13 ECHR (right to an effective remedy). In the case *Cariello*, the applicant raised an additional ground of incompatibility with articles 8 and 6(2) ECHR (presumption of innocence) on account of the publication of parts of the intercepted conversations. The

ECtHR dismissed both cases as manifestly ill-founded. As regards the compatibility of the interceptions with the article 8 ECHR, in particular, the Court noted that these were governed by a domestic rule sufficiently accessible and foreseeable. Moreover, in addition to being fully justified to pursue a legitimate aim such as the ascertainment of the truth, under domestic law wiretappings are authorised only if it is absolutely necessary for the continuation of the investigation. As for the publication of parts of intercepted communications covered by secrecy which, according to the applicants in the case *Cariello* constituted a violation of article 8 ECHR, the Court found that the interference to the applicants' right to a private life could not be attributed to the national authorities. This was all the more true, as the latter, the Court noted, had conducted an effective investigation on the leak.

In the cases *Caldarella v. Italy* (No. 29703/06) and *De Carolis and Lolli v. Italy* (No. 33359/05), the Court confirmed its settled case-law regarding the incompatibility between the rules on bankruptcy before the reform introduced by legislative decree No. 5/2006 and article 8 ECHR. Indeed, the norms, now abrogated, providing for the registration of the individual declared bankrupt in a special register and the associated inability to apply for rehabilitation until five years after termination of the bankruptcy proceedings had again been declared contrary to ECHR standards on the right to private life. In the case *Caldarella*, the Court also found a violation of the right to an effective remedy (article 13 ECHR) as the applicants had had no effective remedy by which to complain of the restrictions resulting from entry in the bankruptcy register.

The case *Oliari and others* (Nos. 18766/11, 36030/11), communicated to the parties in 2013, concerned the prohibition to contract marriage or to enter into any other type of civil union for same-sex couples. The applicants alleged they are being discriminated against as a result of their sexual orientation in breach of article 14 (prohibition of discrimination), in conjunction with articles 8 (right to respect for family life and family life) and 12 (right to marry) of the Convention. The same provisions were invoked in another case communicated to the parties in 2013. In the case *Orlandi and others* (Nos. 26431/12, 26742/12, 44057/12, 60088/12), the applicants, all same-sex couples, complained about the authorities' refusal to register their marriage contracted abroad.

In the second case *Parrillo* (No. 43028/05), communicated to the parties in 2013, the applicant complained that the exclusion from the Cross of Honour ceremony dedicated to the memory of her partner, killed as a consequence of the terrorist attack in Nasiriya in 2003, on account of the mere fact that she was not legally married to him had violated her right to respect for private and family life. For the same reason, the applicant further alleged a violation of 14 ECHR (non-discrimination).

Again on the subject of family rights, in 2013 the Italian Government was invited to submit its comments on the case *Cusan and Fazzo* (No. 77/07). This was a case lodged by an Italian married couple who claimed the right to give their new-born the mother's name. After their request was dismissed by the register of births, marriages and deaths and having exhausted all possible domestic remedies, the applicants alleged that the impossibility under domestic legislation to register their child under the mother's name violated their right to respect for private life and family (article 8 ECHR) in conjunction with article 14 ECHR (prohibition of discrimination) as well as article 5 Protocol VII ECHR (equality between spouses).

In *Tarantino and others v. Italy*, the applicants are eight students who failed the entrance examination to study at the Faculty of Medicine and Dentistry. Relying on article 2 Protocol I ECHR, they complained that the current system of limited access to university studies constituted a breach of their right to education. According to the applicants, in particular, the criteria used to limit admission to university studies (entrance examination and *numerus clausus*) neither pursued a legitimate aim nor were proportionate to the goal of ensuring the adequate preparation of future professionals. In considering the case, the ECtHR first of all reiterated that the right to education is not absolute and that Contracting States enjoy a certain margin of appreciation in the regulation of educational institutions. Considering that the restrictions chosen by the Italian State conform to the legitimate aim of achieving high levels of professionalism, the Court then found that the measures imposed were not disproportionate. In particular, as for the first restriction (entrance examination), the Court noted that this could be considered a proportionate measure designed to ensure a minimum and adequate education level in universities. With regard to the second one (*numerus clausus*), the Strasbourg Court examined both criteria used for applying such limitation, that is the capacity and resource potential of universities, and the society's need for a particular profession. While stressing that the latter is confined to a national outlook and appeared to be short-sighted, the Court concluded that the second limitation was also proportionate. It followed that there had not been a violation of article 2 Protocol I ECHR.

In the case *Asquini Bisconti v. Italy* (No. 10009/06), the applicants complained that the compulsory inclusion of Catholic religious education in the public nursery school curriculum interferes with their freedom of thought, conscience and religion and with their right as parents to ensure that their daughter receives an education which is in line with their philosophical convictions (article 9 ECHR). They also complained that the only means of obtaining exemption from compulsory Catholic religious education being by written request constituted a further violation of the Convention under its articles 9 and 10 ECHR, as the applicants were obliged to take a formal stand with regard to their personal beliefs. Noting that the applicants did not raise their complaints before neither the school governing body nor the national administrative courts, the ECtHR declared the case inadmissible for non-exhaustion of domestic remedies.

Italy in the Case-law of the Court of Justice of the European Union

A. Persons with Disabilities and Equal Treatment in Employment

In its judgment C-312/11, 4 July 2013, the Court of Justice of the European Union (ECJ) declared that, by not introducing a requirement for all employers to make reasonable adjustments, where needed in a particular case, for all persons with disabilities, Italy had failed to fulfil its obligation to ensure the correct and full implementation of directive 2000/78/EC of 27 November 2000 establishing a general framework for equal treatment in employment and occupation.

The Court's ruling stemmed from an infringement procedure brought in 2006 by the European Commission against Italy and culminated in 2011 with the referral of Italy to the ECJ for its failure to fulfil its obligation to implement, fully and correctly, article 5 of directive 2000/78/EC which places Member States under an obligation of general application to make reasonable accommodation to enable persons with a disability to have access to, to participate in, or to advance in employment, or to undergo training.

Indeed, according to the European Commission (EC), contrary to EU law, the Italian provisions on employment of people with disabilities do not concern all disabled persons; they are not enforceable against all employers and they do not concern all the various aspects of the employment relationship. Furthermore, the EC pleaded that the Italian system of promotion of employment of disabled people was essentially based on a set of incentives and grants in aid and not, as required by EU law, by placing all employers under an obligation to make reasonable accommodation for all disabled persons.

The Court of Luxembourg, first of all, dismissed the Italian Government's submission according to which an equally acceptable and correct implementation of article 5 of directive 2000/78 may consist of organising a public and private system assisting employers and persons with disabilities. Inasmuch as it considered that the full and correct implementation of article 5 of directive 2000/78 requires States to place all employers under an obligation to make reasonable accommodation for all disabled persons concerning all the various aspects of the employment relationship, the ECJ granted the European Commission's action brought against Italy. Indeed, even considering the system of national and regional laws in force in Italy integrating the level of assurance and facilitation offered to persons with disabilities by l. 68/1999, the ECJ found that Italy has not fully and correctly implemented article 5 of directive 2000/78/EC.

B. Application of the "Return Directive"

By the order of 21 March 2013 in the case C-522/11, the ECJ tackled again the compatibility with directive 2008/115 (the so-called "Return Directive") of article 10-bis of the Consolidated immigration act (lgs.d. 286/1998).

The case stemmed from a request for a preliminary ruling from the Lecce justice of peace in the context of criminal proceedings brought against Mr Mbaye, a Senegalese citizen prosecuted for the offence of illegal residence. In addressing the issue, the ECJ retraced its settled case-law on the compatibility of the Return directive with national laws penalising the illegal residence of third-country nationals.

With regard to the first question formulated by the referring court, the ECJ reiterated what it affirmed in *Achughbabian* (C-329/11, 6 December 2011) about the interpretation of article 2 of the relevant directive. More specifically, it confirmed that the criminalisation of the conduct of illegal stay cannot exclude from the scope of the "return directive" a third-country nationals accused or convicted of such an offence.

As for the second question referred, the Court, recalling its case-law in *Sagor* (see *2013 Yearbook*, pp. 379–380), ruled that, although the conversion of a fine into immediate expulsion (that is without the period for voluntary departure as provided for by the directive) is not in principle contrary to the directive, such a replacement can only operate under the conditions of article 7(4) of the directive (risk of absconding, risk to public policy, public security or national security).

C. Fixed-term Work, Non-discrimination, Compensation

By its order of 7 March 2013 in the case C-393/11, the ECJ answers the request for a preliminary ruling submitted by the Council of State in the context of a dispute between the Italian Regulatory Authority for Electricity and Gas (AEEG) and some of its employees. The question, very similar to that raised in the case *Rosanna Valenza et al. v. AGCM* decided by the ECJ on October 18, 2012 (see *2013 Yearbook*, p. 380), concerned the refusal of the Authority to take into account, in order to determine the applicants' length of service upon their recruitment on a permanent basis as career civil servants (which took place under a stabilisation procedure for the public sector employees provided by l. 296/2006) periods of service previously completed with the same public agency under fixed-term employment contracts. As in the *Rosanna Valenza* case, the referring court asked the ECJ to consider whether the national legislation which completely disregards length of service under fixed-term working contracts in cases where the workers concerned are recruited under a stabilisation procedure is contrary to EU law and specifically to the Framework agreement on fixed-term work annexed to directive 1999/70/EC.

The Court, reaffirming the principles established in the case *Rosanna Valenza*, reiterates at the outset that the principle of non-discrimination recognised in the Framework agreement provides that fixed-termed workers cannot be treated less favourably then permanent workers that are in a comparable situation, unless there are objective grounds justifying a difference in treatment. In the event that the nature of the duties performed by the applicants and the quality of the experience they have acquired in the years during which they worked for the AEEG under fixed-term employment contracts make it possible for the national court to determine that they are in a situation comparable with that of career civil servants, the ECJ concluded that the mere fact that the fixed-term worker completed those periods of service on the basis of a fixed-term employment contract does not constitute such an objective ground. It is then up to the national court to determine whether or not there are other "objective reasons" to justify any difference in treatment.

Another reference for a preliminary ruling decided by the ECJ concerning the compatibility of the Italian legislation with article 4 of the Framework agreement on fixed-term work annexed to directive 1999/70/EC is case C-361/12. The request, made in proceedings between Ms Carratù and Poste Italiane (National postal service) concerning the insertion of a fixed-term clause into the employment contract they had concluded, relates to the disparity between the compensation to be paid to the employee engaged unlawfully under a fixed-term contract and that afforded to unlawfully dismissed worker employed under a contract of indefinite duration. The referring court, in particular, asks the ECJ to assess the compatibility of l. 183/2010 (Provisions on fixed-term work) with article 4 (principle of non-discrimination) of the Framework agreement to the extent that the compensation scheme provided by national law seems to have a punitive effect on the fixed-term worker. In particular, the referring court noted that, irrespective of the length of the proceedings and the point at which the worker is reinstated, a worker engaged unlawfully under a fixed-term contract is afforded less favourable protection than either that afforded to an unlawfully dismissed worker employed under a contract of indefinite duration.

After having clarified that the provisions of the Framework agreement may be relied on directly against a State body such as Poste Italiane and that the concept of "employment conditions" covers the compensation that the employer must pay to an employee on account of the unlawful insertion of a fixed-term clause into his employment contract, the ECJ concluded that article 4 of the Framework agreement does not apply in the present case. This, the Luxembourg Court observed, because the principle of equal treatment apply only whether the persons concerned can be regarded as being in a comparable situation while the present case concerns workers whose employment contract was concluded unlawfully and workers who have been dismissed. Consequently, while the Framework agreement does not preclude Member States from granting fixed-term workers more favourable treatment than that provided for by the Framework agreement, EU law must be interpreted as not requiring the compensation paid in respect of the unlawful insertion of a fixed-term clause into an employment relationship to be treated in the same way as that paid in respect of the unlawful termination of a permanent employment relationship.

> Directive 1999/70/EC and the Framework agreement must be interpreted as not applying neither to the fixed-term employment relationship between a temporary worker and a temporary employment business nor to the employment relationship between such a worker and a user undertaking. That's the ECJ's finding in the case C-290/12 of 11 April 2013.

Finally, with the order of 12 December 2013, *Rocco Papalia v. City of Aosta* (C-50/13), the ECJ rules on the compatibility of lgs.d. 165/2001 (General rules on the organisation of employment by the Government) with article 5 of the Framework annexed to directive 1999/70/EC on the prevention of misuse. The request for a preliminary ruling, submitted by the Court of Aosta, stems from a dispute between Mr Papalia and the City of Aosta on the compensation for the damage the applicant had suffered as a result of the misuse of successive fixed-term employment contracts. Taking into account that in such a circumstance the Italian legislation does not only excludes any transformation of the fixed-term employment relationship into an employment relationship for an indefinite period, but that the right to that compensation is subject to the obligation on that worker to prove that he was forced to forego better work opportunities, the referring national court asks the ECJ to determine the compatibility of the Italian legislation with the relevant EU law.

Even though the settled case-law of the ECJ exclude that States are under an obligation to transform fixed-term contracts into an employment relationship for an indefinite period, the ECJ reiterated that provisions of domestic law aimed at penalising the misuse of successive fixed-term employment contracts shall not render impossible in practice or excessively difficult the exercise of the rights conferred by European Union law. In the present case, it is for the referring court to assess whether the obligation on the worker to prove the damage he considers himself to have incurred renders excessively difficult the exercise of his right to compensation.

Legal Approach to the Chairperson-Rapporteur's Draft Declaration in Light of the Current Debate on the Right of Peoples to Peace

By Ambassador Christian Guillermet Fernández[1]
and Dr. David Fernández Puyana[2]

1. Introduction

Since the inception of the Human Rights Council in 2006 part of the international community, with the exception of the Group of Eastern and Western European and Others States, has actively been engaged in the promotion of the right to peace through the adoption of several resolutions. However, it should be noted that the promotion of the right of peoples to peace within the UN human rights bodies started at the Commission on Human Rights in 2001. Although many of the States have supported the on-going process, some of them have not recognized the existence of the right to peace under international law. In particular, the Western States and associated countries have constantly showed their opposition to this UN process by arguing that this notion is not correctly linked to human rights. From 2003 to 2005, the Commission on Human Rights decided to change the mandate of this topic by introducing the title of "Promotion of peace as a vital requirement for the full enjoyment of all human rights by all" with the purpose of introducing a more human rights approach to this topic. The purpose of this paper is to analyse this debate by taking into account the positions showed by the different stakeholders. Additionally, the different consultations convened by the Chairperson-Rapporteur on the Open Ended Working Group on the Right to Peace will also studied. Finally, the paper will analyse the draft Declaration elaborated by the Chairperson-Rapporteur in light of the following elements: firstly, international law and human rights law; secondly, the points of concurrences among all delegations and thirdly, outcome of the consultations held in the context of the on-going process. Finally, the notion of the right to life in a context of peace, human rights and development will be proposed as a means to overcome the political differences among all regional groups and to elaborate this notion in the context of the current mandate of the Human Rights Council in the field of human rights.

2. Debate

2.1. *Commission on Human Rights*

From 2001 to 2003 the CHR has adopted two resolutions entitled "promotion of the right of peoples to peace"[3]. In particular, at the 78th meeting, the representative of Cuba, introduced draft resolution E/CN.4/2001/L.95, sponsored by several countries[4] and said that the text aimed to consolidate and promote the international community's conviction that "life without war serve(d) as the primary international prerequisite for the material well-being, development and progress of countries, and for the full implementation of the rights and fundamental freedoms proclaimed by the United Nations", as enshrined in the Declaration on the Right of Peoples to Peace. He added that following extensive open-ended consultations, a significant part of the text and the original title ("human rights and disarmament") had been modified to ensure that the draft resolution would be widely acceptable[5].

In the explanation of vote before the vote, the representative of Belgium, speaking in explanation of the position of the European Union (hereinafter, EU) and its associated countries[6], said that some of the issues raised in the draft resolution were better dealt with in other forums. International Peace and Security were essential for the realization of all human rights, including the right to development, but military spending continued to be high. There was therefore a need for Governments to set priorities in favour of development and the promotion and protection of human rights. He added that the draft resolution dealt only with the relationship between States and not with the relationship between a State and its citizens, which was the Commission's core mandate. Moreover, the Declaration on the Right of Peoples to Peace had not been agreed to by consensus. The Union was also uncomfortable with the idea that there was a right to peace, which was not established in any international human rights instrument[7].

At the request of the representative of Belgium, a roll-call vote was taken on the draft resolution, which was adopted by 29 votes[8] to 16[9], with 7 abstentions[10].

In explanation of vote after the vote, the representative of India said that, although the text contained agreed-upon language from various international instruments and although her delegation noted in particular the second preambular paragraph and paragraph 4, it did not consider the Commission to be the appropriate forum for examining disarmament issues[11].

Afterwards, the representative of Costa Rica said that she did not agree with the preceding speaker. The Commission was indeed the appropriate forum to address such issues, since disarmament was crucial to the protection of human rights. The draft resolution complemented other resolutions adopted by the Commission with the aim of promoting a culture of peace. Costa Rica possessed no army, having opted to devote its national resources to education and development[12].

Afterwards, at the 56th meeting of the Commission, the representative of Cuba introduced draft resolution E/CN.4/2002/L.90, sponsored by several countries by saying that the absence of war is the primary international prerequisite for the material well-being, development and progress of countries, and for the full implementation of the rights and fundamental human freedoms, and in particular the right to life. To ensure the exercise of the right of peoples to peace the policies of States should be directed towards the elimination of the threat of war, the renunciation of the use or threat of use of force in international relations, the settlement of international disputes by peaceful means, the respect of the principle of territorial integrity and the respect of independence of States on the basis of the Charter of the United Nations. In addition, the international community should do their utmost to achieve general and complete disarmament under effective international control, as well as to ensure that the resources released by effective disarmament measures are used for comprehensive development, in particular that of the developing countries[13].

In the explanation of vote before the vote, the representative of Spain, speaking in explanation of the position of the EU and its associated countries[14], said that some of the issues raised in the draft resolution were better dealt with in other forums. He added that the draft resolution dealt only with the relationship between States and not with the relationship between a State and its citizens, which was the Commission's core mandate. The Union was also uncomfortable with the idea that there was a right to peace, which was not established in any international human rights instrument[15].

At the request of the representative of Spain, a roll-call vote was taken on the draft resolution, which was adopted by 33 votes[16] to 15[17], with 5 abstentions[18].

As a consequence of introducing a more human rights approach to the right of peoples to peace, in 2003 the Commission changed the title of the three following resolutions as follows "Promotion of peace as a vital requirement for the full enjoyment of all human rights by all"[19].

In 2003 and 2004 the CHR slowly began to elaborate the component of human rights in this topic jointly to the principles of international law – Art 2 of the UN Charter – by emphasizing that an international system should be "based on respect of the principles enshrined in the Charter of the United Nations and the promotion of all human rights and fundamental freedoms"[20]. After that, the Commission urged "all States to respect and to put into practice the principles and purposes of the Charter of the United Nations in their relations with all other States, irrespective of their political, economic or social systems"[21] and to promote the peaceful settlement of disputes "as a vital requirement for the promotion and protection of all human rights of everyone and all peoples"[22].

In particular, at the 61st meeting, the representative of Cuba, introduced draft resolution E/CN.4/2003/L.76, sponsored by several countries[23] and said that it reaffirms the commitment of all States to promoting peace and underlined the importance of enhancing the role and effectiveness of the United Nations in strengthening international peace and security. In addition, it rejects the use of violence in pursuit of political aims and stressed that only peaceful political solutions could assure a stable and democratic future for peoples throughout the world and urged all States to respect the principles enshrined in the Charter of the United Nations and international law. He stated that Paragraph 1 was a new element, stressing that peace was a vital requirement for the promotion and protection of human rights for all[24].

In the explanation of vote before the vote, the representative of the United States of America said that a draft resolution on the topic of promoting peace was inappropriate for the Commission[25].

The representative of Ireland, speaking on behalf of the member States of the EU that were members of the Commission and of Poland, with the endorsement of the whole EU, the acceding countries and the associated countries, said that some of the issues raised in the draft resolution were better dealt with in other forums. Moreover, the draft resolution dealt only with the relationship between States and not the relationship between the State and its citizens or the exercise of individuals' human rights vis-à-vis the State, which was the core mandate of the Commission[26].

Afterwards, the representative of Algeria said he hoped that the draft resolution would be adopted by a large majority because the strengthening of peace was also a means of strengthening human rights[27].

At the request of the representative of the United States of America, a roll-call vote was taken on the draft resolution, which was adopted by 33 votes[28] to 16[29], with 4 abstentions[30].

In the last resolution on this topic presented before the CHR in 2005[31], the human rights approach to the right of peoples to peace was again elaborated. In particular, the resolution stressed that "peace is a vital requirement for the promotion and protection of all human rights for all"[32] and also invited "States and relevant United Nations human rights mechanisms and procedures to continue to pay attention to the importance of mutual cooperation, understanding and dialogue in ensuring the promotion and protection of all human rights"[33]. Finally, it "calls upon the United Nations High Commissioner for Human Rights to carry out a constructive dialogue and consultations with Member States, specialized agencies and inter-governmental organizations on how the CHR could work for the promotion of an international environment conducive to the full realization of the right of peoples to peace, and encourages non-governmental organizations to contribute actively to this endeavour".

At the request of the representative of the United States of America, a roll-call vote was taken on the draft resolution, which was adopted by 32 votes[34] to 15[35], with 6 abstentions[36]. The explanation of Member States before the vote was again the same[37].

The CHR was a functional commission within the overall framework of the United Nations from 1946 until it was replaced by the Human Rights Council (HRC) in 2006. It was the UN's principal mechanism and international forum concerned with the promotion and protection of human rights. On 15 March 2006, the UNGA voted overwhelmingly to replace the Commission with the HRC.

2.2. Human Rights Council

In accordance with the resolution 60/251, the HRC is exclusively focused on those who truly suffer in a conflict: human beings and peoples. It is a forum for dialogue, not confrontation, which always works by and for the victims. In accordance to its Preamble, development, peace and security and human rights are interlinked and mutually reinforcing. However, the UNGA clearly decided that the Council should address situations of gross and systematic violations of human rights and also contribute, through dialogue and cooperation, towards the prevention of human rights violations and respond promptly to human rights emergencies. Additionally, in accordance with the operative section of the resolution, the mandate of the HRC is to promote and protect human rights, but not directly peace.

Since 2008 the HRC has been working on the "Promotion of the right of peoples to peace" inspired by previous resolutions on this issue approved by the UNGA and the former CHR, particularly the GA resolution 39/11 of 12 November 1984, entitled "Declaration on the Right of Peoples to Peace" and the United Nations Millennium Declaration. The Group of Eastern and Western European and Others States continued with its traditional position showed at the Commission on Human Rights.

In 2008, the HRC reiterated the traditional position, according to which "peoples of our planet have a sacred right to peace"[38], and that preservation and protection of this right constitutes a fundamental obligation of each State (paragraph 2). Therefore, States should direct their policies towards the elimination of the threat of war, particularly nuclear war, the renunciation of the use or threat of use of force in international relations and the settlement of international disputes by peaceful means on the basis of the Charter of the United Nations (paragraph 5).

The resolution also stresses that peace is a vital requirement for the promotion and protection of all human rights for all (paragraph 3) and that the cleavage that divides human society, between the rich and the poor, and the ever-increasing gap between the developed and developing worlds pose a major threat to global prosperity, peace, security and stability (paragraph 4).

Additionally, the HRC reiterated the OHCHR to convene a workshop on the right of peoples to peace, which was finally held on 15–16 December 2009 in Geneva. In this workshop the current deep division about the existence of the right to peace could be seen even at the academic level. In fact, some well-known legal practitioners who participated at the *Workshop on the right of peoples to peace* held on 9–10 December 2009 in Geneva stated that the right to peace had never been explicitly formalized into a treaty, including the UN Charter, and that the UN human rights instruments had not given proper expression to this enabling right[39].

The opening statement of the workshop was delivered by Ms. Kyung-Wha Kang (Deputy High Commissioner for Human Rights). She recalled that peace and human rights were intricately related and that the Charter of the United Nations provided that strengthening universal peace and promoting and encouraging respect for human rights without discrimination were among the main purposes of the Organization. She also pointed out that human rights treaties also contained references to the importance of peace as a precondition for the full enjoyment of fundamental human rights, as well as to the impact of respect for human rights on the creation of a peaceful society. She concluded by recalling that "respect for human rights was often more critical in times of conflict, noting that many of the worst human rights violations… occurred in situations of armed conflict and other forms of violent situations. Accountability for gross human rights violations was a crucial component of human rights and could often be conducive to peace"[40].

On 17 June 2010, the HRC adopted resolution 14/3 on the right of peoples to peace, which explicitly requested "the Advisory Committee, in consultation with Member States, civil society, academia and all relevant stakeholders, to prepare a draft declaration on the right of peoples to peace, and to report on the progress thereon to the Council at its seventeenth session"[41].

Furthermore, the resolution 14/3 explicitly recognizes the "... the important work being carried out by civil society organizations for the promotion of the right of peoples to peace and the codification of that right"[42]; recalls "the United Nations Declaration and Programme of Action on Culture of Peace, 1999, and the UNGA resolution 53/25 proclaiming 2001–10 as the International Decade for a Culture of Peace and Non-Violence for the children's of the world;[43] "calls upon States and relevant United Nations bodies to promote effective implementation of the United Nations Declaration and Programme of Action on Culture of Peace"[44]; and finally, "supports the need to further promote the realization of the right of peoples to peace" and in that regard requests "the Advisory Committee, in consultation with Member States, civil society, academia and all relevant stakeholders, to prepare a draft declaration on the right of peoples to peace, and to report on the progress thereon to the Council at its seventeenth session"[45].

On 17 June 2011, the HRC adopted the resolution 17/16 by which "takes note of the progress report of the HRC Advisory Committee on the right of peoples to peace (A/HRC/17/39), which include more than 40 possible standards for inclusion in the draft declaration on the right of peoples to peace" (paragraph 14); "supports the need to further promote the realization of the right of peoples to peace and, in that regard, requests the Advisory Committee, in consultation with Member States, civil society, academia and all relevant stakeholders, to present a draft declaration on the right of peoples to peace, and to report on progress thereon to the Council at its twentieth session" (paragraph 15); and finally "requests the OHCHR to retransmit the questionnaire prepared by the Advisory Committee in the context of its mandate on the issue of the right of peoples to peace, seeking the views and comments of Member States, civil society, academia and all relevant stakeholders" (paragraph 16).

On 29 June 2012 the plenary of the HR Council discussed the (third) AC draft declaration on the right to peace. In the general debate representatives of 9 States[46], 3 International Organisations[47] and 10 civil society organisations (CSOs)[48] took the floor. On 5 July 2012 the HR Council took action on draft resolution L.16 (The promotion of the right to peace) as orally revised by Cuba on behalf of the co-sponsors. It was adopted by a registered vote of 34 votes in favour[49], 12 abstentions[50] and one against[51].

On 5 July 2012, the HRC adopted resolution 20/15 on "The promotion of the right to peace". The resolution established an open-ended working group (hereinafter: OEWG) with the mandate of progressively negotiating a draft UN Declaration on the right to peace on the basis of the draft submitted by the Advisory Committee, and without prejudging relevant past, present and future views and proposals.

The resolution further decided that the working group shall hold its first session for four working days in 2013, before the twenty-second session of the HR Council (March 2013); and requested the President of the HRC to invite the Chairperson of the Advisory Committee's drafting group to participate in the first session of the working group.

The OEWG concluded in its first session that there were some governmental delegations and other stakeholders that recognize the existence of the right to peace. They argued that this right was already recognized by soft-law instruments (such as UNGA res. 39/11 of 1984 entitled, "Declaration on the Right of Peoples to Peace"). On the other hand, several other delegations stated that a stand-alone "right to peace" does not exist under international law. In their view, peace is not a human right, but a consequence of the full implementation of all human rights.

At its 23rd session (June 2013), the HR Council had before it the first progress report of the OEWG. On 7 June 2013 the plenary of the HR Council discussed the report of the first session of the OEWG on the draft United Nations Declaration on the right to peace prepared by Mr. Christian Guillermet, Chairperson-Rapporteur of the OEWG. In the general debate, representatives of seven States[52], two International Organizations[53] and eight CSOs[54] took the floor.

Mr. Guillermet stated that our challenge is to address the difficulties in a spirit of cooperation, good faith and transparency in view to reaching an agreement in favour of the promotion and protection of human rights. Persisting in not negotiating or rejecting an initiative because it does not respond to one's interests or national legal system is not a constructive approach to the matter. Since this year we celebrate the 20th anniversary of the Vienna Declaration and Plan of Action, it would be contradictory to deny the progressive development of human rights and the need to move toward a better, more just and respectful human rights environment[55].

On 13 June 2013, the HRC adopted resolution 23/16 at the initiative of the CELAC by 30 votes in favour[56], 9 against[57] and 8 abstentions[58]. The HRC "*decided* that the working group shall hold its second session for five working days in 2014, before the twenty-fifth session of the HRC". It also "*requested* the Chairperson-Rapporteur of the working group to conduct informal consultations with Governments, regional groups and relevant stakeholders before the second session of the working group". Finally, it "*requested* the Chairperson-Rapporteur of the working group to prepare a new text on the basis of the discussions held during the first session of the working group and on the basis of the inter-sessional informal consultations to be held, and to present it prior to the second session of the working group for consideration and further discussion thereat".

The representative of the United States of America said that human rights are universal and are held and exercised by individuals. The United States does not agree with attempts to develop a collective "right to peace" or to position it as an "enabling right" that would in any way modify or stifle the exercise of existing human rights. They do, however, remained open to the possibility of discussing, for instance, the relationship between human rights and peace or how respect for human rights contributes to a culture of peace, including in this OEWG[59].

Afterwards, the Permanent Representative of Ireland said that the following explanation of vote was agreed on by the EU as a whole. The EU firmly believes in peace and human rights, and its close linkage. Peace and human rights can be mutually reinforced. There is no legal basis for the right to peace in international law and it is not possible to find a common definition of this right. If the new text to be prepared by the Chairperson-Rapporteur well reflects their position on the relationship between peace and the enjoyment of human rights, then they will take into serious consideration taking part in the negotiation process, including the second session of the OEWG[60].

2.3. Consultations

On 22 October 2013, the Office of the High Commissioner for Human Rights sent a Note Verbale to all Permanent Missions in Geneva and non-governmental organizations by informing them that pursuant to resolution A/HRC/RES/23/16, the Chairperson-Rapporteur of the Working Group on a Draft United Nations Declaration on the Right to Peace would like to conduct informal consultations with Governments, regional groups and relevant stakeholders before the second session of the working group.

In this connection, a Note prepared by the Chairperson-Rapporteur of the Working Group, was attached to this Note Verbale. In this note the Chairperson-Rapporteur addressed the following questions to States and non-governmental organizations: 1. What are the main international human rights themes, which should be considered in the future text of the Draft Declaration to be presented by the Chairperson-Rapporteur?; 2. What is your opinion about the human rights themes proposed by the Chairperson-Rapporteur as set out below? Would they positively contribute to an open and constructive discussion on the text of a Declaration and eventually to agreement among all different stakeholders?

The proposal of themes were the following: human security and enjoyment of economic, social and cultural rights, including the right to health and environment; racism, racial discrimination, xenophobia and related intolerance; education; freedom of expression, religion or belief and prohibition of propaganda of war; development; protection of victims, transitional justice and prevention of conflicts; peacekeeping, peacemaking and peace-building; disarmament; terrorism; measures aimed to increasing the awareness of the Declaration. This list was not exhaustive.

On 31 October and 1 November 2013, the Chairperson-Rapporteur of the open-ended inter-governmental Working Group convened informal consultations with Member States.

On 18–19 November 2013, the Chairperson-Rapporteur organized with the support of the Finn Church Aid and the World Council of Churches a closed meeting about the future Declaration at the Ecumenical Institute (Bossey, Canton of Vaud, Switzerland). Some 25 delegates representing the UN Secretariat (OHCHR[61]), funds and programmes (UNHCR[62], UNEP[63], UNDP[64], UNICEF[65], UNFPA[66]), specialized agencies (FAO[67], ILO[68], UNESCO[69], WHO[70]), research and training institutes (UNIDIR[71]), inter-governmental organizations (IOM[72]), human rights treaty bodies (HR Committee[73]), special procedures (Working Group on Mercenaries) and international humanitarian organizations (IFRC[74]) were invited to participate at the closed meeting to give inputs to the on-going process.

On 9 May 2014, the Chairperson-Rapporteur held an informal consultation with governments, regional groups and civil society organizations, in which he stated that a resolution adopted by consensus will necessarily carry more weight than one supported by a majority of States. In addition, a future Declaration will be a useful tool to generate widespread and consistent State practice and/or provide evidence of *opinio juris* of customary rule. Additionally, soft-law instruments can be vehicles for focusing consensus on rules and principles, and for mobilizing a general response on the part of States.

The preliminary ideas of the Chairperson-Rapporteur disclosed at the previous consultation were included the "Letter from the Chairperson-Rapporteur of the open-ended inter-governmental working group on a draft United Nations declaration on the right to peace, addressed to the members of the working group"[75], which circulated as an official document at the second session of the OEWG. In accordance with the above letter, the following points of concurrence among all delegations were highlighted by the Chairperson-Rapporteur:

1. The declaration should be short and concise and should provide an added value to the field of human rights on the basis of consensus and dialogue.

2. The declaration should be guided by international law, basing itself on the Charter of the United Nations and the promotion of human rights and fundamental freedoms.

3. The legal basis of the human rights legal system is the concept of human dignity.

4. Human rights and fundamental freedoms, in particular the right to life, are massively violated in the context of war and armed conflict. In addition, there is no possibility to exercise fundamental rights in a context of armed violence.

5. Cooperation, dialogue and the protection of all human rights are fundamental to the prevention of war and armed conflict.

6. The promotion, protection and prevention of violations of all human rights would make a profound contribution to peace.

7. Human rights, peace and development are interdependent and mutually reinforcing.

8. Many concepts of human rights included in the draft declaration elaborated by the Advisory Committee are new and unclear, which results in the risk that the current process will become an unproductive, futile and frivolous exercise. Many notions have already been addressed in other more appropriate forums, some under the Human Rights Council, and some not.

Having identified the above points of concurrence and after consulting with different stakeholders[76], the Chairperson-Rapporteur considers that the draft declaration below could be acceptable to all members of the working group.

3. Analysis

In this section, the different components of the text proposed by the Chairperson-Rapporteur[77], in particular its Preamble and Operative Part, will be deeply analysed in light of the following elements: firstly, international law and human rights law; secondly, the points of concurrences among all delegations and thirdly, outcome of the consultations held in the context of the on-going process.

3.1. Preamble

3.1.1. Charter of the United Nations

Guided by the purposes and principles of the Charter of the United Nations.

Sources: Art. 1 and 2 of the Charter.

The *United Nations Conference on International Organization* (UNCIO) had as its purpose to review and rewrite the *Dumbarton Oaks*

agreements of 1944, in which international leaders formulated and negotiated the future architecture of the United Nations[78]. The formulation
of the *Dumbarton Oaks agreements* was the first important step taken to
carry out the *Moscow Declaration* of 1943, which recognized the necessity of ensuring a rapid and orderly transition from war to peace[79] and
the need for a postwar international organization to succeed the League
of Nations[80].

For the first time the linkage between economic and social matters,
human rights and peace, was recognized in Art. IX of the *Dumbarton
Oaks agreements*: "With a view to the creation of conditions of stability
and well-being which are necessary for peaceful and friendly relations
among nations, the Organization should facilitate solutions of international economic, social and other humanitarian problems and promote
respect for human rights and fundamental freedoms...."[81].

Ever since, the United Nations has been always guided by a conception of peace understood in a wider and more positive way, in which the
well-being of individuals and societies, including economic welfare, social security and human rights, has a clear prevalence over a conception
of peace related exclusively to use of violence or force[82].

On 26 June 1945, the Charter of the United Nations was signed at
the San Francisco War Memorial and Performing Arts Centre in San
Francisco (United States of North-America) by 50 of the original member
countries[83]. It entered into force on 24 October 1945, after being ratified
by the five permanent members of the Security Council – the Republic of
China[84], France, the Union of Soviet Socialist Republics[85], the United
Kingdom, and the United States – and a majority of the other signatories.
Today, the 193 member States of the United Nations[86] have undertaken
"...to save succeeding generations from the scourge of war..."[87].

The United Nations' purposes, spelled out in article 1 of the Charter,
and the principles as set out in article 2 express the ideas which will guide
the States parties when ratifying the Charter. Certain elements of article 1
(1) and 1 (2) are considered principles binding under customary international law (i.e. prohibition of aggression, the prohibition of other breaches
of peace, an obligation to settle disputes by peaceful means and respect
for human rights)[88].

The International Court of Justice (hereinafter: ICJ) stated in the
Advisory Opinion on *certain expenses*[89] that "The purposes of the United
Nations are set forth in Article 1 of the Charter. The first two purposes as
stated in paragraphs 1 and 2, maybe summarily described as pointing to
the goal of international peace and security and friendly relations. The
third purpose is the achievement of economic, social, cultural and humanitarian goals and respect for human rights.... The primary placed

ascribed to international peace and security is natural, since the fulfilment of the other purposes will be dependent upon the attainment of that basic condition…"

3.1.2. Notion of universal peace

Recalling the determination of the peoples of the United Nations to live to-gether in peace with one another as good neighbours in order to save succeed-ing generations from the scourge of war, and to take appropriate measures to strengthen universal peace.

Sources: Preamble, para. 1 and Art. 1(2) of the UN Charter.

At the opening session of the *United Nations Conference on International Organization* (UNCIO), which took place in San Francisco (United States) on 25 April 1945, President Truman stated in his inaugural speech that "if we do not want to die together in war, we must learn to live together in peace"[90].

Life has traditionally been linked to peace and security matters. However, the linkage between the concept of life and peace was included for the first time in a speech delivered by President Roosevelt on 4 March 1933 before the United States Capitol in Washington[91]. This elaboration was later inserted in both the Preamble of the UN Charter[92] without being discussed in substance in the San Francisco Conference and the North Atlantic Treaty[93]. The UNGA has quite often referred to this commitment[94]. However, some resolutions use the term "neighbours" in a narrow geographical sense[95], while others have a more far-reaching meaning[96].

The United Nations is a response to the two world wars and the intention of the member States to suppress war[97]. The maintenance of international peace and security is the most important goal of the United Nations in accordance with Art. 1(1)[98]. Chapter VII grants the Security Council extensive powers in this field. The conditions to use these powers remain very vague, mainly due to the very broad notions used in Art. 39[99]. The Security Council enjoys considerable discretion in the determination whether a threat to the peace, a breach of peace, or an act of discretion exists[100]. Although the International Criminal Tribunal for the former Yugoslavia has recognized the Council's broad discretion, it has also emphasized that it is not unlimited[101].

The Charter recognizes that peace is more than the absence of war and therefore, it includes outstanding legal provisions of international human rights law to be applied by the international community as a whole, which should be aimed to eliminating progressively those issues likely to cause war. The analysis of international human rights instruments confirms the conviction that respect for human rights is at the basis of peace[102].

After a lively debate during the negotiation process of the Charter[103], a consensus was reached among all States that the efforts should no longer be limited to stopping direct threats of war, but should also include to fight against its roots causes, including "poverty, disease, ignorance, insecurity, unemployment, inequality and not least lawless tyranny and lack of human dignity"[104].

Recent practice has stressed the strong linkage and interdependence of peace and security with broader conditions of social development. As indicated by the Security Council declaration, adopted at the level of Head of State and Government in 1992, "peace and prosperity are indivisible and lasting peace and security require effective cooperation for the eradication of poverty and the promotion of a better life for all in larger freedom"[105].

Although the Preamble is an integral part of the Charter, it does not set forth any basic obligation of the member States[106]. It only serves as an interpretative guideline for the provisions of the Charter[107]. The first part of the Preamble contains basically two ideas: maintenance of peace and international security[108] and respect for human rights[109]. Additionally, it refers to some but not all of the purposes of the Organization (i.e. equal rights of nations or peoples[110], enhancement of the friendly relations among States[111] and the limitation of the use of force[112]). In the second part, it declares that governments of these peoples have agreed to the Charter, which addresses the contractual element of the Charter[113].

Article 1 (2) of the UN Charter proclaims that the purpose of the United Nations is to "… take other appropriate measures to strengthen universal peace". In this provision peace or universal peace can be found separately from security. The degree of overlapping between peace and security depends very much upon whether the term peace is narrowly or broadly defined. If peace is narrowly defined as the mere absence of a threat or use of force against the territorial integrity or political independence of any State (Art. 2(4)), the term security will contain parts of what is usually referred to as notion of positive peace.

This latter notion is understood as encompassing the activity which is necessary for maintaining the conditions of peace[114]. Therefore, Art. 1 (2) is often considered key in including the positive notion of peace, which goes beyond the negative absence of the use of force by establishing the linkage between peace and human rights.

The positive approach of peace goes in the line of the wide notion of peace supported by the former Secretary-General Kofi Annan in his report "In larger freedom": "The threats to peace and security in the twenty-first century include not just international war and conflict but civil violence, organized crime, terrorism and weapons of mass destruction. They also include poverty, deadly infectious disease and environmental degradation..."[115].

Taking into account that peace and human rights are a cornerstone of the further elaboration of the human security framework and that this concept is inseparable from conditions of peace[116], it could safely be concluded that the broader meaning of peace deals with the generic causes of conflict[117]. As one human right expert highlighted, "real peace is much more than stability, order or absence of war: peace is transformative, about individual and societal progress and fulfilment; and peace within and between societies is as much about justice as anything else"[118]. Thus, an integrated approach to human security would be related to the deepest causes of war, such as economic despair, social injustice and political oppression[119].

Among the key structural causes of instability and conflict are poverty, inequality and lack of economic opportunity. Although diplomacy might be useful in the short-term effort to maintain peace, long-term solutions require economic development and greater social justice[120]. As the *Declaration and Programme of Action on Culture of Peace* indicates, the anti-poverty strategies, the assurance of equity in development and the pursuit of food security are elements of peacebuilding.

As to the protection of human rights, Art. 1 (3) of the Charter states that "to achieve international co-operation in solving international problems of an economic, social, cultural, or humanitarian character, and in promoting and encouraging respect for human rights and for fundamental freedoms for all without distinction as to race, sex, language, or religion".

This provision has been textually invoked with respect to the improvement of the effective enjoyment of human rights and fundamental freedoms within the United Nations system[121], the political rights of women[122], the question of racial conflict in South Africa resulting from apartheid[123], the elimination of racial discrimination[124], the elimination of all forms of intolerance and discrimination based on religion and beliefs[125], enhancement of international cooperation in the field of human rights[126], and the strengthening of the rule of law[127].

In terms of the progressive elaboration of human rights, one of the main achievements reached at the San Francisco Conference was the inclusion in Art. 1 of the provision, which highlights that "the peaceful and friendly relations among nations" is based on two fundamental principles, namely: "... respect for the principle of equal rights and self-determination of peoples"[128] and the "... respect for human rights and for fundamental freedoms for all without distinction as to race, sex, language or religion"[129].

Arts. 55[130] and 56[131] of the Charter affirm that the United Nations is built on the understanding that peace needs to be secured by economic and social welfare and by the realization of human rights and that the Organization and its members should cooperate to this end[132]. Furthermore, Art. 55 reaffirm the program of cooperation in the field of human rights as set out in the Preamble and Art. 1 (3) of the Charter.

Art. 55 is also considered key in reflecting the positive notion of peace, which describes "a state of peaceful and friendly relations among nations and the necessary preconditions which may prevent conflicts from arising or allow for their peaceful settlement"[133].

3.1.3. *Universal Declaration of Human Rights and International Covenants*

Guided also by the Universal Declaration of Human Rights and the International Covenants on Civil, Political, Economic, Social and Cultural Rights as a common standard of achievement for all peoples and all nations.

The Universal Declaration of Human Rights (UDHR) is a declaration adopted by the United Nations UNGA on 10 December 1948 at Palais de Chaillot, Paris. The Declaration arose directly from the experience of the Second World War and represents the first global expression of rights to which all human beings are inherently entitled.

It consists of 30 articles which have been elaborated in subsequent international treaties, regional human rights instruments, national constitutions and laws. The "International Bill of Human Rights" consists of the Universal Declaration of Human Rights, the ICESCR, and the International Covenant on Civil and Political Rights (hereinafter: ICCPR). As of 2013, they have been ratified by 160 and 167 States, respectively[134].

As indicated by Prof. Eide, "the package of rights contained in the Declaration was not simply the historical product of real-life legal evolution in the positivistic sense, but a set of normative aspirations elaborated in 1948 with the hope that they would, over time, become real rights and, as such, effectively recognized and enjoyed .... The rights in the UDHR were formulated in highly general and abstract terms. This was delivery done in order to maintain a degree of flexibility for States during the required transformation of their internal systems"[135].

3.1.4. *Principles of international law*

Recalling that the friendly relations among nations are based on respect for the principle of equal rights and self-determination of peoples, and international cooperation to solve international problems of an economic, social, cultural or humanitarian character and to promote and encourage respect for human rights and fundamental freedoms for all.

Sources: Preamble, paragraph 1, Resolution 60/251
on the Human Rights Council adopted by the
General Assembly on 15 March 2006.

The principles codified in Art. 2 of the Charter[136] constitute the basic foundational principles of the whole body of international law. The *Dumbarton Oaks Proposals* already listed most of the principles, with the exception of the principle that protects matters essentially within the domestic matters[137].

The seven principles of international law recognised by the UN Charter in its Art. 2 are the following: 1. Prohibition of the threat or use of force against the territorial integrity or political independence of any State; 2. Settlement of international disputes by peaceful means; 3. Prohibition to intervene in matters within the domestic jurisdiction of any State; 4. Cooperation among States; 5. Self-determination of peoples; 6. Sovereign equality of States and 7. The fulfilment in good faith of international obligations.

In the resolution 2625 (XXV) of 1970 on "Declaration on Principles of International Law concerning Friendly Relations and Co-operation among States in accordance with the Charter of the United Nations", the UNGA emphasized that "... the paramount importance of the Charter of the United Nations for the maintenance of international peace and security and that... the adoption of the Declaration...would contribute to the strengthening of world peace and constitute a landmark in the development of international law and of relations among States..."[138].

The relationship between the full respect of principles enshrined in Art. 2 of the UN Charter and the maintenance of peace and security as a purpose was reaffirmed in the Draft Declaration on Rights and Duties of States of 1949 elaborated by the International Law Commission as follows: "... primary purpose of the United Nations is to maintain international peace and security, and the reign of law and justice is essential to the realization of this purpose"[139].

Additionally, the promotion of human rights[140] and peace[141] are considered as essential purposes, whose realization should be jointly promoted by Member States of the United Nations in conjunction with the full respect of those principles included in the UN Charter. Therefore, the Charter is considered as the constitution of the international community[142]. It follows that all countries have included this perspective in both national constitutions and regional instruments.

3.1.5. *Human dignity as foundation of freedom, justice and peace*

Recalling also that the inherent dignity and of the equal and inalienable rights of all members of the human family is the foundation of freedom, justice and peace in the world.

Sources: Preamble, paragraph 1,
Universal Declaration of Human Rights.

In accordance with the first recital of the Preamble of the UDHR[143], those who want a world with freedom, peace and justice must recognize that all members of the human family have inherent dignity. The wanting of this peace does not make for or create these inherent rights, but that these rights are inherent and inalienable and that therefore, our recognition will help humankind bring the desired freedom, justice and peace in the world[144].

The first recital speaks of "inherent dignity" and of "inalienable rights", both of which phrases are closely linked to Enlightenment ways of thinking[145]. The drafters of the Declaration had an Enlightenment view of human rights "as somehow located in human beings simply by virtue of their own humanity and for no other extraneous reason"[146]. As indicated by René Cassin, the French representative, before the UNGA, "in common with the 1789 Declaration, (the Universal Declaration) was founded upon the great principles of liberty, equality and fraternity".

The UDHR proclaimed in its article 1 that "all human beings are born free and equal in dignity and rights. They are endowed with reason and conscience and should act towards one another in a spirit of brotherhood". The drafters wanted to stress that all members of the human family have inherent dignity because they are born with equal and inalienable rights. No person or political body gave these rights to human beings, because they were born with them. In addition, reason and conscience are the vehicles by which human beings should treat one another in brotherhood.

Article 1 was approved by the UNGA with 45 favourable votes and 9 abstentions. It affirms the existence of three main principles in international law, namely: liberty, equality and brotherhood. As stated by René Cassin, the Declaration had to incorporate the following principles: firstly, unity of the human race or of the human family; secondly, the idea that every human being has the right to be treated as every other human being and thirdly, the concept of solidarity or brotherhood among peoples[147].

In its judgment in *Furundzija*, the International Criminal Tribunal for the former Yugoslavia had recourse to the general principle of human dignity when providing a definition of rape as a crime against humanity. It held that the "General principle of respect for human dignity is the basic underpinning and indeed the very raison d'être of international humanitarian law and human rights law; indeed, in modern times it has become of such paramount importance as to permeate the whole body of international law. This principle is intended to shield human beings from outrages upon their personal dignity"[148].

Human dignity has become a ubiquitous idea and central concern of international law[149]. As a foundational norm within the United Nations, "human dignity served to signify that moral consensus, indeed universality, was a necessary response to the war's atrocities"[150]. The inclusion of human dignity in the contemporary international law is a response to the widespread revulsion of the horrors of the Second World War[151]. Therefore, it prohibits the worst excesses possible in war[152] and claims the observance of minimal standards of civil, political and social recognition[153]. Consequently, human dignity is a basic norm which "can be read as a reaction against pre-war sovereigntist conceptions of legality which allowed positive law to become the tool of crimes against humanity apparently without contradiction"[154].

Human dignity and human rights are closely connected, like the two sides of a coin. It is part of the core content of fundamental rights and the foundation for all truly fundamental rights. It also possesses a universalist ambition, representing the fabric that binds together the human family.

The *Vienna Declaration and Programme of Action* of 1993 recognised and affirmed that all human rights derive from dignity in the following terms:

"Recognizing and affirming that all human rights derive from the dignity and worth inherent in the human person, and that the human person is the central subject of human rights and fundamental freedoms, and consequently should be the principal beneficiary and should participate actively in the realization of these rights and freedoms"[155].

Human dignity has played an important role in several social and political movements that occurred in the 20th century. It has been shaped by the reaction against Nazi ideology, dictatorships and communism[156]. Therefore, it was not surprising that three of the main responsibles of the Second World War incorporated this concept in their national constitutions[157], or that it came to the fore with the fall of several dictatorships in Europe[158]. The most dramatic increase came in the 1990s following the fall of the Berlin Wall and the transition to democracy in central and Eastern Europe under the influence of Germany[159]. This latter country also played a major role in the drafting of the new South African constitution post-apartheid[160].

In addition, the term is featured in a wide range of declarations and treaties[161]. Human dignity has become a central and recurrent concept in the reasoning of supreme courts and constitutional courts throughout the world[162] and many domestic constitutions. All of them stated that "human dignity is not as an autonomous right, but instead as a legal principle with constitutional status"[163].

The *Declaration and Programme of Action on a Culture of Peace* adopted by the UNGA in 1999 recognised the importance of human dignity in the education process as follows: "Ensure that children, from an early age, benefit from education on the values, attitudes, modes of behaviour and ways of life to enable them to resolve any dispute peacefully and in a spirit of respect for human dignity and of tolerance and non-discrimination"[164].

In accordance with report *In Larger Freedom* prepared by Kofi Annan "All human beings have the right to be treated with dignity and respect... No security agenda and no drive for development will be successful unless they are based on the sure foundation of respect for human dignity"[165].

3.1.6. Disregard of human rights and breach of peace

Recalling that disregard and contempt for human rights have resulted in barbarous acts which have outraged the conscience of mankind.

Sources: Preamble, paragraph 2, Universal Declaration of Human Rights.

The second recital of the Preamble of the Universal Declaration of Human Rights stated that "Whereas disregard and contempt for human rights have resulted in barbarous acts which have outraged the conscience of mankind..." The experience of the Holocaust and the Second World War shocked the drafters in the elaboration of the whole Declaration, and in particular the drafting of this recital.

The ECOSOC held its first meeting in February 1946. It decided to begin to fulfil its human rights mandate by authorizing a preparatory group to be called the Nuclear Commission on Human Rights (hereinafter: CHR). That Commission met in April/May 1946. Mrs. Roosevelt was elected Chairman by acclamation[166].

Since the beginning of the Nuclear Commission, all governmental delegates recognized that the violation of human rights is one of the main causes of war. Mr. Henri Laugier, Assistant Secretary-General of Social Affairs, opened the first meeting as follows: "Ladies and gentlemen, it is a new thing and it is a great thing in the history of humanity that the international community organized after a war which destroyed material wealth and spiritual wealth accumulated by human effort during centuries has constituted an international mechanism to defend the human rights in the world".

Furthermore, he stated that "it is difficult to define the violation of human rights within a nation, which would constitute a menace to the security and peace of the world and the existence of which is sufficient to put in movement the mechanism of the United Nations for the maintenance of peace and security. However, if this machinery had existed a few years ago, if it had been powerful and if the universal support of the public opinion had give it authority, international action would have been mobilized against the first authors and supporters of fascism and Nazism"[167].

After, Mr. Laugier delivered other opening remarks, in which he stated that "the task of the Human Rights Commission amounted to following up in the field of peace the fight which free humanity had waged in the field of war, defending against all offensive attacks the rights and dignity of man, and establishing, upon the principles of the United Nations Charter a powerful international recognition of rights"[168].

In accordance with the Representative of the United Kingdom at the CHR "the establishment of human rights and fundamental freedoms as part of international law, with obligations on each state to observe and maintain them, is an essential safeguard against the danger of war"[169].

As to the relationship between war, human rights and peace, Mr. Malik (Lebanon) stated that the promotion of respect for human rights was closely linked to the maintenance of peace and security. It follows that "the violation of human rights was one of the causes of war, and, if the first aim of the United Nations was to be attained, the observance of human rights must be guaranteed"[170].

3.1.7. Social and international order

Recalling in particular that everyone is entitled to a social and international order in which the rights and freedoms set forth in the Universal Declaration of Human Rights can be fully realized.

Sources: Art. 28, Universal Declaration of Human Rights.

While articles 3 to 27 enumerate the catalogues of rights contained in the UDHR, article 1 provides its foundation in connection implicitly with the right to life[171] and article 28 its ultimate or utopian aspiration[172]. Art. 28 requires that "social and international conditions be so structured as to make possible the equal enjoyment throughout the world of all the rights listed"[173]. This provision refers to the transformation of ideals into normative standards. Therefore, the rights contained in the Declaration constitute an integrated, interdependent, and to a large extent, indivisible normative system of rights[174].

The conception of human rights and freedoms contained in article 28 was firstly presented by the then President of the United States,

Franklin D. Roosevelt in his "Four Freedoms"[175] speech delivered before the Congress on 6 January 1941: "In the future days, which we seek to make secure, we look forward to a world founded upon four essential human freedoms...".

Art. 28 corresponds to the vision of peace, freedom and human rights underlying the creation of the United Nations. In particular, Art. 55 of the UN Charter states that ".... to achieve international co-operation in solving international problems of an economic, social, cultural or humanitarian character, and in promoting and encouraging respect for human rights and/or fundamental freedoms for all without distinction as to race, sex, language, or religion".

In addition, to move forward a social and international order in which the rights and freedoms contained in the Declaration can be fully realized, it is necessary to advance in an increasingly peaceful and co-operative world. This requires a link between the three main purposes of the organization as set out in article 1 of the Charter, namely: maintenance and advancement of peace, international co-operation in the solution of economic, social, humanitarian and cultural problems, and the promotion of human rights for all[176].

As indicated by Prof. Eide, "some might say that article 28 is a utopian aspiration. It is preferable, however, to see it as a vision to be pursued with determination, while taking into account that it will only gradually and partially be achieved in practice ... Art. 28 deals with the process of realization. To clarify this concept, some words may be required on the three stages which human rights concerns traverse: idealization, positivization and realization"[177].

On several occasions, the UNGA has stated that the codification of the rules of international law and their progressive development would assist in promoting the "purposes and principles" of the Charter of the United Nations. In particular, the UNGA resolution 1505 (XV) on the *Future work in the field of the codification and progressive development of international law* stated that: "the conditions prevailing in the world today give increased importance to the role of international law ... in strengthening international peace, developing friendly and co-operative relations among the nations, settling disputes by peaceful means and advancing economic and social progress throughout the world"[178].

The UNGA reaffirmed in its resolution 54/27 of 19 January 2000[179] on the *outcome of the action dedicated to the 1999 centennial of the first International Peace Conference*, the commitment of the United Nations and its Member States to the adherence to, and the development of international law as a basis for conducting international relations. Furthermore, for a number of years, the UNGA has reiterated its conviction that peaceful settlement of disputes and the progressive elaboration of international law constitute one of the foundation stones of the rule of law and a clear means to also establish a just and lasting peace all over the world[180].

3.1.8. All human rights are universal, indivisible, interrelated, interdependent and mutually reinforcing

Recalling that the Vienna Declaration on Human Rights stated that all human rights are universal, indivisible, interrelated, interdependent and mutually reinforcing, and that all human rights must be treated in a fair and equal manner, on the same footing and with the same emphasis.

Sources: Part. I, Art. 5, Vienna Declaration and Programme of Action on Human Rights.

The Vienna Declaration and Programme of Action emphasizes that all human rights are of equal importance, seeking to end the qualitative division between civil and political rights and economic, social and cultural rights, which was pronounced during the Cold War era. Part I, para 5 states that "All human rights are universal, indivisible and interdependent and interrelated. The international community must treat human rights globally in a fair and equal manner, on the same footing, and with the same emphasis. While the significance of national and regional particularities and various historical, cultural and religious backgrounds must be borne in mind, it is the duty of States, regardless of their political, economic and cultural systems, to promote and protect all human rights and fundamental freedoms." This phrase is also cited by Declaration of Montreal as well as The Yogyakarta Principles[181] and the Convention on the Rights of Persons with Disabilities[182]. To this end, Part II, para. 75 also encourages the Commission on Human Rights, in accordance with the Committee on Economic, Social and Cultural Rights, to continue the examination of Optional Protocol to the International Covenant on Economic, Social and Cultural Rights on equal basis of the Optional Protocols to the International Covenant on Civil and Political Rights.

3.1.9. Pillars of the United Nations system

Recalling that peace and security, development and human rights are the pillars of the United Nations system and the foundations for collective security and well-being, and recognizing that development, peace and security and human rights are interlinked and mutually reinforcing.

Sources: Art. 72, World Summit Outcome Document, Doc. 60/1, General Assembly, 24 October 2005.

The resolution which created the Human Rights Council acknowledged in its Preamble that "... peace and security, development and human rights are the pillars of the United Nations system and the foundations for collective security and well-being, and recognizing that development, peace and security and human rights are interlinked and mutually reinforcing"[183].

As indicated by the Human Rights Committee, the strengthening of international peace constitutes the most important condition and guarantee for the safeguarding of the right to life. It follows that as stated by the CHR, the safeguarding of this foremost right is an essential condition for the enjoyment of the entire range of economic, social and cultural, as well as civil and political rights. In addition, it should be noted that the right to life requires that the three main pillars of the United Nations (i.e. peace, human rights and development) are fully respected in order to achieve better conditions of life.

The linkage between life and the three pillars of the United Nations as a preventive measure to avoid war and armed conflict was elaborated in the Constitutions of the UN Specialized Agencies (i.e. ILO[184], FAO[185], WHO[186] and UNESCO[187]); the 2000 UN Millennium Declaration[188] and the 2005 World Summit Outcome Document; the Security Council resolutions 1325 (2000), 1820 (2008), 1888 and 1889 (2009) on women, peace and security. Additionally, this linkage was included in several peace movements and ideas that have marked over the history of humankind (i.e. the 1999 Hague Agenda for Peace and Justice for the Twenty-first Century; the 2000 Earth Charter; and the 2010 Universal Declaration of the Rights of Mother Earth).

The final outcome document of the International Conference on the Relationship between disarmament and development[189] concluded that true and lasting peace and security in this interdependent world demand rapid progress in both disarmament and development, since they are the most urgent challenges facing the world today and the pillars on which should be built enduring international peace and security.

3.1.10. Poverty, development and peace

Recalling the world commitment to eradicate poverty and promote sustained economic growth, sustainable development and global prosperity for all.

Sources: Art. 17, World Summit Outcome Document, Doc. 60/1,
General Assembly, 24 October 2005.

Several declarations and instruments support the relationship between development and peace, for instance, the Millennium Declaration[190], the Declaration on the Right to Development[191] and the 2005 World Summit Outcome Document[192]. In addition, a transformed partnership based on equality between women and men is needed as a condition for people-centred sustainable development and world peace[193]. In addition, the role played by men and boys in advancing gender equality is vital[194].

In accordance with the resolution 7/4 of 2008 the HRC decided to create the mandate of the independent expert on the effects of foreign debt and other related international financial obligations of States on the full enjoyment of all human rights, particularly economic, social and cultural rights. It was adopted by a recorded vote of 34 in favour[195] to 13 against[196].

The World Conference on Human Rights held in Vienna in 1993 reaffirmed "the right to development, as established in the Declaration on the Right to Development, as a universal and inalienable right and an integral part of fundamental human rights. As stated in the Declaration on the Right to Development, the human person is the central subject of development. While development facilitates the enjoyment of all human rights, the lack of development may not be invoked to justify the abridgement of internationally recognized human rights. States should cooperate with each other in ensuring development and eliminating obstacles to development. The international community should promote an effective international cooperation for the realization of the right to development and the elimination of obstacles to development. Lasting progress towards the implementation of the right to development requires effective development policies at the national level, as well as equitable economic relations and a favourable economic environment at the international level"[197].

Additionally, the Declaration and Programme of Action of Vienna focused the implementation of the right to development on the least developed countries[198] and particular groups of people, such as women[199], indigenous people[200], minorities[201] and children[202].

In accordance with the UNESCO transdisciplinary project entitled "Towards a culture of peace" of 1996, "Development is the most secure basis for peace", as "without development, there is no prospect for lasting peace". Sustainability of development is only possible in a framework of justice and freedom of expression. It requires the "intellectual and moral solidarity of mankind", as phrased in the Constitution of UNESCO. Reciprocally, peace is a fundamental dimension of development as there is no development without stability and security. Development must preserve the environment in a "true partnership... between humanity and nature"[203].

The *Declaration and Programme of Action on a Culture of Peace* proclaimed that development is part of the culture of peace: "a culture of peace is a set of values, attitudes, traditions and modes of behaviour and ways of life based on ... (f) Respect for and promotion of the right to development"[204]. Additionally, the Declaration and Programme of Action proposed some specific actions to promote sustainable economic and social development (i.e. eradicate poverty, reduce inequalities, external debt, food security, full participation, women and children, post-conflict situation, preservation of natural resources and self-determination).

Development, peace, security and human rights are mutually reinforcing and peace and justice encompass an economic dimension in accordance with the 1974 Universal Declaration on the Eradication of Hunger and Malnutrition[205], and the 2005 Outcome World Summit Document[206]. In addition, it should be recalled the UN Secretary-General reports entitled "An agenda for peace. Preventive diplomacy, peacemaking and peace-keeping" of 1992[207] and "In Larger Freedom: Towards Development, Security and Human Rights for All" of 2005[208].

Additionally, it should be recalled that the concept of human security is closed linked with the right life. In particular, the Universal Declaration on the Eradication of Hunger and Malnutrition[209] and the Outcome World Summit Document[210] recognized it in connection with the fight against poverty.

The *World Conference on Human Rights* expressed "its dismay and condemnation that gross and systematic violations and situations that constitute serious obstacles to the full enjoyment of all human rights continue to occur in different parts of the world. Such violations and obstacles include ... poverty, hunger and other denials of economic, social and cultural rights ..."[211].

Additionally, the *Declaration and Programme of Action on a Culture of Peace* recognised that the eradication of poverty is close linked to a culture of peace as follows: "The fuller development of a culture of peace is integrally linked to: ... (f) Eradicating poverty and illiteracy and reducing inequalities within and among nations"[212]and on the actions to promote sustainable economic and social development it stressed the following: "(a) Undertake comprehensive actions on the basis of appropriate strategies and agreed targets to eradicate poverty through national and international efforts, including through international cooperation"[213].

3.1.11. Women and peace

Recalling that the full and complete development of a country, the welfare of the world and the cause of peace require the maximum participation of women on equal terms with men in all fields.

> Sources: Preamble, paragraph 12, Convention on the Elimination of All Forms of Discrimination against Women (CEDAW).

In the 2005 World Summit Outcome the UNGA acknowledged that peace and security, development and human rights were the foundations for collective security and well-being. Moreover, peace and respect for human rights, along with the right to the rule of law and gender equality, among others, were interlinked and mutually reinforcing[214].

A transformed partnership based on equality between women and men is needed as a condition for people-centred sustainable development and world peace[215]. In addition, the role played by men and boys in advancing gender equality is vital[216].

Although the relationship between gender and disarmament is not immediately apparent, gender mainstreaming represents a different approach to the traditionally complex and politically sensitive fields of security, disarmament, non-proliferation and arms control[217]. The Beijing Declaration and Platform for Action stated that full participation of women in decision-making, conflict prevention and resolution and any other peace initiative is essential to the realization of lasting peace[218]. Besides, Security Council resolution 1325 (2000) on women, peace and security, recognized gender mainstreaming as a major global strategy to promote gender equality by indicating that "all those involved in the planning for disarmament, demobilization and reintegration should consider the different needs of female and male ex-combatants".

3.1.12. The role of human rights in the prevention of armed conflicts

Recalling the importance of prevention of armed conflict in accordance with the purposes and principles of the Charter and the commitment to promote a culture of prevention of armed conflict as a means of effectively addressing the interconnected security and development challenges faced by peoples throughout the world.

Sources: Art. 74, World Summit Outcome Document, Doc. 60/1, General Assembly, 24 October 2005.

On 31 January 1992, the first ever Summit Meeting of the Security Council was convened at the Headquarters of the United Nations in New York. Thirteen of the fifteen Heads of State and Government members of the Council attended the Summit.

As indicated by Boutros Boutros-Ghali, former Secretary-General of the United Nations, in his report on the Agenda for Peace, "the January 1992 Summit therefore represented an unprecedented recommitment, at the highest level, to the Purposes and Principles of the Charter"[219]. He also stressed that the sources of conflict and war are pervasive and deep and that to eliminate them will require efforts to enhance respect of human rights and fundamental freedoms and also to promote the sustainable economic and social development for wider prosperity[220].

Pursuant to the UNGA resolution 47/120 on an Agenda for peace: preventive diplomacy and related matters of 1993, the building of peace and security can be only construed within the United Nations in an integrated manner:

> "... international peace and security must be seen in an integrated manner and that the efforts of the Organization to build peace, justice, stability and security must encompass not only military matters, but also, through its various organs within their respective areas of competence, relevant political, economic, social, humanitarian, environmental and developmental aspects"[221].

The former Secretary-General of the United Nations highlighted that the United Nations was created with a great and courageous vision. According to him, now is the time, for its nations and peoples, to seize the moment for the sake of the future[222].

Armed conflicts continue to bring fear and horror to humanity. Since the creation of the United Nations in 1945 until 1992, over 100 major conflicts have left some 20 million dead. In order to prevent, contain and bring conflicts to an end, the international community should respect —among other measures— the foundation stones of the United Nations, such as the principles of sovereignty and integrity of States and the full respect of human rights for all. In addition, Member States should bring their attention to the deepest causes of conflicts (i.e. economic despair and social injustice) as a means to prevent and resolve conflicts and preserve the universal peace in the world[223].

In the supplement document to an Agenda for Peace of 1995, the Secretary-General of the United Nations stressed that "... demilitarization, the control of small arms, institutional reform, improved police and judicial systems, the monitoring of human rights, electoral reform and social and economic development can be as valuable in preventing conflict as in healing the wounds after conflict has occurred"[224].

The Preamble of the UN Charter states that the cardinal mission of the United Nations remains "... to save succeeding generations from the scourge of war". Additionally, as set forth in its Art. 1, paragraph 1, Member States are obligated "to take effective collective measures for the prevention and removal of threats to the peace...".

As indicated in the report on Prevention of Armed Conflict of 2001, the Secretary General stressed that the Charter provides the United Nations with a strong mandate for preventing armed conflict. He added that the prevention is more desirable to ensure lasting peace and security than trying to stop it or alleviate its symptoms. It follows that conflict prevention becomes the cornerstone of the UN collective security system[225].

A new approach to the concept of peace has emerged in recent years because it has included a broader focus on the nature of sustainable peace, such as social and economic development, good governance and democratization, the rule of law and respect of human rights. The Secretary-General also stated that in the twenty-first century, collective security should imply an obligation to address tensions, grievances, inequality, injustice, intolerance and hostilities at the earliest stage possible, before the conflict erupts. He also indicated that this understanding brings the United Nations back to its roots due to the Charter, and in particular Art. 55[226], creates the basis for elaborating a more comprehensive and long-term approach to conflict prevention[227].

Both the United Nations Millennium Declaration adopted by the UNGA in its resolution 55/2[228] and the resolution 1318 (2000) adopted by the Security Council[229] recognized the vital role of all parts of the United Nations system in conflict prevention, peaceful resolution of disputes, peacekeeping, post-conflict peace-building and reconstruction and also pledged to enhance the effectiveness of the United Nations in this field. Furthermore, in its resolution 53/243 on the Declaration and Programme of Action on a Culture of Peace, the UNGA calls upon Member States, civil society and the whole United Nations system to promote activities related to conflict prevention[230].

As recognised by the Secretary General, the promotion and protection of all human rights is an important legal tool aimed at preventing armed conflicts in the world:

> "Sustainable and long-term prevention of armed conflict must include a focus on strengthening respect for human rights and addressing core issues of human rights violations, wherever these occur. Efforts to prevent armed conflict should promote a broad range of human rights, including not only civil and political rights but also economic, social and cultural rights, including the right to development"[231].

On 18 July 2003, the UNGA adopted upon consensus the resolution 57/337 on prevention of armed conflict, by which it recognized that "the need for mainstreaming and coordinating the prevention of armed conflict throughout the United Nations system, and calls upon all its relevant organs, organizations and bodies to consider, in accordance with their respective mandates, how they could best include a conflict prevention perspective in their activities"[232].

3.1.13. The role of Human Rights Council in the prevention of human rights violations

Recalling that the Human Rights Council shall contribute, through dialogue and cooperation, towards the prevention of human rights violations and respond promptly to human rights emergencies.

Sources: Art. 5, paragraph f, Resolution 60/251 on the Human Rights Council adopted by the General Assembly on 15 March 2006.

The *Vienna Declaration and Programme of Action* included a provision in which the Conference on Human Rights calls upon the UN Centre for Human Rights to provide technical assistance and qualified expertise in the field of prevention and resolution of disputes[233]. *Afterwards, in its resolution 48/141 of 1993, the* UNGA *requested the Office of the United Nations High Commissioner for Human Rights to play an active role in* removing the current obstacles and in meeting the challenges to the full realization of all human rights and in preventing the continuation of human rights violations throughout the world[234].

In the report on the *Follow-up to the World Conference on Human Rights* presented before the CHR, the High Commissioner stressed the importance of strengthening preventive strategies in many different areas of human rights (i.e. genocide, racism and racial discrimination, development, civil and political rights, slavery, impunity, women and children). In its concluding observations, the High Commissioner stated that "... the universal implementation of human rights, economic, social and cultural as well as civil and political, is the surest preventive strategy and the most effective way of avoiding the emergence of conflict"[235].

Among the possible preventive measures in the field of human rights, the High Commissioner highlighted the following: urgent appeals by special Rapporteurs and thematic mechanisms; requests by treaty bodies for emergency reports; the indication of interim measures of protection under petition procedures for which treaty bodies are responsible; the urgent dispatch of personal envoys of the Secretary-General, the High Commissioner for Human Rights, or of other organizations; the urgent dispatch of human rights and humanitarian observers or fact-finders; the establishment of international courts; and proposals for the establishment of a rapid reaction force[236].

The special procedures of the Council are a useful way "...to monitor the human rights situation in the countries and take all action to avoid a repetition of past patterns when conflicts ravaging a country have made international headlines, only to be forgotten until a new crisis emerges"[237]. Human rights violations are often a root cause of conflict and human rights are always an indispensable element in achieving peace and reconciliation. It follows that the failure to adequately address the root causes of the conflict will risk leading to further outbreaks of large-scale violence[238]. The priority of the special procedures is that the interests of justice are served and to assist in ensuring that all human rights are protected[239].

By virtue of their independence and the nature of their mandates, the different mandate holders are "well placed to function as early warning mechanisms, as alarm bells," according to the High Commissioner for Human

Rights, Navi Pillay[240]. Since those special procedures cover all types of human rights, they are able to help defuse tensions at an early stage. The mandates focus on specific situations and make recommendations to governments to address problems, wherever they occur in the world.

Finally, on 21 February 2014, the UNGA adopted *upon consensus* the resolution 68/160 on enhancement of international cooperation in the field of human rights, by *which* considered that "international cooperation in the field of human rights, in conformity with the purposes and principles set out in the Charter of the United Nations and international law, should make an effective and practical contribution to the urgent task of preventing violations of human rights and fundamental freedoms"[241].

3.1.14. The linkage between education and peace

Recalling also that the wide diffusion of culture, and the education of humanity for justice and liberty and peace are indispensable to the dignity of man and constitute a sacred duty which all the nations must fulfil in a spirit of mutual assistance and concern.

Sources: Preamble, paragraph 4, Constitution of UNESCO.

The right to education on peace and human rights is deeply rooted in international human rights instruments (i.e. the Universal Declaration of Human Rights[242], the UN Convention on the Rights of the Child[243], the ICESCR[244]) and the Declaration on the Preparation of Societies for Life in Peace[245]. At the regional level, reference should be made to the 2000 Dakar Framework for Action, Education for All[246] and the Protocol of San Salvador on Economic, Social and Cultural Rights[247].

As stated by the former Special Rapporteur on the Right to Education, gender inequality and other forms of social, religious, ethnic and racial discrimination impede social mobility and impact negatively on the full realization of all human rights, including development, peace and security[248].

The World Conference on Human Rights held in 1993 in Vienna reaffirmed that States are duty-bound "… to ensure that education is aimed at strengthening the respect of human rights and fundamental freedoms …"[249] and emphasized "… the importance of incorporating the subject of human rights education programmes and calls upon States to do so. Education should promote understanding, tolerance, peace and friendly relations between the nations and all racial or religious groups and encourage the development of United Nations activities in pursuance of these objectives. Therefore, education on human rights and the dissemination of proper information, both theoretical and practical, play an important role in the promotion and respect of human rights…"[250].

Additionally, the Declaration and Programme of Action of Vienna emphasized the obligation to facilitate access to education for people with disabilities[251], vulnerable groups – in particular migrant workers–[252] and women[253]. As to the human rights education, the Declaration should promote the values of peace, social justice, democracy, tolerance and development[254].

In accordance with the UNESCO transdisciplinary project entitled "Towards a culture of peace" of 1996, "Education, seen broadly, is the most important process by which people gain the values, attitudes and behaviours of a culture of peace…"[255].

The *Declaration and Programme of Action on a Culture of Peace* recognised education as a part of the culture of peace: "education at all levels is one of the principal means to build a culture of peace. In this context, human rights education is of particular importance"[256]. In addition, it identifies specific actions to promote the culture of peace through education (i.e. international cooperation, children, women, curricula, dialogue, conflict prevention and higher education).

3.1.15. Education and training on human rights

Recalling the United Nations Declaration on Human Rights Education and Training, which proclaimed that everyone has the right to know, seek and receive information about all human rights and fundamental freedoms and should have access to human rights education and training.

> Sources: Art. 1, United Nations Declaration on
> Human Rights Education and Training.

The Preamble of the Declaration indicates that "… everyone has the right to education, and that education shall be directed to the full development of the human personality and the sense of its dignity, enable all persons to participate effectively in a free society and promote understanding, tolerance and friendship among all nations and all racial, ethnic or religious groups, and further the activities of the United Nations for the maintenance of peace, security and the promotion of development and human rights".

3.1.16. The relationship between culture of peace
and human rights

Recalling the Declaration and Programme of Action on a Culture of Peace, which recognized that culture of peace is a set of values, attitudes, traditions and modes of behaviour and ways of life based on, among others, the full respect for and promotion of all human rights and fundamental freedoms.

> Sources: Art. 1(c), Declaration and Programme of
> Action on Culture of Peace.

The *Declaration on a Culture of Peace* clearly defines a culture of peace as a set of values, attitudes, traditions and modes of behaviour and ways of life, which is based on some elements, and also indicates that its full development is integrally linked to several important fields. Moreover, it identifies the main actors responsible to implement the Declaration and the role played by education in the construction of a culture of peace.

Pursuant to UNGA resolution 56/5 on the International Decade for a Culture of Peace and Non-Violence for the Children of the World (2001–2010), proclaimed in Assembly resolution 53/2, the Secretary-General transmitted in July a report of the UNESCO Director-General covering implementation of the Programme of Action.

The report identified the eight areas of the *Programme of Action*: fostering a culture of peace through education; promotion of sustainable economic and social development; respect for all human rights; equality between men and women; democratic participation; understanding, tolerance and solidarity; participatory communication and the free flow of information and knowledge; and international peace and security. Regarding formal and non-formal education for a culture of peace, the report recommended a coordinated effort by specialized agencies and UN funds and programmes, with a view to developing a comprehensive strategy for the Decade. It proposed inviting civil society to adopt a distinct programme of activities along the same lines as those undertaken by NGOs in consultative status with UNESCO, which had adopted a Plan of Action for the Decade and invited their members to implement it through national and local branches[257].

3.1.17. *Elimination of war and armed violence*

Solemnly invites all stakeholders to guide themselves in their activities by recognizing the supreme importance of practicing tolerance, dialogue, cooperation and solidarity among all stakeholders as a means to promote world peace through human rights and to end, reduce and prevent progressively war and armed violence, in particular, by observing the following.

> Sources: this provision describes some possible means
> aimed at enhancing human rights law with the
> purpose of ending conflicts.

In accordance to the Preamble of resolution 60/251 of the HRC, development, peace and security and human rights are interlinked and mutually reinforcing[258]. However, the UNGA clearly decided that the Council should address situations of gross and systematic violations of human rights[259] and also contribute, through dialogue and cooperation, towards the prevention of human rights violations and respond promptly to human rights emergencies[260].

Because of human rights violations in conflict situation, the HRC has convened several special sessions at the request of one third of the membership of the Council[261]. Most of these sessions have finished with the adoption upon consensus of a resolution, by which the Council decided to dispatch a Fact-Finding Mission or independent commission of inquiry with the mandate to assess the human rights situation in the specific country in conflict. These missions are usually comprised by one or several highly qualified persons, whose are appointed by the President of the HRC after consulting with the members of the Council.

In particular, the HRC has created upon consensus in its special sessions some human rights mechanisms to monitor the implementation of the respective resolutions in Darfur[262], Myanmar[263], Democratic Republic of the Congo[264], Cote d'Ivoire[265], Libyan Arab Jamahiriya[266] and Central African Republic[267].

The positive added value of the HRC, and in particular its special sessions, is to focus on those who truly suffer in a conflict: human beings and people. It is a forum for dialogue, not confrontation, which always works, by and for the victims[268]. Its primary objective is to safeguard the human rights of all persons[269] and to address the desperate human rights crisis[270]. It follows that the obligation of the Council is to respond, examine, denounce, intervene and react to egregious human rights violations in concert with other UN bodies, putting an immediate end to ongoing violence[271] and finding a peaceful and durable solution to the specific conflict[272]. Furthermore, it is imperative of the Council to have a greater understanding of the causes and consequences of conflict in order to decrease and alleviate the suffering of victims[273] through the adoption of particular recommendations[274].

On the other hand, the Security Council is the only competent body to determine the existence of any threat to the peace, breach of the peace, or act of aggression and to make recommendations, or decide what measures to be taken[275]. Although the Security Council has recognised the increasing linkage between human rights and peace and security, the operative section of resolutions in Darfur[276], Democratic Republic of the Congo[277], Cote d'Ivoire[278], Libyan Arab Jamahiriya[279] and Central African Republic[280] has not focused on specific matters of human rights, with the exception of a reference to the obligation of States to protect women and children in armed conflict, or even the population in general. The main purpose of the above resolutions is to make a call for all parties to the conflict to end violence, strengthen dialogue, sign a peace agreement, foster a transition process or create humanitarian corridors to assist population.

As indicated by the HRC, in a context of war and armed conflict, there is always a gross and systematic violation of all human rights and fundamental freedoms, including extrajudicial killings, summary executions, sexual violence, looting, forced displacement, large-scale of arrest, abductions, forced recruitment of children, beatings, disappearance, torture, arbitrary detention, forced labour practices or lack of fundamental economic rights (i.e. food, water, medicines). In particular, the right to life and security of people and their fundamental dignity is always under threat, even violated, in this type of dreadful situation. To achieve a genuine peace and stability, the country in conflict should firstly immediately cease all type of violence (i.e. cease-fire). Secondly, States should re-establish again the full respect and implementation of fundamental rights and freedom and thirdly, to identify the most appropriate solutions for a peaceful settlement of the crisis and to promote a national dialogue and reconciliation.

Additionally, the HRC has stressed that the roots of conflicts which have recently shaken some specific countries, where population live below poverty, are not new. In accordance with the statements delivered by the different stakeholders during the Special Sessions, States should apply long-term strategies for development, reduce poverty, finish with the impunity/rule of law and strengthen international cooperation with the human rights mechanism and among nations in order to reduce the cycle of violence and consolidate universal peace.

3.2. Operative Part

3.2.1. Right to live in peace, human rights and development

Everyone is entitled to the promotion, protection and respect for all human rights and fundamental freedoms, in particular the right to life, in a context in which all human rights, peace and development are fully implemented.

> Sources: This language is the proposal by the Chairperson-Rapporteur
> to add value to the draft Declaration. There exists a
> consensus in the recognition of the right to life.

The right to life as a fundamental and universal human right of everyone has been spelled out in the UDHR[281], ICCPR[282], the African Charter on Human and Peoples' Rights (ACHPR)[283], the European Convention on Human Right (ECHR)[284] and the American Convention on Human Rights (ACHR)[285]. In accordance with these legal provisions, States Parties are expressly obligated to protect the right to life by law and to take positive measures to ensure it.

The right to life has properly been characterized as the supreme human right, since without effective guarantee of this right, all other rights of the human being would be devoid of meaning[286]. Since the right to life is non-derogable right in accordance with Art. 4(2) of the ICCPR[287], it may never be suspended in time of public emergency which threatens the life of the nation. In addition, the right to life has been deemed *ius cogens* under international law[288].

The Human Rights Committee has issued two General Comments interpreting the content of Art. 6 on the right to life contained in the ICCPR. Both comments focus on the duty of States to prevent mass violence such as war and emphasize the duty of States to adopt positive measures to protect the right to life[289].

In the first of these General Comments, adopted on 27 July 1982 (16th session), the Committee pointed out that: "… every effort they make to avert the danger of war, especially thermonuclear war, and to strengthen international peace and security would constitute the most important condition and guarantee for the safeguarding of the right to life…"[290]. In its second General Comment, adopted on 2 November 1984 (23rd session), the Committee, after expressing its concern by the toll of human life taken by conventional weapons in armed conflicts, noted that: "… the very existence and gravity of this threat (nuclear weapons) generates a climate of suspicion and fear between States, which is in itself antagonistic to the promotion of universal respect for and observance of human rights and fundamental freedoms in accordance with the Charter of the United Nations and the International Covenants on Human Rights"[291].

This latter General Comment met with vehement criticism in the Social, Humanitarian Cultural Affairs Committee (GA Third Committee) because of the big opposition coming from Western States. Committee members Ermacora and Errera stated that the demand that the production and possession of nuclear weapons be recognized as crimes against humanity exceeds the Committee's competence. On the other hand, other members Opsahl, Coté-Harper, Dimitrijevic and Tomuschat considered that "the Committee should take care not to undermine its own authority as the most important quasi-judicial organ of human rights protection within the framework of the United Nations by making political decisions in the area of "soft" international law"[292].

As to the inter-relationship between the right to life and other human rights, including the enabling right to peace, energy is sometimes unnecessarily spent on the question of which should come first – either right to life or right to peace, or vice versa –. About the position regarding the inter-relationship between both rights appears to have been correctly stated in the Preamble to the UDHR, namely that "Whereas recognition of the inherent dignity and of the equal and inalienable rights of all members of the human family is the foundation of freedom, justice and peace in the world". Therefore, the enabling right to peace would seem to be a derivative of the right to life rather than vice versa. It follows that the right to life is not only the legal foundation for other rights, but also an integral part of all the rights which are essential to guarantee a better life for all human beings.

Consequently, this perspective was used in the adoption of the "Istanbul Declaration" by the Red Cross in its Twenty-first International Conference held in 1969 in the following terms[293]: "*Man has a right to enjoy lasting peace, that it is essential for him to be able to have a full and satisfactory life founded on respect of his rights and of his fundamental liberty*"[294].

In accordance with the operative section of the resolution 60/251, the mandate of the HRC is to promote and protect human rights, but not directly peace. It follows that peace should be elaborated in light of some fundamental human right, which has already been recognised by the international community as a whole, such as the right to life.

The right to life in peace is more linked to human rights than the so called right to peace in both its individual and collective dimension. It follows that the linkage between the right to life and peace could be much more acceptable for all countries. Therefore, instead of re-creating new rights without the necessary consensus or unanimity, the international community should progressively elaborate existing and already consolidated rights in international law in the line of the Commonwealth experience. As indicated previously, the linkage between the right to life and peace was unanimously recognised in Art. 1 of the *Declaration on the Preparation of Societies for Life in Peace*.

The added value of the new Declaration is not only to recall again the linkage between the right to life and peace, but also to elaborate the right to life in connection to peace, including also human rights and development, which has not still elaborated in international law. The United Nations does not need to re-invent the wheel, but only to strengthen the right to life linked to peace, human rights and development. Therefore, the recognition of the right to life and the affirmation of the right to live in peace, human rights and development are intended to ensure that the authorities take measures to guarantee that life may be lived in a natural and dignified manner and that the individual has every possible means for this purpose. The elaboration of the right to life in this direction would help to further develop the right of everyone to live in a context in which the three pillars of the United Nations is fully respected. In fact, the right to live in peace is a holistic concept which goes beyond the strict absence of armed conflicts. It is also positive, since it is linked to the eradication of structural violence as a result of the economic and social inequalities in the world and to the effective respect for all human rights without discrimination.

The elaboration of the right to live in a context of peace, human rights and development will surely contribute to the strengthening of international cooperation and multilateralism and will also influence the current objectives of the United Nations and Commonwealth as a fundamental step towards the promotion of peace, tolerance, friendship and brotherhood among all peoples.

3.2.2. *Principles of international law derived from the notion of human dignity*

States should enhance the principles of freedom from fear and want, equality and non-discrimination and justice and rule of law as a means to build peace within societies. In this regard, States should undertake measures to bring about, maintain and enhance conditions of peace to benefit people in need, particularly in situations of humanitarian crisis.

Human dignity can be divided into three components: "*intrinsic values*, which identify the special status of human beings in the world; *autonomy*, which expresses the right of every person, as a moral being and as free and equal individual, to make decisions and pursue his own idea of the good life; and *community value*, conventionally defined as the legitimate state and social interference in the determination of the boundaries of personal autonomy"[295].

3.2.2.1. *Intrinsic values*

As to the *intrinsic values* of human dignity, it should be noted that intrinsic value is the origin of a set of fundamental rights. The first of these rights is the right to life, a basic pre-condition for the enjoyment of any other right. Another right related to intrinsic value is equality before and under the law. This means not being discriminated against due to race, colour, ethnic or national origin, sex or age. The last fundamental right is the right to integrity, both physical and mental[296].

Respect for the integrity of the person requires states to protect the right to life and respect the prohibition of torture and ill-treatment. The rights to integrity are of utmost importance. This is reflected by the fact that unlike some other rights which contain clauses permitting their restriction on grounds such as the need to maintain public order it is never possible to justify restrictions to these rights. A second important attribute of the rights to integrity is that they cannot be derogated in time of public emergency. The right to life and its linkage to peace have been already dealt in the section 3.4.

Equality and non-discrimination are held to be positive and negative statements of the same principle. One is treated equally when one is not discriminated against and one is discriminated against when one is not treated equally[297]. Equality and non-discrimination are better understood as distinct norms that are in creative tension with each other than subsumed under the human rights concept. This is founded in equal moral status and equal moral status is realized through individual human rights[298]. As principle, it is never defined in a single and uniform fashion.

In his dissenting opinion to the ICJ judgment in the South West African Cases, Judge Tanaka undertook to examine whether the legal principles of non-discrimination and equality, denying apartheid, can be recognized as general principles. He came to maintain the position that

> "The principle of equality before the law, however, is stipulated in the list of human rights recognized by the municipal system of virtually every state no matter whether the form of government be republican or monarchical and in spite of any differences in the degree of precision of the relevant provision. This principle has become an integral part of the constitutions of most civilized countries of the world"[299].

The principles of 'elementary considerations of humanity', 'human dignity' and 'equality before the law' have considerably broadened the scope of human rights law and its link with other fields of written und unwritten international law[300].

The *Vienna Declaration and Programme of Action* of 1993 recognised the concept of equality as a principle of international law in the following terms:

> "Considering the major changes taking place on the international scene and the aspirations of all the peoples for an international order based on the principles enshrined in the Charter of the United Nations, including promoting and encouraging respect for human rights and fundamental freedoms for all and respect for the principle of equal rights and self-determination of peoples, peace, democracy, justice, equality, rule of law, pluralism, development, better standards of living and solidarity"[301].

The *Declaration and Programme of Action on a Culture of Peace* adopted by the UNGA in 1999 recognised the importance of equality between men and women as follows: "Actions to ensure equality between women and men..."[302] and the non-discrimination principle in connection with education: "Ensure that children, from an early age, benefit from education on the values, attitudes, modes of behaviour and ways of life to enable them to resolve any dispute peacefully and in a spirit of respect for human dignity and of tolerance and non-discrimination"[303].

The *World Summit Outcome document* considered equality as a fundamental value in international relations in the following terms: "we reaffirm that our common fundamental values, including freedom, equality, solidarity, tolerance, respect for all human rights, respect for nature and shared responsibility, are essential to international relations" and "we are determined to establish a just and lasting peace all over the world in accordance with the purposes and principles of the Charter. We rededicate ourselves to support all efforts to uphold the sovereign equality of all States…"[304].

3.2.2.2. Autonomy

The idea of autonomy in the human dignity is the concept of existential minimum, also referred to as social minimum or freedom from want, or the basic right to the provision of adequate living conditions. This requires access to some essential utilities, such as basic education and health services, as well as some elementary necessities, such as food, water, clothing and shelter[305]. In addition, autonomy is the ability to make personal decisions and choices in life without undue external influences. It would be linked to the freedom from fear.

The *World Summit Outcome document* considered freedom as a fundamental value in international relations in the following terms: "we reaffirm that our common fundamental values, including freedom, equality, solidarity, tolerance, respect for all human rights, respect for nature and shared responsibility, are essential to international relations"[306].

The *Declaration and Programme of Action on a Culture of Peace* recognised the respect of fundamental freedoms as a part of culture of peace as follows: "a culture of peace is a set of values, attitudes, traditions and modes of behaviour and ways of life based on…: (c) Full respect for and promotion of all human rights and fundamental freedoms" and … "(i) Adherence to the principles of freedom, justice, democracy, tolerance, solidarity, cooperation, pluralism, cultural diversity, dialogue and understanding at all levels of society and among nations [307].

Additionally, the *Vienna Declaration and Programme of Action* of 1993 recognised that "… the human person is the central subject of human rights and fundamental freedoms, and consequently should be the principal beneficiary and should participate actively in the realization of these rights and freedoms"[308].

The freedom from fear and want refers to the proclamation made by the President Franklin Roosevelt in his 1941 message to Congress by which proposed those four fundamental freedoms that people "everywhere in the world" ought to enjoy, namely: freedom of speech, freedom of worship, freedom from want and freedom from fear. The declaration of the

Four Freedoms as a justification for war would resonate through the remainder of the war, and for decades longer as a frame of remembrance[309].

The phrase of "freedom from fear and want" derived from the Atlantic Charter of 1941, which proclaimed in its Preamble "Sixth, after the final destruction of the Nazi tyranny, they hope to see established a peace which will afford to all nations the means of dwelling in safety within their own boundaries, and which will afford assurance that all the men in all lands may live out their lives in freedom from fear and want".

In accordance with second recital of the Universal Declaration of Human Rights "... freedom from fear and want has been proclaimed as the highest aspiration of the common people". Additionally, both the International Covenant on Civil, Political, Economic, Social and Cultural Rights recognized in its Preamble that "... the ideal of free human beings enjoying civil and political freedom and freedom from fear and want can only be achieved if conditions are created whereby everyone may enjoy his civil and political rights, as well as his economic, social and cultural rights".

Dag Hammarskjöld, second UN Secretary General, stated that "the work for peace is essentially working for the most elementary human right: the right to security and freedom from fear". Therefore, in his view, the UN had a "responsibility to assist governments in protecting this essential human right without them having to hide behind a shield of weapons"[310].

As indicated by the "Human Development Report" prepared by the United Nations Development Program (hereinafter: UNDP) in 1994, in the process of establishing an international organization like the United Nations, the questions were first, how to "maintain international peace and security" and secondly, how to pursue "freedom from fear and want". The peace of the world could be established not only through preventing war and military conflicts among sovereign states, but also by taking initiatives to "achieve international cooperation in solving international problems of an economic, social, cultural, or humanitarian character, and in promoting and encouraging respect for human rights and for fundamental freedoms for all without distinction as to race, sex, language, or religion"[311].

As spelled out by the *World Summit Outcome document*, "we recognize that all individuals, in particular vulnerable people, are entitled to freedom from fear and freedom from want, with an equal opportunity to enjoy all their rights and fully develop their human potential"[312].

When Kofi Annan launched *In Larger Freedom*[313] in 2005, the title was deliberately chosen so as to "stress the enduring relevance of the Charter of the United Nations". The report acknowledges that there is much work that still needs to be done in order to achieve the goals set by the Millennium Declaration. Specifically, he highlights several key areas that need substantial work, including goals relating to freedom from want (such as financing for development and meeting Millennium Development Goals), and freedom from fear (preventing catastrophic terrorism, the proliferation of biological, chemical, and especially nuclear weapons, building a lasting peace in war torn lands), goals ensuring the freedom to live in dignity (such as establishing the rule of law), and the strengthening of the United Nations.

In accordance with the Annan's report "larger freedom implies that men and women everywhere have the right to be governed by their own consent, under law, in a society where all individuals can, without discrimination or retribution, speak, worship and associate freely. They must also be free from want – so that the death sentences of extreme poverty and infectious disease are lifted from their lives – and free from fear – so that their lives and livelihoods are not ripped apart by violence and war. Indeed, all people have the right to security and to development"[314].

Freedom from want addresses development and encompasses the eight Millennium Development Goals (i.e. eradicate extreme poverty and hunger; achieve universal primary education; promote gender equality and empower of women; reduce child mortality; improve maternal health; combat AIDS, Malaria and other diseases; ensure environmental sustainability and develop a global partnership for development). Freedom from fear bears on collective security (i.e. terrorism prevention; nuclear, biological and chemical weapons; reduced risk and prevalence of war; use of force; peacekeeping and peacebuilding; disarmament and mercenarism)[315].

3.2.2.3. Community values

The third and final element of human dignity is community values, which is related to the social dimension of dignity. It emphasizes "the role of the state and community in establishing collective goals and restrictions on individual freedoms and rights on behalf of a certain idea of good life"[316]. The pursuit of peace through justice is one of the most important objectives to be progressively realized by States as spelled out in their national constitutions.

Justice is one of the most important moral and political concepts. The word comes from the Latin *jus*, meaning right or law. This aspect of the concept of justice is based upon the rights and duties of the individual person. The liberal concept of justice is an interpersonal one – resolution of conflicts between individuals.

In accordance with Art. 29 of the UDHR: "Everyone has duties to the community in which alone the free and full development of his personality is possible". Additionally, the African Charter of the Rights of Man and of Peoples states in its article 27 that every individual "shall have duties towards his family and society, the State and other legally recognized communities and the international community". Additionally, as indicated by Mary Robinson, former High Commissioner for Human Rights, the message of article 29 is clear: the individual must work to improve human rights, whether individually or in the community or as a member of a non-governmental organizational group in its widest sense[317].

The *World Summit Outcome document* considered justice as a fundamental principle in international relations in the following terms: "We re-dedicate ourselves ... to uphold resolution of disputes by peaceful means and in conformity with the principles of justice and international law"[318].

The *Declaration and Programme of Action on a Culture of Peace* included justice is part of the culture of peace: "a culture of peace is a set of values, attitudes, traditions and modes of behaviour and ways of life based on ...adherence to the principles of freedom, justice, democracy, tolerance, solidarity, cooperation, pluralism, cultural diversity, dialogue and understanding at all levels of society and among nations; and fostered by an enabling national and international environment conducive to peace"[319].

The delicate balance between peace and justice laid out in the Charter had quickly been tested by the Nuremberg trials, because several issues that have proved problematic for peacemakers left unresolved during the drafting process, namely: the retroactive application of law, human rights observance as a necessary condition to enduring peace and the situation of past accountability in contemporary discussions of post-war justice[320].

The post-War World II collective system had to reconcile and link two central goals: to maintain peace and security in the world and at the same time foster respect for human rights within the domestic legal system. These twin goals are described in the Preamble of the Charter, which declares that the United Nations are determined "to save succeeding generations from the scourge of war", "to reaffirm faith in fundamental human rights, in the dignity and worth of the human person, in the equal rights of men and women and of nations large and small", as well as, "to establish conditions under which justice and respect for the obligations arising from treaties and other sources of international law can be maintained".

The World Conference on Human Rights held in Vienna in 1993 stressed that "all persons who perpetrate or authorize criminal acts associated with ethnic cleansing are individually responsible and accountable for such human rights violations, and that the international community should exert every effort to bring those legally responsible for such violations to justice"[321].

In accordance with the UNESCO transdisciplinary project entitled "Towards a culture of peace" of 1996, "Justice – there is no justice without freedom – is essential to peace-building. Injustice lies at the very roots of conflict and without justice there can be no peace..."[322].

The Preamble of the UDHR does not declare that the deprivation of rights caused the war, but it does make note that the "disregard and contempt" for rights occurred both and during the war[323].

The rule of law is a form of government, in which people enjoy rights to be free from oppression, interference and discrimination and in which they may exercise rights of free expression, conscience and belief. Some topics related to the rule of law are good governance, the adherence to the principles of supremacy of law, equality before the law, accountability to the law, fairness in the application of the law, separation of powers, participation in decision-making, legal certainty, avoidance of arbitrariness and procedural and legal transparency[324].

The *Vienna Declaration and Programme of Action* of 1993 recognised the concept of rule of law as a principle of international law in the following terms:

> "Considering the major changes taking place on the international scene and the aspirations of all the peoples for an international order based on the principles enshrined in the Charter of the United Nations, including promoting and encouraging respect for human rights and fundamental freedoms for all and respect for the principle of equal rights and self-determination of peoples, peace, democracy, justice, equality, rule of law, pluralism, development, better standards of living and solidarity"[325].

In addition, as indicated by the *World Summit Outcome document*, the linkage between human rights, rule of law and democracy is very closed. It states that:

> "We recommit ourselves to actively protecting and promoting all human rights, the rule of law and democracy and recognize that they are interlinked and mutually reinforcing and that they belong to the universal and indivisible core values and principles of the United Nations, and call upon all parts of the United Nations to promote human rights and fundamental freedoms in accordance with their mandates"[326].

Since 2006 the UNGA has regularly adopted a resolution without vote entitled "The rule of law at the national and international levels"[327] by which it reaffirmed that rule of law and international law is essential for peaceful coexistence and cooperation among States[328]; that it is essential for the realization of economic growth, sustainable development, the eradication of poverty and hunger and the protection of all human rights[329] and that it should guide the activities of the United Nations and of its Member States[330].

3.2.3. Positive measures

Every state, the United Nations and the specialized agencies, as well as other interested international, regional and national organizations, and civil society, should adopt all possible actions, including the establishment and enhancement of national institutions and related infrastructures, with the purpose of implementing, strengthening and elaborating this Declaration.

Sources: Part III, Declaration on Preparation of Societies for
Life in Peace and Art. 34 and 83, Vienna Declaration and
Programme of Action.

Positive action is a concept of great importance in the context of anti-discrimination laws, which have been adopted by several international human rights instruments and openly applied by courts[331]. It includes all measures aimed to make positive steps to alter existing social practices so as to eliminate patterns of group exclusion and disadvantage[332]. These actions were introduced for first time in Europe and North America in the aftermath of the First and Second World Wars to reserve particular posts for persons with disabilities because of the very large number of seriously wounded survivors of both wars[333]. In international human rights law there is a broad consensus that permits the use of temporary and proportionate positive action measures, and even may impose certain obligations upon states to use positive action[334].

As part of the social development, it has become apparent that achieving progress requires that special measures are taken to ensure socially excluded groups are able to participate in decision-making by public authorities and important areas of social life. Without such participation, social exclusion would remain a persistent problem. Active steps to promote a better life are required to reach a peaceful world.

The "right to life" and the "right to live" are not – or should not be – terms with necessarily different meanings and legal content by being considered as equivalent, interdependent and interrelated. However, the right to life is the manifest aspect of the right to live, and the right to live exists and is exercised as a result of recognition of, and respect for, the right to life[335]. In other words, the right to live is the active exercise of inalienable right to life, which has as a main purpose the full and free development of the human dignity and personality[336]. Therefore, the "recognition of the right to life and the affirmation of the right to live are intended to ensure that the authorities take measures to guarantee that life may be lived in a natural and dignified manner and that the individual has every possible means at his disposal for this purpose"[337].

In order to progressively eliminate armed conflict and war over the earth and consequently to live in a context of peace, the protection of human rights and dignity should be in the centre of all decision-making processes in both the national and international level. It follows that different stakeholders should adopt positive measures in the economic, social and cultural fields on peace matters through the promotion of human rights and human dignity.

3.2.4. Principle of pro-homine

The provisions included in this Declaration shall be interpreted in light of the Charter of the United Nations, the Universal Declaration of Human Rights and other international instruments ratified by countries.

The Inter American Commission observed in the case Azocar v. Chile that in case of doubt, the ambiguity should be interpreted in favour of the victims' rights. This principle of *pro-homine*, as the Inter-American Court has stated, is a controlling guideline for interpreting the Convention, and in human rights law in general[338].

The *pro homine* or *pro persona* principle is a very new Latin maxim, never used in international law before, and not even mentioned in Roman law. The interpretation obtained by the application of this principle is similar to that obtained by means of other, traditional Latin maxims[339].

4. Conclusions

The promotion of the right of peoples to peace within the UN human rights bodies started at the Commission on Human Rights in 2001. Afterwards, in 2008 the Human Rights Council decided to continue with this topic. Throughout this long period of time, part of the international community, with the exception of the Group of Eastern and Western European and Others States, has actively been engaged in the promotion of this matter through the adoption of several resolutions. However, it should be noted that although many of the States have supported the ongoing process, some of them have not recognized the existence of the right to peace under international law. In particular, the Western States and associated countries have constantly showed their opposition to this UN process by arguing that this notion is not correctly linked to human rights and that the Human Rights Council is not the competent body to deal with it. From 2003 to 2005, the Commission on Human Rights decided to change the mandate of this topic by introducing the title of "Promotion of peace as a vital requirement for the full enjoyment of all human rights by all" with the purpose of introducing a more human rights approach to this topic. In June 2013, the Human Rights Council adopted resolution 23/16 requesting the Chairperson-Rapporteur of the Working Group to prepare a new text on the basis of the discussions held during the first session of the Working Group and on the basis of the inter-sessional informal consultations. In order to find more consensual positions, the Chairperson-Rapporteur on the Open Ended Working Group on the right to peace convened several consultations with different stakeholders.

The paper analysed the draft Declaration elaborated by the Chairperson-Rapporteur in light of the following elements: firstly, international law and human rights law; secondly, the points of concurrences among all delegations and thirdly, outcome of the consultations held in the context of the on-going process.

In particular, the Chairperson-Rapporteur recalled in the Preamble of his text the Charter of the United Nations, the Universal Declaration of Human Rights and International Covenants. Additionally, he stressed the importance to make a reference to the following notions and ideas: universal peace; principles of international law; human dignity as foundation of freedom, justice and peace; the disregard of human rights and breach of peace; the social and international order; the universality, interdependence and interrelation among all human rights; the pillars of the United Nations system; poverty, development and peace; women and peace; the role of human rights in the prevention of armed conflicts; the role of the Human Rights Council in the prevention of human rights violations; the linkage between education and peace; the relationship between culture of peace and human rights and the elimination of war and armed violence.

Afterwards, the Chairperson-Rapporteur stressed the importance of including in the operative part of his declaration a reference to the right to live in peace, human rights and development; the three principles of international law derived from the notion of human dignity (i.e. intrinsic values, autonomy and community values); possible positive measures and the principle of pro-homine. In conclusion, it should be noted that the notion of the right to life in a context of peace, human rights and development could become the means to overcome the political differences among all regional groups and to elaborate this notion in the context of the current mandate of the Human Rights Council in the field of human rights.

Annex I

[United Nations Declaration on the right to peace]

Preamble

The General Assembly,

Guided by the purposes and principles of the Charter of the United Nations,

Guided also by the Universal Declaration of Human Rights and the International Covenants on Civil, Political, Economic, Social and Cultural Rights as a common standard of achievement for all peoples and all nations,

Recalling the determination of the peoples of the United Nations to live together in peace with one another as good neighbours in order to save succeeding generations from the scourge of war, and to take appropriate measures to strengthen universal peace,

Recalling that the friendly relations among nations are based on respect for the principle of equal rights and self-determination of peoples, and international cooperation to solve international problems of an economic, social, cultural or humanitarian character and to promote and encourage respect for human rights and fundamental freedoms for all,

Recalling also that the inherent dignity and of the equal and inalienable rights of all members of the human family is the foundation of freedom, justice and peace in the world,

Recalling that disregard and contempt for human rights have resulted in barbarous acts which have outraged the conscience of mankind,

Recalling in particular that everyone is entitled to a social and international order in which the rights and freedoms set forth in the Universal Declaration of Human Rights can be fully realized,

Recalling that the Vienna Declaration and Programme of Action stated that all human rights are universal, indivisible, interrelated, interdependent and mutually reinforcing, and that all human rights must be treated in a fair and equal manner, on the same footing and with the same emphasis,

Recalling that peace and security, development and human rights are the pillars of the United Nations system and the foundations for collective security and well-being, and recognizing that development, peace and security and human rights are interlinked and mutually reinforcing,

Recalling the world commitment to eradicate poverty and promote sustained economic growth, sustainable development and global prosperity for all,

Recalling that the full and complete development of a country, the welfare of the world and the cause of peace require the maximum participation of women on equal terms with men in all fields,

Recalling the importance of prevention of armed conflict in accordance with the purposes and principles of the Charter and the commitment to promote a culture of prevention of armed conflict as a means of effectively addressing the interconnected security and development challenges faced by peoples throughout the world,

Recalling that the Human Rights Council shall contribute, through dialogue and cooperation, towards the prevention of human rights violations and respond promptly to human rights emergencies,

Recalling also that the wide diffusion of culture, and the education of humanity for justice and liberty and peace are indispensable to the dignity of man and constitute a sacred duty which all the nations must fulfil in a spirit of mutual assistance and concern,

Recalling the United Nations Declaration on Human Rights Education and Training, which proclaimed that everyone has the right to know, seek and receive information about all human rights and fundamental freedoms and should have access to human rights education and training,

Recalling the Declaration and Programme of Action on a Culture of Peace, which recognized that culture of peace is a set of values, attitudes, traditions and modes of behaviour and ways of life based on, among others, the full respect for and promotion of all human rights and fundamental freedoms,

Inviting solemnly all stakeholders to guide themselves in their activities by recognizing the supreme importance of practicing tolerance, dialogue, cooperation and solidarity among all stakeholders as a means to promote world peace through human rights and to end, reduce and prevent progressively war and armed violence, in particular, by observing the following:

Article 1

Everyone is entitled to the promotion, protection and respect for all human rights and fundamental freedoms, in particular the right to life, in a context in which all human rights, peace and development are fully implemented.

Article 2

States should enhance the principles of freedom from fear and want, equality and non-discrimination and justice and rule of law as a means to build peace within societies. In this regard, States should undertake measures to bring about, maintain and enhance conditions of peace, particularly to benefit people in need in situations of humanitarian crises.

Article 3

States, the United Nations including its specialized agencies, as well as other interested international, regional, national and local organizations and civil society, should adopt all possible actions with the purpose of implementing, strengthening and elaborating this Declaration, including the establishment and enhancement of national institutions and related infrastructures.

Article 4

The provisions included in this Declaration shall be interpreted in light of the Charter of the United Nations, the Universal Declaration of Human Rights and other relevant international instruments ratified by countries.

End

Notes

[1] Deputy Permanent Representative of Costa Rica to the United Nations in Geneva and Chairperson/Rapporteur of the Working Group on the right to peace.

[2] PhD and LLM, Legal assistant of the Chairperson/Rapporteur, Permanent Mission of Costa Rica in Geneva.

[3] Commission on Human Rights resolution 2001/69, 25 April 2001 and resolution 2002/71, 25 April 2002.

[4] Algeria, Angola, Burundi, Cuba, the Democratic People's Republic of Korea, the Democratic Republic of the Congo, Ghana, Haiti, the Libyan Arab Jamahiriya, the Republic of the Congo, Rwanda, the Sudan and Togo. Kenya, Madagascar, Panama, Tunisia and Yemen subsequently joined the sponsors.

[5] Doc. E/CN.4/2001/SR.78, Summary record of the 78th session, 1 May 2001, p. 20–21.

[6] Members of the European Union that are members of the Commission – France, Germany, Italy, Portugal, Spain and the United Kingdom of Great Britain and Northern Ireland; the associated countries that are members of the Commission – the Czech Republic, Latvia, Poland and Romania – aligned themselves with the statement).

[7] Doc. E/CN.4/2001/SR.78, Summary record of the 78th session, 1 May 2001, p. 23–24.

[8] Algeria, Burundi, China, Costa Rica, Cuba, Democratic Republic of the Congo, Ecuador, Indonesia, Kenya, Libyan Arab Jamahiriya, Madagascar, Malaysia, Mauritius, Mexico, Niger, Nigeria, Pakistan, Peru, Qatar, Russian Federation, Saudi Arabia, South Africa, Swaziland, Syrian Arab Republic, Thailand, Uruguay, Venezuela, Viet Nam, Zambia.

[9] Belgium, Canada, Czech Republic, France, Germany, Italy, Japan, Latvia, Norway, Poland, Portugal, Republic of Korea, Romania, Spain, United Kingdom of Great Britain and Northern Ireland, United States of America.

[10] Argentina, Brazil, Cameroon, Colombia, Guatemala, India, Senegal.

[11] Doc. E/CN.4/2002/SR.56, Summary record of the 56th session, 1 May 2001, p. 30.

[12] Doc. E/CN.4/2001/SR.56, *op. cit.*, note 11, p. 31.

[13] Doc. E/CN.4/2001/SR.78, Summary record of the 78th session, 9 August 2002, p. 44.

[14] Members of the European Union that are members of the Commission – France, Germany, Italy, Portugal, Spain and the United Kingdom of Great Britain and Northern Ireland; the associated countries that are members of the Commission – the Czech Republic, Latvia, Poland and Romania – aligned themselves with the statement).

[15] Doc. E/CN.4/2001/SR.78, *op. cit.*, note 13, p. 48.

[16] Algeria, Armenia, Bahrain, Burundi, Cameroon, Chile, China, Costa Rica, Cuba, Democratic Republic of the Congo, Ecuador, Indonesia, Kenya, Libyan Arab Jamahiriya, Malaysia, Mexico, Nigeria, Pakistan, Peru, Russian Federation,

Saudi Arabia, Sierra Leone, South Africa, Sudan, Swaziland, Syrian Arab Republic, Thailand, Togo, Uganda, Uruguay, Venezuela, Viet Nam, Zambia.

[17] Austria, Belgium, Canada, Croatia, Czech Republic, France, Germany, Italy, Japan, Poland, Portugal, Republic of Korea, Spain, Sweden, United Kingdom of Great Britain and Northern Ireland.

[18] Argentina, Brazil, Guatemala, India, and Senegal.

[19] Commission on Human Rights resolution 2003/61, 24 April 2003; resolution 2004/65, 21 April 2004 and resolution 2005/56, 20 April 2005.

[20] Paragraph 4, resolution 2003/61, 24 April and paragraph 6, resolution 2004/65, 21 April 2004.

[21] Paragraph 5, resolution 2003/61, 24 April and paragraph 6, resolution 2004/65, 21 April 2004.

[22] Paragraph 6, resolution 2004/65, 21 April 2004.

[23] Algeria, China, Cuba, Democratic Republic of the Congo, Kenya, Libyan Arab Jamahiriya, Sierra Leone, Swaziland, Sudan, Syrian Arab Republic, Togo and Zimbabwe and the observers for Angola, Belarus, Botswana, Burundi, Equatorial Guinea, Haiti, Iran (Islamic Republic of), Iraq, Mozambique, People's Democratic Republic of Korea, Qatar, Rwanda and Tunisia.

[24] Doc. E/CN.4/2003/SR.61, Summary record of the 61st session, 26 May 2003, p. 48.

[25] Doc. E/CN.4/2003/SR.61, *op. cit.*, note 24, p. 26.

[26] Doc. E/CN.4/2003/SR.61, *op. cit.*, note 24, p. 27.

[27] Doc. E/CN.4/2003/SR.61, *op. cit.*, note 24, p. 28.

[28] Algeria, Armenia, Bahrain, Brazil, Burkina Faso, Cameroon, China, Cuba, Democratic Republic of the Congo, Gabon, Guatemala, Kenya, Libyan Arab Jamahiriya, Malaysia, Mexico, Pakistan, Peru, Russian Federation, Saudi Arabia, Senegal, Sierra Leone, South Africa, Sri Lanka, Sudan, Swaziland, Syrian Arab Republic, Thailand, Togo, Uganda, Uruguay, Venezuela, Viet Nam, Zimbabwe.

[29] Australia, Austria, Belgium, Canada, Croatia, France, Germany, Ireland, Japan, Paraguay, Poland, Republic of Korea, Sweden, Ukraine, United Kingdom of Great Britain and Northern Ireland, United States of America.

[30] Argentina, Chile, Costa Rica, India.

[31] Doc. E/CN.4/2004/SR.57, Summary record of the 57th session, 27 April 2004, p. 34–39.

[32] Paragraph 1, resolution 2005/56, 20 April 2005.

[33] Paragraph 10, resolution 2005/56, 20 April 2005.

[34] Bhutan, Brazil, Burkina Faso, China, Congo, Cuba, Dominican Republic, Ecuador, Egypt, Eritrea, Ethiopia, Gabon, Guatemala, Guinea, Indonesia, Kenya, Malaysia, Mauritania, Nepal, Nigeria, Pakistan, Paraguay, Peru, Qatar, Russian Federation, Saudi Arabia, South Africa, Sri Lanka, Sudan, Swaziland, Togo, Zimbabwe.

[35] Australia, Canada, Finland, France, Germany, Hungary, Ireland, Italy, Japan, Netherlands, Republic of Korea, Romania, Ukraine, United Kingdom of Great Britain and Northern Ireland, United States of America.

[36] Argentina, Armenia, Costa Rica, Honduras, India, Mexico.

[37] Doc. E/CN.4/2005/SR.57, Summary record of the 57th session, 27 March 2006, p. 36–40.

[38] Para. 1 of the operative part of HR Council res. 8/9, adopted on 18 June 2008 by 32 votes in favour, 13 against and 2 abstentions (India and Mexico).

[39] A/HRC/14/38 of 17 March 2010.

[40] *Ibidem* No. 39, par. 3–8.

[41] Doc. resolution A/HRC/14/L.12, par. 15.

[42] Last paragraph of the preamble of the res. 14/3 cit.

[43] Doc. resolution A/HRC/14/L.12, par. 4 of Preamble.

[44] Doc. resolution A/HRC/14/L.12, par. 11.

[45] Doc. resolution A/HRC/14/L.12, par. 15.

[46] Algeria, Bolivia, China, Cuba, Costa Rica, Ecuador, Sudan, Viet Nam and Venezuela (Bolivarian Republic of).

[47] Denmark (on behalf of the European Union), Senegal (on behalf of the African Group) and the representative of the Organization of the Islamic Cooperation.

[48] International Association of Peace Messenger Cities (in association with SSIHRL), Associazione Comunità Papa Giovanni XXIII, International Association of Democratic Lawyers, International Buddhist Relief Organisation, Rencontre Africaine de Défense des Droits de l'Homme, Worldwide Organization for Women, Commission africaine des promoteurs de la santé et des droits de l'homme, Verein Sudwind Entwicklungspolitik, Nord Sud XXI and Comité International pour le Respect et l'Application de la Charte Africaine des Droits de l'Homme et de Peuples.

[49] Angola, Bangladesh, Benin, Botswana, Burkina Faso, Cameroun, Chile, China, Congo, Costa Rica, Cuba, Djibouti, Ecuador, Guatemala, Indonesia, Jordan, Kuwait, Kyrgyzstan, Libya, Malaysia, Maldives, Mauritania, Mauritius, Mexico, Nigeria, Peru, Philippines, Qatar, Russian Federation, Saudi Arabia, Senegal, Thailand, Uganda and Uruguay.

[50] Austria, Belgium, Czech Republic, Hungary, India, Italy, Norway, Poland, Republic of Moldova, Romania, Spain and Switzerland.

[51] United States of America.

[52] Algeria, Bolivia, China, Cuba, Holy See, Morocco and Venezuela.

[53] Organization of the Islamic Cooperation and the Community of the Latin America and Caribbean States (CELAC).

[54] International Association of Democratic Lawyers, International Association of Peace Messenger Cities, Japanese Workers for Committee, Japanese Federation of Bar Associations, Indian Council of South America, Maarij Foundation for Peace and Development, World Barua Organization and the World Federation of Democratic Youth.

[55] The complete oral statement delivered can be found in the extranet of the HRC, 23th regular session, http://www.ohchr.org/EN/HRBodies/HRC/Pages/HRCRegistration.aspx, user name: HRC extranet, password: 1 session.

[56] Angola, Bangladesh, Benin, Botswana, Burkina Faso, Cameroon, Chile, Congo, Costa Rica, Djibouti, Ecuador, Guatemala, Indonesia, Jordan, Kuwait, Kyrgyzstan, Libya, Malaysia, Maldives, Mauritania, Mauritius, Mexico, Nigeria, Peru, Philippines, Qatar, Saudi Arabia, Thailand, Uganda, Uruguay.

[57] Austria, Czech Republic, Estonia, Germany, Japan, Montenegro, Republic of Korea, Spain and the United States of America.

[58] India, Ireland, Italy, Kazakhstan, Poland, Republic of Moldova, Romania and Switzerland.

[59] *Ibidem* 55.

[60] *Ibidem* 55.

[61] Office of the United Nations High Commissioner for Human Rights.

[62] United Nations High Commissioner for Refugees.

[63] United Nations Environment Programme.

[64] United Nations Development Programme.

[65] United Nations Children's Fund.

[66] United Nations Population Fund.

[67] Food and Agriculture Organization of the United Nations.

[68] International Labour Organization.

[69] United Nations Educational, Scientific and Cultural Organization.

[70] World Health Organization.

[71] United Nations Institute for Disarmament Research.

[72] International Organization for Migration.

[73] Human Rights Committee.

[74] International Federation of Red Cross and Red Crescent Societies.

[75] Letter from the Chairperson-Rapporteur of the open-ended intergovernmental working group on a draft United Nations declaration on the right to peace, Christian Guillermet-Fernández, addressed to the members of the working group, Doc. A/HRC/WG.13/2/2, 13 May 2014.

[76] On 2–3 June 2014, the Chairperson-Rapporteur organized with the support of the Finn Church Aid and the World Council of Churches a closed meeting about the future Declaration at the Caux Foundation (Caux-sur-Montreaux, Switzerland). Some 25 governmental delegates from different regional groups participated to give their inputs to the process. Additionally, on 4 June 2014, the Chairperson-Rapporteur organized another closed meeting with NGO at the Permanent Mission of Costa Rica with the same purpose.

[77] The text can be found in the Annex of this paper.

[78] Conclusions of the Washington Conversations on International Peace and Security Organization. 7 October 1944. See in http://www.ibiblio.org/pha/policy/1944/441007a.html.

[79] Paragraph 3 of the Preamble: "Recognizing the necessity of insuring a rapid and orderly transition from war to peace and of establishing and maintaining international peace and security with the least diversion of the world's human and economic resources for armaments". See in http://avalon.law.yale.edu/wwii/moscow.asp.

[80] Paragraph 3 of the dispositive section: "That they recognize the necessity of establishing at the earliest practicable date a general international organization, based on the principle of the sovereign equality of all peace-loving states, and open to membership by all such states, large and small, for the maintenance of international peace and security". See in http://avalon.law.yale.edu/wwii/moscow.asp.

[81] See in http://www.ibiblio.org/pha/policy/1944/441007a.html.

[82] LIVA TEHINDRAZANARIVELO, D. and KOLB, R., "Peace, Right to, International Protection", Max Planck Encyclopedia of Public International Law, December 2006, p. 12.

[83] Argentina, Australia, Belarus, Belgium, Bolivia (Plurinational State of), Brazil, Canada Chile, China, Colombia, Costa Rica, Cuba, Denmark, Dominican Republic, Ecuador, Egypt, El Salvador, Ethiopia, France, Greece, Guatemala, Haiti, Honduras, India, Iran (Islamic Republic of), Iraq, Lebanon, Liberia, Luxembourg, Mexico, Netherlands, New Zealand, Nicaragua, Norway, Panama, Paraguay, Peru, Philippines, Poland, Russian Federation, Saudi Arabia, South Africa, Syrian Arab Republic, Turkey, Ukraine, United Kingdom of Great Britain and Northern Ireland, United States of America, Uruguay and Venezuela (Bolivarian Republic of). See in http://treaties.un.org/Pages/ViewDetails.aspx?src=TREATY&mtdsg_no=I-1&chapter=1&lang=en.

[84] Currently by the People's Republic of China.

[85] Later replaced by the Russian Federation.

[86] See in http://www.un.org/en/members/index.shtml.

[87] Preamble, para. 1.

[88] SIMMA, B., KHAN, D.E. and PAULUS, A., The Charter of the United Nations, A commentary, Oxford Commentaries on international law, third edition, Volume II, November 2012, p. 108–109.

[89] Case Certain expenses of the United Nations (1962, rep. 167–168) of the International Court of Justice. See in http://www.icj-cij.org/docket/files/49/5259.pdf.

[90] See in http://www.ibiblio.org/pha/policy/1945/450425a.html.

[91] "In the field of world policy I would dedicate this Nation to the policy of the good neighbour – the neighbour who resolutely respects himself and, because he does so, respects the rights of others – the neighbour who respects his obligations and respects the sanctity of his agreements in and with a world of neighbours". Statement delivered in the First inaugural Address on 3 March 1933. See in http://en.wikisource.org/wiki/Franklin_Roosevelt%27s_First_Inaugural_Address.

[92] Preamble, paragraph 5: "...to practice tolerance and live together in peace with one another as good neighbours..."

[93] Preamble, paragraph 1: "The Parties to this Treaty reaffirm their faith in the purposes and principles of the Charter of the United Nations and their desire to live in peace with all peoples and all governments..." Signed in Washington on 4 April 1949. See in http://www.nato.int/cps/en/natolive/official_texts_17120.htm.

[94] Doc. UNGA Res. entitled "Peaceful and neighbourly relations among States", A/RES/1236(XII) (14 December 1957); UNGA Res. entitled "Measures aimed at the implementation and promotion of peaceful and neighbourly relations among States", A/RES/1301 (XIII) (10 December 1958) and UNGA Res. entitled "Development and strengthening of good neighbourliness between States", A/RES/34/99 (14 December 1979).

[95] Doc. UNGA Res entitled "Development and strengthening of good neighbourliness between States: 34/99 (14 December 1979); 36/101 (9 December 1981) and 37/117 (16 December 1982).

[96] Doc. UNGA Res 2625 (XXV) of 24 October 1970.

[97] SIMMA, B., KHAN, D.E. and PAULUS, *op. cit.*, note 88, p. 102.

[98] Art. 1.1: "To maintain international peace and security, and to that end: to take effective collective measures for the prevention and removal of threats to the peace, and for the suppression of acts of aggression or other breaches of the peace, and to bring about by peaceful means, and in conformity with the principles of justice and international law, adjustment or settlement of international disputes or situations which might lead to a breach of the peace".

[99] Art. 39: "The Security Council shall determine the existence of any threat to the peace, breach of the peace, or act of aggression and shall make recommendations, or decide what measures shall be taken in accordance with Articles 41 and 42, to maintain or restore international peace and security".

[100] SIMMA, B., KHAN, D.E. and PAULUS, A., *op. cit.*, note 88, p. 1.275.

[101] Prosecutor v. Dusko Tadic, para. 28.

[102] SYMONIDES, J., "Towards the Universal Recognition of the human right to peace", International Affairs Review, 2006, No. 1 (153), p. 6.

[103] The Soviet Union initially supported the position that the "primary and indeed the only task of the international organization should be the maintenance of peace and security and for the economic and social matters a separate organization should be created", in HILDEBRAND, R., Dumbarton Oaks: The Origins of the United Nations and the Search for Postwar Security, University of North Carolina Press, 1990, p. 87–88.

[104] MACLAURIN, J., The United Nations and Power Politics, George Allen and Unwin Ltd, 1951, p. 10.

[105] UNSC Presidential Note (31 January 1992), UN Doc. S/23500, 5.

[106] SIMMA, B., KHAN, D.E. and PAULUS, A., *op. cit.*, note 88, p. 105.

[107] Report of the Rapporteur of the Commission 1/1 UNCIO VI, Doc. 944 1/1/34 (1), 446–47. As to the legal function of the Preambles see art. 31.2 of the Vienna Convention on the Law of Treaties (1969): "The context for the purpose of the interpretation of a treaty shall comprise, in addition to the text, including its preamble and annexes". In addition, it should be recalled the following cases of the International Court of Justice: Asylum (1950, rep. 282) and Rights of Nationals of the United States of America in Morocco (1952, rep. 196).

[108] Art. 2.2: "... to unite our strength to maintain international peace and security..."

[109] Art. 1.2: "... to reaffirm faith in fundamental human rights, in the dignity and worth of the human person, in the equal rights of men and women..."

[110] Art. 1.2: "...to reaffirm faith ... in the equal rights ... of nations large and small..."

[111] Art. 2.1: "...to practice tolerance and live together in peace with one another as good neighbours..."

[112] Art. 2.3: "... to ensure, by the acceptance of principles and the institution of methods, that armed force shall not be used, save in the common interest..."

[113] "Accordingly, our respective Governments, through representatives assembled in the city of San Francisco, who have exhibited their full powers found to be in good and due form, have agreed to the present Charter of the United Nations and do hereby establish an international organization to be known as the United Nations.

[114] SIMMA, B., KHAN, D.E. and PAULUS, A., *op. cit.*, note 88, p. 109–110.

[115] In Larger Freedom – Towards Development, Security and Human Rights for All, Report of the Secretary-General of the United Nations for decision by Heads of State and Government in September 2005. Doc. A/59/2005 of 21 March 2005, para. 78. See in http://www.un.org/largerfreedom/

[116] HAYDEN, P., "Constraining war: human security and the human right to peace", Human Rights Review, 6(1) Oct./Dec. 2004, p. 46.

[117] LINARELLI, J., "Peace-building", Denver Journal of International Law and Policy, Vol. 24, 1996, p. 253–83.

[118] CORNISH, P., "Terrorism, Insecurity and Underdevelopment", *Journal of Conflict, Security and Development*, Vol. 30, 2001, p. 147–52.

[119] Report of the Secretary-General: An agenda for peace. Preventive diplomacy, peacemaking and peace-keeping. Doc. A/47/277 – S/24111 of 17 June 1992, paragraphs 43–44.

[120] MCFARLANE, H. and FOONG KHONG, Y., Human security and the UN: A critical history. Bloomington, Ind.: Indiana University Press, 2006, p. 151.

[121] UNGA Resolutions entitled Alternative approaches and ways and means within the United Nations system for improving the effective enjoyment of human rights and fundamental freedoms: Res. 34/46, 23 November 1979; Res. 36/133 (14 December 1981); Res. 38/124 (16 December 1983); Res. 339/145 (14 December 1984); Res. 40/124 (13 December 1985).

[122] UNGA Resolutions entitled Political rights of women: Res. 56 (1) (11 December 1946); Res. 36/2263 (XXII) (7 November 1967); Res. 34/180 (18 December 1979); Res. 36/131 (14 December 1984); Res. 40/124 (13 December 1985).

[123] UNGA Resolutions entitled The question of race conflict in South Africa resulting from the policies of apartheid of the Government of the Union of South Africa: Res. 616 A (VII) (5 December 1952); Res. 820 (14 December 1954); Res. 1016 (XI) (30 January 1957); Res. 1248 (XIII) (30 October 1958); Res. 1375 (XIV) (17 November 1959).

[124] UNGA Res. 1904 (XVIII) (20 November 1963) (Declaration on the Elimination of All Forms of Racial Discrimination) and Res. 2647 (XXV) (17 December 1970).

[125] UNGA Res. 36/55 (25 November 1981).

[126] UNGA Resolutions entitled Enhancement of international cooperation in the field of human rights: Res. 51/100 (12 December 1996); Res. 53/154 (9 December 1998); Res. 54/181 (17 December 1999); Res. 55/109 (4 December 2000); Res. 56/149 (8 February 2002); Res. 57/224 (18 February 2002); Res. 58/170 (22 December 2003); Res. 59/187 (20 December 2004); Res. 60/156 (23 November 2005); Res. 61/168 (19 December 2006); Res. 62/160 (18 December 2007); Res. 63/180 (18 December 2008).

[127] UNGA Res 48/132 (20 December 1993).

[128] Art. 1 (2).

[129] Art. 1 (3).

[130] Art. 55 (c): "With a view to the creation of conditions of stability and well-being which are necessary for peaceful and friendly relations among nations based on respect for the principle of equal rights and self-determination of peoples, the United Nations shall promote: .... universal respect for, and observance of, human rights and fundamental freedoms for all without distinction as to race, sex, language, or religion".

[131] Art. 56: "All Members pledge themselves to take joint and separate action in co-operation with the Organization for the achievement of the purposes set forth in Article 55".

[132] SIMMA, B., KHAN, D.E. and PAULUS, A., *op. cit.*, note 88, p. 1537.

[133] SIMMA, B., KHAN, D.E. and PAULUS, A., *op. cit.*, note 88, p. 1540.

[134] See at https://treaties.un.org/Pages/Treaties.aspx?id=4&subid=A&lang=en.

[135] EIDE, A., "Article 28", in ALFREDSSON, G. and A. EIDE, A., The Universal Declaration of Human Rights: a common standard of achievement, Martinus Nijhoff Publishers, The Hague/Boston/London, 1999, p. 606–607.

[136] In accordance with the Resolution 1815 (XVII) the principles are as a follows: 1. States shall refrain in their international relations from the threat or use of force against the territorial integrity or political independence of any State; 2. States shall settle their international disputes by peaceful means in such a manner that international peace and security and justice are not endangered; 3. The duty not to intervene in matters within the domestic jurisdiction of any State; 4. The duty of States to co-operate with one another; 5. The equal rights and self-determination of peoples; 6. The sovereign equality of States and 7. States shall fulfil in good faith the obligations assumed by them in accordance with the Charter.

[137] Art. 2: "In pursuit of the purposes mentioned in Chapter I the Organization and its members should act in accordance with the following principles:

1. The Organization is based on the principle of the sovereign equality of all peace-loving states.

2. All members of the Organization undertake, in order to ensure to all of them the rights and benefits resulting from membership in the Organization, to fulfil the obligations assumed by them in accordance with the Charter.

3. All members of the Organization shall settle their disputes by peaceful means in such a manner that international peace and security are not endangered.

4. All members of the Organization shall refrain in their international relations from the threat or use of force in any manner inconsistent with the purposes of the Organization.

5. All members of the Organization shall give every assistance to the Organization in any action undertaken by it in accordance with the provisions of the Charter.

6. All members of the Organization shall refrain from giving assistance to any state against which preventive or enforcement action is being undertaken by the Organization".

[138] Doc. A/RES/25/2625, Declaration on Principles of International Law concerning Friendly Relations and Co-operation among States in accordance with the Charter of the United Nations, 24 October 1970, para. 3.

[139] Full text appears in the annex to General Assembly resolution 375 (IV) of 6 December 1949.

[140] Art. 1.3 of the UN Charter: "to achieve international co-operation in solving international problems of an economic, social, cultural, or humanitarian character, and in promoting and encouraging respect for human rights and for fundamental freedoms for all without distinction as to race, sex, language, or religion".

[141] Art. 1.2 of the UN Charter: "to develop friendly relations among nations based on respect for the principle of equal rights and self-determination of peoples, and to take other appropriate measures to strengthen universal peace".

[142] FASSBENDER, The UN Charter as Constitution of the International Community, Leiden/Boston, Martinus Nijhoff Publishers, Koninklijke Brill NV, 2009.

[143] Preamble, first paragraph: "Peace in the world, together with freedom and justice, are founded on the recognition of the inherent dignity and inalienable rights of all members of the human family, as enshrined in the Universal".

[144] MORSINK, J., The Universal Declaration of Human Rights: origins, drafting and intent, University of Pennsylvania, Philadelphia, 1999, p. 313.

[145] Virginia Declaration of Rights of 1776, section 1: "That all men are by nature equally free and independent and have certain inherent rights, of which, when they enter into a state of society…"; Declaration of Independence of USA of 1776: "… that all men are created equal…" and Declaration of the Rights of Man of 1789, article 1: "Men are born and remain free and equal in rights….".

[146] MORSINK, J., *op. cit.*, note 144, p. 281.

[147] Doc. E/CN4/AC1/SR.2, p. 2.

[148] Furundzija, ICTY, Trial Chamber II, Judgment of 10 December 1998, at §185.

[149] RABKIN, J., "What we can learn about human dignity from international law", Harvard Journal of Law and Public Policy, Fall 2003, No. 27, p. 145–147.

[150] RILEY, S., "Human dignity: comparative and conceptual debates", International Journal of Law in context, 2010, No. 6, p. 119.

[151] WICKS, E., "The meaning of life: dignity and the right to life in international human rights treaties", *Human Rights Law Review*, 2012, Vol. 12:2, p. 206.

[152] International humanitarian law.

[153] Human Rights law.

[154] RILEY, S., *op. cit.*, note 150, p. 123–124.

[155] Doc. A/CONF.157/23, Vienna Declaration and Programme of Action, 12 July 1993, para. 2.

[156] MCCRUDDEN, C., "Human dignity and judicial interpretation of human rights", *The European Journal of International Law*, 2008, Vol. 19, No. 4, p. 662.

[157] Japan, art. 24: "... laws shall be enacted from the standpoint of individual dignity and the essential equality of the sexes"; Italy, art. 3: "All citizens have equal social dignity and are equal before the law, without distinction of sex, race, language, religion, political opinions, personal and social conditions...."; art. 27: "...Punishment cannot consist in treatments contrary to human dignity and must aim at rehabilitating the convicted..." and art. 41: "There is freedom of private economic initiative. It cannot be conducted in conflict with social utility or in a manner that could damage safety, liberty, and human dignity"; Germany, art. 1.1: "Human dignity shall be inviolable. To respect and protect it shall be the duty of all state authority".

[158] Greece, art. 7.2: "Torture, any bodily maltreatment, impairment of health or the use of psychological violence, as well as any other offence against human dignity are prohibited and punished as provided by law"; Spain, art. 10.1: "The human dignity, the inviolable and inherent rights, the free development of the personality, the respect for the law and for the rights of others are the foundation of political order and social peace"; Portugal, art. 1: "Portugal shall be a sovereign Republic, based on the dignity of the human person and the will of the people and committed to building a free, just and solidary society", art. 26.2: "The law shall lay down effective guarantees against the procurement and misuse of information concerning persons and families and its use contrary to human dignity".

[159] MCCRUDDEN, C., *op. cit.*, note 156, p. 673.

[160] The Republic of South Africa is one, sovereign, democratic state founded on the following values: a. "Human dignity, the achievement of equality and the advancement of human rights and freedoms".

[161] UN Charter, Charter of Fundamental Rights of European Union, Convention on the rights of the Child, Convention against Torture, African Charter on Human and Peoples' Rights, International Convention on the Elimination of All Forms of Discrimination against Women, American Convention on Human Rights, International Covenant on Civil and Political, and Economic,

Social and Cultural Rights, International Convention on the Elimination of All Forms of Racial Discrimination.

[162] Germany, India, USA, South Africa, France, Colombia, Israel, and Canada.

[163] BARROSO, L.R., "Here, there and everywhere: human dignity in contemporary and in the transitional discourse", International and Comparative Law Review, 2012, No. 331, p. 354.

[164] Declaration and Programme of Action on a Culture of Peace, UNGA Doc. A/RES/53/243, 6 October 1999, art. 9.b.

[165] Report of the Secretary-General: In Larger Freedom: Towards Development, Security and Freedom for All, UN Doc. A/59/2005, 21 March 2005, paragraph 127–128.

[166] JOHNSON, G. AND SYMONIDES, J., "The Universal Declaration of Human Rights: a history of its creation and implementation", Human Rights in Perspective, UNESCO Publishing, May 1998, p. 33.

[167] Doc. E/HR/6, 1 May 1946 – 1st Meeting held on Monday, 29 April 1946, p. 1–3.

[168] Doc. E/CN.4/SR.1, 28 January 1947, Summary Record of the 1st Meeting, held at Lake Success, New York, on Monday, 27 January 1947, p. 1–2.

[169] Doc. E/CN.4/38, 25 November 1947, Statement Regarding the Possible Ways In Which the Recommendations of the Human Rights Commission Might Be Presented to the General Assembly, submitted by the Representative of the United Kingdom on the Commission on Human Rights, p. 2.

[170] Doc. E/CN.4/SR.50, 4 June 1948, 50th Meeting, Held on Thursday, 27 May 1948, p. 4.

[171] Art. 1 of the UDHR: "All human beings are born free and equal in dignity and rights. They are endowed with reason and conscience and should act towards one another in a spirit of brotherhood".

[172] Art. 28 of the UDHR: "Everyone is entitled to a social and international order in which the rights and freedoms set forth in this Declaration can be fully realized".

[173] ALFREDSSON, G. and EIDE, A. (eds.), The Universal Declaration of Human Rights: a common standard of achievement, Martinus Nijhoff Publishers, Hague, 2004, p. 597.

[174] ALFREDSSON, G. and EIDE, A. (eds.), *op. cit.*, note 173, p. 606.

[175] Four Freedoms: speech, worship, fear and want.
See in http://americanrhetoric.com/speeches/fdrthefourfreedoms.htm.

[176] ALFREDSSON, G. and EIDE, A. (eds.), *op. cit.*, note 173, p. 614.

[177] EIDE, A., *op. cit.*, note 135, p. 597–604.

[178] Preamble, para. 1, Doc. UNGA Res. 1505 (XV), Future work in the field of the codification and progressive development of international law, 12 December 1960.

[179] Doc. UNGA, Res. Adopted by the General Assembly [on the report of the Sixth Committee (A/54/609)] 54/27. Outcome of the action dedicated to

the 1999 centennial of the first International Peace Conference, 19 January 2000, A/RES/54/27.

[180] UNGA Res. entitled The rule of law at the national and international levels: 61/39 (4 December 2006); Res. 62/70 (6 December 2007); Res. 63/128 (11 December 2008); Res. 64/116 (16 December 2009); Res. 65/32 (6 December 2010).

[181] Art. 1.a: "Embody the principles of the universality, interrelatedness, interdependence and indivisibility of all human rights in their national constitutions or other appropriate legislation and ensure the practical realisation of the universal enjoyment of all human rights".

[182] Preamble, paragraph c: "Reaffirming the universality, indivisibility, interdependence and interrelatedness of all human rights and fundamental freedoms and the need for persons with disabilities to be guaranteed their full enjoyment without discrimination".

[183] Preamble, para. 6, UNGA Res. 60/251, 3 April 2006, Human Rights Council.

[184] The Constitution of International Labour Organisation (ILO) says that "lasting peace can be established only if it is based on social justice". It also states in its Preamble that "Whereas also the failure of any nation to adopt humane conditions of labour is an obstacle in the way of other nations which desire to improve the conditions in their own countries; The High Contracting Parties, moved by sentiments of justice and humanity as well as by the desire to secure the permanent peace of the world".

[185] The Constitution of the Food and Agriculture Organization (FAO) states that it is aimed to the improvement of the levels of life and nutrition of all peoples, as well as to the eradication of hunger.

[186] The Constitution of the World Health Organization (WHO) states that "the enjoyment of the highest attainable standard of health is one of the fundamental rights of every human being without distinction of race, religion, political belief, economic or social condition"; "the health of all peoples is fundamental to the attainment of peace and security" and "healthy development of the child is of basic importance; the ability to live harmoniously in a changing total environment is essential to such development".

[187] The Preamble to the Constitution of the United Nations Educational, Scientific and Cultural Organization (UNESCO) states that "since wars begin in the minds of men, it is in the minds of men that the defences of peace must be constructed". In addition, it states that "For these reasons, the States Parties to this Constitution, believing in full and equal opportunities for education for all, in the unrestricted pursuit of objective truth, and in the free exchange of ideas and knowledge, are agreed and determined to develop and to increase the means of communication between their peoples and to employ these means for the purposes of mutual understanding and a truer and more perfect knowledge of each other's lives".

[188] Para. 32 states that the United Nations is the common house of the entire human family, where it should realize its universal aspirations for peace, cooperation and development.

[189] Report of the International Conference on the Relationship between disarmament and development, New York, 24 August-11 September 1987, A/CONF.130/39, of 22 September 1987.

[190] Paragraph 32 states that United Nations is the common house of the entire human family, where it should realize its universal aspiration for peace, cooperation and development.

[191] Preamble states that "international peace and security are essential elements for the realization of the right to development". Furthermore, article 1.1. indicates that "the right to development is an inalienable human right by virtue of which every human person and all peoples are entitled to participate in, contribute to, and enjoy economic, social, cultural and political development, in which all human rights and fundamental freedoms can be fully realized".

[192] The World Summit Outcome Document restated that human rights, peace and development are interrelated and interdependent and that the fostering of one promotes the realization of the others.

[193] Beijing Declaration and Platform for Action, Fourth World Conference on Women, 15 September 1995, A/CONF.177/20 (1995) and A/CONF.177/20/Add.1 (1995), paragraphs 1 and 132.

[194] Report of the Expert Group Meeting that took place in Brasilia, Brazil from 21 to 24 October 2003: The role of men and boys in achieving gender equality. United Nations Division of Advancement of Women, EGM/MEN-BOYS-GE/2003/REPORT, 12 January 2004; Report of the Secretary General, Thematic issue before the Commission: the role of men and boys in achieving gender equality, Commission on the Status of Women, E/CN.6/2004/9, 22 December 2003.

[195] Angola, Azerbaijan, Bangladesh, Bolivia, Brazil, Cameroon, China, Cuba, Djibouti, Egypt, Gabon, Ghana, Guatemala, India, Indonesia, Jordan, Madagascar, Malaysia, Mali, Mauritius, Mexico, Nicaragua, Nigeria, Pakistan, Peru, Philippines, Qatar, Russian Federation, Saudi Arabia, Senegal, South Africa, Sri Lanka, Uruguay and Zambia.

[196] Bosnia and Herzegovina, Canada, France, Germany, Italy, Japan, Netherlands, Republic of Korea, Romania, Slovenia, Switzerland, Ukraine, and United Kingdom of Great Britain and Northern Ireland.

[197] Doc. A/CONF.157/23, Vienna Declaration and Programme of Action, 12 July 1993, art. 10.

[198] Doc. A/CONF.157/23, Vienna Declaration and Programme of Action, 12 July 1993, art. 9: "The World Conference on Human Rights reaffirms that least developed countries committed to the process of democratization and economic reforms, many of which are in Africa, should be supported by the international community in order to succeed in their transition to democracy and economic development".

[199] Doc. A/CONF.157/23, Vienna Declaration and Programme of Action, 12 July 1993, art. 18: "...Gender-based violence and all forms of sexual harassment and exploitation, including those resulting from cultural prejudice and international trafficking, are incompatible with the dignity and worth of

the human person, and must be eliminated. This can be achieved by legal measures and through national action and international cooperation in such fields as economic and social development, education, safe maternity and health care, and social support...."

[200] Doc. A/CONF.157/23, Vienna Declaration and Programme of Action, 12 July 1993, art. 20: "The World Conference on Human Rights recognizes the inherent dignity and the unique contribution of indigenous people to the development and plurality of society and strongly reaffirms the commitment of the international community to their economic, social and cultural well-being and their enjoyment of the fruits of sustainable development..."

[201] Doc. A/CONF.157/23, Vienna Declaration and Programme of Action, 12 July 1993, art. 27: "Measures to be taken, where appropriate, should include facilitation of their (minorities) full participation in all aspects of the political, economic, social, religious and cultural life of society and in the economic progress and development in their country".

[202] Doc. A/CONF.157/23, Vienna Declaration and Programme of Action, 12 July 1993, art. 45: "The World Conference on Human Rights reiterates the principle of "First Call for Children" and, in this respect, underlines the importance of major national and international efforts, especially those of the United Nations Children's Fund, for promoting respect for the rights of the child to survival, protection, development and participation".

[203] Report of the Director-General of the UNESCO entitled on "Towards a culture of peace", Doc. A/51/395, 23 September 1996, para. 11.

[204] Declaration and Programme of Action on a Culture of Peace, UNGA Doc. A/RES/53/243, 6 October 1999, art. 1.

[205] Principle h) states that "... Peace and justice encompass an economic dimension helping the solution of the world economic problems, the liquidation of under-development, offering a lasting and definitive solution of the food problem for all peoples..."

[206] Paragraph 72 states that "... no State can best protect itself by acting entirely alone and that all States need an effective and efficient collective security system pursuant to the purposes and principles of the Charter".

[207] Paragraphs 43–44 of the "An agenda for peace. Preventive diplomacy, peacemaking and peacekeeping" indicated that an integrated approach to human security would be related to the deepest causes of war, such as economic despair, social injustice and political oppression.

[208] In paragraph 25–126 of "In Larger Freedom: Towards Development, Security and Human Rights for All" the former Secretary-General stated that this concept is linked to the twin values of freedom from fear and freedom from want.

[209] Preambular paragraph a): "... the grave food crisis .... acutely jeopardizes the most fundamental principles and values associated with the right to life and human dignity ..."

[210] Paragraph 143 on human security: "... we stress the right of people to live in freedom and dignity, free from poverty and despair. We recognize that all

individuals, in particular vulnerable people, are entitled to freedom from fear and freedom from want, with an equal opportunity to enjoy all their rights and fully develop their human potential..."

[211] Doc. A/CONF.157/23, Vienna Declaration and Programme of Action, 12 July 1993, Art. 30.

[212] Declaration and Programme of Action on a Culture of Peace, UNGA Doc. A/RES/53/243, 6 October 1999, art. 3.

[213] Declaration and Programme of Action on a Culture of Peace, UNGA Doc. A/RES/53/243, 6 October 1999, art. 10.

[214] Opening statement by the Deputy High Commissioner, A/HRC/14/38, paragraph 6.

[215] Beijing Declaration and Platform for Action, Fourth World Conference on Women, 15 September 1995, A/CONF.177/20 (1995) and A/CONF.177/20/Add.1 (1995), paragraphs 1 and 132.

[216] Report of the Expert Group Meeting that took place in Brasilia, Brazil from 21 to 24 October 2003: The role of men and boys in achieving gender equality. United Nations Division of Advancement of Women, EGM/MEN-BOYS-GE/2003/REPORT, 12 January 2004; Report of the Secretary General, Thematic issue before the Commission: the role of men and boys in achieving gender equality, Commission on the Status of Women, E/CN.6/2004/9, 22 December 2003.

[217] Briefing note issued by the Office for Disarmament Affairs in collaboration with the Office of the Special Adviser on Gender Issues and the Advancement of Women of the Department for Economic and Social Affairs, http://disarmament.un.org/gender.htm, 2008.

[218] The United Nations Fourth World Conference on Women: Action for equality, development and peace, Beijing, China, September 1995, par. 22.

[219] An agenda for peace, preventive diplomacy, peacemaking and peace-keeping, Report of the Secretary-General pursuant to the statement adopted by the Summit Meeting of the Security Council on 31 January 1992, Doc. A/47/277, S/24111, 17 June 1992, p. 2.

[220] An agenda for peace, *op. cit.*, note 219, p. 5.

[221] An agenda for peace: preventive diplomacy and related matters, Doc. A/RES/47/120, General Assembly, 10 February 1993.

[222] An agenda for peace, *op. cit.*, note 219, p. 86.

[223] An agenda for peace, *op. cit.*, note 219, p. 13–18.

[224] Supplement to an Agenda for Peace: position paper of the Secretary-General on the occasion of the fiftieth anniversary of the United Nations, Doc. A/50/60-S/1995/1, 3 January 1995, p. 47.

[225] Prevention of armed conflict, Report of the Secretary-General, Doc. A/55/985-S/2001/574, 7 June 2001, p. 18–19.

[226] Art. 55: "With a view to the creation of conditions of stability and well-being which are necessary for peaceful and friendly relations among nations based on respect for the principle of equal rights and self-determination of

peoples, the United Nations shall promote: a) higher standards of living, full employment, and conditions of economic and social progress and development; b) solutions of international economic, social, health, and related problems; and international cultural and educational cooperation; and c) universal respect for, and observance of, human rights and fundamental freedoms for all without distinction as to race, sex, language, or religion".

[227] Prevention of armed conflict, *op. cit.*, note 225, p. 19.

[228] Art. 9: "To make the United Nations more effective in maintaining peace and security by giving it the resources and tools it needs for conflict prevention, peaceful resolution of disputes, peacekeeping, post-conflict peace-building and reconstruction. In this context, we take note of the report of the Panel on United Nations Peace Operations and request the General Assembly to consider its recommendations expeditiously".

[229] Art. 2: "Pledges to enhance the effectiveness of the United Nations in addressing conflict at all stages from prevention to settlement to post-conflict peace-building".

[230] Art. 9.G: "Actions to foster a culture of peace through education ... g) Strengthen the ongoing efforts of the relevant entities of the United Nations system aimed at training and education, where appropriate, in the areas of conflict prevention and crisis management, peaceful settlement of disputes, as well as in post-conflict peace-building".

[231] Prevention of armed conflict, *op. cit.*, note 917, p. 18–94.

[232] Doc. UNGA Resolution 57/337 on Prevention of armed conflict, 18 July 2003, p. 11.

[233] Vienna Declaration and Programme of Action, adopted by the World Conference on Human Rights in Vienna on 25 June 1993, p. 25.

[234] Doc. UNGA 48/141 on the High Commissioner for the promotion and protection of all human rights, 20 December 1993, p. 4 (f).

[235] Doc. E/CN.4/2000/12, Report of the United Nations High Commissioner for Human Rights and follow-up to the World Conference on Human Rights, 28 December 1999, p. 92.

[236] Doc. E/CN.4/2000/12, *op. cit.*, note 927, p. 94.

[237] Statement by Chaloka Beyani, Chairperson of the Coordination Committee of Special Procedures, Twentieth Special Session of the Human Rights Council on the situation of human rights in the Central African Republic, 20 January 2014.

[238] Statement by Manuela Carmena Castrillo, Chairperson of the Coordination Committee of Special Procedures, Eight Special Session of the Human Rights Council on the situation of human rights in the East of the Democratic Republic of Congo, 28 November 2008.

[239] Statement by Jose Luis Gomez del Prado, Chairperson of the Coordination Committee of Special Procedures, Eight Special Session of the Human Rights Council on the situation of human rights in the Libyan Arab Jamahiriya, 25 February 2011.

[240] In http://www.ohchr.org/EN/NewsEvents/Pages/KeyRoleEarlyWarning.aspx.

[241] Doc. UNGA Resolution 68/160 on enhancement of international cooperation in the field of human rights, 21 February 2014, p. 6.

[242] Article 26.2 UDHR states that "education shall be directed to the full development of the human personality and to the strengthening of respect for human rights and fundamental freedoms. It shall promote understanding, tolerance and friendship among all nations, racial or religious groups, and shall further the activities of the United Nations for the maintenance of peace".

[243] Article 29 CRC states that children's education should develop each child's personality, talents and abilities to the fullest. It should encourage children to respect others, human rights and their own and other cultures. It should also help them learn to live peacefully, protect the environment and respect other people. Children have a particular responsibility to respect the rights their parents, and education should aim to develop respect for the values and culture of their parents.

[244] Article 13 ICESCR states that "... recognize the right of everyone to education. They agree that education shall be directed to the full development of the human personality and the sense of its dignity, and shall strengthen the respect for human rights and fundamental freedoms. They further agree that education shall enable all persons to participate effectively in a free society, promote understanding, tolerance and friendship among all nations and all racial, ethnic or religious groups, and further the activities of the United Nations for the maintenance of peace".

[245] Article 1 states that "... to ensure that their policies relevant to the implementation of the present Declaration, including educational processes and teaching methods as well as media information activities, incorporate contents compatible with the task of the preparation for life in peace of entire societies and, in particular, the young generations".

[246] Goal 6 states that "Education, both formal and non-formal, is therefore a key element to achieving sustainable development, peace and stability within and among countries, by fostering social cohesion and empowering people to become active participants in social transformation".

[247] Article 13 states that "... education should be directed towards the full development of the human personality and human dignity and should strengthen respect for human rights, ideological pluralism, fundamental freedoms, justice and peace. They further agree that education ought to enable everyone to participate effectively in a democratic and pluralistic society and achieve a decent existence and should foster understanding, tolerance and friendship among all nations and all racial, ethnic or religious groups and promote activities for the maintenance of peace".

[248] Report submitted by the Special Rapporteur on the Right to Education, Mr. Vernor Muñoz Villalobos, E/CN.4/2006/45, 8 February 2006, par. 18.

[249] Doc. A/CONF.157/23, Vienna Declaration and Programme of Action, 12 July 1993, Preamble, art. 33.

[250] Doc. A/CONF.157/23, Vienna Declaration and Programme of Action, 12 July 1993, Preamble, art. 33.

[251] Doc. A/CONF.157/23, Vienna Declaration and Programme of Action, 12 July 1993, Art. 63: "The World Conference on Human Rights reaffirms that all human rights and fundamental freedoms are universal and thus unreservedly include persons with disabilities. Every person is born equal and has the same rights to life and welfare, education and work, living independently and active participation in all aspects of society..."

[252] Doc. A/CONF.157/23, Vienna Declaration and Programme of Action, 12 July 1993, Art. 24: "Great importance must be given to the promotion and protection of the human rights of persons belonging to groups which have been rendered vulnerable, including migrant workers, the elimination of all forms of discrimination against them, and the strengthening and more effective implementation of existing human rights instruments. States have an obligation to create and maintain adequate measures at the national level, in particular in the fields of education, health and social support, for the promotion and protection of the rights of persons in vulnerable sectors of their populations and to ensure the participation of those among them who are interested in finding a solution to their own problems".

[253] Doc. A/CONF.157/23, Vienna Declaration and Programme of Action, 12 July 1993, Art. 18: "...Gender-based violence and all forms of sexual harassment and exploitation, including those resulting from cultural prejudice and international trafficking, are incompatible with the dignity and worth of the human person, and must be eliminated. This can be achieved by legal measures and through national action and international cooperation in such fields as economic and social development, education, safe maternity and health care, and social support....";

[254] Doc. A/CONF.157/23, Vienna Declaration and Programme of Action, 12 July 1993, Art. 79: "States should strive to eradicate illiteracy and should direct education towards the full development of the human personality and to the strengthening of respect for human rights and fundamental freedoms. The World Conference on Human Rights calls on all States and institutions to include human rights, humanitarian law, democracy and rule of law as subjects in the curricula of all learning institutions in formal and non-formal settings"; art. 80: "Human rights education should include peace, democracy, development and social justice, as set forth in international and regional human rights instruments, in order to achieve common understanding and awareness with a view to strengthening universal commitment to human rights" and art. 82: "Governments, with the assistance of intergovernmental organizations, national institutions and non-governmental organizations, should promote an increased awareness of human rights and mutual tolerance...."

[255] Report of the Director-General of the UNESCO entitled on "Towards a culture of peace", Doc. A/51/395, 23 September 1996, para. 22.

[256] Declaration and Programme of Action on a Culture of Peace, UNGA Doc. A/RES/53/243, 6 October 1999, art. 4.

[257] Doc. Yearbook of the United Nations, 2002, p. 651.

[258] Para. 6: "peace and security, development and human rights are the pillars of the United Nations system and the foundations for collective security and well-being, and recognizing that development, peace and security and human rights are interlinked and mutually reinforcing". Doc. A/RES/60/251 on the Human Rights Council, 3 April 2006.

[259] Doc. A/RES/60/251 on the Human Rights Council, 3 April 2006. Art. 3.

[260] Doc. A/RES/60/251, *op. cit.*, note 259. Art. 5.f.

[261] Doc. A/RES/60/251, *op. cit.*, note 259. Art. 10.

[262] Doc. A/HRC/S-4/101, situation of human rights in Darfur, 13 December 2006.

[263] Doc. A/HRC/S-5/1, situation of human rights in Myanmar, 2 October 2007.

[264] Doc. A/HRC/S-8/1, situation of human rights in the east of the Democratic Republic of the Congo, 1 December 2008.

[265] Doc. A/HRC/S-14/1, situation of human rights in Cote d'Ivoire in relation to the conclusion of the 2010 presidential election, 23 December 2010.

[266] Doc. A/HRC/S-15/1, situation of human rights in the Libyan Arab Jamahiriya, 25 February 2011.

[267] Doc. A/HRC/S-20/1, situation of human rights in the Central Africa Republic and technical assistance in the field of human rights, 20 January 2014.

[268] Statement delivered by Spain, HRC special session on Darfur, 12 December 2006; Chile on Democratic Republic of the Congo, 28 November 2008.

[269] Statement delivered by Sierra Leone, HRC special session on the Central African Republic, 20 January 2014; Philippines, Peru on Myanmar, 2 October 2007; Mexico and Chile on Cote d'Ivoire, 23 December 2010; Nigeria on behalf of African Group and Spain on Libyan Arab Jamahiriya, 25 February 2011.

[270] Statement delivered by the European Union, African Group, Pakistan, France, New Zealand, Latvia on Myanmar, 2 October 2007; Netherland and Republic of Korea on Democratic Republic of the Congo, 28 November 2008; Jordan, European Union, Sweden, Spain and Austria on Cote d'Ivoire, 23 December 2010; France, Norway, Chile, Bulgaria, Honduras, Denmark, Belgium, Republic of Korea, Slovakia, United States of America, Thailand and United Kingdom on Libyan Arab Jamahiriya, 25 February 2011; Israel on the Central African Republic, 20 January 2014.

[271] Statement delivered by Germany, Republic of Korea, Switzerland, Greece, Denmark, Liechtenstein, on Myanmar, 2 October 2007; Pakistan, the United Kingdom, Switzerland, Bolivia and Italy on Democratic Republic of the Congo, 28 November 2008; Peru, Republic of Korea and United Kingdom on Cote d'Ivoire, 23 December 2010; Iran and Canada on Libyan Arab Jamahiriya, 25 February 2011; Latvia, Liechtenstein and Thailand on the Central African Republic, 20 January 2014.

[272] Statement delivered by Niger, HRC special session on the Central African Republic, 20 January 2014.

[273] Statement delivered by Mexico, HRC special session on Democratic Republic of the Congo, 28 November 2008.

[274] Statement delivered by Argentina on Myanmar, 2 October 2007.

[275] Art. 39 of the UN Charter.

[276] Doc. S/RES/1714 (2006), 6 October 2006.

[277] Doc. S/RES/1857 (2008), 22 December 2008.

[278] Doc. S/RES/1962 (2010), 20 December 2010.

[279] Doc. S/RES/2016 (2011), 27 October 2011.

[280] Doc. S/RES/2134 (2014), 28 January 2014.

[281] Art. 3: "Everyone has the right to life, liberty and security of person".

[282] Art. 6 (1): "Every human being has the inherent right to life. This right shall be protected by law. No one shall be arbitrarily deprived of his life". Adopted and opened for signature, ratification and accession by General Assembly resolution 2200A (XXI) of 16 December 1966, entry into force 23 March 1976.

[283] Art. 4: "Human beings are inviolable. Every human being shall be entitled to respect for his life and the integrity of his person. No one may be arbitrarily deprived of this right". Adopted June 27, 1981, OAU Doc. CAB/LEG/67/3 rev. 5, 21 I.L.M. 58 (1982), entered into force Oct. 21, 1986.

[284] Art. 2 (1): "Everyone's right to life shall be protected by law..." Signed on 4 November 1950 in Rome.

[285] Art. 4 (1): "1. Every person has the right to have his life respected. This right shall be protected by law and, in general, from the moment of conception. No one shall be arbitrarily deprived of his life". Signed at the Inter-American Specialized Conference on Human Rights, San Jose, Costa Rica, 22 November 1969.

[286] NOWAK, M., U.N. Covenant on Civil and Political Rights: CCPR Commentary, Engel Publisher, Kehl/Strasbourg/Arlington, 2005, p. 104.

[287] Art. 4 (2): "No derogation from articles 6, 7, 8 (paragraphs I and 2), 11, 15, 16 and 18 may be made under this provision".

[288] RAMCHARAN, B., "The Right to Life", Netherlands International Law Review (NILR), 1983.

[289] MOLLER, J. TH. and ZAYAS, A. United Nations Human Rights Committee Case Law 1977–2008: a Handbook, Kehl/Strasbourg, Engel Publisher, 2009, p. 144.

[290] Doc. General Comment No. 6: The right to life (art. 6): 30 April 1982, para. 2.

[291] Doc. General Comment No. 14: The right to life (art. 6): 9 November 1984, para. 5.

[292] NOWAK, M., *op. cit.*, note 286, p. 109.

[293] RAMCHARAN, B., *op. cit.*, note 288, p. 307–308.

[294] *International Review of Red Cross*, Ninth year, No. 104, 1969, Para. 1 and 2, p. 620. See in http://www.loc.gov/rr/frd/Military_Law/pdf/RC_Nov-1969.pdf.

[295] BARROSO, L.R., "Here, there and everywhere: human dignity in contemporary and in the transitional discourse", *International and Comparative Law Review*, 2012, p. 392.

[296] BARROSO, L.R., *op. cit.*, note 296, p. 363–364.

[297] MCCRUDDEN, C., Equality and Non-Discrimination, in English Public Law, Oxford, David Feldman ed., 2004 and BAYEFSKY, A., "The principle of Equality and Non-discrimination in International law", *Human Rights Quarterly*, 1990, Vol. 11, p. 5–19.

[298] BESSON, S., "International Human Rights and Political Equality-Implications for Global Democracy", in EMAN, E. & NASSTROM, S. (eds.), *Equality in Transnational and Global Democracy*, London, Palgrave, 2013.

[299] South West African cases, ICJ Reports, 1966, para. 299.

[300] BEDI, The Development of Human Rights Law by the Judges of the International Court of Justice, Portland Oregon, Hart Publishing, Oxford, 2007, p. 107.

[301] Doc. A/CONF.157/23, Vienna Declaration and Programme of Action, 12 July 1993, para. 9.

[302] Declaration and Programme of Action on a Culture of Peace, UNGA Doc. A/RES/53/243, 6 October 1999, art. 12.

[303] Declaration and Programme of Action on a Culture of Peace, *op. cit.*, note 302, art. 9.b.

[304] Doc. A/RES/60/1, World Summit Outcome document, General Assembly, 24 October 2005, paragraph 4–5.

[305] BARROSO, L.R., *op. cit.*, note 295, p. 371.

[306] Doc. A/RES/60/1, World Summit Outcome document, General Assembly, 24 October 2005, paragraph 4.

[307] Declaration and Programme of Action on a Culture of Peace, UNGA Doc. A/RES/53/243, 6 October 1999, art. 1.

[308] Doc. A/CONF.157/23, Vienna Declaration and Programme of Action, 12 July 1993, Preamble, para. 2.

[309] BODNAR, J., The "Good War" in American Memory, Maryland, Johns Hopkins University Press, 2010, p. 11.

[310] D. Hammarskjöld, Tal, Ett urval redigerat av Wilder Foot (Speeches, A selection Edited by Wilder Foot) (Norstedt, Stockholm, 1962, p. 144.

[311] OKUBO, S., "Freedom from Fear and Want" and "the Right to Live in Peace", and "Human Security", Ritsumeikan International Affairs, 2007, Vol. 5, p. 1–15, p. 5.

[312] Doc. A/RES/60/1, World Summit Outcome document, General Assembly, 24 October 2005, paragraph 143.

[313] Report of the Secretary-General: In Larger Freedom: Towards Development, Security and Freedom for All, UN Doc. A/59/2005, 21 March 2005.

[314] Report of the Secretary-General: In Larger Freedom: Towards Development, Security and Freedom for All, UN Doc. A/59/2005, 21 March 2005, par. 15.

[315] KANG, G., "The three freedoms of the United Nations in Northeast Asia", Korea Observer, Vol. 36, 2005, No. 4, p. 719–720.

[316] BARROSO, L.R., *op. cit.*, note 295, p. 374.

[317] ROBINSON, M., "From Human Rights to People's Rights: fifty years after the Universal Declaration", Diritti dell'uomo, diritti dei popoli, 2002, p. 29.

[318] Doc. A/RES/60/1, World Summit Outcome document, General Assembly, 24 October 2005, paragraph 5.

[319] Declaration and Programme of Action on a Culture of Peace, UNGA Doc. A/RES/53/243, 6 October 1999, art. 1.i.

[320] MCGUINNESS, M., "Peace v. Justice: The Universal Declaration of Human Rights and the Modern Origins of the Debate", Diplomatic History, Vol. 35, No. 5, p. 750–752.

[321] Doc. A/CONF.157/23, Vienna Declaration and Programme of Action, 12 July 1993, art. 23.

[322] Report of the Director-General of the UNESCO entitled on "Towards a culture of peace", Doc. A/51/395, 23 September 1996, para. 12.

[323] Paragraph 2, UDHR: "Whereas disregard and contempt for human rights have resulted in barbarous acts which have outraged the conscience of mankind ..."

[324] MCGUINNESS, M., *op. cit.*, note 320, p. 764.

[325] Doc. A/CONF.157/23, Vienna Declaration and Programme of Action, 12 July 1993, para. 9.

[326] Doc. A/RES/60/1, World Summit Outcome document, General Assembly, 24 October 2005, paragraph 5.

[327] Doc. A/RES/61/39, 18 December 2006; A/RES/62/70, 8 January 2008; A/RES/63/70, 15 January 2009; A/RES/64/70, 15 January 2010; A/RES/65/32, 10 January 2011; A/RES/66/102, 13 January 2012 and A/RES/67/07, 14 January 2013.

[328] Paragraph 3: "Reaffirming further the need for universal adherence to and implementation of the rule of law at both the national and international levels and its solemn commitment to an international order based on the rule of law and international law, which together with the principles of justice, is essential for peaceful coexistence and cooperation among States".

[329] Paragraph 4: "Convinced that the advancement of the rule of law at the national and international levels is essential for the realization of sustained economic growth, sustainable development, the eradication of poverty and hunger and the protection of all human rights and fundamental freedoms, and acknowledging that collective security depends on effective cooperation, in accordance with the Charter and international law, against transnational threats".

[330] Paragraph 6: "Convinced that the promotion of and respect for the rule of law at the national and international levels, as well as justice and good governance, should guide the activities of the United Nations and of its Member States".

[331] European Court of Human Rights and Constitutional Courts: USA, Germany, South-Africa.

[332] BELL, C. HEGARTY, A. AND LIVINGSTONE, S. "The Enduring Controversy: Developments on Affirmative Action Law in North America" (1996), International Journal of Discrimination and the Law 233, at p. 234.

[333] WADDINGTON, L. "Reassessing the Employment of People with Disabilities in Europe From Quotas to Anti-Discrimination Laws", 1996, 18 Comparative Labour Law Review 62.

[334] O'CINNEIDE, Positive action, University College, London, p. 23.

[335] GROSS ESPIELL, H., "Right to life and right to live", in D. Premont, Essays on the right to life, Association of International Consultants on Human Rights, Brussels, 1988, p. 43 and OKECHUKWU, H., The right to life and the right to live: Ethics of international solidarity, Series XXIII, Theology, Vol./Bd. 387, European University Studies, Paris.

[336] BALANDA, L., "Le droit de vivre"; VEUTHEY, M., "Le droit à la survie, fundament du droit humanitaire" and P. RICHARD, P., "Droits de l'homme, paix et désarmement. Éléments essentiels de la garantie du droit de vivre", in PREMONT, D., Essays on the right to life, Brussels, Association of International Consultants on Human Rights, 1988.

[337] GROSS ESPIELL, H., *op. cit.*, note 335, p. 43–45.

[338] A.A. Azocar v. Chile, IACommHR (1999), Report No. 137/99, Case 11,863, at para. 146, available at: www.cidh.oas.org/annualrep/99eng/Merits/Chile11.863.htm (last visited 15 Dec. 2009). On the Vienna Convention and the pro homine principle see the Separate Opinion of García-Ramírez in Mayagna (Sumo) Awas Tingni Community v. Nicaragua, Merits, Reparations and Costs, IACtHR (Ser. C), No. 79 (2001), at para. 2.

[339] VILLAREAL. A., 'El principio pro homine: interpretación extensiva vs. el consentimento del estado', 5 Int'l L Rev colombiana der. int. (2005) 337; Pinto, 'El principio pro homine. Criterios de hermenéutica y pautas para la regulación de los derechos humanos', in C. Abregú and M. Courtis, La aplicación de los tratados sobre derechos humanos por los tribunales locales (2nd edn, 1998), at 163. A reference to this principle can be read in some separate opinions of the Inter American Court: see, e.g., Bámaca-Velásquez v. Guatemala, Merits, IACtHR (2000) Ser. C, No. 70, Concurring Opinion of García Ramírez, at para. 3.

Index

Abruzzo, Region of: 59-61, 63, 132, 137, 286
Afghanistan: 88, 89, 107, 161, 203, 270
Albania: 97, 137, 155, 194, 201, 239, 242,246, 270, 282
Algeria: 202, 248
Andorra: 201, 203, 239
Angola: 168, 201, 203
Apulia, Region of: 61, 63, 132, 137, 195, 216
Arab Spring: 30, 186, 188, 197, 220
Argentina: 166, 169, 173, 182, 205, 248
Armed conflicts: 46, 122
Armenia: 174, 204, 227, 239, 242, 248
Asylum, refugees, stateless persons: 18, 30, 35, 46, 53, 55, 58, 71, 73, 76, 80-81, 88-89, 91-92, 147, 159, 163, 184-185, 192-197, 202, 208-209, 216, 220-222, 242-244, 251, 279-282, 293-294, 296, 321-322
Austria: 166, 169, 173-176, 201, 203-204, 246, 259, 276, 322
Azerbaijan: 170, 200, 204, 227, 239, 242, 247-248

Bahamas: 169
Bahrain: 172
Balkans: 202, 270
Bangladesh: 90, 107, 170
Barbados: 169
Basilicata, Region of: 132, 137, 300
Belarus: 168, 181, 201-202, 220, 248, 252

Belgium: 174, 177, 201, 210, 227, 246, 251, 261
Belize: 201
Benin: 168, 203
Bioethics, biomedicine: 23, 42, 65, 95, 100, 120, 126, 129, 211-212, 217
Bolivia: 163, 201, 204
Bolzano, Autonomous Province of: 63, 132, 137, 296-297
Bosnia and Herzegovina: 201, 203, 227, 242, 247-248, 251, 265, 270
Botswana: 168-169, 176
Brazil: 91, 100, 169, 172, 175-176, 181-182, 213, 248
Bulgaria: 219, 221, 242
Burkina Faso: 168, 170, 201-202, 204

Calabria, Region of: 61-63, 72, 132, 137, 195, 216, 298
Cambodia: 177, 203
Cameroon: 163, 166-167, 170, 280
Campania, Region of: 25, 62, 132, 137, 256, 287, 299, 300
Canada: 163, 168, 170, 181, 213, 248
Cape Verde: 170, 203
Central African Republic: 171, 177, 181, 183
Chad: 171, 202
Children and adolescents: 22-24, 27, 30, 36-37, 42, 44-46, 50, 53, 56-57, 59, 61, 65, 69, 71, 74-76, 90-92, 95, 97, 99-100, 102, 105-109, 111-113, 116-119, 124, 133, 137-138, 143, 146, 148-150,

153-154, 159, 161, 163, 170,
174-177, 180, 184, 186-188, 196,
198-199, 204-205, 207, 215-217,
222-223, 225, 241, 244-245, 251,
278, 284-287, 289-290, 300-302,
322, 324, 331
Chile: 169, 202, 248
China: 97, 155, 171, 201, 204
Civil society organisations: 28-29,
32-33, 35, 39, 17, 59, 61, 71, 74,
98, 100, 102, 106-108, 118-119,
131, 137, 139-140, 144, 147, 168,
185-186, 208, 210, 219, 227, 231,
241-243 251, 257-258, 260, 265,
283, 316-317
Colombia: 74, 100, 170, 175, 203,
204
Congo, Democratic Republic of:
168, 177, 203
Congo, Republic of: 171
Conscientious objection: 90, 177,
238, 241
Constitutional Court (Italian):
26-27, 33, 69, 101, 110, 275-276,
278, 283-288, 290-292, 295-298,
300, 303, 307-309, 312-314,
317-318, 323
Corruption: 22, 41-43, 50, 134,
175, 217-218, 252-253, 331
Costa Rica: 20-21, 33, 169,
172-174, 177, 182
Court of Justice of the EU: 33, 51,
110, 186, 211-219, 221- 226,
248-249, 258, 260, 275, 278,
283, 290- 294, 299, 303-308,
312-314, 318-321, 323-339
Croatia: 177
Cuba: 164-165, 167, 170, 172, 178,
180-182, 203, 282
Cultural heritage: 22, 50, 57, 84,
121-122, 125, 290
Culture of peace: 19, 58-59, 131,
140-141, 143-145, 147

Cyprus: 118, 194, 202, 203, 227, 270
Czech Republic: 169, 176, 201,
242, 259

Death penalty: 93, 119, 162, 170,
174, 258, 281
Democracy, rule of law: 15-17, 90,
110, 125, 143, 161, 167, 190, 192,
211, 217-221, 225, 245-247, 257,
270, 282, 323
Denmark: 164, 174, 200, 210, 242,
259
Disabilities – see Persons with
disabilities
Diversity and intercultural
dialogue: 165, 180, 190, 211
Djibouti: 170, 173, 181, 201
Dominican Republic: 202-203

Ecuador: 169, 172-173, 176, 182
Education, training, research: 16,
19-21, 24, 28, 30, 32, 35, 38-39,
41, 44, 56-57, 59, 61, 63-65,
70-73, 79, 84, 92, 96-98,
100-101, 104-105, 107-109, 111,
113-114, 116, 120-129, 131,
133-135, 137, 139, 140-141,
143-154, 166, 172-173, 175,
185-186, 189, 194, 202, 205,
208-209, 211-215, 217-219, 228,
233-234, 243-244, 255, 257, 259,
263, 270-271, 284-285, 297, 299,
328, 331, 333, 335
Egypt: 56, 107, 164, 166, 185, 201,
245, 248, 271, 311
El Salvador: 204
Elderly people: 183
Elections: 43, 52, 74, 79-82, 165,
189, 218, 263-264, 328, 330
Emilia-Romagna, Region of: 60,
62-63, 96, 132, 137, 141, 150, 154
Enforced disappearances: 23, 35,
39, 42, 204

Environment, pollution, waste: 19, 57, 133-135, 137, 177, 214, 224, 228-229, 234, 238, 241, 255-256, 286, 288, 290-291
Eritrea: 30, 181, 193, 197, 222
Estonia: 169, 201, 227, 242, 246
Ethiopia: 100, 133, 168, 173
EU citizens: 52, 97, 296-298
European Court of Human Rights: 23-24, 26-27, 33, 44, 51, 79, 87, 91, 94, 109-110, 186, 217-219, 221-226, 248-249, 260, 278, 290-292, 294, 299, 303-308, 312-314, 318-334
Expropriation: 297, 299-300, 326-327

Female genital mutilation: 99, 162
Fiji: 162, 164
Finland: 163-164, 201, 246, 264, 276
Former Yugoslav Republic of Macedonia: 203
Former Yugoslavia: 29
France: 166, 176, 197
Freedom of expression, pluralism in the media: 183, 190, 219, 248-249, 264, 329-330
Friuli-Venezia Giulia, Region of: 60, 62-63, 132, 297

Gabon: 168, 172, 174, 176-177, 180-182
Gender, gender discrimination: see Women, equal opportunities, gender issues
Georgia: 74, 227, 239, 246, 248, 270, 281
Germany: 165-166, 169-170, 173,175, 177, 197, 210, 227, 242, 246, 256, 258, 261, 263, 276
Greece: 165, 184, 194, 203, 219, 227, 242, 259, 261
Guatemala: 169, 182, 201

Guinea: 176, 204
Guinea-Bissau: 204
Guyana: 204

HIV/AIDS: 215
Holy See: 194, 248
Homophobia, trans phobia: 76, 88, 190
Homosexuality, transsexuality: 248
Horn of Africa: 271, 321
Human dignity: 16, 26, 91, 95, 212, 215, 308, 309
Human rights defenders: 17, 159, 174
Hungary: 172, 175, 177, 203, 220, 227, 245, 248, 261

Iceland: 227, 248
Independent institutions for the protection of human rights: 24-25, 36, 39, 43, 59, 61, 65, 72-73, 77-78, 88, 111, 116-119, 132-139, 143, 148-151, 159, 184, 189, 227, 261-262
India: 97, 168-169
Indonesia: 168, 201
International Criminal Court: 43, 257
International solidarity, development cooperation: 24, 32, 59, 65, 74, 102, 131, 141, 143-144, 146-147, 180, 210, 214
Iran: 160, 168, 172, 175, 180-182, 200
Iraq: 269-270
Ireland: 169, 172, 176-181, 246-247, 251, 261
Israel: 74, 171, 179, 204, 248
Ivory Coast: 168, 281

Jamaica: 200, 202
Japan: 168-169, 177-178, 200-201, 212, 248
Jordan: 171, 173, 175

Kazakhstan: 71-72, 81, 168-169, 192, 248
Kenya: 168, 201
Kosovo: 155, 247, 270
Kuwait: 168, 173, 175, 201, 204
Kyrgyzstan: 201-202, 248

Latin America and Caribbean: 169, 172, 188
Latvia: 201, 227, 242, 247, 251, 261
Lazio, Region of: 63, 96, 107, 132-133, 137, 150, 227, 256, 283, 303
Lebanon: 271
Liberia: 163
Libya: 90, 168, 174, 184, 194, 222 260, 271
Liechtenstein: 246
Liguria, Region of: 62, 132-133, 137
Lithuania: 163, 166, 167, 204, 247
Lombardy, Region of: 62, 64, 96, 107, 132, 134, 137, 154

Malawi: 163
Malaysia: 168, 171
Maldives: 168, 173
Mali: 169, 174, 183, 269, 271
Malta: 194, 197, 204, 227, 246, 251, 259
Marche, Region of: 59, 60-61, 64, 132, 137, 262
Marginalisation, social exclusion: 105, 109, 119, 122, 153, 240
Mauritania: 168, 201
Mauritius, Republic of: 202
Mexico: 167, 171, 174-176. 178, 181-182, 248
Middle East: 140, 221
Migrants, foreigners: 27, 30-31, 35, 37, 43, 46, 55, 57-58, 60-71, 73, 75-76, 79-88, 90-92, 96-98, 102-103, 106, 135, 141, 143, 146, 154-155, 183-189, 191- 196, 208-209, 215-216, 220, 232, 242, 245, 255, 257, 260, 266, 284, 292-297, 302, 336
Minorities: 24, 29-30, 35, 39, 59-60, 88, 166, 174, 189, 216-218, 221, 246-247, 263-264
Moldova, Republic of: 97, 155, 169, 203, 219, 239, 242, 246, 248
Molise, Region of: 60, 64, 132, 137, 287
Monaco, Principality of: 204, 227, 248
Mongolia: 162
Montenegro: 155, 169, 175, 227, 247-248
Morocco: 97, 155, 173-175, 204, 221, 248
Mozambique: 175, 201
Myanmar: 160, 167,178

Netherlands: 177, 194, 201, 210, 246-247, 321
New Zealand: 202
Nigeria: 104, 171, 181, 188, 197, 280-282
Non-discrimination: 23, 30-31, 33, 35, 37-38, 41, 44, 60, 72, 79, 85-86, 88, 94-98, 103, 106, 117, 134, 159, 161-164, 170, 175, 180, 182, 191, 198-203, 205-208, 211-212, 218, 221, 237, 239-241, 246, 259-261, 283-285, 298, 315-316, 322-323, 332-333, 336-337
Norway: 162, 167, 173-174, 201, 210, 251, 264

Palestine, Occupied Palestinian territories: 74, 140, 172, 179, 271
Pakistan: 172, 179-180, 197, 203, 255, 281
Paraguay: 201, 204

Parliamentary immunity: 317
"Peace human rights" norm: 20,
58-59, 131
Personal freedom and prison
conditions: 25-28, 37-38, 44,
78, 90, 94, 118, 134, 139, 224,
228-232, 289, 294, 307-308, 311,
314-315, 319-321
Persons with disabilities: 24, 41,
44, 59, 61, 65, 69, 71, 76, 88, 90,
99, 102-103, 105, 108-109, 119,
134, 153, 174, 190, 198, 204,
233, 260,283, 285-286, 298,
302, 335, 336
Peru: 162, 169, 172, 176, 182,
201, 248
Philippines: 97, 169, 175
Piedmont, Region of: 65, 96, 128,
132, 134, 136-137
Poland: 100, 169, 177, 201, 219,
225, 227, 246-247, 251
Portugal: 174-175, 194, 201, 227,
246, 251
Poverty: 63-64, 75, 105, 119, 153,
160, 191, 225, 237, 240, 297

Qatar: 166, 169, 172-173,
175-176, 270

Reasonable length of proceedings:
26, 44, 223, 242, 304,
322-325
Right to health: 71, 76, 87, 137,
287-288
Right to housing: 29, 31, 96-97,
202, 243
Right to peace: 15, 20-21, 33, 42,
169, 181
Right to private and family life:
222, 276, 278, 285, 295, 299,
322, 328, 331-333
Roma, Sinti and Travellers: 35, 73,
88, 99, 202, 207

Romania: 97, 169, 173, 175,
219-220, 246, 324
Russian Federation: 100, 176, 202,
219, 227, 239, 242, 245-246, 248
Rwanda: 200, 204

Sahel: 161, 271
San Marino: 194, 227, 246
Sao Tome and Principe: 204
Sardinia, Region of: 20, 58, 60,
62, 64, 132, 137, 195, 290
Saudi Arabia: 171, 175
Senegal: 162, 171, 173
Serbia: 155, 169, 203, 220, 245,
247-248
Sicily, Region of: 20, 60, 93, 107,
132, 195, 216, 225
Slavery, trafficking: 30, 36-37, 44,
52, 54, 74, 99, 101, 120, 160,
168, 175-176, 188, 191, 215, 217-
218, 250-251, 263, 266-267, 310
Slovak Republic: 227, 246
Slovenia: 173, 204, 227, 246, 261,
263
Social security, pensions: 23-24,
53, 62-63, 133, 135, 209, 225,
236, 239, 242, 284, 291-292, 298
Social services: 60, 107, 124, 150,
153, 237, 240, 322, 331
Somalia: 171-173, 181, 197, 222,
271
South Africa: 74, 172, 179-180,
182, 192, 248
South Korea: 248
South Sudan: 181, 271
Spain: 93, 165, 169, 173, 177, 205,
212, 214, 220, 227, 242, 251,
256, 259, 311-312
Sri Lanka: 174
Stalking: 45, 60
Statute of limitations: 306, 309,
325, 326
Sudan: 182, 271

Sweden: 173, 175, 197, 202, 212, 259, 261
Switzerland: 169, 173-174, 246, 291, 322
Syria: 88-89, 93, 160, 170-172, 220, 269

Tajikistan: 201, 203, 248
Terrorism: 167, 178, 256, 310-312
Thailand: 169, 177
Togo: 200
Torture, inhuman treatments: 218, 226-227, 231, 245, 294-295, 307-312, 319-322
Trent, Autonomous Province of: 60, 63-64, 132, 135, 137, 141, 145
Trentino-Alto Adige, Region of: 62, 132. 137
Tunisia: 172, 175, 177-178, 185, 248, 260
Turkey: 173-175, 219-220, 227, 242, 311
Turkmenistan: 170
Tuscany, Region of: 63-65, 72, 96, 132, 136-138
Tuvalu: 170, 204

Uganda: 71, 168
Ukraine: 97, 100, 177, 201, 219-220, 227, 239, 247-248, 311
Umbria, Region of: 63, 132, 137, 154
United Arab Emirates: 169, 173, 270
United Kingdom: 173, 176, 201 203, 246, 259, 261

United States of America: 169, 172-176, 215, 245, 270
Universal Periodic Review (UPR): 35, 37, 39, 42, 71, 168, 172, 183
University Human Rights Centre (University of Padua): 20-21, 32, 41, 59, 73, 104, 120-121, 124, 137, 140, 146, 147, 148, 150-151, 211
Uruguay: 178, 180, 201, 205, 248
Uzbekistan: 170, 201, 204

Valle d'Aosta, Region of: 60-61, 64, 132, 135
Veneto, Region of: 32, 58-59, 60-61, 63, 96, 132, 135, 137, 140, 143-144, 146-155, 247, 262, 289
Venezuela: 169, 202
Volunteering: 88-90, 95, 98, 147, 153

Women, equal opportunities, gender issues: 24, 30, 31, 38, 44, 56, 58-60, 63, 65, 69, 72, 88, 95-96, 98-99, 102, 111, 134, 143-144, 152, 207-208, 214, 251, 255, 275-277, 280-283, 289
Workers' rights: 16, 23-25, 42, 51, 58-65, 79, 113, 204-210, 235, 237, 241, 287-288, 337-338

Yemen: 173, 177

Zambia: 163

Table of Cases

Constitutional Court

Judg. 25 November 2005, No. 425: 278
Judg. 26 February 2010, No. 80: 286
Judg. 8 July 2010, No. 250: 293
Judg. 21 July 2010, No. 265: 314
Judg. 9 February 2011, No. 40: 297
Judg. 11 March 2011, No. 80: 313
Judg. 12 May 2011, No. 164: 314
Judg. 11 November 2011, No. 303: 313
Judg. 5 April 2012, No. 78: 290
Judg. 18 January 2013, No. 2: 296
Judg. 18 January 2013, No. 4: 299
Judg. 15 March 2013, No. 40: 284
Judg. 29 March 2013, No. 57: 314
Judg. 9 May 2013, No. 85: 287
Judg. 22 May 2013, No. 92: 291
Judg. 29 May 2013, No. 103: 290
Judg. 7 June 2013, No. 135: 308
Ord. 7 June 2013, No. 136: 300
Judg. 20 June 2013, No. 143: 318
Judg. 4 July 2013, No. 170: 290
Judg. 17 July 2013, No. 197: 284
Judg. 18 July 2013, No. 202: 295
Judg. 18 July 2013, No. 203: 285
Judg. 18 July 2013, No. 210: 313
Judg. 18 July 2013, No. 214: 318
Judg. 19 July 2013, No. 222: 297
Judg. 23 July 2013, No. 235: 312
Judg. 22 November 2013, No. 278: 278
Judg. 22 November 2013, No. 279: 307

Judg. 12 December 2013, No. 305: 317
Judg. 17 December 2013, No. 308: 290
Judg. 17 December 2013, No. 313: 317

Court of Cassation, Civil Division

Ord. Sec. VI, 9 January 2013, No. 359: 282
Ord. Sec. VI, 10 January 2013, No. 563: 279
Judg. Sec. II, 14 January 2013, No. 705: 299
Judg. Sec. VI, 16 January 2013, No. 1007: 304
Judg. Sec. I, 28 January 2013, No. 1804: 299
Judg. Sec. VI, 15 February 2013, No. 3740: 304
Judg. Sec. III, 19 February 2013, No. 4030: 277
Judg. Sec. VI, 20 February 2013, No. 4230: 296
Ord. Sec. VI, 27 March 2013, No. 7654: 305
Ord. Sec. VI, 4 April 2013, No. 8281: 280
Judg. Sec. VI, 8 April 2013, No. 8561: 305
Judg. Sec. VI, 18 April 2013, No. 9500: 281
Judg. Sec. un., 22 April 2013, No. 9687: 283
Ord. Sec. VI, 6 May 2013, No. 10460: 298
Ord. Sec. VI, 14 May 2013, No. 11451: 296
Judg. Joint Sec., 16 May 2013, No. 11833: 306
Ord. Sec. VI, 17 May 2013, No. 12134: 282
Sent. Sec., 22 May 2013, No. 12531: 275
Ord. Sec. VI, 23 May 2013, No. 12751: 279
Ord. Sec. VI, 28 May 2013, No. 13172: 280
Judg. Sec. I, 6 June 2013, No. 14329: 275
Judg. Joint Sec., 10 June 2013, No. 14501: 294
Judg. Joint Sec., 10 June 2013, No. 14502: 293
Judg. Sec. VI, 12 June 2013, No. 14777: 306
Judg. Sec. VI, 13 June 2013, No. 14786: 305
Judg. Joint Sec., 17 June 2013, No. 15115: 293
Ord. Sec. VI, 20 June 2013, No. 15512: 294
Ord. Sec. VI, 24 June 2013, No. 15757: 281
Judg. Sec. III, 17 September 2013, No. 21166: 285
Judg. Sec. III, 17 September 2013, No. 21255: 277

Judg. Sec. VI, 20 September 2013, No. 21667: 295

Judg. Sec. I, 27 September 2013, No. 22292: 302

Judg. Sec. Employment, 27 September 2013, No. 22269: 292

Judg. Sec. VI, 1 October 2013, No. 22449: 291

Judg. Sec. Employment, 2 October 2013, No. 22549: 291

Judg. Sec. Employment, 2 October 2013, No. 22550: 291

Judg. Sec. Employment, 2 October 2013, No. 22551: 291

Judg. Sec. Employment, 3 October 2013, No. 22620: 291

Judg. Sec. Employment, 4 October 2013, No. 22740: 291

Judg. Sec. Employment, 8 October 2013, No. 22874: 291

Judg. Sec. Employment, 8 October 2013, No. 22877: 291

Judg. Sec. II, 8 October 2013, No. 22885: 305

Judg. Sec. Employment, 18 October 2013, No. 23703: 291

Judg. Sec. Employment, 21 October 2013, No. 23779: 291

Judg. Sec. VI, 22 October 2013, No. 23887: 304

Judg. Sec. VI, 22 October 2013, No. 23879: 304

Ord. Sec. VI, 24 October 2013, No. 24064: 280

Ord. Sec. VI, 24 October 2013, No. 24066: 280

Judg. Sec. VI, 29 October 2013, No. 24411: 305

Judg. Sec. VI, 5 November 2013, No. 24840: 305

Judg. Sec. I, 8 November 2013, No. 25212: 282

Judg. Sec. I, 11 November 2013, No. 25288: 306

Judg. Sec. V, 14 November 2013, No. 25577: 305

Ord. Sec. VI, 18 November 2013, No. 25873: 280

Judg. Sec. VI, 20 November 2013, No. 26071: 305

Judg. Sec. VI, 21 November 2013, No. 26181: 306

Judg. Sec. VI, 22 November 2013, No. 26192: 305

Judg. Sec. VI, 22 November 2013, No. 26196: 305

Judg. Sec. VI, 22 November 2013, No. 26197: 305

Judg. Sec. VI, 22 November 2013, No. 26198: 305

Judg. Sec. VI, 22 November 2013, No. 26200: 305

Ord. Sec. VI, 26 November 2013, No. 26380: 298

Judg. Sec. II, 26 November 2013, No. 26442: 304

Judg. Sec. VI, 26 November 2013, No. 26471: 305

Judg. Sec. II, 26 November 2013, No. 26453: 305

Judg. Sec. II, 26 November 2013, No. 26437: 305

Judg. Sec. II, 26 November 2013, No. 26444: 305

Judg. Sec. VI, 26 November 2013, No. 26476: 306

Judg. Sec. II, 28 November 2013, No. 26644: 305

Judg. Sec. II, 28 November 2013, No. 26650: 305

Judg. Sec. VI, 28 November 2013, No. 26701: 305

Judg. Sec. VI, 28 November 2013, No. 26702: 305

Judg. Sec. VI, 28 November 2013, No. 26703: 305

Judg. Sec. VI, 28 November 2013, No. 26704: 305

Judg. Sec. VI, 28 November 2013, No. 26705: 305

Judg. Sec. VI, 28 November 2013, No. 26706: 305

Judg. Sec. VI, 28 November 2013, No. 26707: 305

Judg. Sec. II, 29 November 2013, No. 26844: 305

Judg. Sec. II, 29 November 2013, No. 26865: 305

Judg. Sec. II, 29 November 2013, No. 26866: 305

Judg. Sec. II, 29 November 2013, No. 26867: 305

Judg. Sec. VI, 29 November 2013, No. 26887: 279

Judg. Sec. VI, 29 November 2013, No. 26896: 305

Judg. Sec. VI, 29 November 2013, No. 26898: 305

Judg. Sec. VI, 29 November 2013, No. 26899: 305

Judg. Sec. VI, 2 December 2013, No. 26996: 305

Judg. Sec. VI, 2 December 2013, No. 26997: 305

Judg. Sec. VI, 2 December 2013, No. 26998: 305

Judg. Sec. VI, 2 December 2013, No. 26999: 305

Judg. Sec. II, 3 December 2013, No. 27046: 304

Judg. Sec. VI, 3 December 2013, No. 27087: 305

Judg. Sec. VI, 3 December 2013, No. 27088: 305

Judg. Sec. VI, 3 December 2013, No. 27089: 305

Judg. Sec. VI, 3 December 2013, No. 27090: 305

Judg. Sec. VI, 3 December 2013, No. 27091: 305

Judg. Sec. VI, 3 December 2013, No. 27092: 305

Judg. Sec. VI, 4 December 2013, No. 27102: 304

Judg. Sec. VI, 4 December 2013, No. 27103: 305

Judg. Sec. VI, 4 December 2013, No. 27104: 305
Judg. Sec. VI, 4 December 2013, No. 27106: 305
Judg. Sec. un., 5 December 2013, No. 27266: 306
Judg. Sec. un., 5 December 2013, No. 27267: 306
Judg. Sec. un., 5 December 2013, No. 27270: 306
Judg. Sec. un., 5 December 2013, No. 27272: 306
Judg. Sec. I, 6 December 2013, No. 27381: 301
Judg. Sec. Employment, 12 December 2013, No. 27856: 306
Judg. Sec. VI, 13 December 2013, No. 27956: 306
Judg. Sec. VI, 18 December 2013, No. 28326: 306
Judg. Sec. I, 18 December 2013, No. 28230: 302
Judg. Sec. VI, 19 December 2013, No. 28483: 305
Judg. Sec. VI, 19 December 2013, No. 28486: 306
Judg. Sec. VI, 19 December 2013, No. 28495: 305
Judg. Sec. VI, 19 December 2013, No. 28499: 305
Judg. Sec. VI, 19 December 2013, No. 28500: 305

Court of Cassation, Criminal Division

Judg. Sec. I, 10 January 2013, No. 42894: 308
Judg. Sec. II, 4 February 2013, No. 26825: 310
Judg. Sec. V, 4 February 2013, No. 30525: 316
Judg. Sec. VI, 27 February 2013, No. 15017: 311
Judg. Sec. VI, 27 February 2013, No. 15018: 311
Judg. Sec. VI, 6 March 2013, No. 10905: 311
Judg. Sec. VI, 28 March 2013, No. 15927: 312
Judg. Sec. VI, 5 April 2013, No. 17605: 311
Judg. Sec. VI, 16 April 2013, No. 18241: 312
Judg. Sec. III, 24 April 2013, No. 33179: 315
Judg. Sec. V, 8 May 2013, No. 37088: 309
Judg. Sec. V, 15 May 2013, No. 25870: 316
Judg. Sec. I, 27 May 2013, No. 27610: 292
Judg. Sec. I, 27 May 2013, No. 27614: 292
Judg. Sec. I, 27 May 2013, No. 27616: 292
Judg. Sec. I, 27 May 2013, No. 27617: 292

Judg. Sec. I, 27 May 2013, No. 27618: 292
Judg. Sec. I, 27 May 2013, No. 27620: 292
Judg. Sec. I, 27 May 2013, No. 27623: 292
Judg. Sec. III, 4 June 2013, No. 29735: 277
Judg. Sec. I, 4 June 2013, No. 39860: 317
Judg. Sec. I, 14 June 2013, No. 30308: 292
Judg. Sec. I, 14 June 2013, No. 30309: 292
Judg. Sec. I, 14 June 2013, No. 30310: 292
Judg. Sec. I, 14 June 2013, No. 30311: 292
Judg. Sec. I, 14 June 2013, No. 30312: 292
Judg. Sec. I, 5 July 2013, No. 40044: 309
Judg. Sec. I, 17 July 2013, No. 35587: 292
Judg. Sec. I, 17 July 2013, No. 35589: 292
Judg. Sec. I, 17 July 2013, No. 35590: 292
Judg. Sec. I, 24 September 2013, No. 42401: 292
Judg. Sec. V, 26 September 2012, No. 41249: 220, 248
Judg. Sec. I, 26 September 2013, No. 42417: 292
Judg. Sec. III, 2 October 2013, No. 12351: 326
Judg. Sec. VI, 15 October 2013, No. 46212: 311
Judg. Sec. VI, 21 October 2013, No. 47561: 311
Judg. Sec. VI, 18 December 2013, No. 3746: 311

Supreme Administrative Council (Consiglio di Stato)

Sec. III, Judg. 17 January 2013, No. 269: 303
Sec. III, Judg. 17 January 2013, No. 270: 303
Sec. V, Judg. 24 April 2013, No. 2279: 300
Sec. V, Judg. 2 May 2013, No. 2391: 287
Sec. IV, Judg. 8 May 2013, No. 2481: 300
Sec. III, Judg. 3 July 2013, No. 3574: 286
Sec. V, Judg. 23 July 2013, No. 3950: 287
Sec. V, Judg. 23 July 2013, No. 3954: 287
Sec. III, Judg. 29 July 2013, No. 3980: 294
Sec. III, Judg. 13 September 2013, No. 4545: 303
Sec. III, Judg. 11 October 2013, No. 4984: 294

Sec. V, Judg. 12 November 2013, No. 5375: 289

Regional Administrative Tribunals (TAR)

TAR Abruzzo Aquila, Sec. I, Judg. 12 September 2013, No. 744: 286
TAR Molise Campobasso, Sec. I, Judg. 12 April 2013, No. 263: 287
TAR Calabria Catanzaro, Sec. II, Judg. 14 June 2013, No. 678: 300
TAR Campania Naples, Sec. IV, Judg. 6 March 2013, No. 1254: 287
TAR Campania Naples, Sec. V, Judg. 16 April 2013, No. 1985: 300
TAR Campania Naples, Sec. V, Judg. 24 July 2013, No. 3879: 300
TAR Campania Naples, Sec. IV, Judg. 18 September 2013, No. 4348: 299
TAR Basilicata Potenza, Sec. I, Judg. 13 March 2013, No. 132: 300
TAR Lazio Rome, Sec. II bis, Judg. 21 January 2013, No. 633: 283
TAR Lazio Rome, Sec. II, Judg. 4 June 2013, No. 5562: 303
TAR Lazio Rome, Sec. II, Judg. 11 September 2013, No. 8206: 283

Ordinary Tribunals

Tribunal of Catanzaro, Sec. I, Judg. 15 January 2013: 285
Court of Appeals of Brescia, Judg. 31 January 2013: 298
Tribunal of Naples, Sec. Pozzuoli, Ord. 20 February 2013, No. 250: 298
Tribunal of Rome, Sec. II, Judg. 15 March 2013, No. 5764: 296
Court of Appeals of Reggio Calabria, Sec. 8 April 2013: 303
Tribunal of Naples, Sec. Pozzuoli, Judg. 24 September 2013, No. 10508: 298
Tribunal of Trieste, Ord. 9 October 2013: 281
Tribunal of Rome, Sec. I, Judg. 14 October 2013, No. 20425: 281
Tribunal of Trieste, Ord. 15 October 2013: 281
Tribunal of Trieste, Ord. 15 October 2013: 281
Tribunal of Rome, Sec. I, Judg. 21 October 2013, No. 20908: 280
Tribunal of Naples, Sec. I, Ord. 25 October 2013: 280
Tribunal of Trieste, Ord. 12 November 2013: 281
Tribunal of Rome, Sec. VI, Judg. 12 November 2013, No. 18931: 315
Tribunal of Trieste, Ord. 20 November 2013, No. 1386: 280

European Court of Human Rights

Abbate v. Italy, No. 29313/09, 7 March 2013: 221
Abubeker v. Austria and Italy, No. 73874/11, 18 June 2013: 322

Andrenelli v. Italy, No. 44109/11, 4 September 2012: 222

Anghel v. Italy, No. 5968/09, 26 June 2013: 324

Arras and Others v. Italy, No. 17972/07, 14 February 2012: 324, 290, 291

Ascierto e Buffolino v. Italy, Nos. 20619/03, 23751/03, 5 November 2013: 325

Asquini e Bisconti v. Italy, No. 10009/06, 5 November 2013: 333

Azenabor v. Italy, No. 25367/11, 8 October 2013: 326

Bassani and Colombo v. Italy, No. 26329/03, 19 June 2012: 222

Belpietro v. Italy, No. 42612/10, 24 September 2013: 249

Bencivenga and Others v. Italy, Nos. 15015/03,19419/03, 19436/03, 19448/03, 19469/03, 19470/03, 5 November 2013: 325

Boadicea Property Services Co. Limited et al. v. Italy, No. 15865/09, 19 February 2013: 328

Brambilla and Others v. Italy, No. 22567/09, 7 November 2013: 330

Caldarella v. Italy, No. 29703/06, 22 January 2013: 332

Capitani and Campanella v. Italy, No. 24920/07, 17 May 2011: 221

Cariello and Others v. Italy, No. 14064/07, 30 April 2013: 332

Caruso v. Italy, No. 24817/03, 2 April 2013: 325

Casacchia and Others v. Italy, No. 23658/07, 15 October 2013: 324

Ceteroni v. Italy, Nos. 22461/93, 22465/93, 15 November 1996: 223

Cirillo v. Italy, No. 36276/10, 29 January 2013: 224, 321

Contessa and Others v. Italy, No. 11004/05, 17 September 2013: 328

Contrada v. Italy, No. 66655/13: 326

Corrado and Others v. Italy, Nos. 32850/02, 32852/02, 34367/02, 34369/02, 34371/02, 34372/02, 34376/02, 34378/02, 34381/02, 34382/02, 34388/02, 16 July 2013: 325

Cusan and Fazzo v. Italy, No. 77/07: 333

D'Auria and Balsamo v. Italy, No. 11625/07, 11 June 2013: 331

De Carolis and Lolli v. Italy, No. 33359/05, 5 March 2013: 332

De Luca v. Italy, No. 43870/04, 24 September 2013: 326

Di Giovanni v. Italy, No. 51160/06, 9 July 2013: 329

Di Pietro and Caruso v. Italy, No. 5868/06, 15 January 2013: 328

Fiocca v. Italy, No. 32968/02, 16 July 2013: 325

Gagliardi and Others v. Italy, No. 29385/03, 16 July 2013: 325

Gaglione and Others v. Italy, No. 45867/07, 21 December 2010:

Galasso and Others v. Italy, Nos. 32740/02, 32742/02, 32743/02, 32748/02, 32848/02, 16 July 2013: 223

Gianquitti and Others v. Italy, No. 36228/02, 22 January 2013: 327

Giuseppe Romano v. Italy, No. 35659/02, 5 March 2013: 327

Godelli v. Italy, No. 33783/09, 25 September 2012: 27, 278

Guiso-Gallisay v. Italy, No. 58858/00, 22 December 2009: 328

H. v. Finland, No. 37359/09, 13 November 2012: 276

Halimi v. Austria and Italy, No. 53852/11, 18 June 2013: 322

Hirsi Jamaa and Others v. Italy [GC], No. 27765/09, 23 February 2012: 186, 187, 222, 260, 294

Hussein Diirshi and Others v. The Netherlands and Italy, Nos. 2314/10, 18324/10,
47851/10, 51377/10, 10 September 2013: 321

Iannelli v. Italy, No. 24818/03, 12 February 2013: 325

Lanteri v. Italy, No. 56578/00, 29 January 2013: 328

Limata and Others v. Italy, Nos. 16412/03, 16413/03, 16414/03, 16415/03, 16416/03,
16417/03, 22294/03, 22351/03, 22353/03, 22354/03, 22355/03, 10 December 2013: 325

Lombardo v. Italy, No. 25704/11, 29 January 2013: 331

Lorenzetti v. Italy, No. 32075/09, 10 April 2012: 318

Luordo v. Italy, No. 32190/96, 17 July 2003: 223

M. C. and Others v. Italy [GC], No. 5376/11, 3 September 2013: 26, 226, 319, 322,

Maffei and De Nigris v. Italy, Nos. 28090/03, 28462/03, 26 November 2013: 325

Maggio and Others v. Italy, Nos. 46286/09, 52851/08, 53727/08, 54486/08, 56001/08,
31 May 2011: 290

Marino and Others v. Italy, Nos. 9743/07, 10692/07, 34901/07, 36180/07, 36181/
07, 36182/07, 36183/07, 15 January 2013: 328

Materazzo and Others v. Italy, No. 34936/07, 15 January 2013: 328

Mercuri v. Italy, No. 14055/04, 22 October 2013: 325

Miruts Hagos v. The Netherlands and Italy, No. 9053/10, 27 August 2013: 321

Mohammed Hassan and Others v. The Netherlands and Italy, Nos. 40524/10, 11746/13, 18764/11, 20355/12, 23696/12, 41993/10, 57531/10, 62865/12, 7903/13, 81839/12, 27 August 2013: 321

Mohammed Hussein and Others v. The Netherlands and Italy, No. 27725/10, 2 April 2013: 321

Mostacciuolo v. Italy, No. 64705/01, 29 March 2009: 223

Musella and Esposito v. Italy, No. 14817/02, 22 January 2013: 327

Natale and Others v. Italy, No. 19264/07, 15 October 2013: 324

Occhetto v. Italy, No. 14507/07, 12 November 2013: 330

Oliari and Others v. Italy, Nos. 18766/11, 36030/11, 3 December 2013: 332

Orlandi and Others v. Italy, Nos. 26431/12, 26742/12, 44057/12, 60088/12, 3 December 2013: 332

Paleari v. Italy, No. 55772/08, 26 July 2011: 221

Parrillo v. Italy, No. 43028/05: 332

Parrillo v. Italy, No. 46470/11, 28 May 2013: 328

Pennino v. Italy, No. 43892/04, 24 September 2013: 326

Plesic v. Italy, No. 16065/09, 2 July 2013: 324

Pozzi v. Italy, No. 55743/08, 26 July 2011: 221

Prestieri v. Italy, No. 66640/10, 29 January 2013: 321

Previti v. Italy, No. 1845/08, 12 February 2013: 326

Quattrone v. Italy, No. 13431/07, 26 November 2013: 325

Ricci v. Italy, No. 30210/06, 8 October 2013: 249, 328, 329

Riina v. Italy, No. 43575/09: 322

Rubortone v. Italy, No. 24891/03, 5 February 2013: 327

Rubortone and Caruso v. Italy, No. 24892/03, 5 February 2013: 327

Ruffolo v. Italy, Nos. 21359/05, 30748/03, 39424/03, 10 May 2012: 222

Santilli v. Italy, No. 51930/10, 17 December 2013: 331

Scoppola v. Italy (2) [GC], No. 10249/03, 17 September 2009: 27, 224 312-314

Segesta sas v. Italy, No. 60901/09, 15 January 2013: 328

Sergi and Others v. Italy, Nos. 17608/03, 17297/04, 31817/03, 37099/03, 19 June

2012: 222

Sneersone and Kampanella v. Italy, No. 14737/09, 12 July 2011: 222

Stea and Others v. Italy, No. 32843/03, 12 March 2013: 327

Sud Fondi srl and Others v. Italy, No. 75909/01, 20 January 2009: 326

Sulejmanovic v. Italy, No. 22635/03, 16 July 2009: 223, 308

Tarakhel and Others v. Switzerland, No. 29217/12: 322

Tarantino and Others v. Italy, Nos. 25851/09, 29284/09, 64090/09, 2 April 2013: 333

Tellissi v. Italy, No. 15434/11, 5 March 2013: 321

Torreggiani and Others v. Italy [GC], Nos. 4357/09, 46882/09, 55400/09; 57875/09, 61535/09, 35315/10,

37818/10, 8 January 2013: 26, 27, 94, 224, 226, 307, 308, 319

Traina v. Italy, No. 37635/05, 15 January 2013: 328

Varvara v. Italy, No. 17475/09, 29 October 2013: 325

Ventura v. Italy, No. 24814/03, 22 January 2013: 327

Court of Justice of the European Union

Judg. C-329/11, 6 December 2011, *Achughbabian*: 293, 336

Judg. C-329/11 (Joined Cases C-302/11, C-303/11, C-304/11, C-305/11), 18 October 2012, *Rosanna Valenza*

e al. v. AGCM: 336, 337

Judg. C-430/11, 6 December 2012, *Sagor*: 293, 336

Ord. C-393/11, 7 March 2013, *Autorità per l'energia elettrica e il gas c. Antonella Bertazzi e altri*: 336-337

Ord. C-522/11, 21 March 2013, *Mbaye*: 293, 336

Judg. C-290/12, 11 April 2013, *Oreste Della Rocca v. Poste Italiane SpA*: 338

Judg. C-312/11, 4 July 2013, *European Commission v. Italy*: 335

Ord. C-50/13, 12 December 2013, *Rocco Papalia v. City of Aosta*: 338

Judg. C-361/12. 12 December 2013, *Carmela Carratù v. Poste Italiane SpA*: 337

European Committee of Social Rights

OMCT v. Italy, No. 19/2003: 242

COHRE v. Italy, No. 58/2009: 240

Confederazione generale italiana del lavoro (CGIL) v. Italy, No. 91/2013: 241

Association for the Protection of All Children (Approach) v. Italy, No. 94/2013: 241

Associazione Nazionale giudici di pace v. Italy, No. 102/2013: 242

Research and Editorial Committee

Andrea Cofelice, MA in Institutions and Policies of Human Rights and Peace, University of Padua. PhD Candidate in Political Science – Comparative and European Politics, University of Siena.

Pietro de Perini, MA in Institutions and Policies of Human Rights and Peace, University of Padua. PhD Candidate, Department of International Politics, City University London.

Paolo De Stefani, Aggregate Professor of International Protection of Human Rights in the Degree Course in Political Science, International Relations and Human Rights at the University of Padua. In the same University he also teaches International Criminal and Humanitarian Law. He is National Director for Italy of the European Master in Human Rights and Democratisation (E.MA).

Marco Mascia, Associate Professor of International Relations and Jean Monnet Chair in Political System of the European Union at the University of Padua. In the same University he is Director of the University Human Rights Centre and Director of the Master's Degree Programme in Human Rights and Multi-level Governance.

Antonio Papisca, Professor Emeritus of the University of Padua and UNESCO Chair in "Human Rights, Democracy and Peace", he promoted in 1982 the establishment of the Human Rights Centre within the University of Padua. In the period between 1994 and 2002 he has been member of the Italian Inter-Ministerial Committee for Human Rights at the Ministry of Foreign Affairs and of the Italian Human Rights Commission at the Presidency of the Council of Ministers.

Claudia Pividori, MA in Institutions and Policies of Human Rights and Peace, University of Padua. PhD in International Order and Human Rights, University of Rome – La Sapienza.

Peter Lang – Italian Yearbook of Human Rights Series

The legal and political significance of human rights has increased enormously at the international and European levels. Awareness has risen that the respect and the promotion of human rights must be at the centre of States and local communities' public policies and that human rights are at the basis of civil society initiatives and movements. There is a large machinery monitoring, at all the levels of governance, the way in which States implement the obligations assumed toward each person under their sovereignty.

The **Italian Yearbook of Human Rights Series** provides year by year, a dynamic and up-to date overview of the measures Italy has taken to adapt its legislation and policies to international human rights law and to comply with commitments voluntarily assumed by the Italian Government at the international level. The Series thus intends to contribute to the continuous monitoring activity on the situation of human rights in Italy undertaken at the local, national and international levels by relevant intergovernmental and civil society actors.

Each volume of this series surveys the activities carried out, during the year of reference, by the relevant national and local Italian actors, including governmental bodies, civil society organisations and universities. It also presents reports and recommendations that have been addressed to Italy by international monitoring bodies within the framework of the United Nations, the Council of Europe and the European Union. Finally, each Yearbook provides a selection of examples from international and national case-law which cast light on Italy's position vis-à-vis internationally recognised human rights.

The Yearbook is edited by the Human Rights Centre of the University of Padua, in cooperation with the UNESCO Chair in Human Rights, Democracy and Peace of the same University, and with the support of the Region of Veneto. The Centre, established in 1982, carries out research and education following a global and interdisciplinary approach. It hosts the Jean Monnet Centre of Excellence on intercultural dialogue, human rights and multi-level governance.

Editorial Board

Léonce Bekemans, *University of Padua*

Bojko Bucar, *University of Ljubljana*

Gabor Halmai, *Eötvös Lóránd University, Budapest*

Jean-Paul Lehners, *Université du Luxembourg*
Gianni Magazzeni, *Office of the UN High Commissioner for Human Rights*
Marco Mascia, *University of Padua*
Antonio Papisca, *University of Padua*
Stelios Perrakis, *Panteion University, Athens*
Ugo Villani, *LUISS University, Rome*
Peter G. Xuereb, *University of Malta*